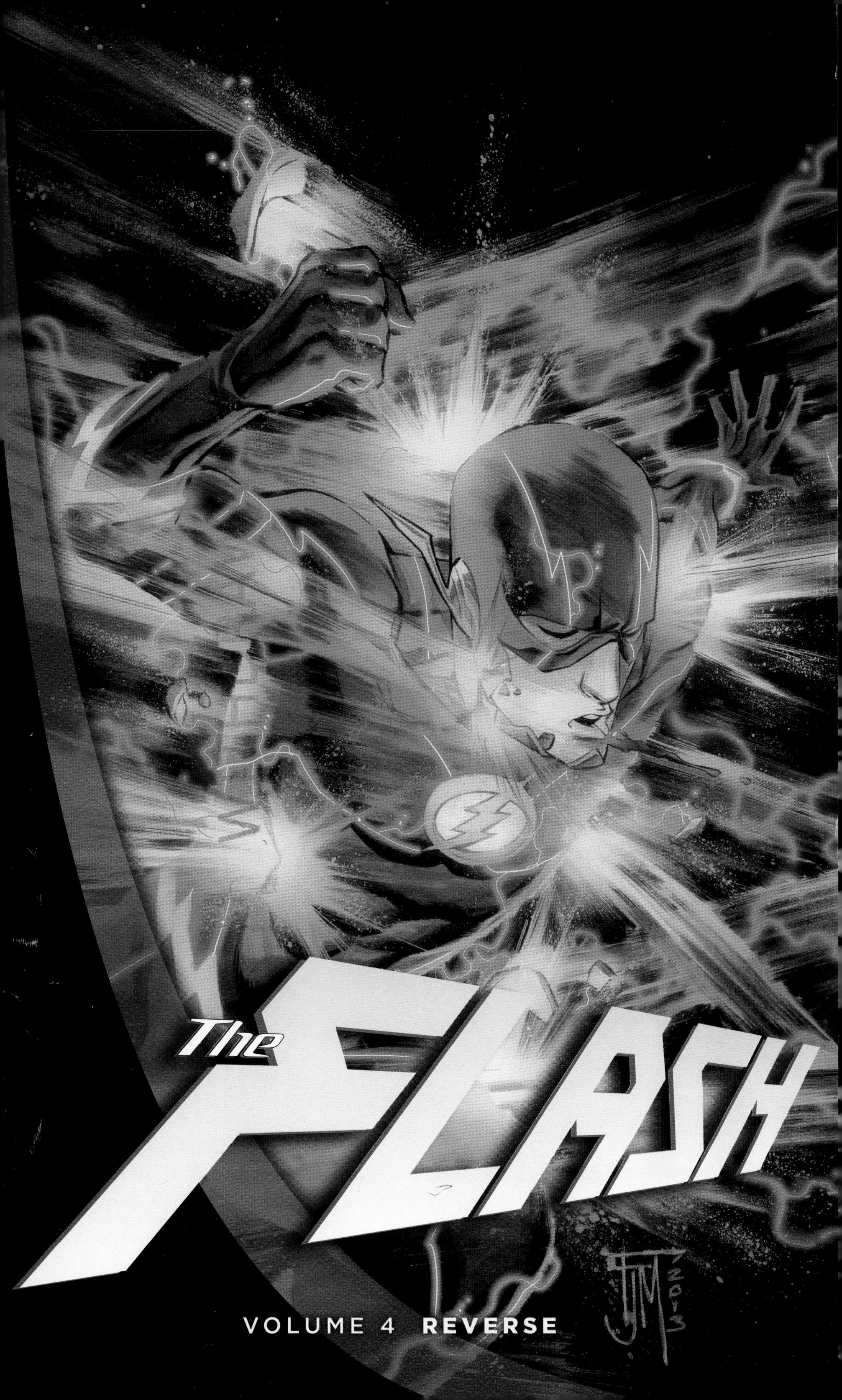
The FLASH
VOLUME 4 REVERSE

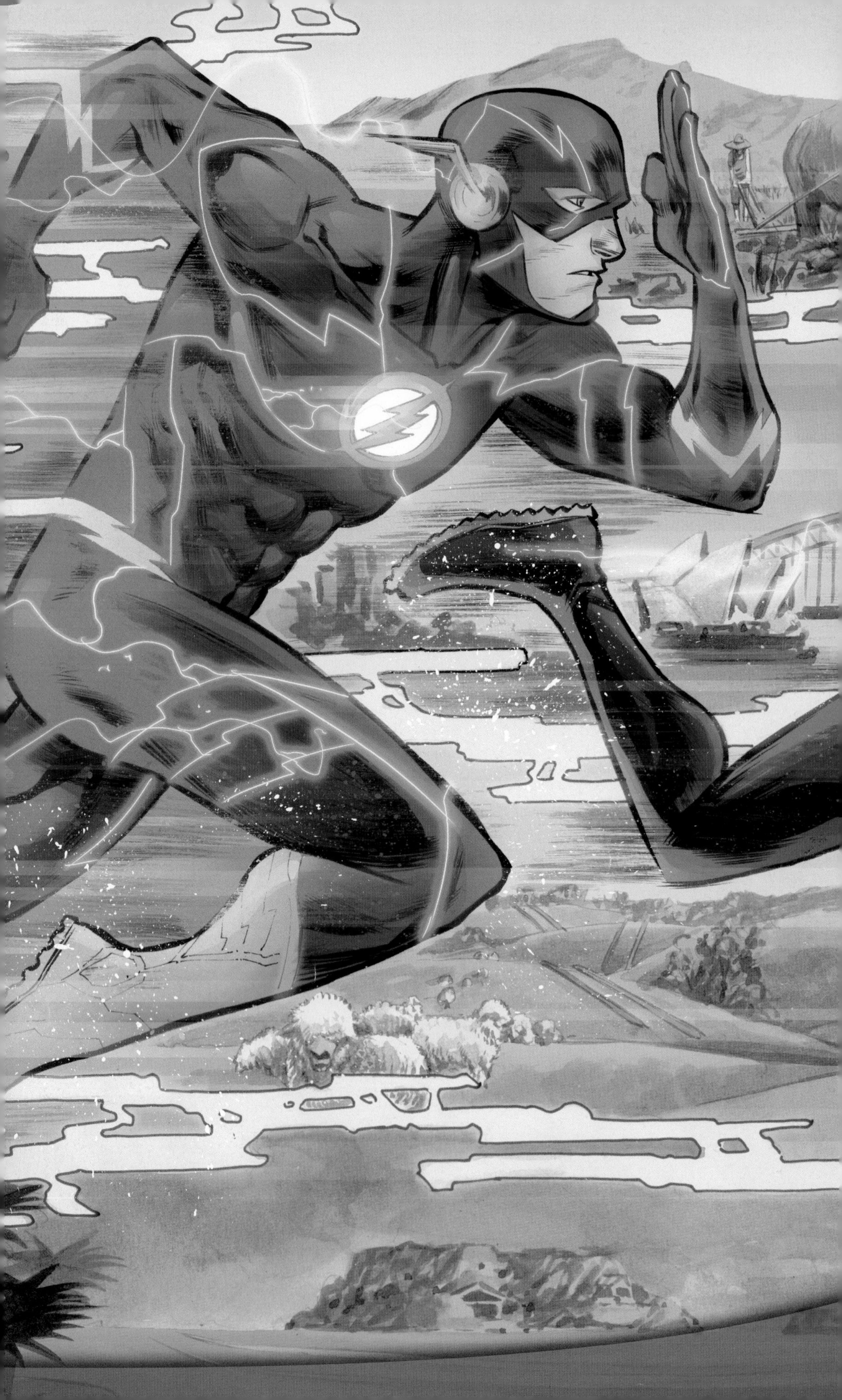

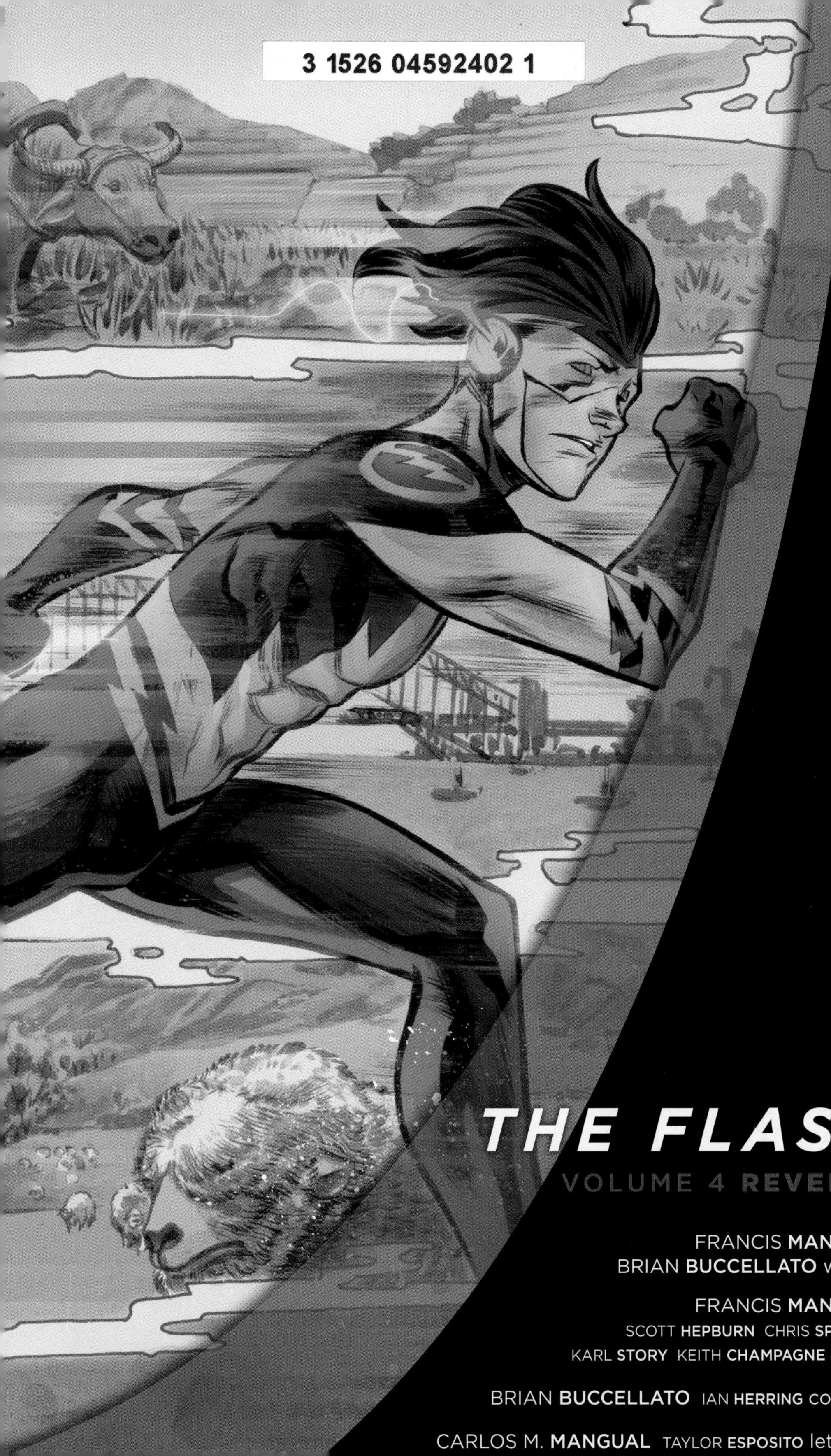

THE FLASH

VOLUME 4 REVERSE

FRANCIS MANAPUL
BRIAN BUCCELLATO writers

FRANCIS MANAPUL
SCOTT HEPBURN CHRIS SPROUSE
KARL STORY KEITH CHAMPAGNE artists

BRIAN BUCCELLATO IAN HERRING colorists

CARLOS M. MANGUAL TAYLOR ESPOSITO letterers

WIL MOSS Editor – Original Series HARVEY RICHARDS Associate Editor – Original Series
ROBIN WILDMAN Editor ROBBIN BROSTERMAN Design Director – Books
ROBBIE BIEDERMAN Publication Design

BOB HARRAS Senior VP – Editor-in-Chief, DC Comics

DIANE NELSON President DAN DIDIO and JIM LEE Co-Publishers GEOFF JOHNS Chief Creative Officer
AMIT DESAI Senior VP – Marketing and Franchise Management
AMY GENKINS Senior VP – Business and Legal Affairs NAIRI GARDINER Senior VP – Finance
JEFF BOISON VP – Publishing Planning MARK CHIARELLO VP – Art Direction and Design
JOHN CUNNINGHAM VP – Marketing TERRI CUNNINGHAM VP – Editorial Administration
LARRY GANEM VP – Talent Relations and Services ALISON GILL Senior VP – Manufacturing and Operations
HANK KANALZ Senior VP – Vertigo and Integrated Publishing JAY KOGAN VP – Business and Legal Affairs, Publishing
JACK MAHAN VP – Business Affairs, Talent NICK NAPOLITANO VP – Manufacturing Administration SUE POHJA VP – Book Sales
FRED RUIZ VP – Manufacturing Operations COURTNEY SIMMONS Senior VP – Publicity BOB WAYNE Senior VP – Sales

THE FLASH VOLUME 4: REVERSE

DC Comics, 1700 Broadway, New York, NY 10019
A Warner Bros. Entertainment Company.
Printed by RR Donnelley, Salem, VA, USA. 7/11/14. First Printing.

HC ISBN: 978-1-4012-4713-3
SC ISBN: 978-1-4012-4949-6

Library of Congress Cataloging-in-Publication Data

Manapul, Francis, author.
The Flash. Volume 4, Reverse / Francis Manapul, Brian Buccellato.
pages cm. — (The New 52!)
ISBN 978-1-4012-4713-3 (hardback)
1. Graphic novels. I. Buccellato, Brian, illustrator. II. Title. III. Title: Reverse.
PN6728.F53M39 2014
741.5'973—dc23
2014011627

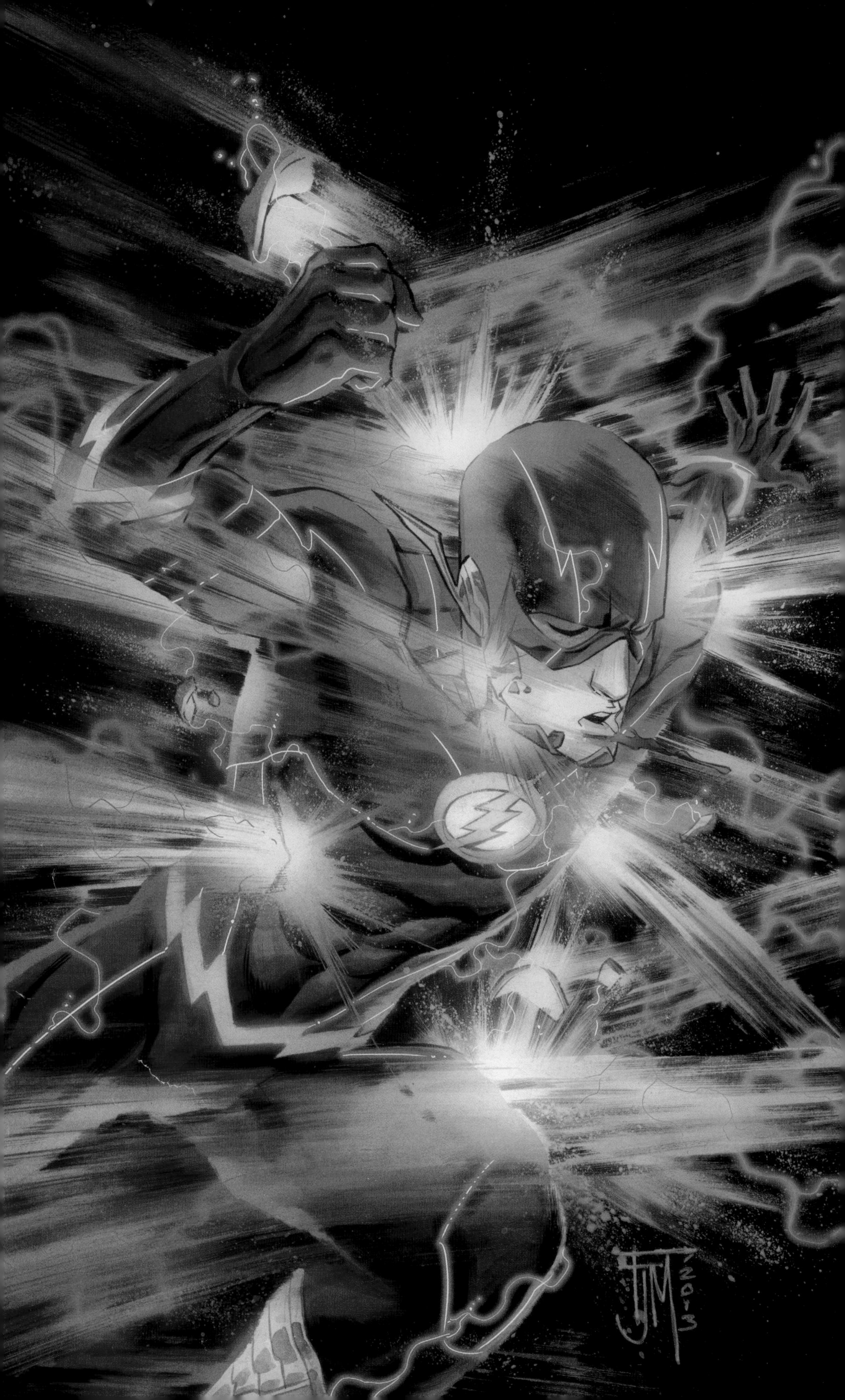

FRANCIS MANAPUL & BRIAN BUCCELLATO writers **FRANCIS MANAPUL** artist

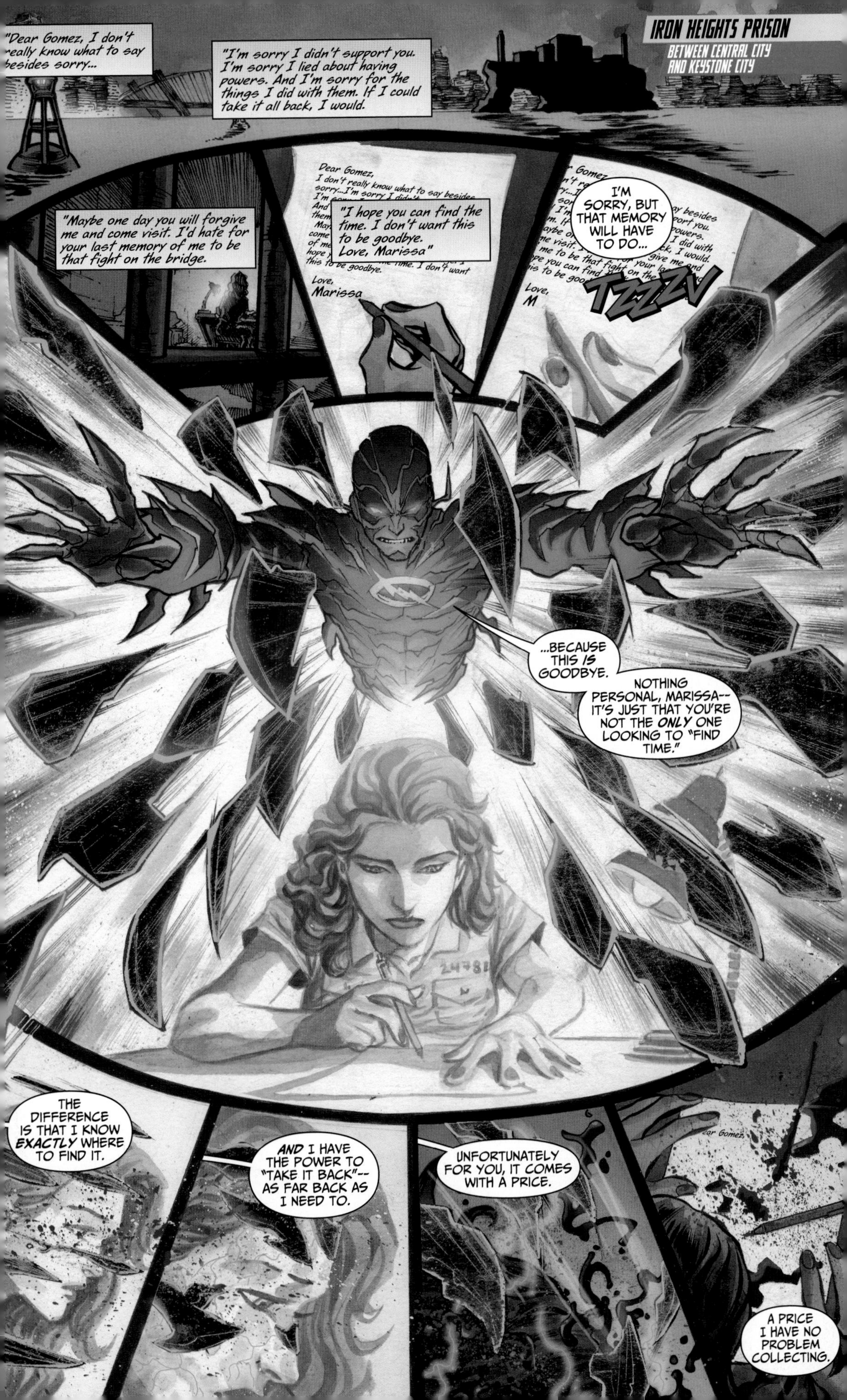

IRON HEIGHTS PRISON
BETWEEN CENTRAL CITY AND KEYSTONE CITY
"Dear Gomez, I don't really know what to say besides sorry...
"I'm sorry I didn't support you. I'm sorry I lied about having powers. And I'm sorry for the things I did with them. If I could take it all back, I would.
"Maybe one day you will forgive me and come visit. I'd hate for your last memory of me to be that fight on the bridge.
"I hope you can find the time. I don't want this to be goodbye. Love, Marissa"
Love, Marissa
I'M SORRY, BUT THAT MEMORY WILL HAVE TO DO...
TZZZV
...BECAUSE THIS IS GOODBYE.
NOTHING PERSONAL, MARISSA-- IT'S JUST THAT YOU'RE NOT THE ONLY ONE LOOKING TO "FIND TIME."
THE DIFFERENCE IS THAT I KNOW EXACTLY WHERE TO FIND IT.
AND I HAVE THE POWER TO "TAKE IT BACK"-- AS FAR BACK AS I NEED TO.
UNFORTUNATELY FOR YOU, IT COMES WITH A PRICE.
A PRICE I HAVE NO PROBLEM COLLECTING.

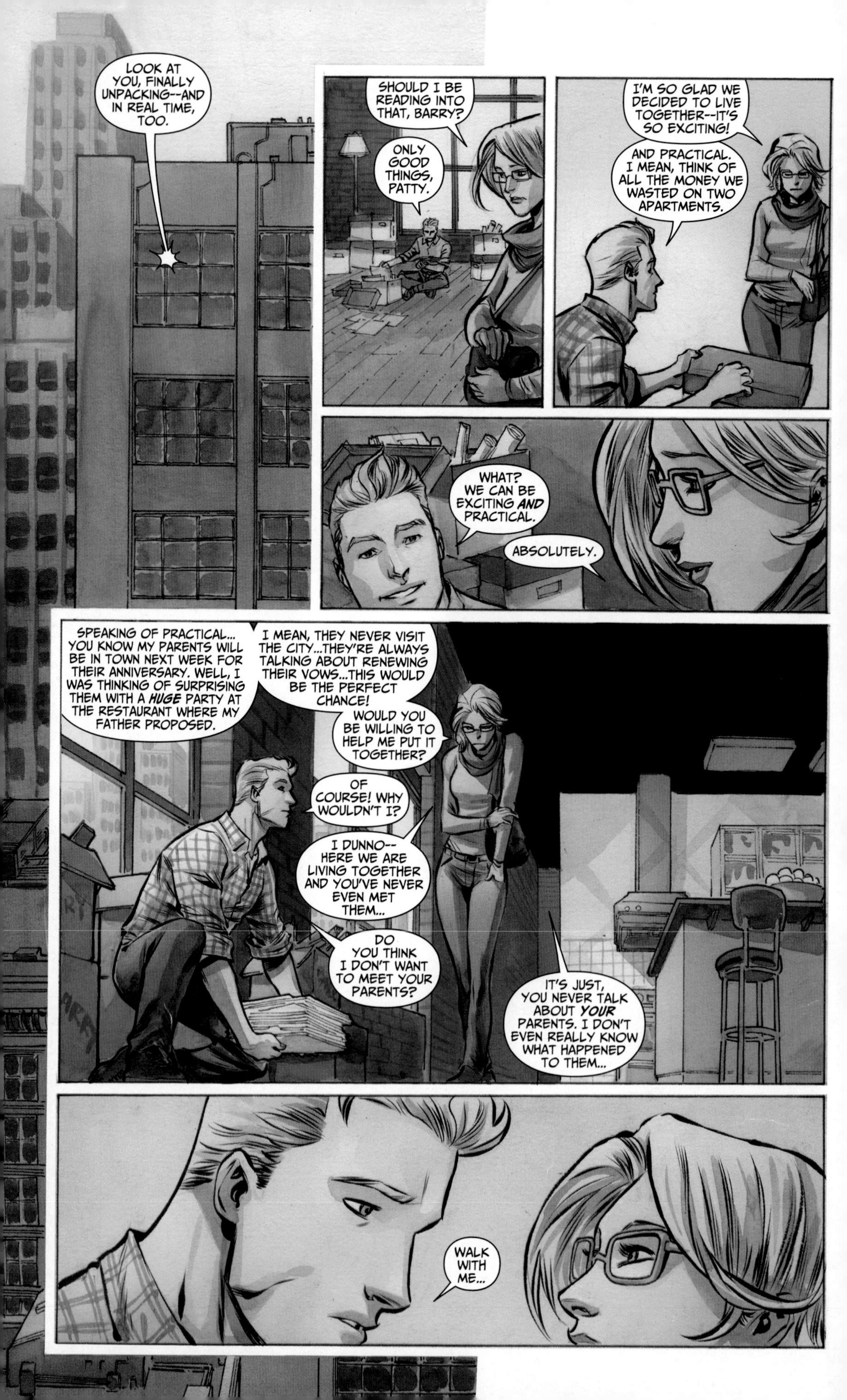
LOOK AT YOU, FINALLY UNPACKING--AND IN REAL TIME, TOO.
SHOULD I BE READING INTO THAT, BARRY?
ONLY GOOD THINGS, PATTY.
I'M SO GLAD WE DECIDED TO LIVE TOGETHER--IT'S SO EXCITING!
AND PRACTICAL. I MEAN, THINK OF ALL THE MONEY WE WASTED ON TWO APARTMENTS.
WHAT? WE CAN BE EXCITING AND PRACTICAL.
ABSOLUTELY.
SPEAKING OF PRACTICAL... YOU KNOW MY PARENTS WILL BE IN TOWN NEXT WEEK FOR THEIR ANNIVERSARY. WELL, I WAS THINKING OF SURPRISING THEM WITH A HUGE PARTY AT THE RESTAURANT WHERE MY FATHER PROPOSED.
I MEAN, THEY NEVER VISIT THE CITY...THEY'RE ALWAYS TALKING ABOUT RENEWING THEIR VOWS...THIS WOULD BE THE PERFECT CHANCE!
WOULD YOU BE WILLING TO HELP ME PUT IT TOGETHER?
OF COURSE! WHY WOULDN'T I?
I DUNNO-- HERE WE ARE LIVING TOGETHER AND YOU'VE NEVER EVEN MET THEM...
DO YOU THINK I DON'T WANT TO MEET YOUR PARENTS?
IT'S JUST, YOU NEVER TALK ABOUT YOUR PARENTS. I DON'T EVEN REALLY KNOW WHAT HAPPENED TO THEM...
WALK WITH ME...

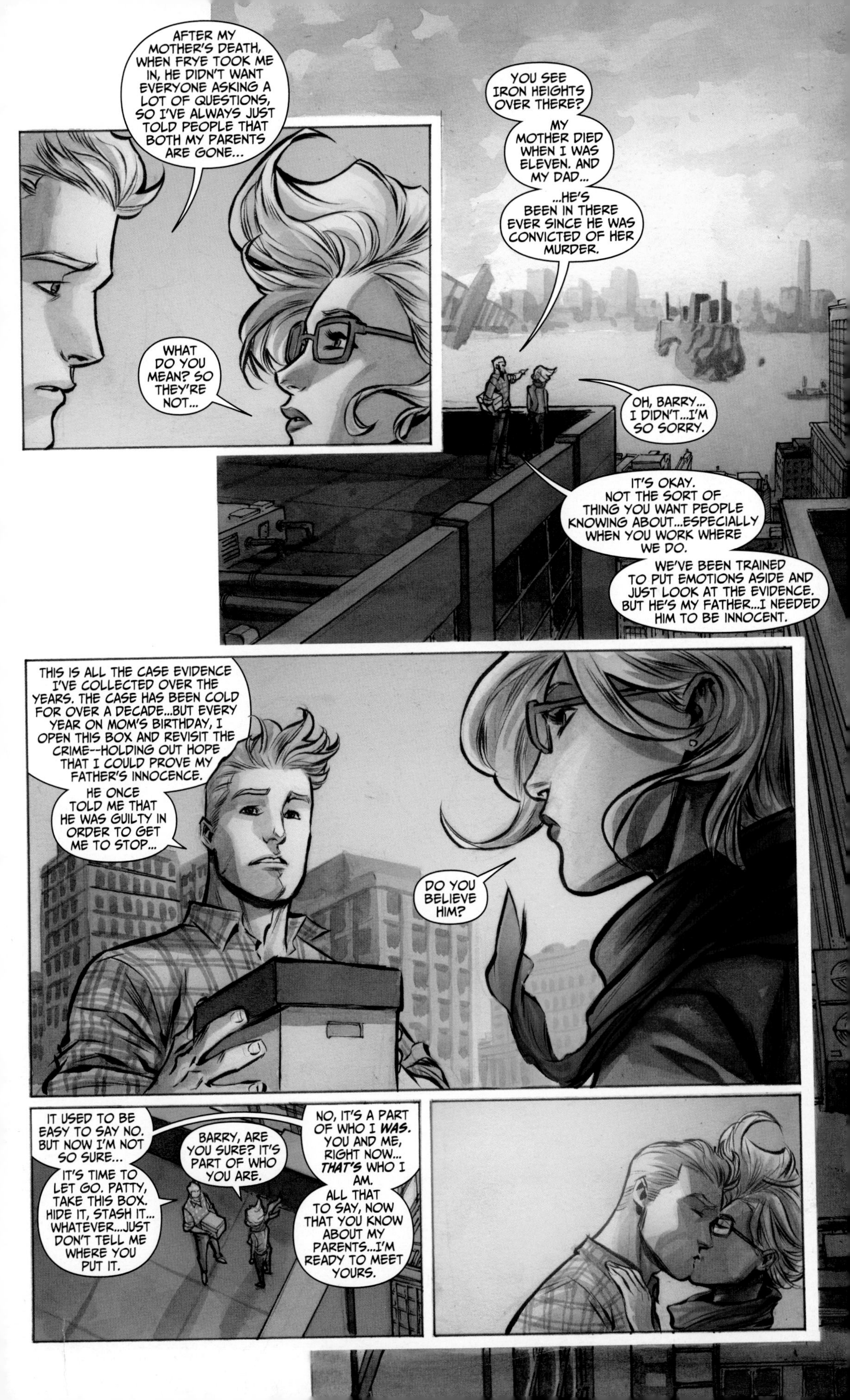
AFTER MY MOTHER'S DEATH, WHEN FRYE TOOK ME IN, HE DIDN'T WANT EVERYONE ASKING A LOT OF QUESTIONS, SO I'VE ALWAYS JUST TOLD PEOPLE THAT BOTH MY PARENTS ARE GONE...
WHAT DO YOU MEAN? SO THEY'RE NOT...
YOU SEE IRON HEIGHTS OVER THERE?
MY MOTHER DIED WHEN I WAS ELEVEN. AND MY DAD...
...HE'S BEEN IN THERE EVER SINCE HE WAS CONVICTED OF HER MURDER.
OH, BARRY... I DIDN'T...I'M SO SORRY.
IT'S OKAY. NOT THE SORT OF THING YOU WANT PEOPLE KNOWING ABOUT...ESPECIALLY WHEN YOU WORK WHERE WE DO.
WE'VE BEEN TRAINED TO PUT EMOTIONS ASIDE AND JUST LOOK AT THE EVIDENCE. BUT HE'S MY FATHER...I NEEDED HIM TO BE INNOCENT.
THIS IS ALL THE CASE EVIDENCE I'VE COLLECTED OVER THE YEARS. THE CASE HAS BEEN COLD FOR OVER A DECADE...BUT EVERY YEAR ON MOM'S BIRTHDAY, I OPEN THIS BOX AND REVISIT THE CRIME--HOLDING OUT HOPE THAT I COULD PROVE MY FATHER'S INNOCENCE.
HE ONCE TOLD ME THAT HE WAS GUILTY IN ORDER TO GET ME TO STOP...
DO YOU BELIEVE HIM?
IT USED TO BE EASY TO SAY NO. BUT NOW I'M NOT SO SURE...
IT'S TIME TO LET GO. PATTY, TAKE THIS BOX. HIDE IT, STASH IT... WHATEVER...JUST DON'T TELL ME WHERE YOU PUT IT.
BARRY, ARE YOU SURE? IT'S PART OF WHO YOU ARE.
NO, IT'S A PART OF WHO I *WAS.* YOU AND ME, RIGHT NOW... *THAT'S* WHO I AM.
ALL THAT TO SAY, NOW THAT YOU KNOW ABOUT MY PARENTS...I'M READY TO MEET YOURS.

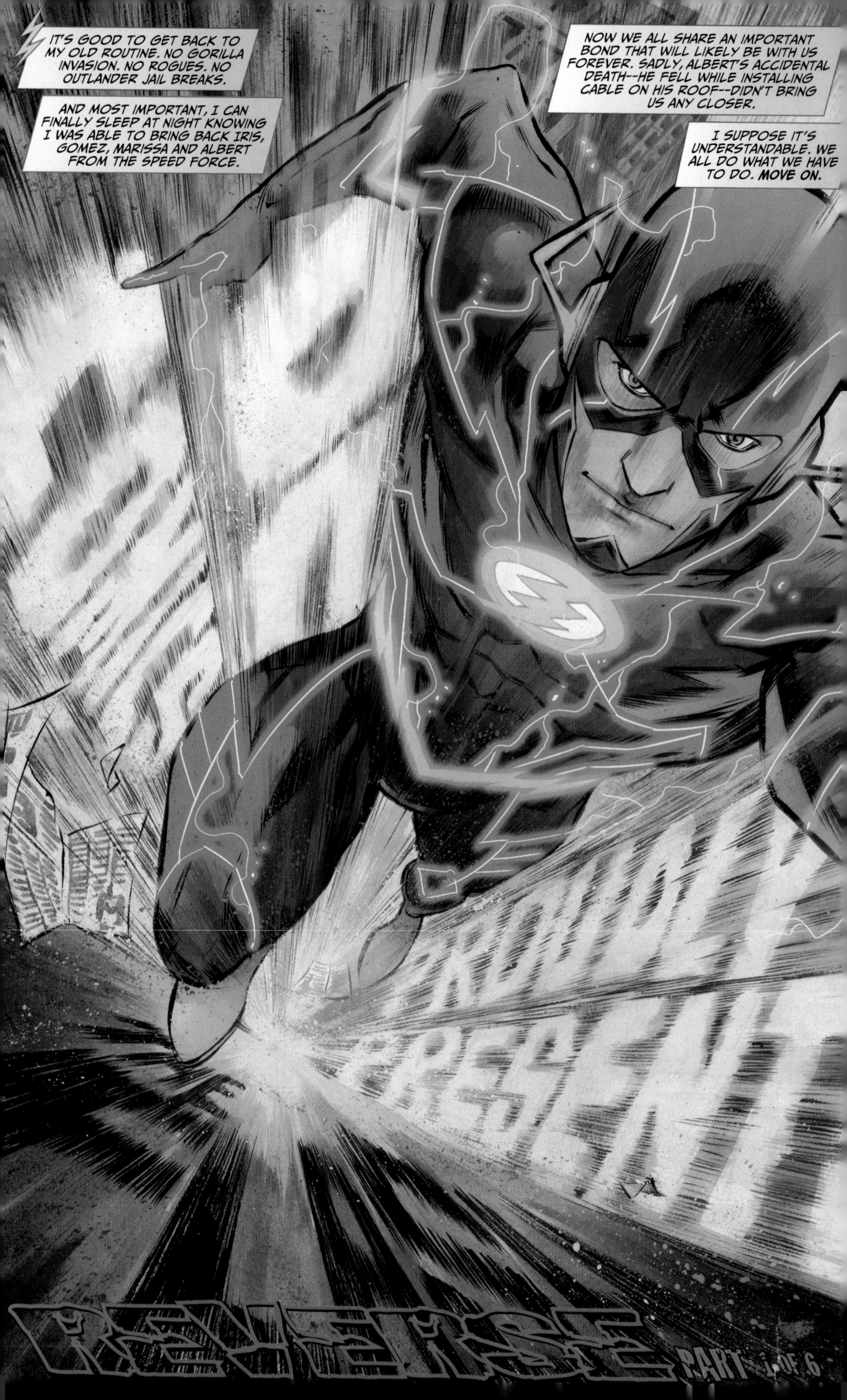
IT'S GOOD TO GET BACK TO MY OLD ROUTINE. NO GORILLA INVASION. NO ROGUES. NO OUTLANDER JAIL BREAKS.
AND MOST IMPORTANT, I CAN FINALLY SLEEP AT NIGHT KNOWING I WAS ABLE TO BRING BACK IRIS, GOMEZ, MARISSA AND ALBERT FROM THE SPEED FORCE.
NOW WE ALL SHARE AN IMPORTANT BOND THAT WILL LIKELY BE WITH US FOREVER. SADLY, ALBERT'S ACCIDENTAL DEATH--HE FELL WHILE INSTALLING CABLE ON HIS ROOF--DIDN'T BRING US ANY CLOSER.
I SUPPOSE IT'S UNDERSTANDABLE. WE ALL DO WHAT WE HAVE TO DO. **MOVE ON.**
REVERSE
PART 1 OF 6

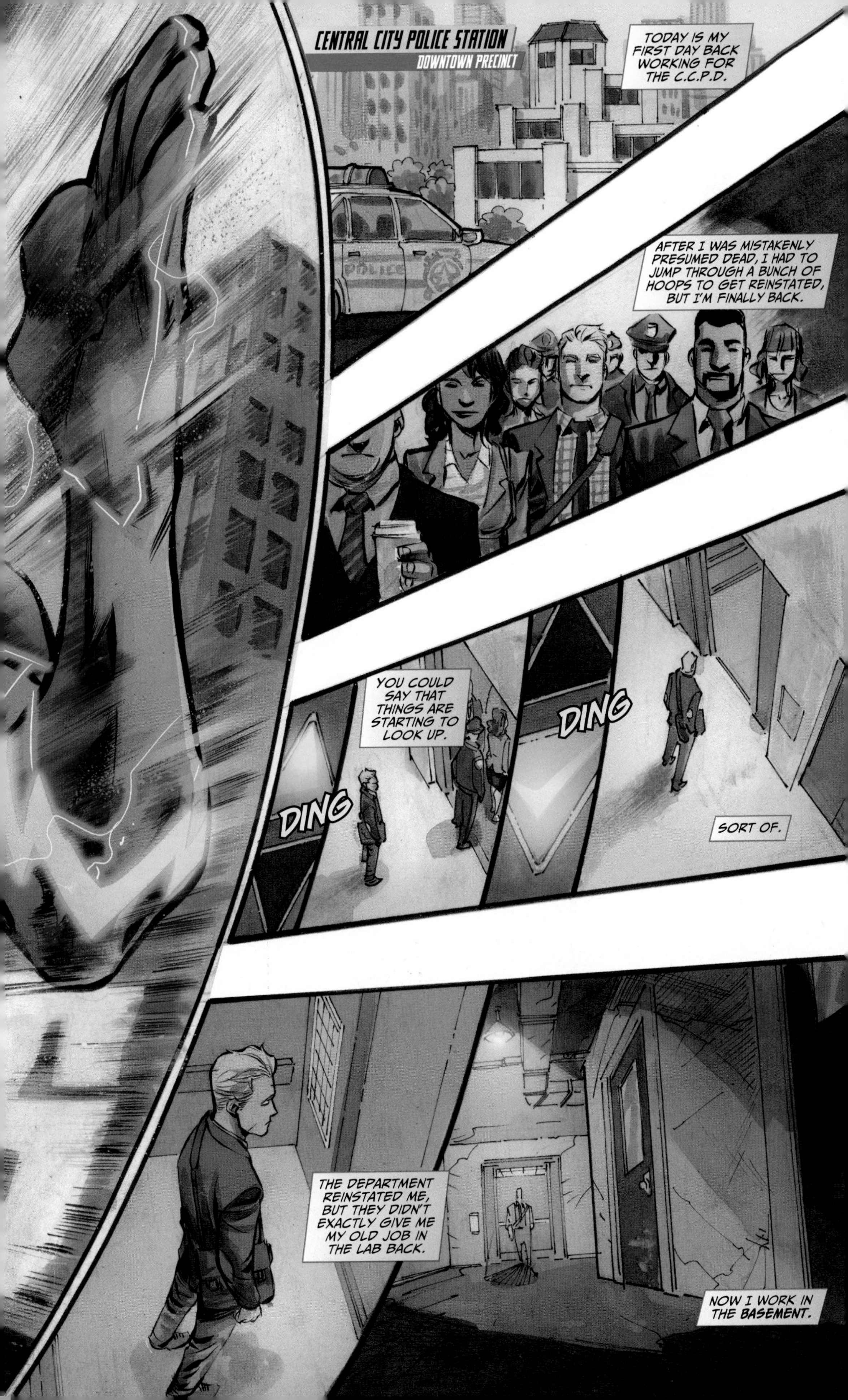

CENTRAL CITY POLICE STATION
DOWNTOWN PRECINCT
TODAY IS MY FIRST DAY BACK WORKING FOR THE C.C.P.D.
AFTER I WAS MISTAKENLY PRESUMED DEAD, I HAD TO JUMP THROUGH A BUNCH OF HOOPS TO GET REINSTATED, BUT I'M FINALLY BACK.
YOU COULD SAY THAT THINGS ARE STARTING TO LOOK UP.
DING
DING
SORT OF.
THE DEPARTMENT REINSTATED ME, BUT THEY DIDN'T EXACTLY GIVE ME MY OLD JOB IN THE LAB BACK.
NOW I WORK IN THE BASEMENT.

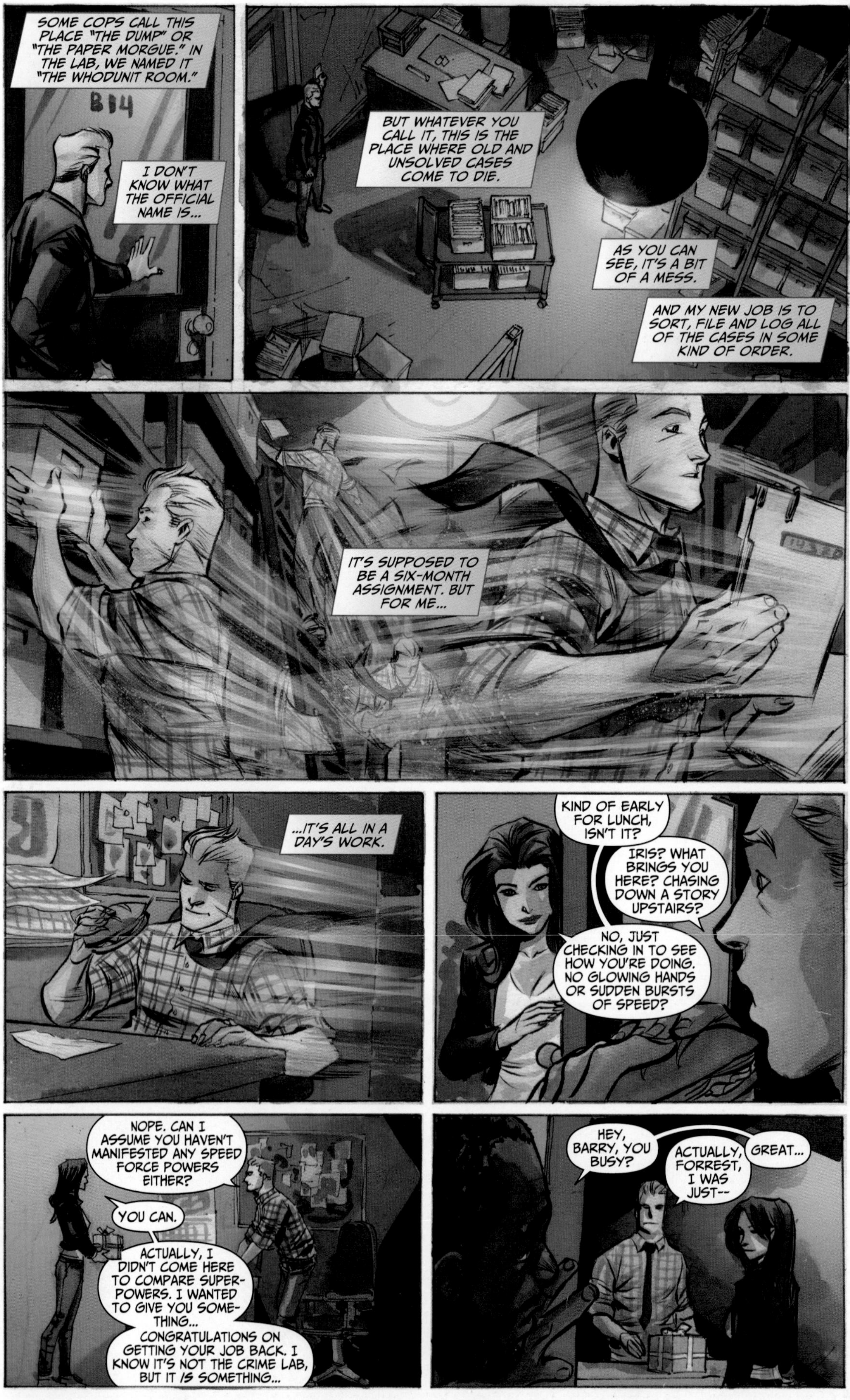
SOME COPS CALL THIS PLACE "THE DUMP" OR "THE PAPER MORGUE." IN THE LAB, WE NAMED IT "THE WHODUNIT ROOM."
B14
I DON'T KNOW WHAT THE OFFICIAL NAME IS...
BUT WHATEVER YOU CALL IT, THIS IS THE PLACE WHERE OLD AND UNSOLVED CASES COME TO DIE.
AS YOU CAN SEE, IT'S A BIT OF A MESS.
AND MY NEW JOB IS TO SORT, FILE AND LOG ALL OF THE CASES IN SOME KIND OF ORDER.
IT'S SUPPOSED TO BE A SIX-MONTH ASSIGNMENT. BUT FOR ME...
...IT'S ALL IN A DAY'S WORK.
KIND OF EARLY FOR LUNCH, ISN'T IT?
IRIS? WHAT BRINGS YOU HERE? CHASING DOWN A STORY UPSTAIRS?
NO, JUST CHECKING IN TO SEE HOW YOU'RE DOING. NO GLOWING HANDS OR SUDDEN BURSTS OF SPEED?
NOPE. CAN I ASSUME YOU HAVEN'T MANIFESTED ANY SPEED FORCE POWERS EITHER?
YOU CAN.
ACTUALLY, I DIDN'T COME HERE TO COMPARE SUPER-POWERS. I WANTED TO GIVE YOU SOME-THING...
CONGRATULATIONS ON GETTING YOUR JOB BACK. I KNOW IT'S NOT THE CRIME LAB, BUT IT IS SOMETHING...
HEY, BARRY, YOU BUSY?
GREAT...
ACTUALLY, FORREST, I WAS JUST--

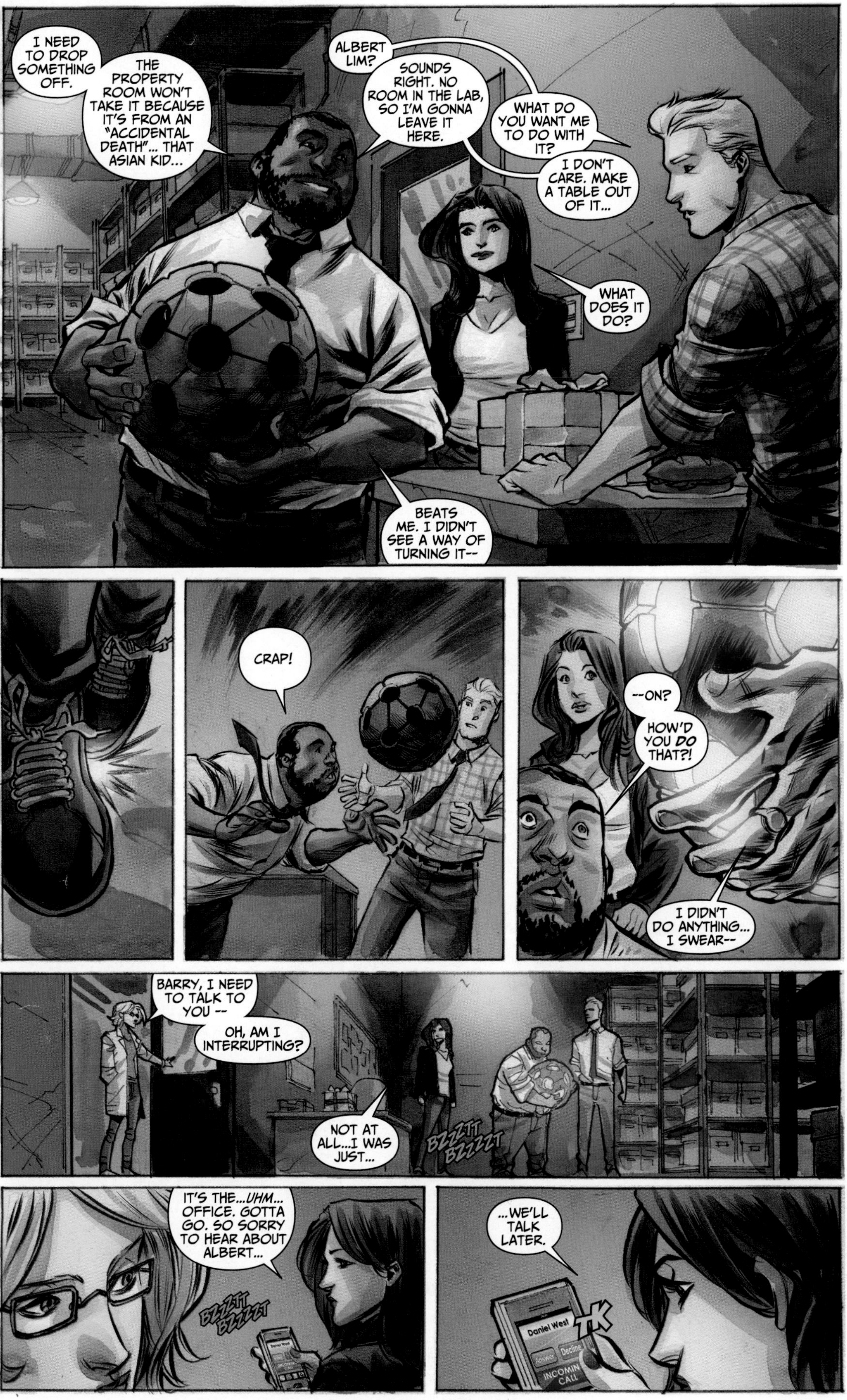
I NEED TO DROP SOMETHING OFF.
THE PROPERTY ROOM WON'T TAKE IT BECAUSE IT'S FROM AN "ACCIDENTAL DEATH"... THAT ASIAN KID...
ALBERT LIM?
SOUNDS RIGHT. NO ROOM IN THE LAB, SO I'M GONNA LEAVE IT HERE.
WHAT DO YOU WANT ME TO DO WITH IT?
I DON'T CARE. MAKE A TABLE OUT OF IT...
WHAT DOES IT DO?
BEATS ME. I DIDN'T SEE A WAY OF TURNING IT--
CRAP!
--ON?
HOW'D YOU DO THAT?!
I DIDN'T DO ANYTHING... I SWEAR--
BARRY, I NEED TO TALK TO YOU --
OH, AM I INTERRUPTING?
NOT AT ALL...I WAS JUST...
BZZZTT BZZZZT
IT'S THE...UHM... OFFICE. GOTTA GO. SO SORRY TO HEAR ABOUT ALBERT...
BZZZTT BZZZZT
...WE'LL TALK LATER.
Daniel West
Answer
Decline
TK

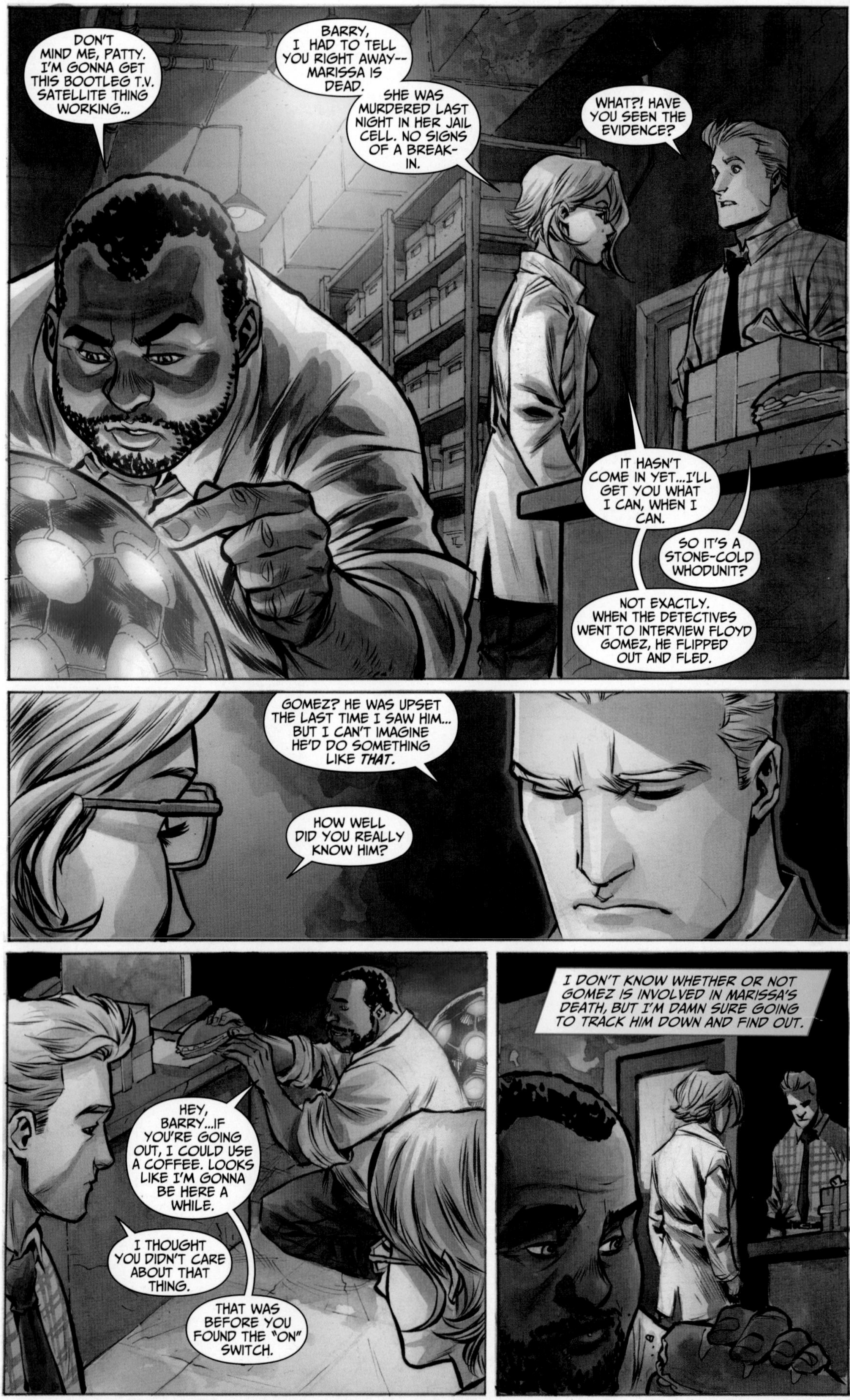
DON'T MIND ME, PATTY. I'M GONNA GET THIS BOOTLEG T.V. SATELLITE THING WORKING...
BARRY, I HAD TO TELL YOU RIGHT AWAY-- MARISSA IS DEAD.
SHE WAS MURDERED LAST NIGHT IN HER JAIL CELL. NO SIGNS OF A BREAK-IN.
WHAT?! HAVE YOU SEEN THE EVIDENCE?
IT HASN'T COME IN YET...I'LL GET YOU WHAT I CAN, WHEN I CAN.
SO IT'S A STONE-COLD WHODUNIT?
NOT EXACTLY. WHEN THE DETECTIVES WENT TO INTERVIEW FLOYD GOMEZ, HE FLIPPED OUT AND FLED.
GOMEZ? HE WAS UPSET THE LAST TIME I SAW HIM... BUT I CAN'T IMAGINE HE'D DO SOMETHING LIKE *THAT.*
HOW WELL DID YOU REALLY KNOW HIM?
HEY, BARRY...IF YOU'RE GOING OUT, I COULD USE A COFFEE. LOOKS LIKE I'M GONNA BE HERE A WHILE.
I THOUGHT YOU DIDN'T CARE ABOUT THAT THING.
THAT WAS BEFORE YOU FOUND THE "ON" SWITCH.
I DON'T KNOW WHETHER OR NOT GOMEZ IS INVOLVED IN MARISSA'S DEATH, BUT I'M DAMN SURE GOING TO TRACK HIM DOWN AND FIND OUT.

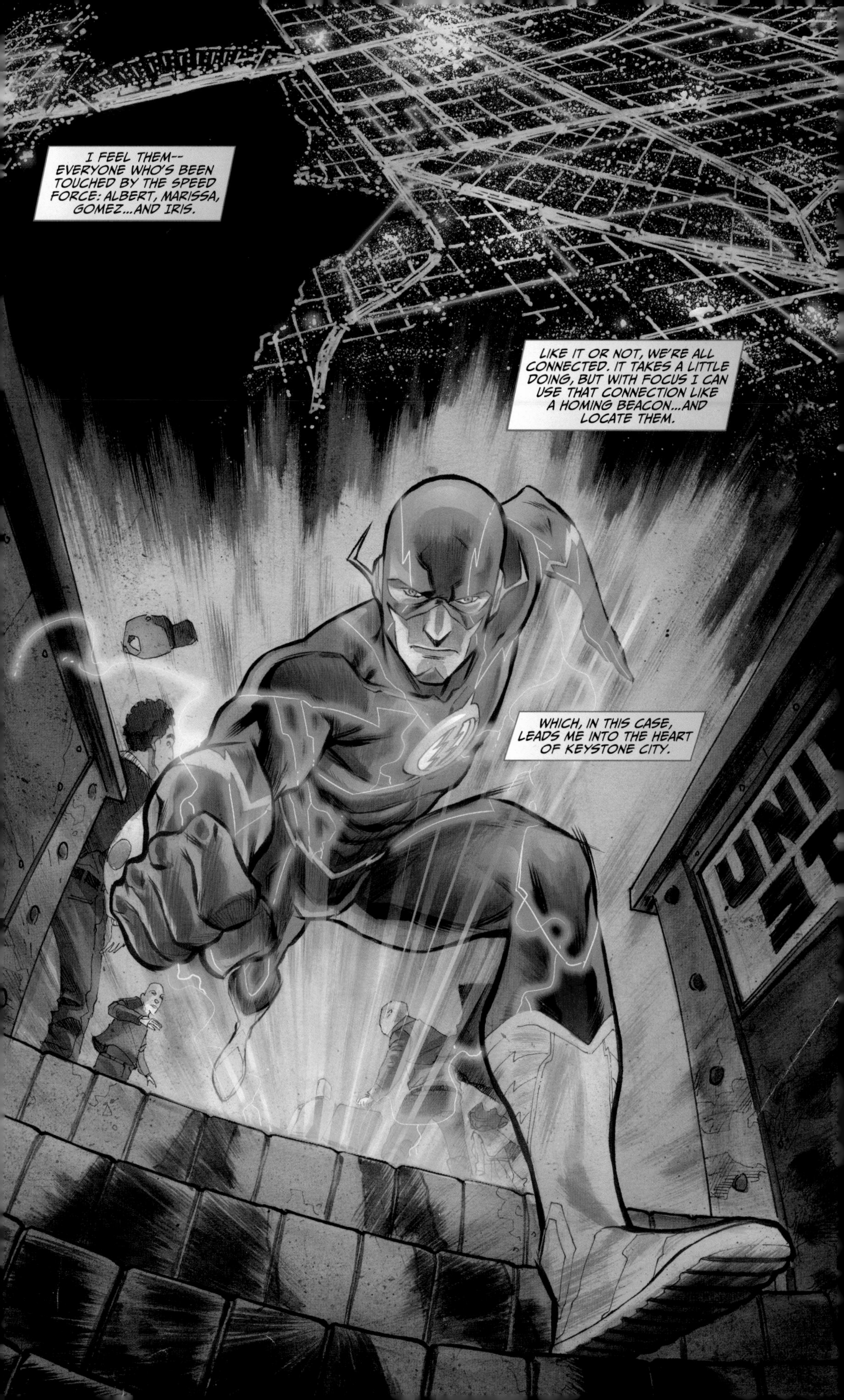
I FEEL THEM--
EVERYONE WHO'S BEEN TOUCHED BY THE SPEED FORCE: ALBERT, MARISSA, GOMEZ...AND IRIS.
LIKE IT OR NOT, WE'RE ALL CONNECTED. IT TAKES A LITTLE DOING, BUT WITH FOCUS I CAN USE THAT CONNECTION LIKE A HOMING BEACON...AND LOCATE THEM.
WHICH, IN THIS CASE, LEADS ME INTO THE HEART OF KEYSTONE CITY.

THERE HE IS.
TRYING TO BE
INCONSPICUOUS...

BUT, TO ME, THAT
JUST MAKES HIM
LOOK SUSPICIOUS.

GOMEZ,
WE NEED TO
TALK--

WHOK

KRENNCH

NO INTEREST IN
TALKING EITHER.

ENNH!
ENNH!

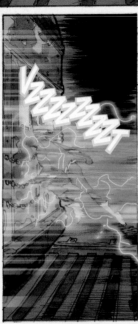

VZZZZZZZT

GOMEZ DEFINITELY
HAS THE LOOK OF
SOMEONE ON THE
RUN.

INNOCENT PEOPLE
DON'T USUALLY
HAVE THAT.

DAMN.

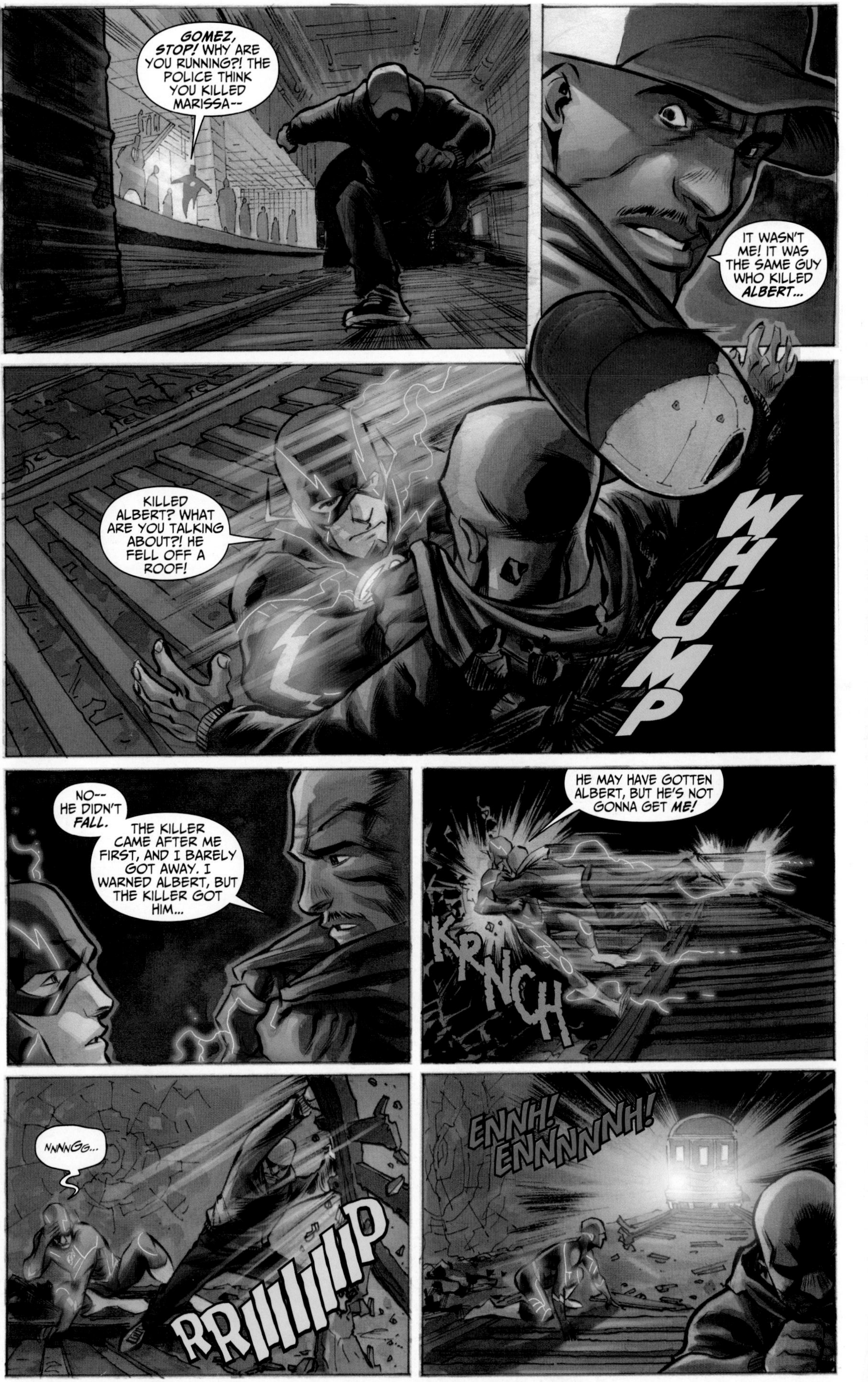
GOMEZ, STOP! WHY ARE YOU RUNNING?! THE POLICE THINK YOU KILLED MARISSA--
IT WASN'T ME! IT WAS THE SAME GUY WHO KILLED ALBERT...
KILLED ALBERT? WHAT ARE YOU TALKING ABOUT?! HE FELL OFF A ROOF!
WHUMP
NO-- HE DIDN'T FALL.
THE KILLER CAME AFTER ME FIRST, AND I BARELY GOT AWAY. I WARNED ALBERT, BUT THE KILLER GOT HIM...
HE MAY HAVE GOTTEN ALBERT, BUT HE'S NOT GONNA GET ME!
KRNCH
NNNNGG...
RRIIIIIIIP
ENNH! ENNNNNH!

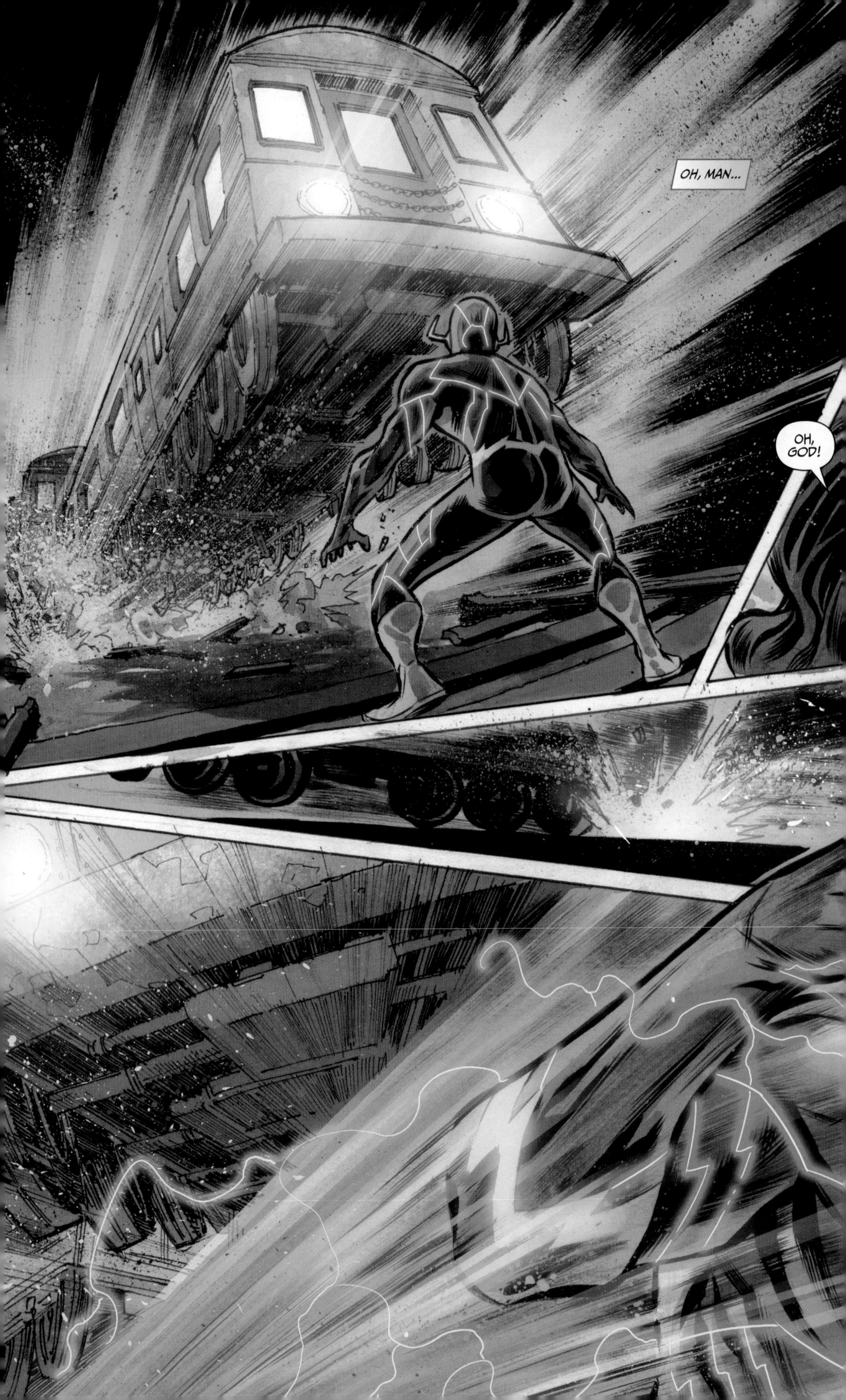
OH, MAN...
OH, GOD!

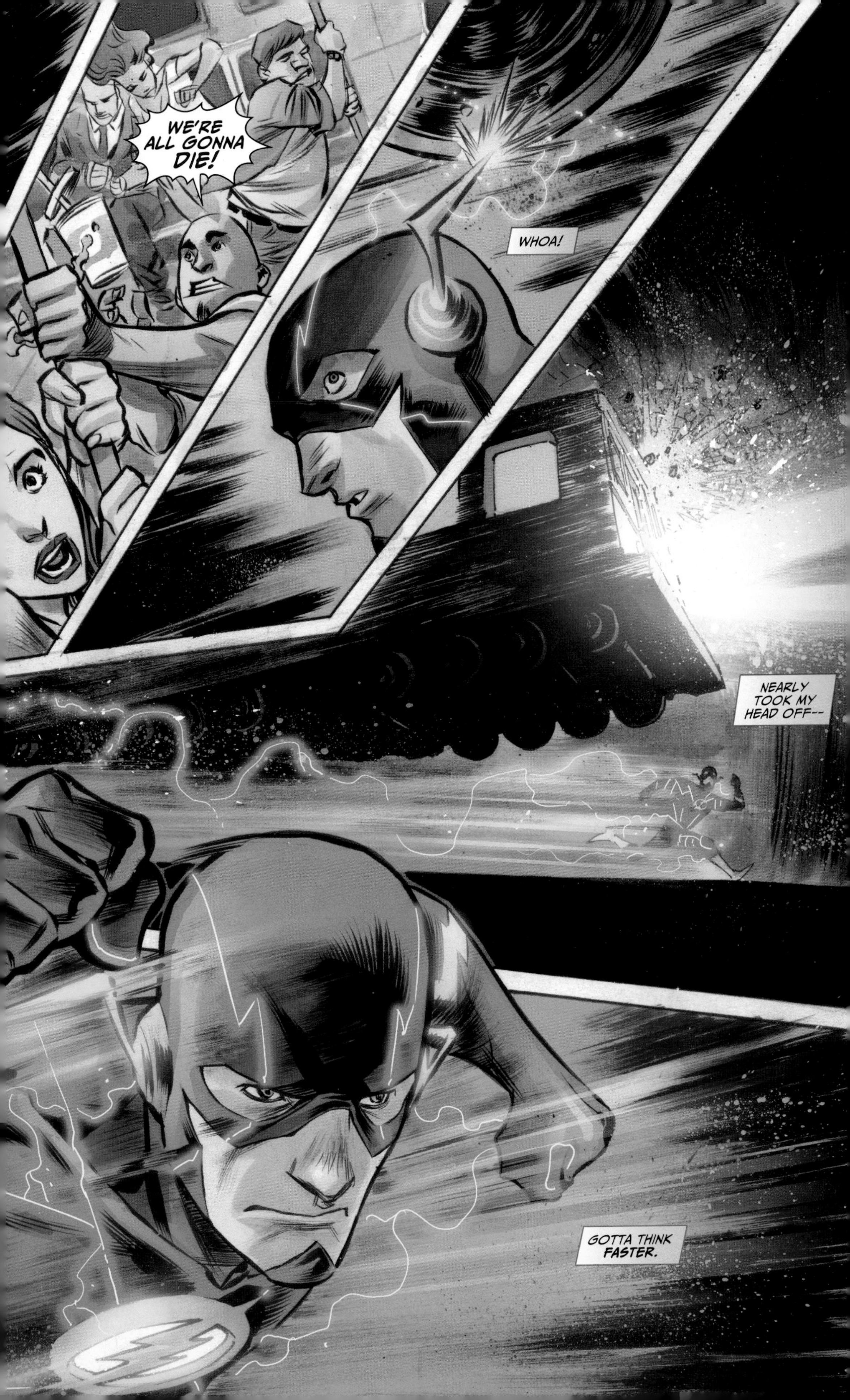
WE'RE ALL GONNA DIE!
WHOA!
NEARLY TOOK MY HEAD OFF--
GOTTA THINK FASTER.

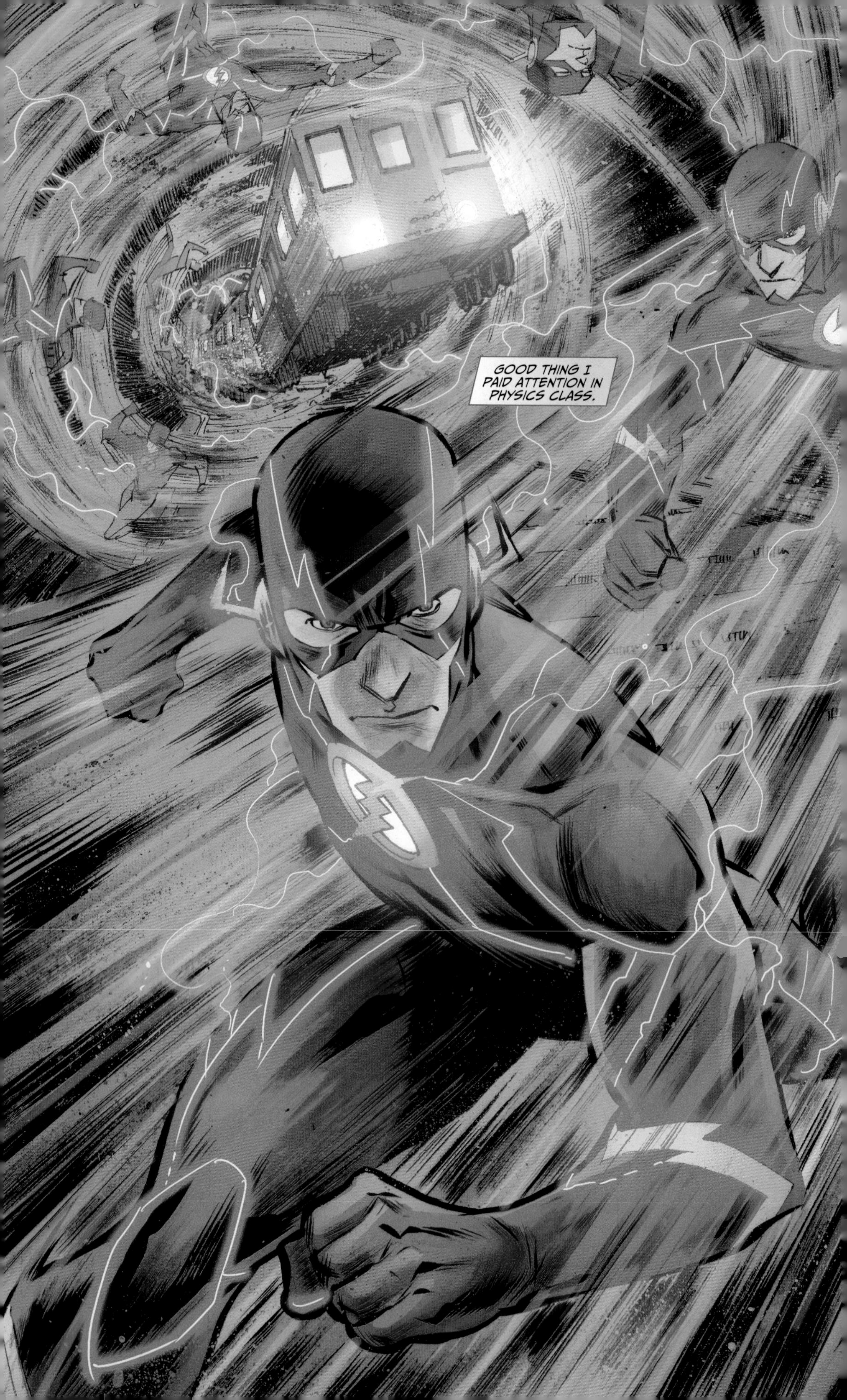
GOOD THING I PAID ATTENTION IN PHYSICS CLASS.

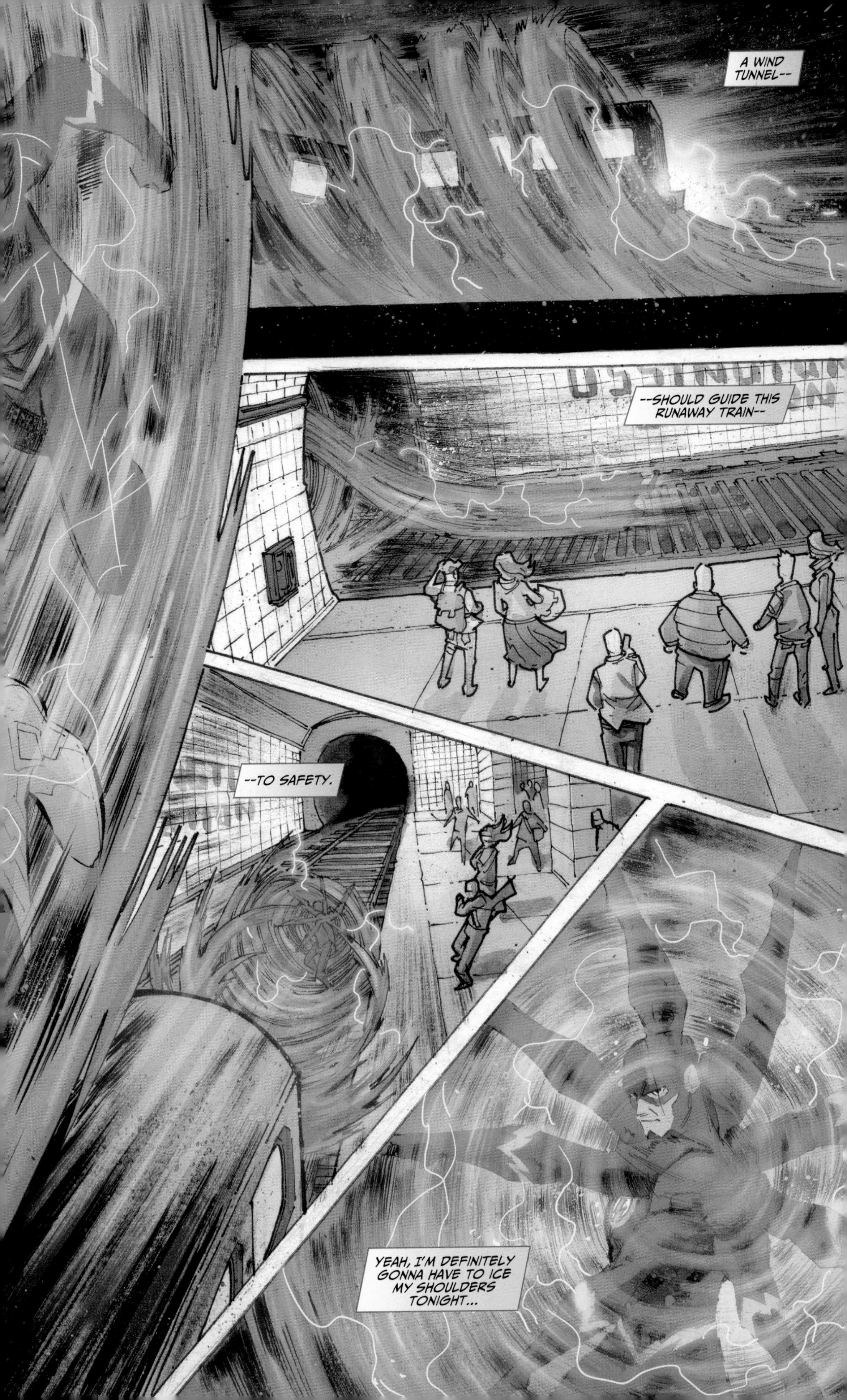
A WIND TUNNEL--
--SHOULD GUIDE THIS RUNAWAY TRAIN--
--TO SAFETY.
YEAH, I'M DEFINITELY GONNA HAVE TO ICE MY SHOULDERS TONIGHT...

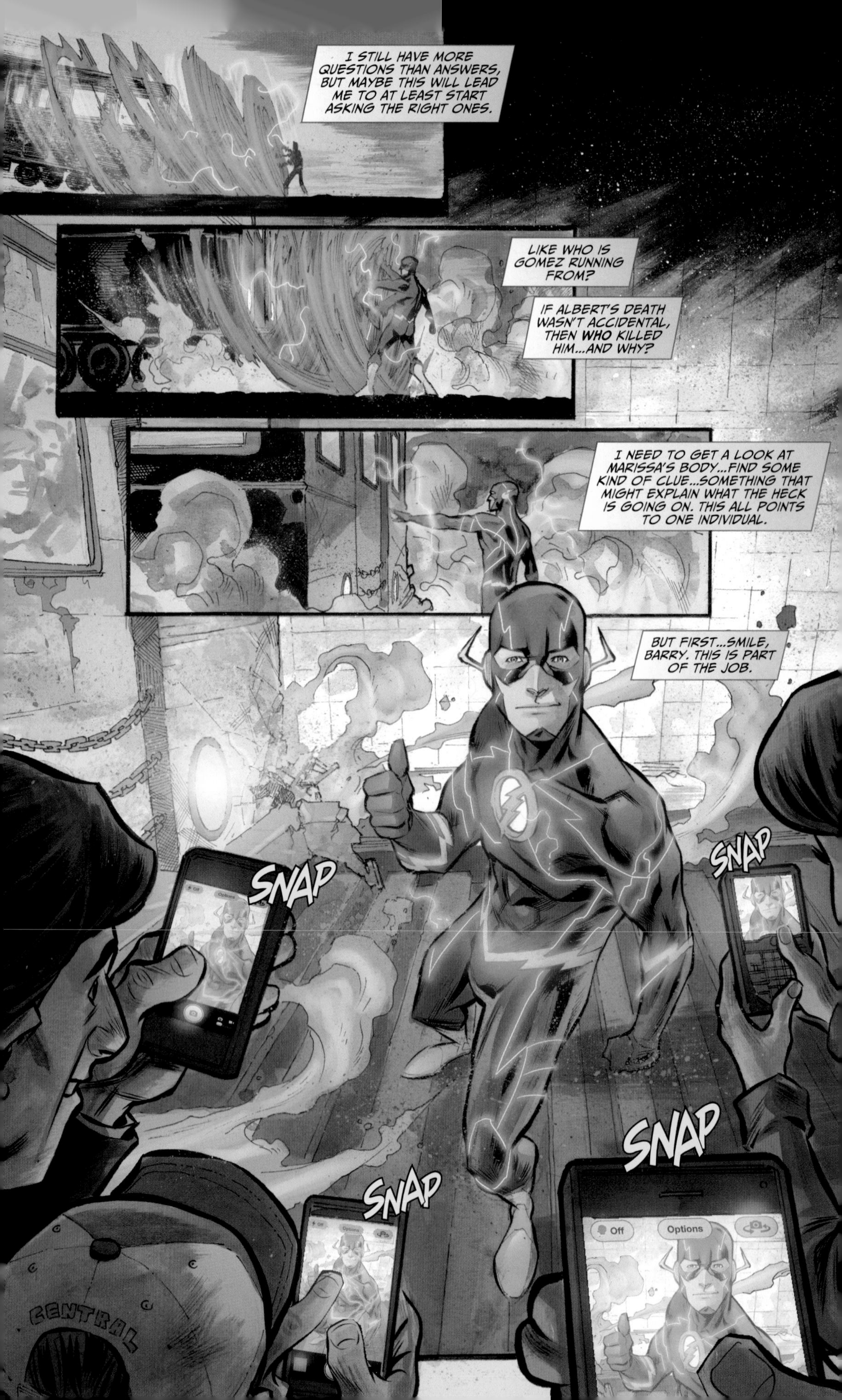
I STILL HAVE MORE QUESTIONS THAN ANSWERS, BUT MAYBE THIS WILL LEAD ME TO AT LEAST START ASKING THE RIGHT ONES.
LIKE WHO IS GOMEZ RUNNING FROM?
IF ALBERT'S DEATH WASN'T ACCIDENTAL, THEN WHO KILLED HIM...AND WHY?
I NEED TO GET A LOOK AT MARISSA'S BODY...FIND SOME KIND OF CLUE...SOMETHING THAT MIGHT EXPLAIN WHAT THE HECK IS GOING ON. THIS ALL POINTS TO ONE INDIVIDUAL.
BUT FIRST...SMILE, BARRY. THIS IS PART OF THE JOB.
SNAP
SNAP
SNAP
SNAP
Off
Options
CENTRAL

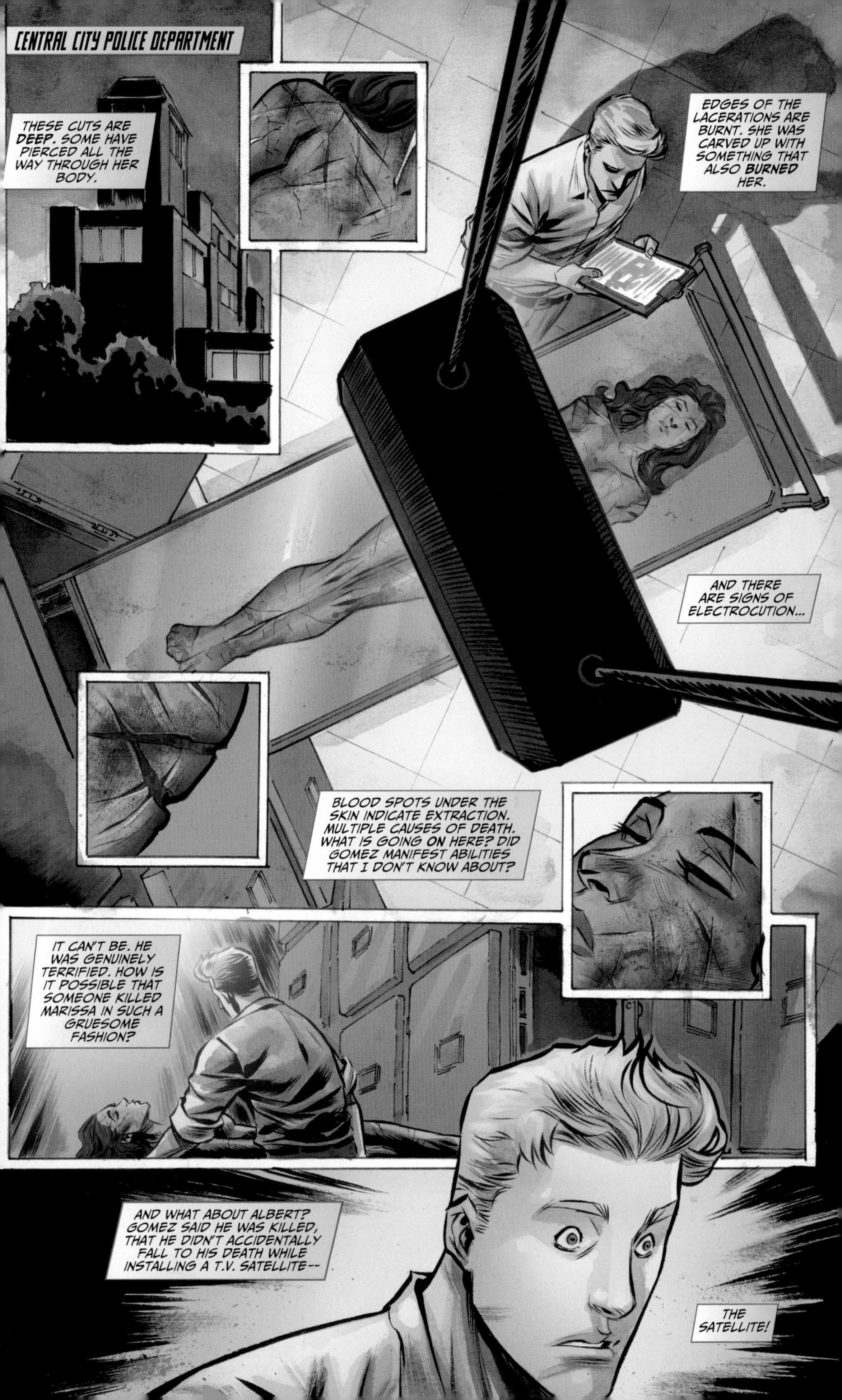
CENTRAL CITY POLICE DEPARTMENT
THESE CUTS ARE DEEP. SOME HAVE PIERCED ALL THE WAY THROUGH HER BODY.
EDGES OF THE LACERATIONS ARE BURNT. SHE WAS CARVED UP WITH SOMETHING THAT ALSO BURNED HER.
AND THERE ARE SIGNS OF ELECTROCUTION...
BLOOD SPOTS UNDER THE SKIN INDICATE EXTRACTION. MULTIPLE CAUSES OF DEATH. WHAT IS GOING ON HERE? DID GOMEZ MANIFEST ABILITIES THAT I DON'T KNOW ABOUT?
IT CAN'T BE. HE WAS GENUINELY TERRIFIED. HOW IS IT POSSIBLE THAT SOMEONE KILLED MARISSA IN SUCH A GRUESOME FASHION?
AND WHAT ABOUT ALBERT? GOMEZ SAID HE WAS KILLED, THAT HE DIDN'T ACCIDENTALLY FALL TO HIS DEATH WHILE INSTALLING A T.V. SATELLITE--
THE SATELLITE!

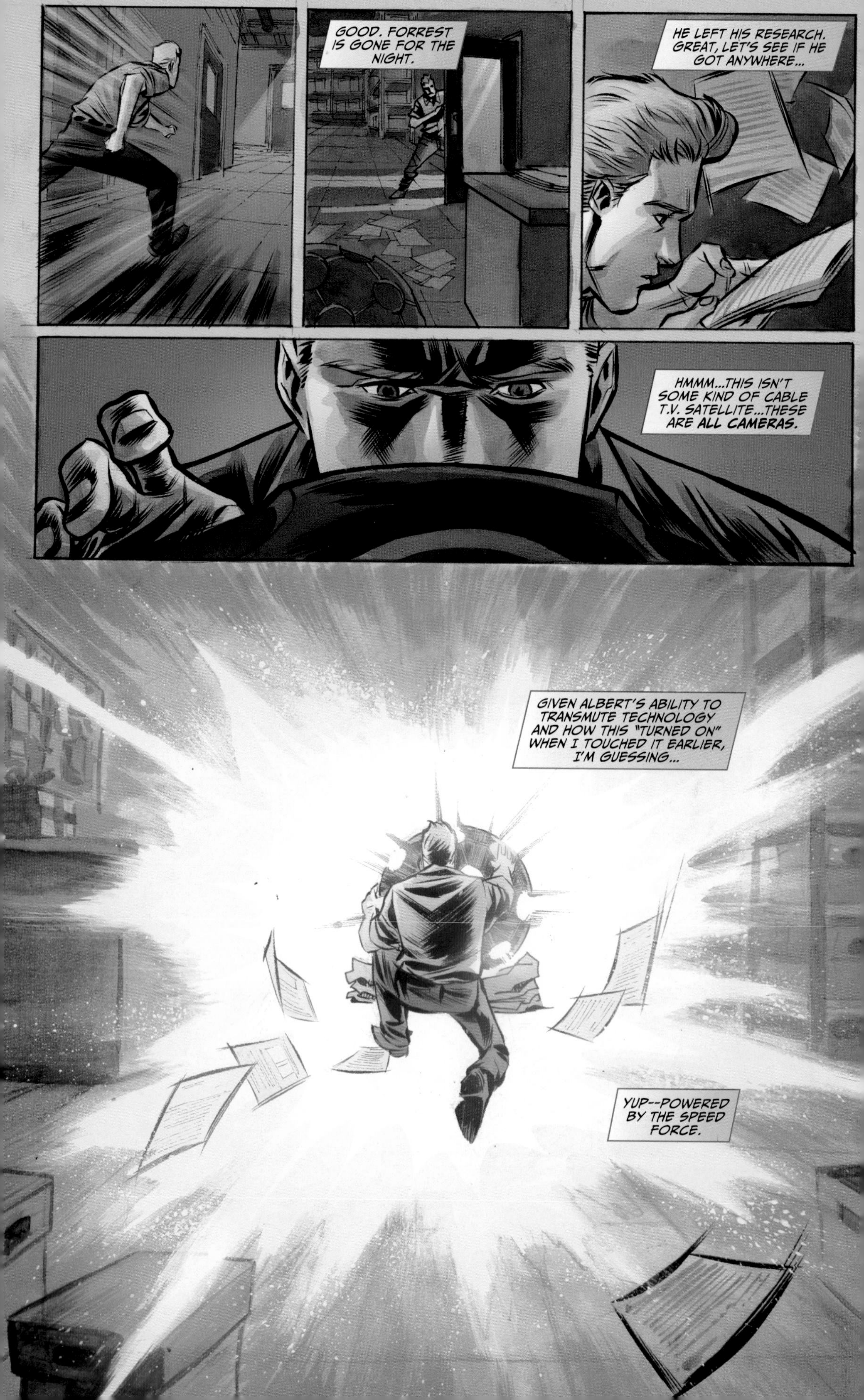
GOOD. FORREST IS GONE FOR THE NIGHT.
HE LEFT HIS RESEARCH. GREAT, LET'S SEE IF HE GOT ANYWHERE...
HMMM...THIS ISN'T SOME KIND OF CABLE T.V. SATELLITE...THESE ARE ALL CAMERAS.
GIVEN ALBERT'S ABILITY TO TRANSMUTE TECHNOLOGY AND HOW THIS "TURNED ON" WHEN I TOUCHED IT EARLIER, I'M GUESSING...
YUP--POWERED BY THE SPEED FORCE.

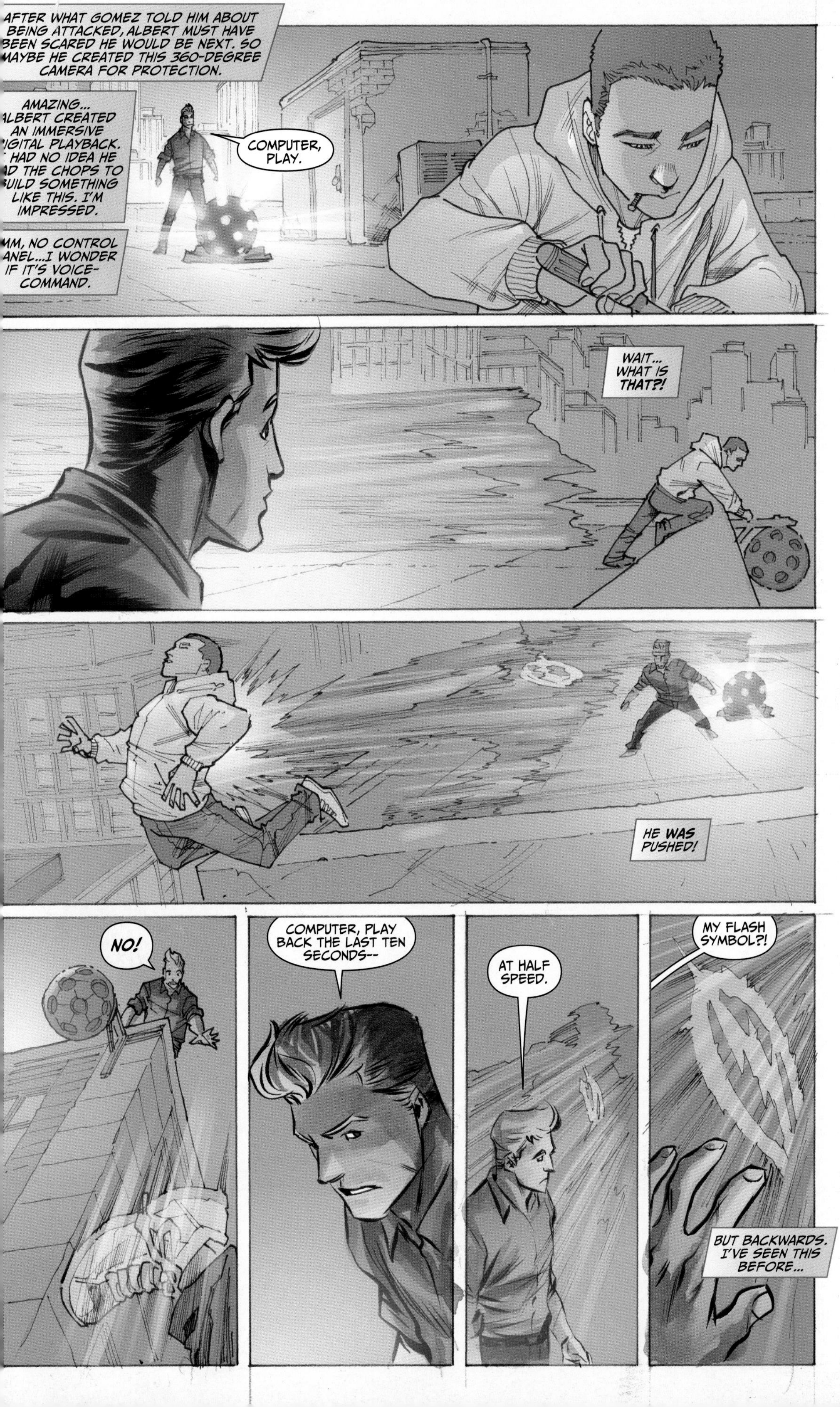
AFTER WHAT GOMEZ TOLD HIM ABOUT BEING ATTACKED, ALBERT MUST HAVE BEEN SCARED HE WOULD BE NEXT. SO MAYBE HE CREATED THIS 360-DEGREE CAMERA FOR PROTECTION.
AMAZING... ALBERT CREATED AN IMMERSIVE DIGITAL PLAYBACK. I HAD NO IDEA HE HAD THE CHOPS TO BUILD SOMETHING LIKE THIS. I'M IMPRESSED.
MM, NO CONTROL ANEL...I WONDER IF IT'S VOICE-COMMAND.
COMPUTER, PLAY.
WAIT... WHAT IS THAT?!
HE WAS PUSHED!
NO!
COMPUTER, PLAY BACK THE LAST TEN SECONDS--
AT HALF SPEED.
MY FLASH SYMBOL?!
BUT BACKWARDS. I'VE SEEN THIS BEFORE...

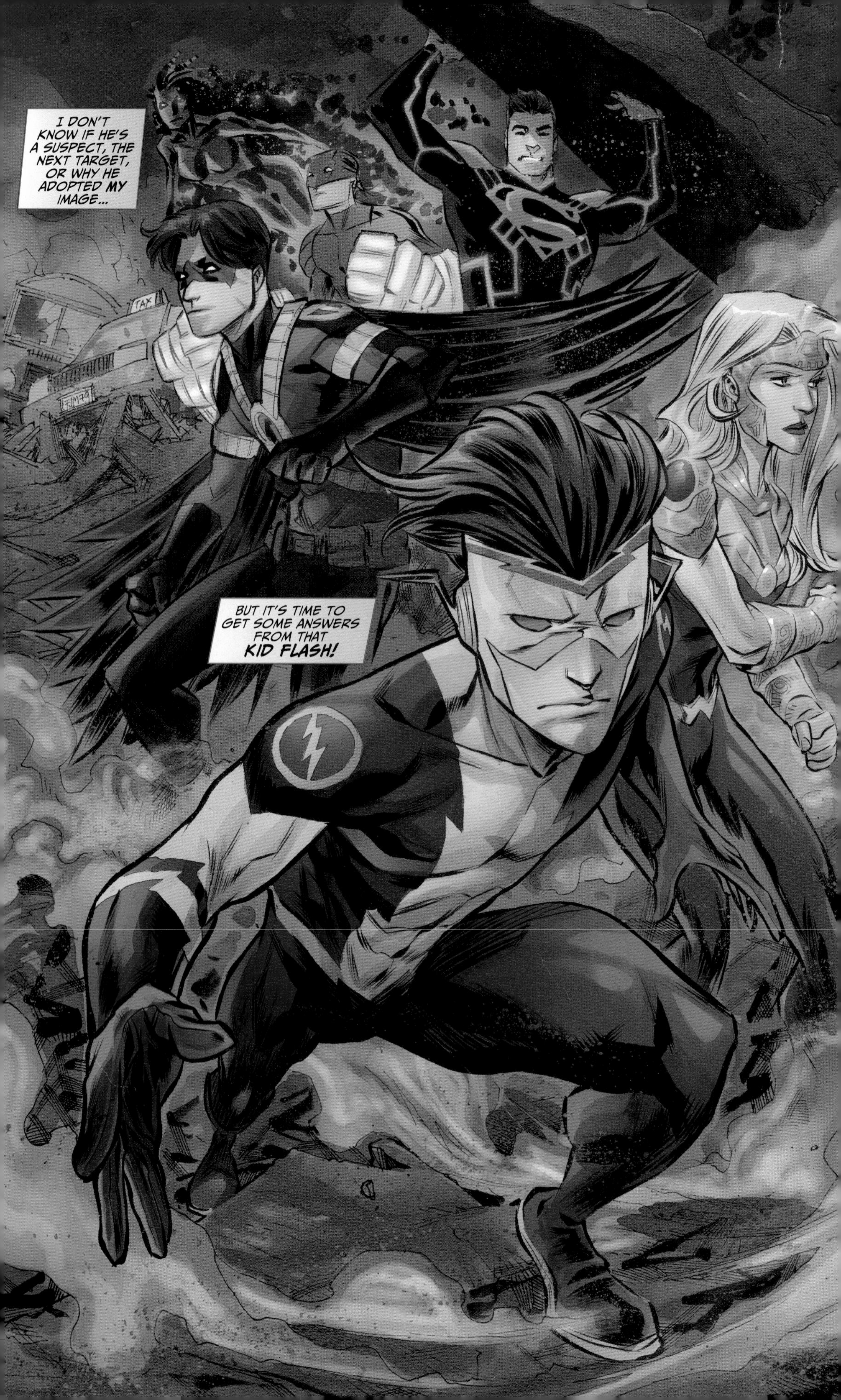
I DON'T KNOW IF HE'S A SUSPECT, THE NEXT TARGET, OR WHY HE ADOPTED MY IMAGE...
BUT IT'S TIME TO GET SOME ANSWERS FROM THAT KID FLASH!

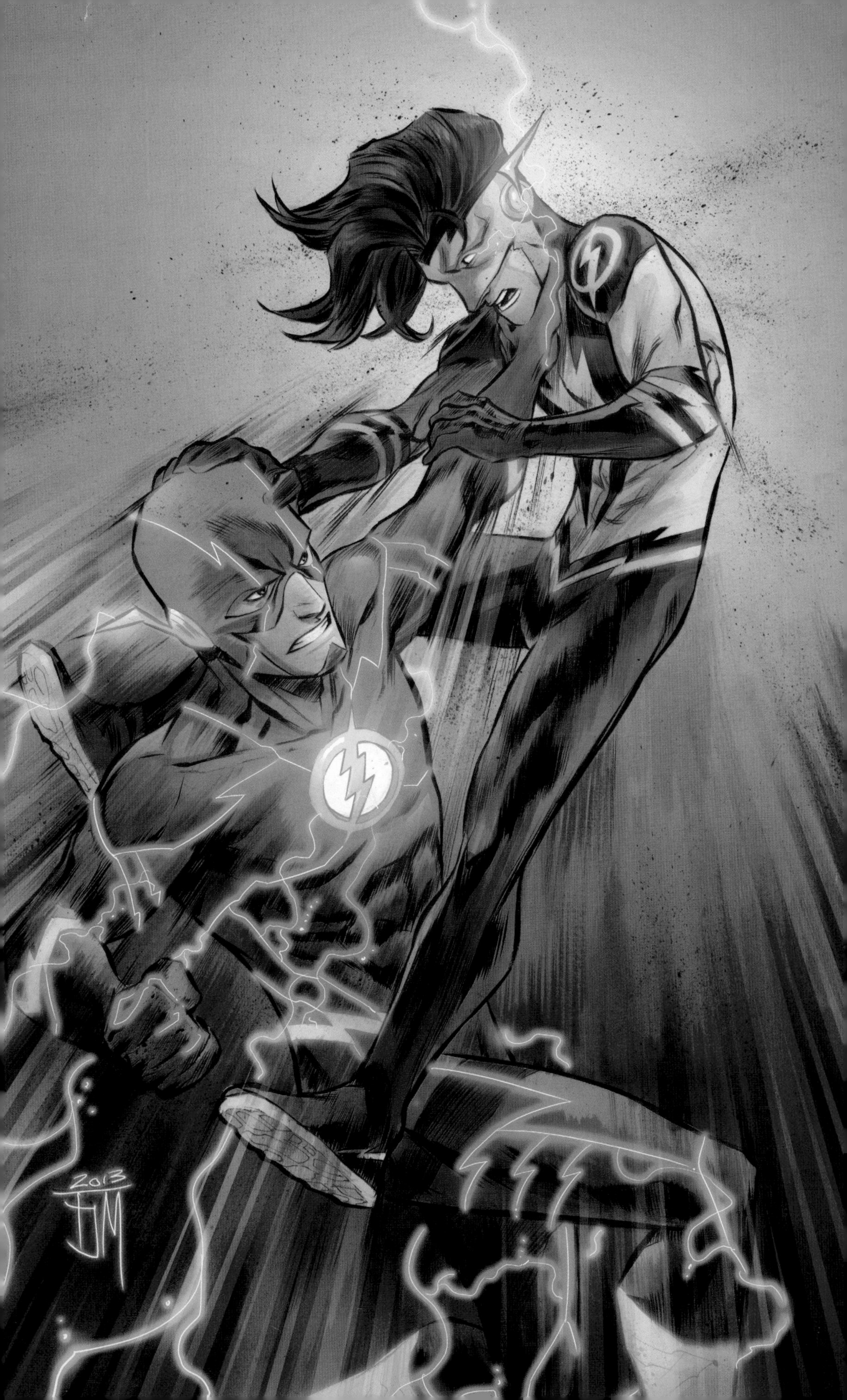
2013

FRANCIS MANAPUL & BRIAN BUCCELLATO writers FRANCIS MANAPUL artist

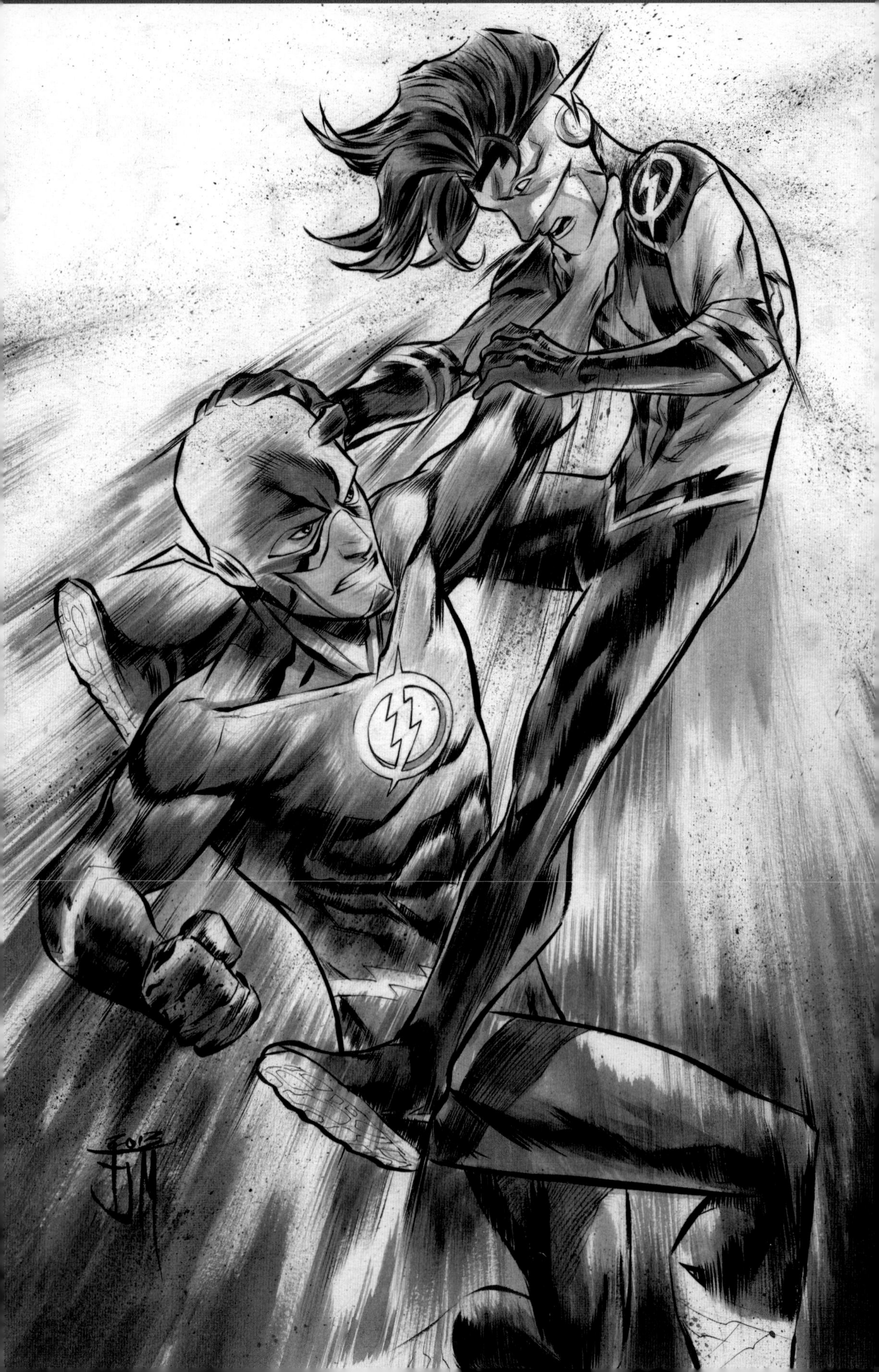

TWO PEOPLE I KNOW WERE RECENTLY MURDERED WITHOUT EXPLANATION.

AND THE ONLY THING THEY HAVE IN COMMON IS THAT THEY WERE BOTH TOUCHED BY THE SPEED FORCE.

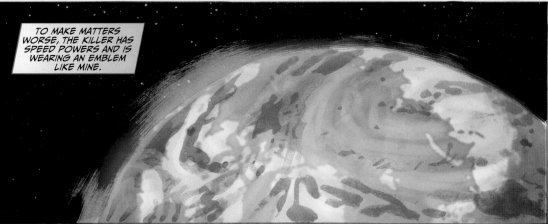

TO MAKE MATTERS WORSE, THE KILLER HAS SPEED POWERS AND IS WEARING AN EMBLEM LIKE MINE.

THAT MAKES IT MY PROBLEM...

IT ALSO MAKES IT MY FAULT.

HAUKADALUR VALLEY, ICELAND.

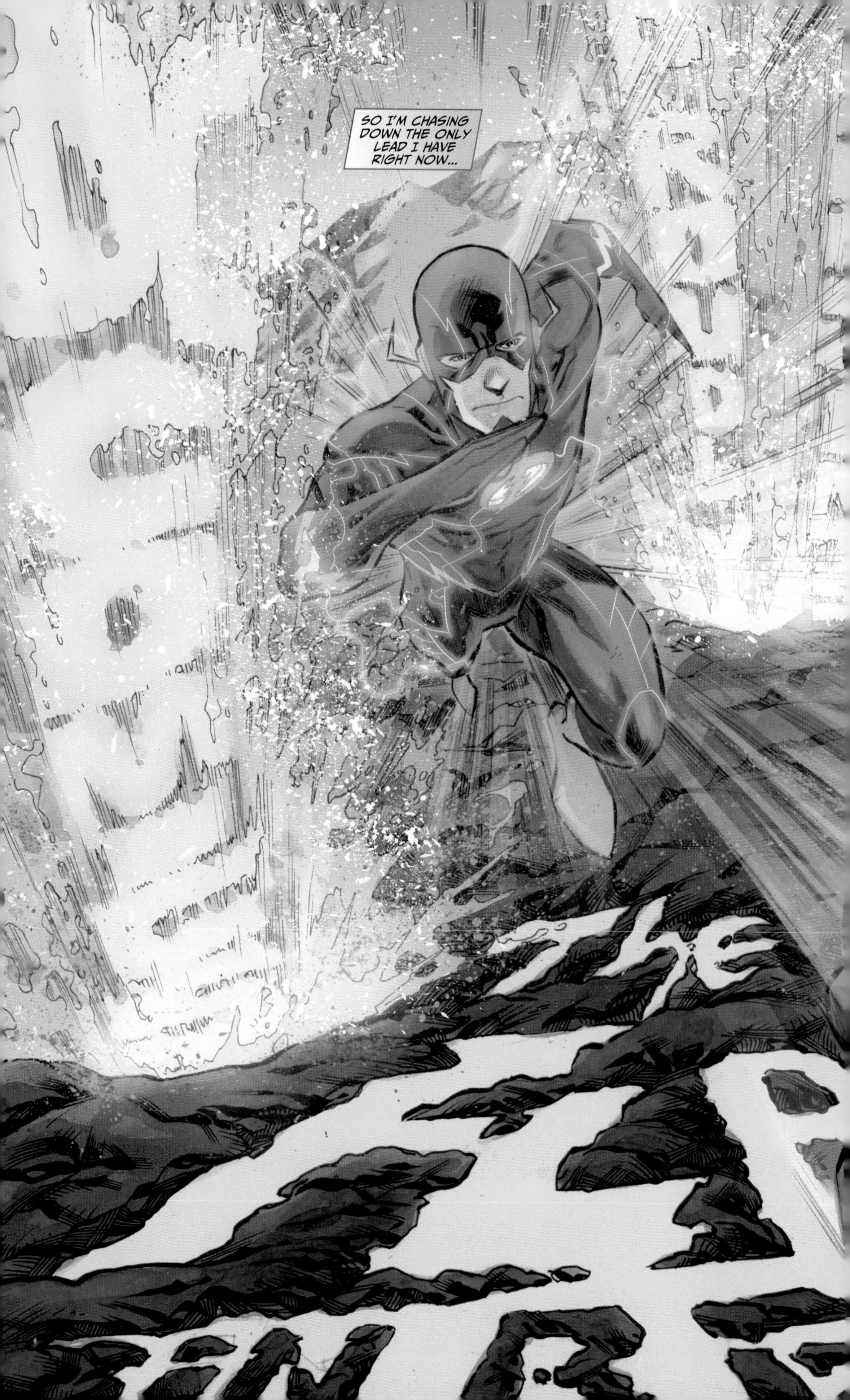
SO I'M CHASING DOWN THE ONLY LEAD I HAVE RIGHT NOW...

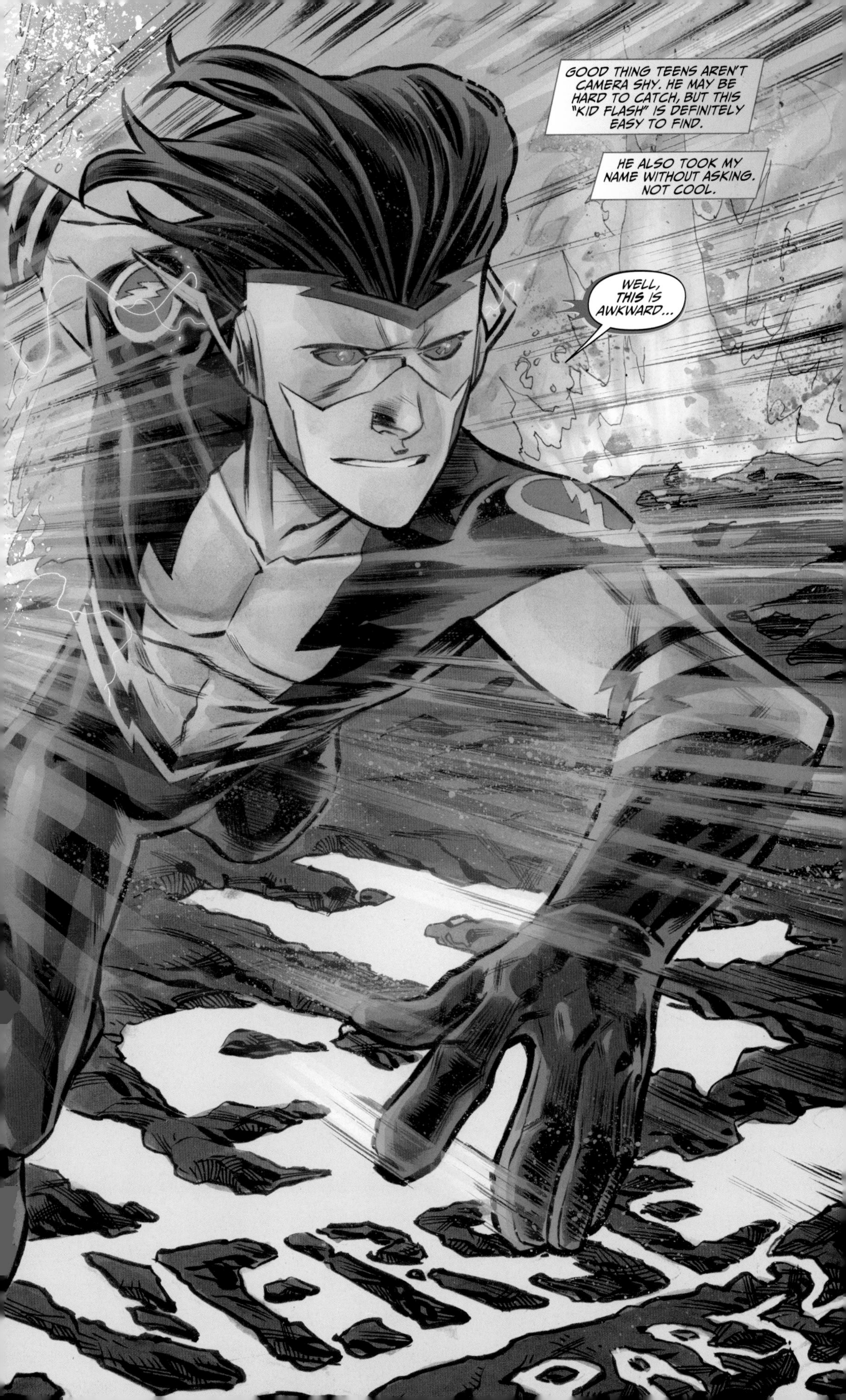
GOOD THING TEENS AREN'T CAMERA SHY. HE MAY BE HARD TO CATCH, BUT THIS "KID FLASH" IS DEFINITELY EASY TO FIND.
HE ALSO TOOK MY NAME WITHOUT ASKING. NOT COOL.
WELL, THIS IS AWKWARD...

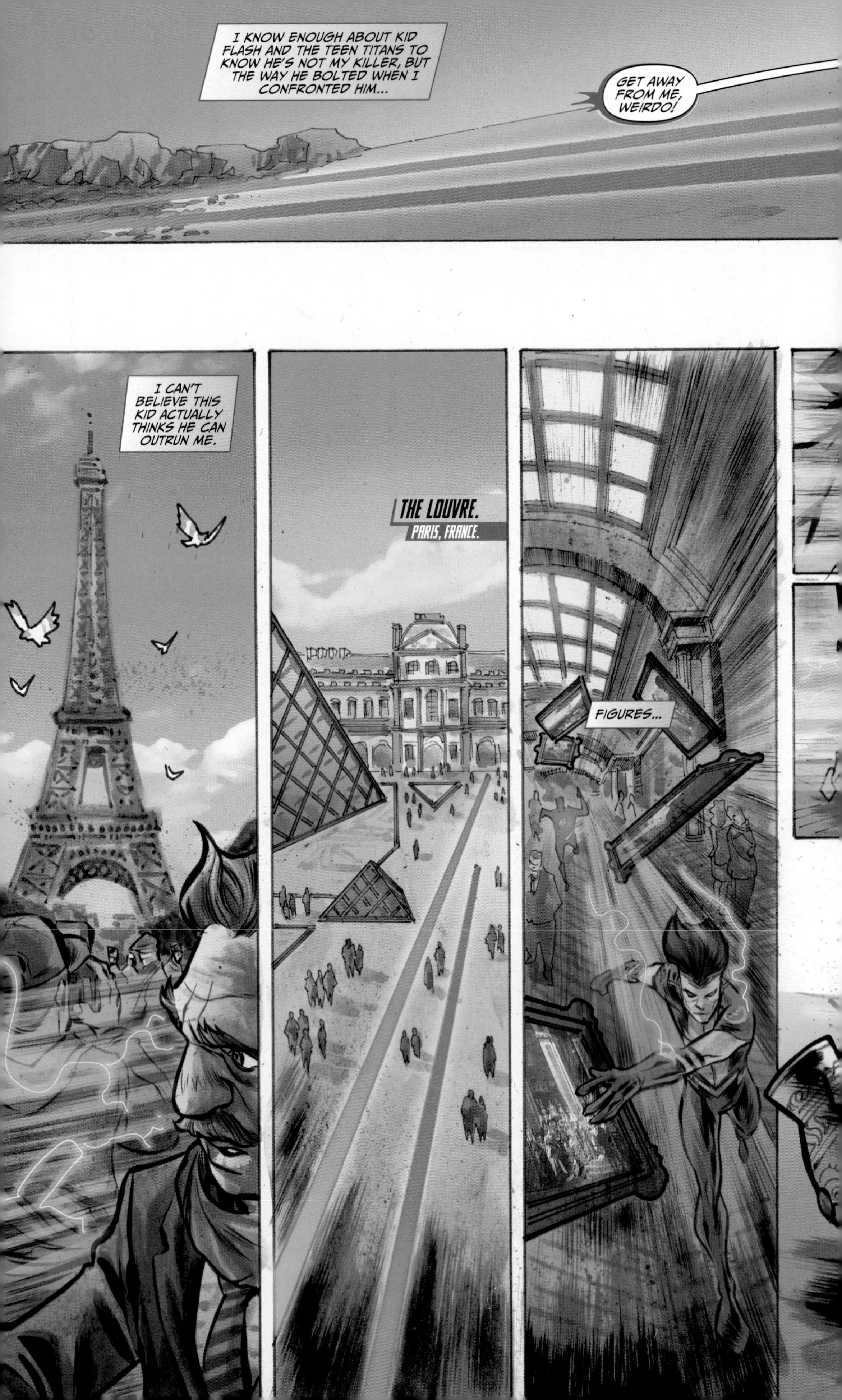
I KNOW ENOUGH ABOUT KID FLASH AND THE TEEN TITANS TO KNOW HE'S NOT MY KILLER, BUT THE WAY HE BOLTED WHEN I CONFRONTED HIM...
GET AWAY FROM ME, WEIRDO!
I CAN'T BELIEVE THIS KID ACTUALLY THINKS HE CAN OUTRUN ME.
THE LOUVRE.
PARIS, FRANCE.
FIGURES...

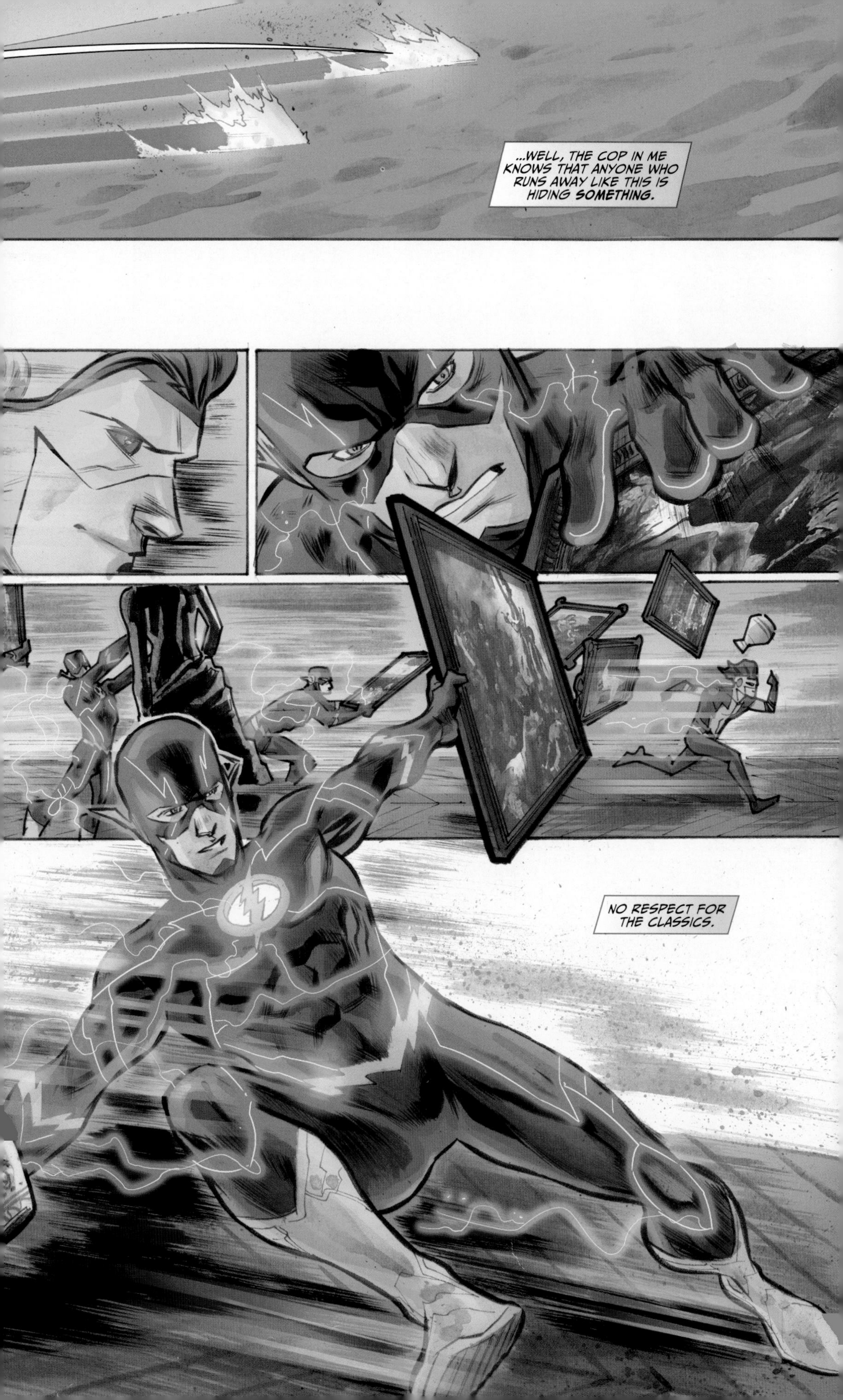
...WELL, THE COP IN ME KNOWS THAT ANYONE WHO RUNS AWAY LIKE THIS IS HIDING SOMETHING.
NO RESPECT FOR THE CLASSICS.

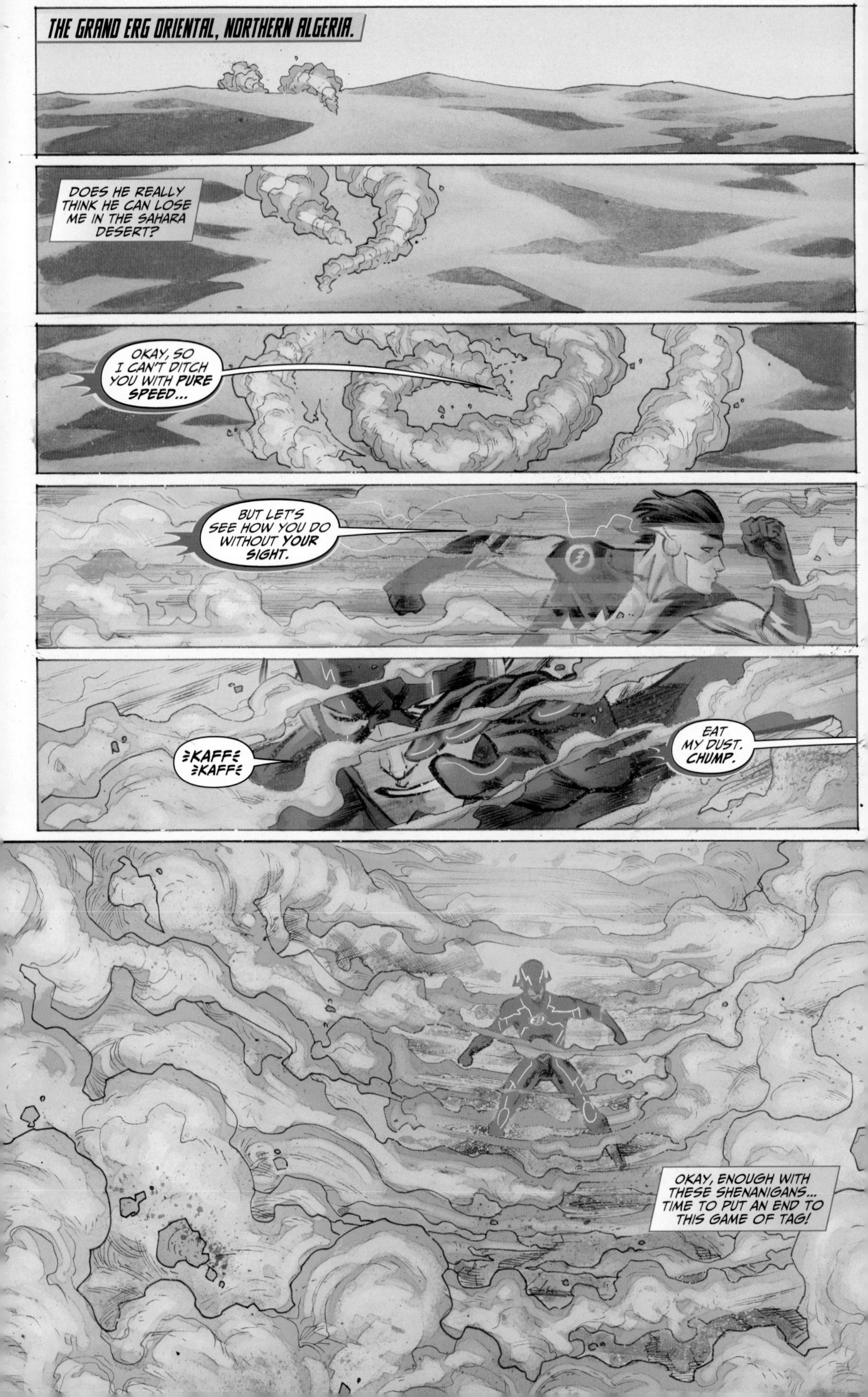
THE GRAND ERG ORIENTAL, NORTHERN ALGERIA.
DOES HE REALLY THINK HE CAN LOSE ME IN THE SAHARA DESERT?
OKAY, SO I CAN'T DITCH YOU WITH PURE SPEED...
BUT LET'S SEE HOW YOU DO WITHOUT YOUR SIGHT.
KAFF KAFF
EAT MY DUST. CHUMP.
OKAY, ENOUGH WITH THESE SHENANIGANS... TIME TO PUT AN END TO THIS GAME OF TAG!

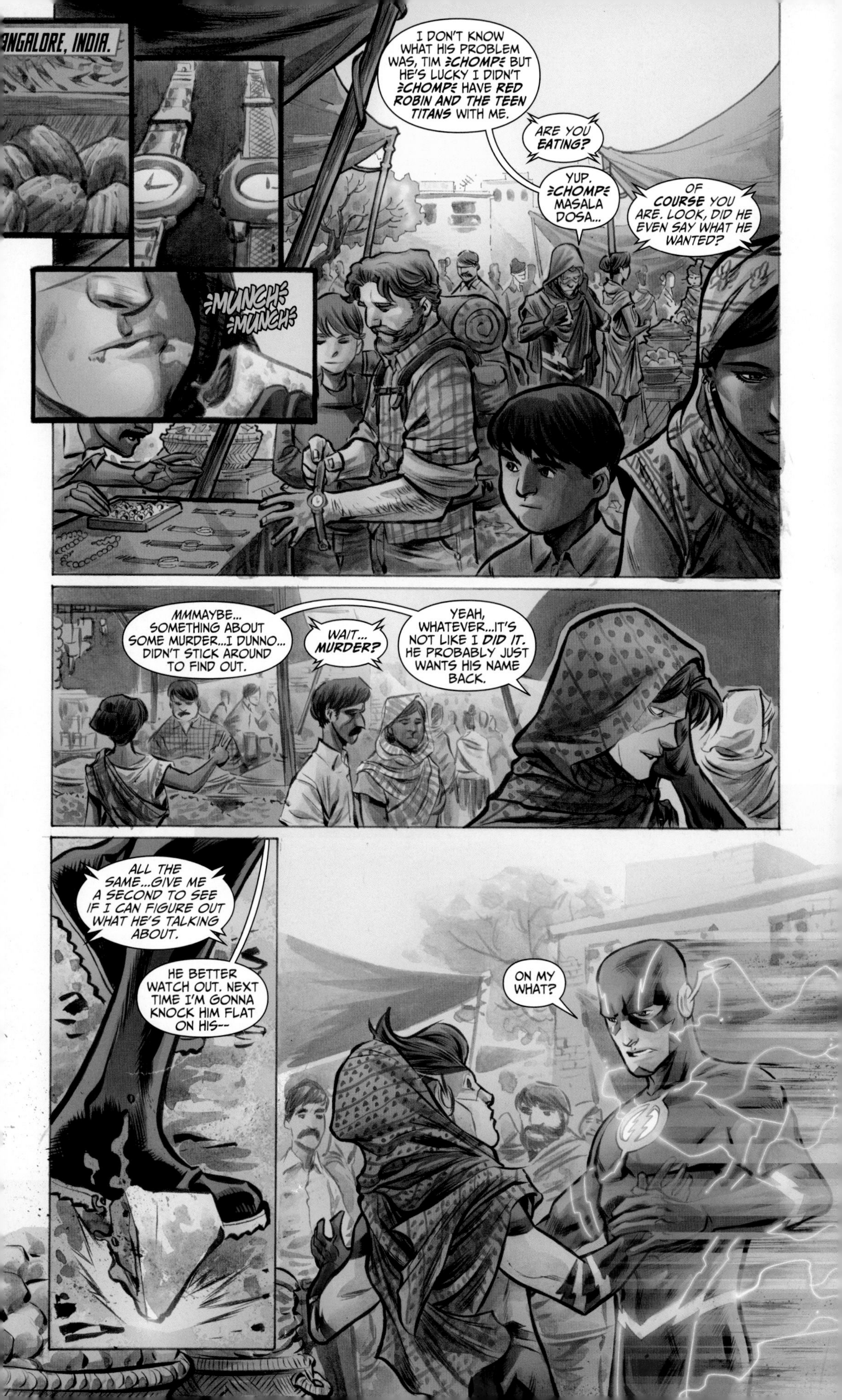

ANGALORE, INDIA.
I DON'T KNOW WHAT HIS PROBLEM WAS, TIM *CHOMP* BUT HE'S LUCKY I DIDN'T *CHOMP* HAVE RED ROBIN AND THE TEEN TITANS WITH ME.
ARE YOU EATING?
YUP. *CHOMP* MASALA DOSA...
OF COURSE YOU ARE. LOOK, DID HE EVEN SAY WHAT HE WANTED?
MUNCH MUNCH
MMMAYBE... SOMETHING ABOUT SOME MURDER...I DUNNO... DIDN'T STICK AROUND TO FIND OUT.
WAIT... MURDER?
YEAH, WHATEVER...IT'S NOT LIKE I DID IT. HE PROBABLY JUST WANTS HIS NAME BACK.
ALL THE SAME...GIVE ME A SECOND TO SEE IF I CAN FIGURE OUT WHAT HE'S TALKING ABOUT.
HE BETTER WATCH OUT. NEXT TIME I'M GONNA KNOCK HIM FLAT ON HIS--
ON MY WHAT?

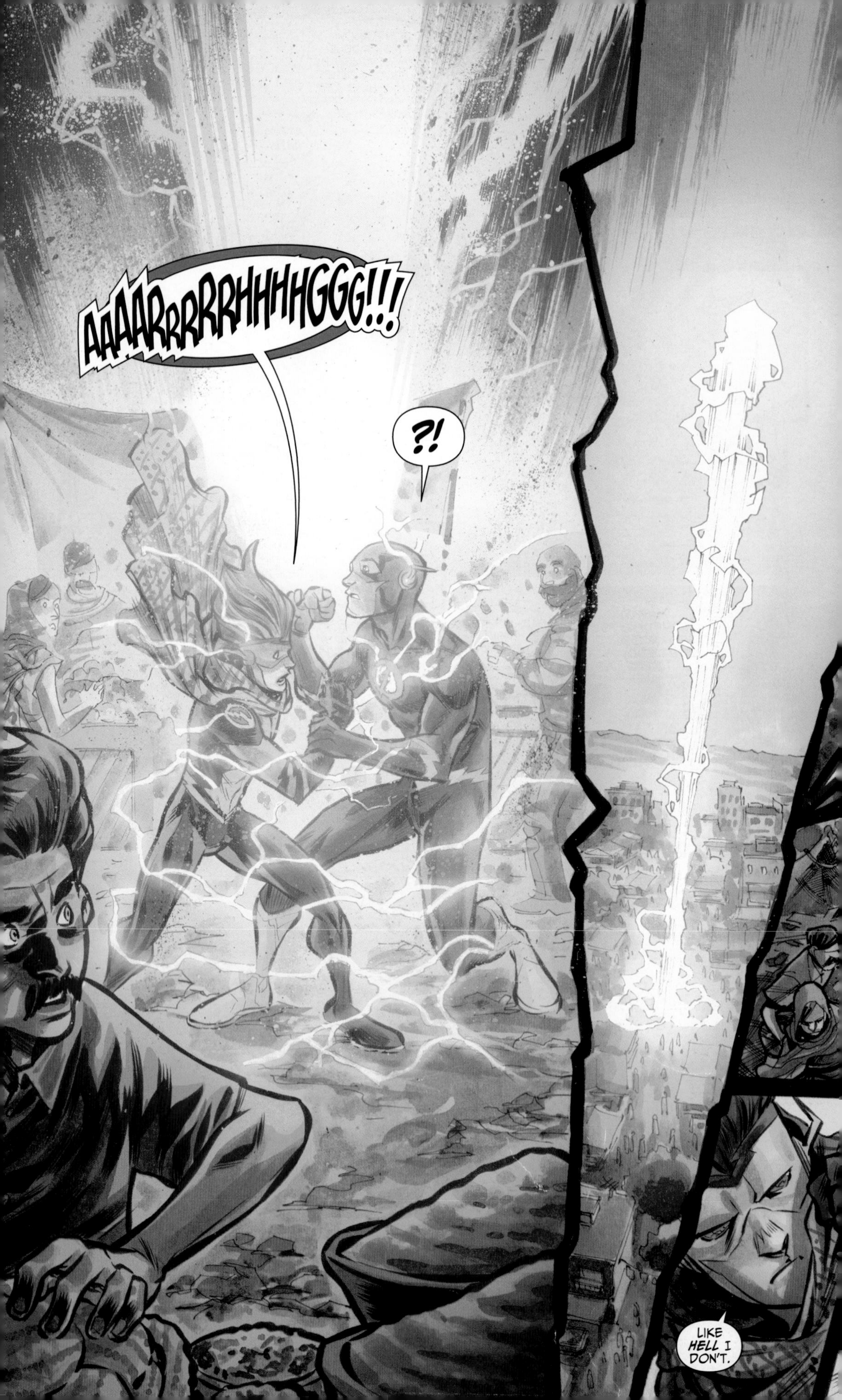
AAAARRRRRHHHHGGG!!!
?!
LIKE HELL I DON'T.

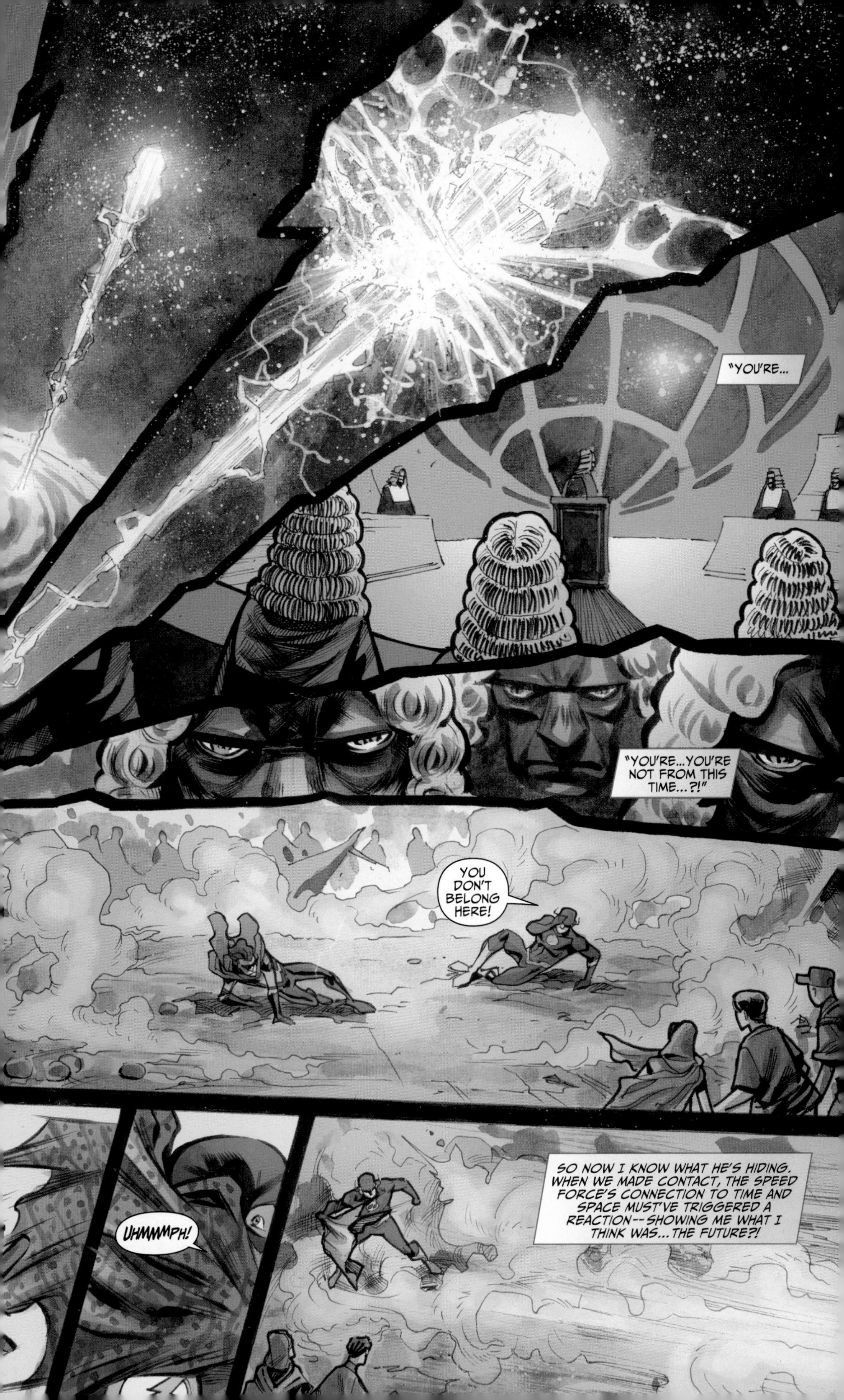
"YOU'RE...
"YOU'RE...YOU'RE NOT FROM THIS TIME...?!"
YOU DON'T BELONG HERE!
UHMMMPH!
SO NOW I KNOW WHAT HE'S HIDING. WHEN WE MADE CONTACT, THE SPEED FORCE'S CONNECTION TO TIME AND SPACE MUST'VE TRIGGERED A REACTION--SHOWING ME WHAT I THINK WAS...THE FUTURE?!

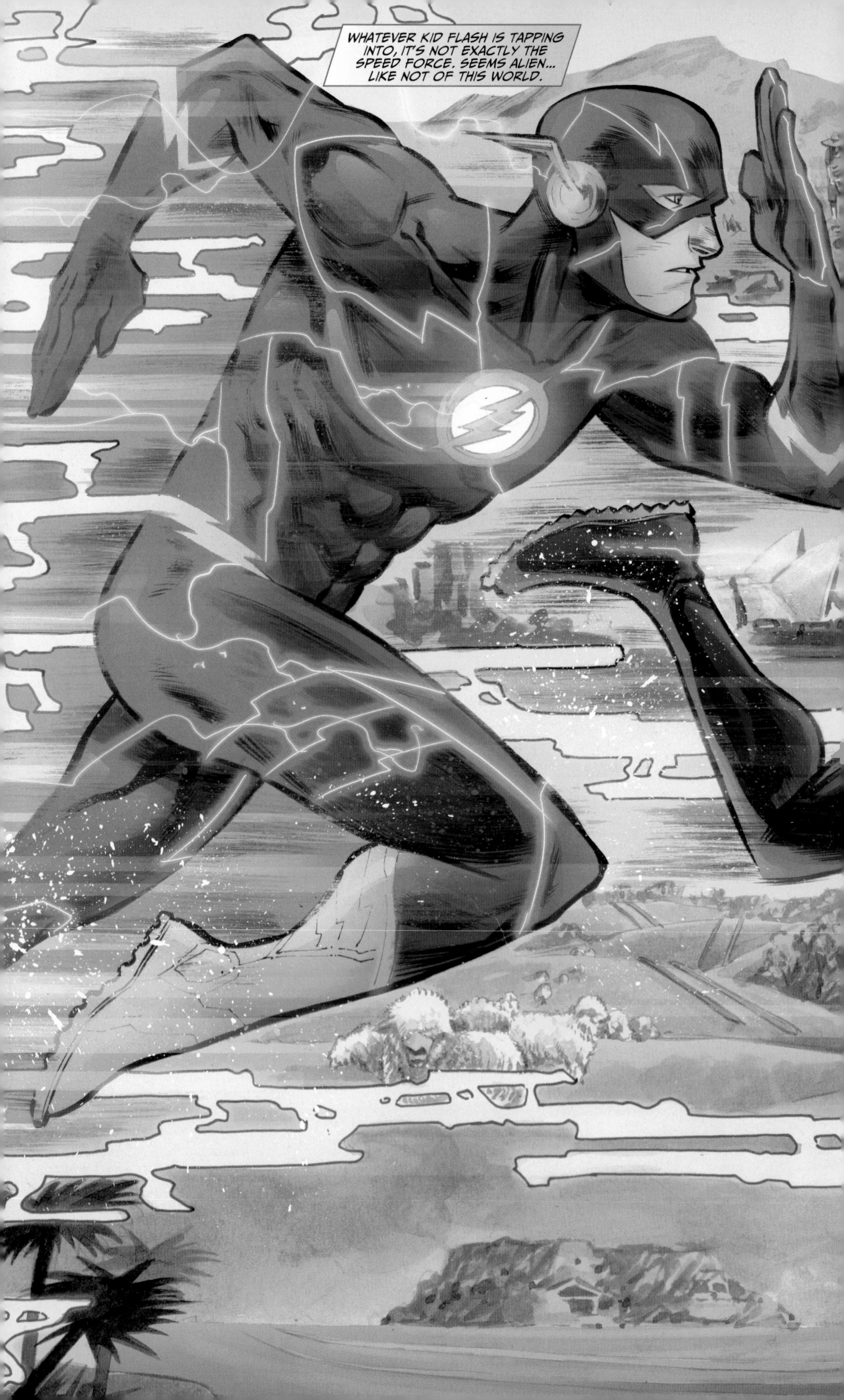
WHATEVER KID FLASH IS TAPPING INTO, IT'S NOT EXACTLY THE SPEED FORCE. SEEMS ALIEN... LIKE NOT OF THIS WORLD.

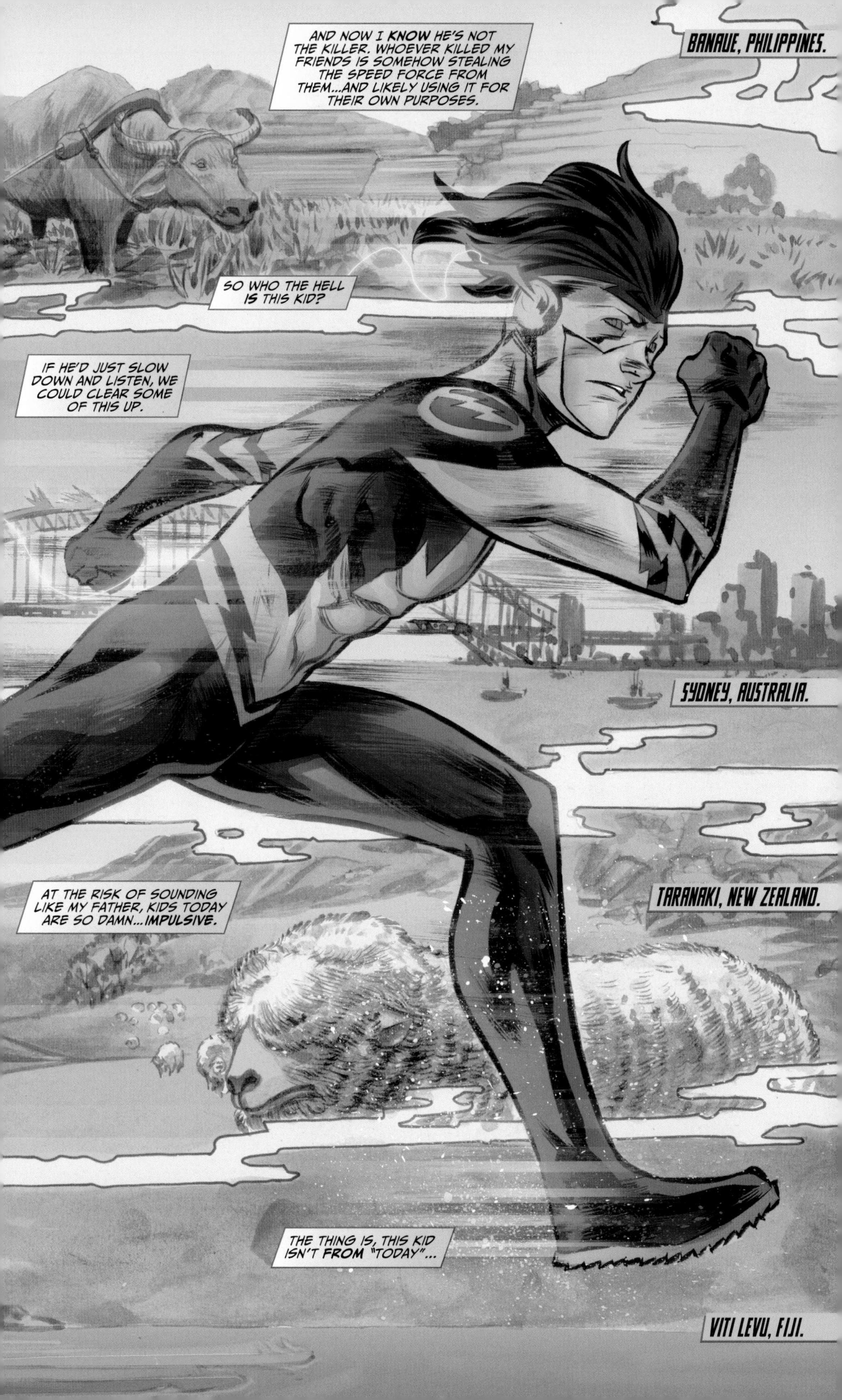

AND NOW I KNOW HE'S NOT THE KILLER. WHOEVER KILLED MY FRIENDS IS SOMEHOW STEALING THE SPEED FORCE FROM THEM...AND LIKELY USING IT FOR THEIR OWN PURPOSES.
BANAUE, PHILIPPINES.
SO WHO THE HELL IS THIS KID?
IF HE'D JUST SLOW DOWN AND LISTEN, WE COULD CLEAR SOME OF THIS UP.
SYDNEY, AUSTRALIA.
TARANAKI, NEW ZEALAND.
AT THE RISK OF SOUNDING LIKE MY FATHER, KIDS TODAY ARE SO DAMN...IMPULSIVE.
THE THING IS, THIS KID ISN'T FROM "TODAY"...
VITI LEVU, FIJI.

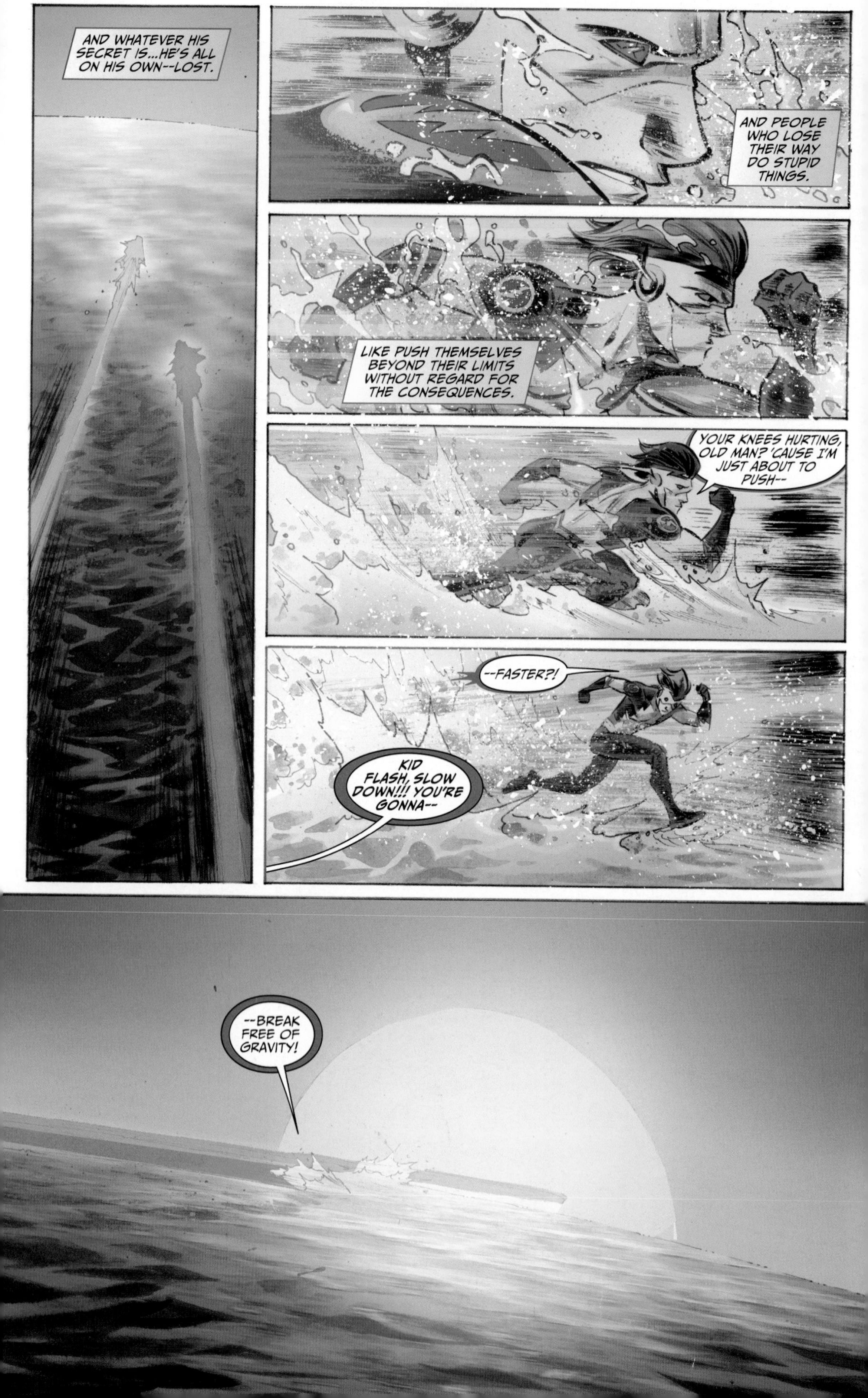
AND WHATEVER HIS SECRET IS...HE'S ALL ON HIS OWN--LOST.
AND PEOPLE WHO LOSE THEIR WAY DO STUPID THINGS.
LIKE PUSH THEMSELVES BEYOND THEIR LIMITS WITHOUT REGARD FOR THE CONSEQUENCES.
YOUR KNEES HURTING, OLD MAN? 'CAUSE I'M JUST ABOUT TO PUSH--
--FASTER?!
KID FLASH, SLOW DOWN!!! YOU'RE GONNA--
--BREAK FREE OF GRAVITY!

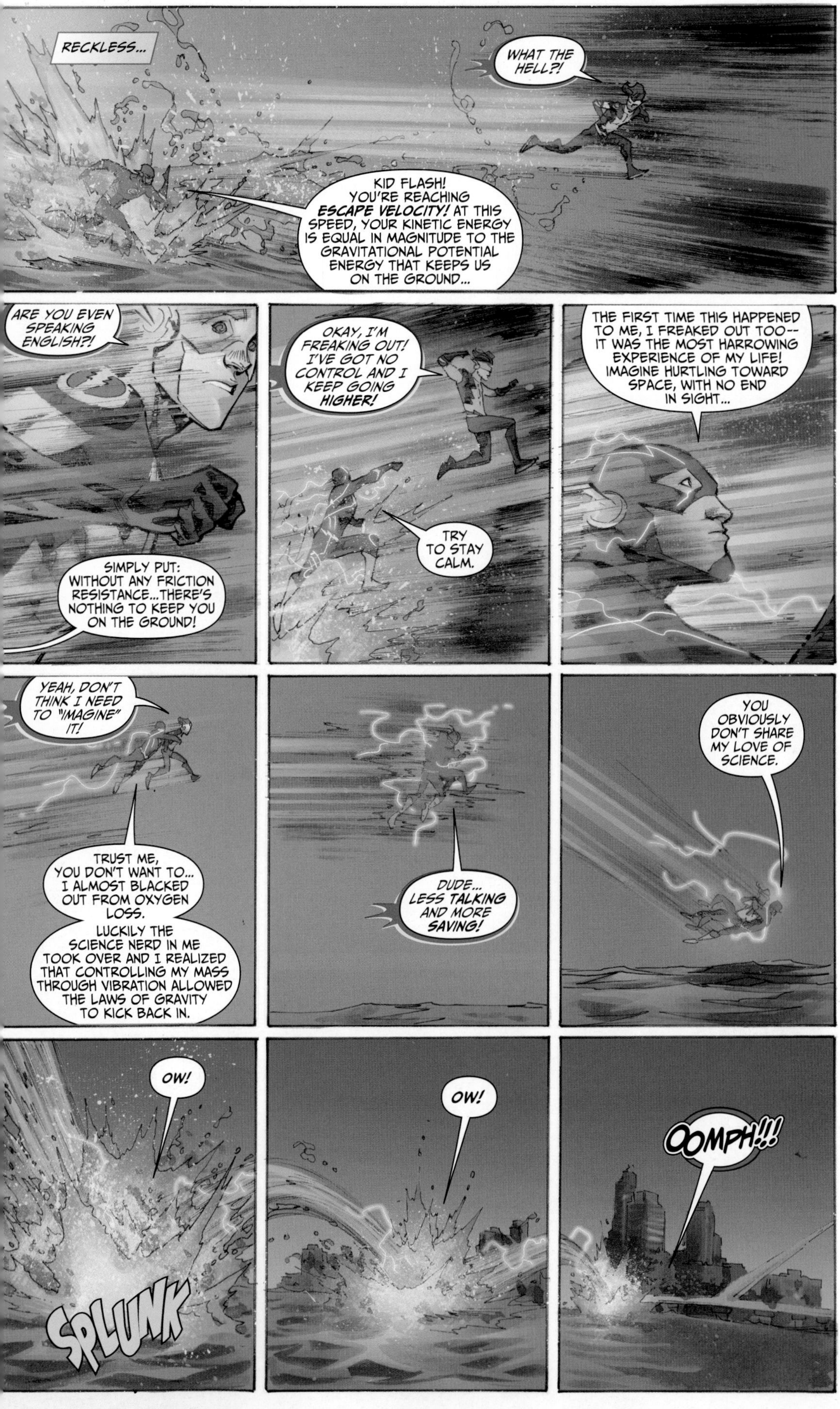

RECKLESS...
WHAT THE HELL?!
KID FLASH! YOU'RE REACHING ESCAPE VELOCITY! AT THIS SPEED, YOUR KINETIC ENERGY IS EQUAL IN MAGNITUDE TO THE GRAVITATIONAL POTENTIAL ENERGY THAT KEEPS US ON THE GROUND...
ARE YOU EVEN SPEAKING ENGLISH?!
SIMPLY PUT: WITHOUT ANY FRICTION RESISTANCE...THERE'S NOTHING TO KEEP YOU ON THE GROUND!
OKAY, I'M FREAKING OUT! I'VE GOT NO CONTROL AND I KEEP GOING HIGHER!
TRY TO STAY CALM.
THE FIRST TIME THIS HAPPENED TO ME, I FREAKED OUT TOO-- IT WAS THE MOST HARROWING EXPERIENCE OF MY LIFE! IMAGINE HURTLING TOWARD SPACE, WITH NO END IN SIGHT...
YEAH, DON'T THINK I NEED TO "IMAGINE" IT!
TRUST ME, YOU DON'T WANT TO... I ALMOST BLACKED OUT FROM OXYGEN LOSS.
LUCKILY THE SCIENCE NERD IN ME TOOK OVER AND I REALIZED THAT CONTROLLING MY MASS THROUGH VIBRATION ALLOWED THE LAWS OF GRAVITY TO KICK BACK IN.
DUDE... LESS TALKING AND MORE SAVING!
YOU OBVIOUSLY DON'T SHARE MY LOVE OF SCIENCE.
OW!
SPLUNK
OW!
OOMPH!!!

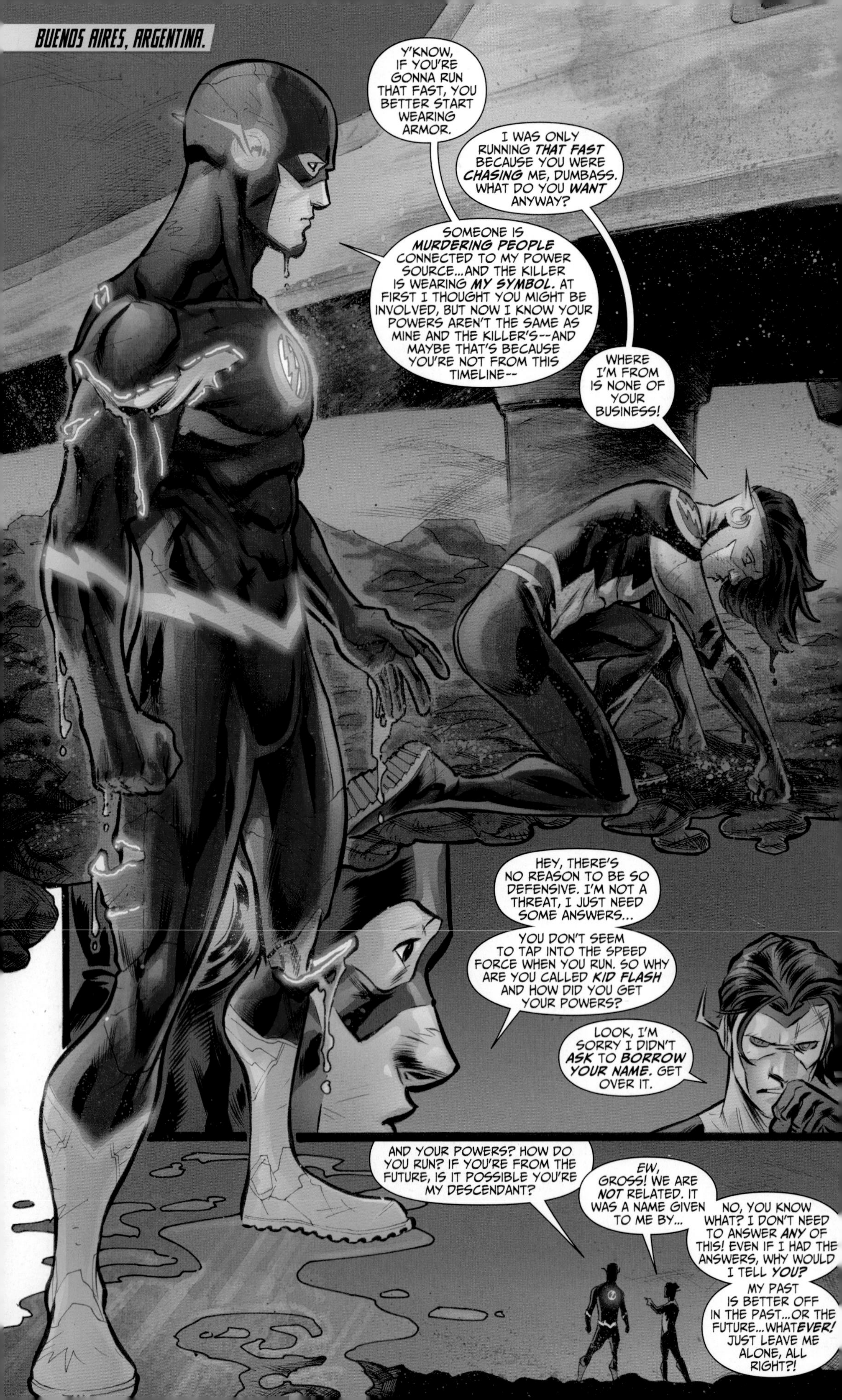
BUENOS AIRES, ARGENTINA.
Y'KNOW, IF YOU'RE GONNA RUN THAT FAST, YOU BETTER START WEARING ARMOR.
I WAS ONLY RUNNING THAT FAST BECAUSE YOU WERE CHASING ME, DUMBASS. WHAT DO YOU WANT ANYWAY?
SOMEONE IS MURDERING PEOPLE CONNECTED TO MY POWER SOURCE...AND THE KILLER IS WEARING MY SYMBOL. AT FIRST I THOUGHT YOU MIGHT BE INVOLVED, BUT NOW I KNOW YOUR POWERS AREN'T THE SAME AS MINE AND THE KILLER'S--AND MAYBE THAT'S BECAUSE YOU'RE NOT FROM THIS TIMELINE--
WHERE I'M FROM IS NONE OF YOUR BUSINESS!
HEY, THERE'S NO REASON TO BE SO DEFENSIVE. I'M NOT A THREAT, I JUST NEED SOME ANSWERS...
YOU DON'T SEEM TO TAP INTO THE SPEED FORCE WHEN YOU RUN. SO WHY ARE YOU CALLED KID FLASH AND HOW DID YOU GET YOUR POWERS?
LOOK, I'M SORRY I DIDN'T ASK TO BORROW YOUR NAME. GET OVER IT.
AND YOUR POWERS? HOW DO YOU RUN? IF YOU'RE FROM THE FUTURE, IS IT POSSIBLE YOU'RE MY DESCENDANT?
EW, GROSS! WE ARE NOT RELATED. IT WAS A NAME GIVEN TO ME BY...
NO, YOU KNOW WHAT? I DON'T NEED TO ANSWER ANY OF THIS! EVEN IF I HAD THE ANSWERS, WHY WOULD I TELL YOU?
MY PAST IS BETTER OFF IN THE PAST...OR THE FUTURE...WHATEVER! JUST LEAVE ME ALONE, ALL RIGHT?!

PLEASE, LET ME HELP YOU. I KNOW WHAT IT'S LIKE. MY NAME IS--

SAVE IT! I DON'T CARE *WHO* YOU ARE OR *WHERE* YOU CAME FROM!

THAT'S FINE, BUT I CARE ABOUT WHO *YOU* ARE.

I'M *SO* NOT GONNA TELL YOU WHO I AM.

LOOK, I'M DOING JUST FINE. I DON'T NEED YOUR HELP. I'M GONNA STAY IN THE PRESENT AND ENJOY THE RIDE!

TAKE IT FROM ME--THE PAST *ALWAYS* CATCHES UP TO YOU. ARE YOU SURE YOU'RE GONNA BE READY WHEN IT DOES?

I WAS *BORN READY.* BESIDES, IF ANYONE MESSES WITH ME...

...I HAVE *MY FRIENDS* TO BACK ME UP.

IT'S GREAT TO HAVE FRIENDS, BUT SOMETIMES YOU NEED SOMEONE WHO UNDER-STANDS WHAT YOU'RE GOING THROUGH. LIKE IT OR NOT, *SOMEHOW* WE ARE CONNECTED.

I'VE GOT A KILLER TO CATCH, BUT AFTERWARDS... WE NEED TO SIT DOWN AND TALK--*FLASH* TO *FLASH.*

WHATEVER. SEE YOU AROUND... *LOSER.*

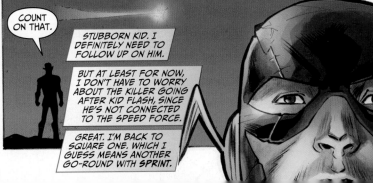

COUNT ON THAT.

STUBBORN KID. I DEFINITELY NEED TO FOLLOW UP ON HIM.

BUT AT LEAST FOR NOW, I DON'T HAVE TO WORRY ABOUT THE KILLER GOING AFTER KID FLASH, SINCE HE'S NOT CONNECTED TO THE SPEED FORCE.

GREAT. I'M BACK TO SQUARE ONE. WHICH I GUESS MEANS ANOTHER GO-ROUND WITH *SPRINT.*

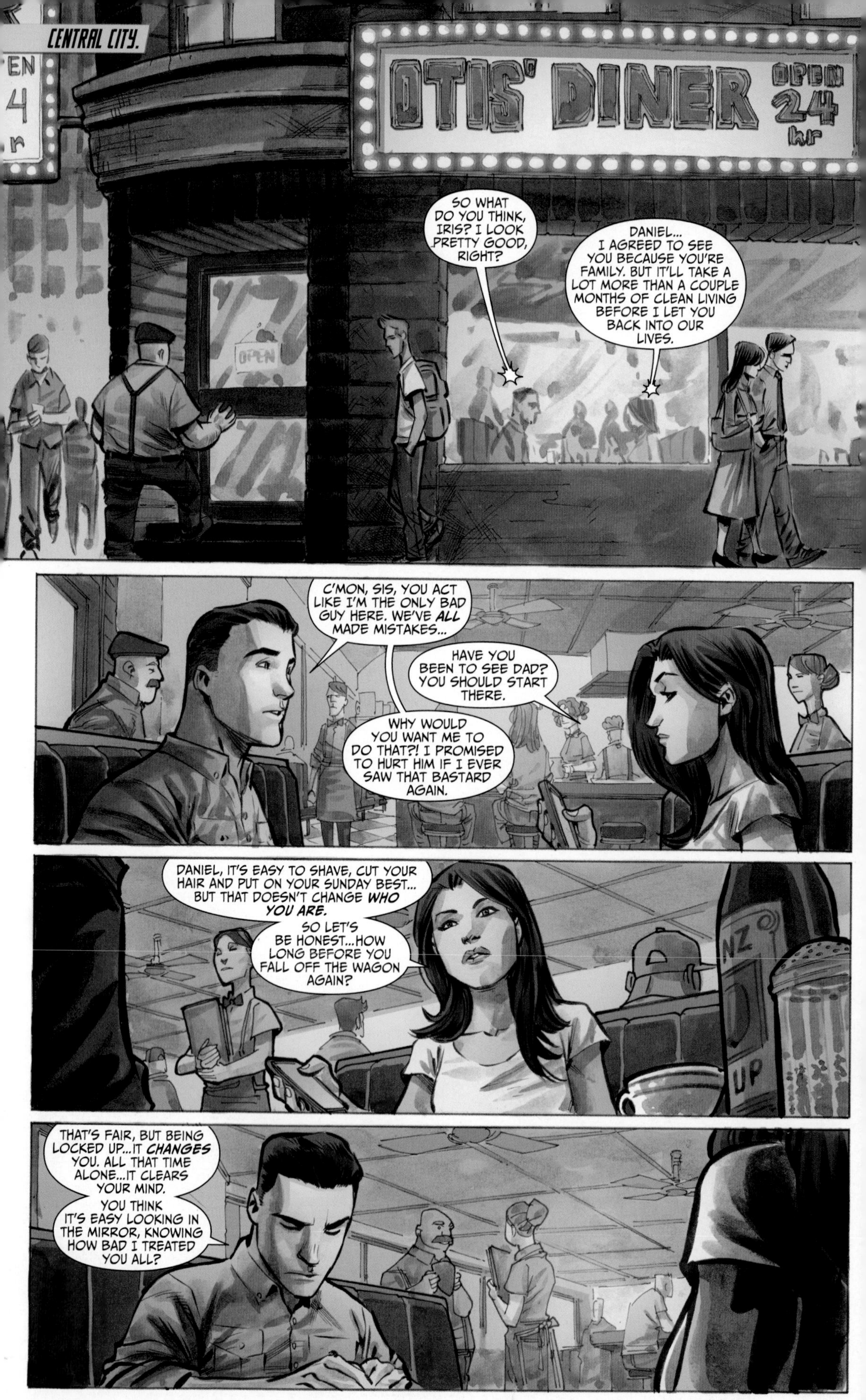
CENTRAL CITY.
OTIS' DINER
OPEN 24 hr
OPEN
SO WHAT DO YOU THINK, IRIS? I LOOK PRETTY GOOD, RIGHT?
DANIEL... I AGREED TO SEE YOU BECAUSE YOU'RE FAMILY. BUT IT'LL TAKE A LOT MORE THAN A COUPLE MONTHS OF CLEAN LIVING BEFORE I LET YOU BACK INTO OUR LIVES.
C'MON, SIS, YOU ACT LIKE I'M THE ONLY BAD GUY HERE. WE'VE *ALL* MADE MISTAKES...
HAVE YOU BEEN TO SEE DAD? YOU SHOULD START THERE.
WHY WOULD YOU WANT ME TO DO THAT?! I PROMISED TO HURT HIM IF I EVER SAW THAT BASTARD AGAIN.
DANIEL, IT'S EASY TO SHAVE, CUT YOUR HAIR AND PUT ON YOUR SUNDAY BEST... BUT THAT DOESN'T CHANGE *WHO YOU ARE.*
SO LET'S BE HONEST...HOW LONG BEFORE YOU FALL OFF THE WAGON AGAIN?
THAT'S FAIR, BUT BEING LOCKED UP...IT *CHANGES* YOU. ALL THAT TIME ALONE...IT CLEARS YOUR MIND.
YOU THINK IT'S EASY LOOKING IN THE MIRROR, KNOWING HOW BAD I TREATED YOU ALL?

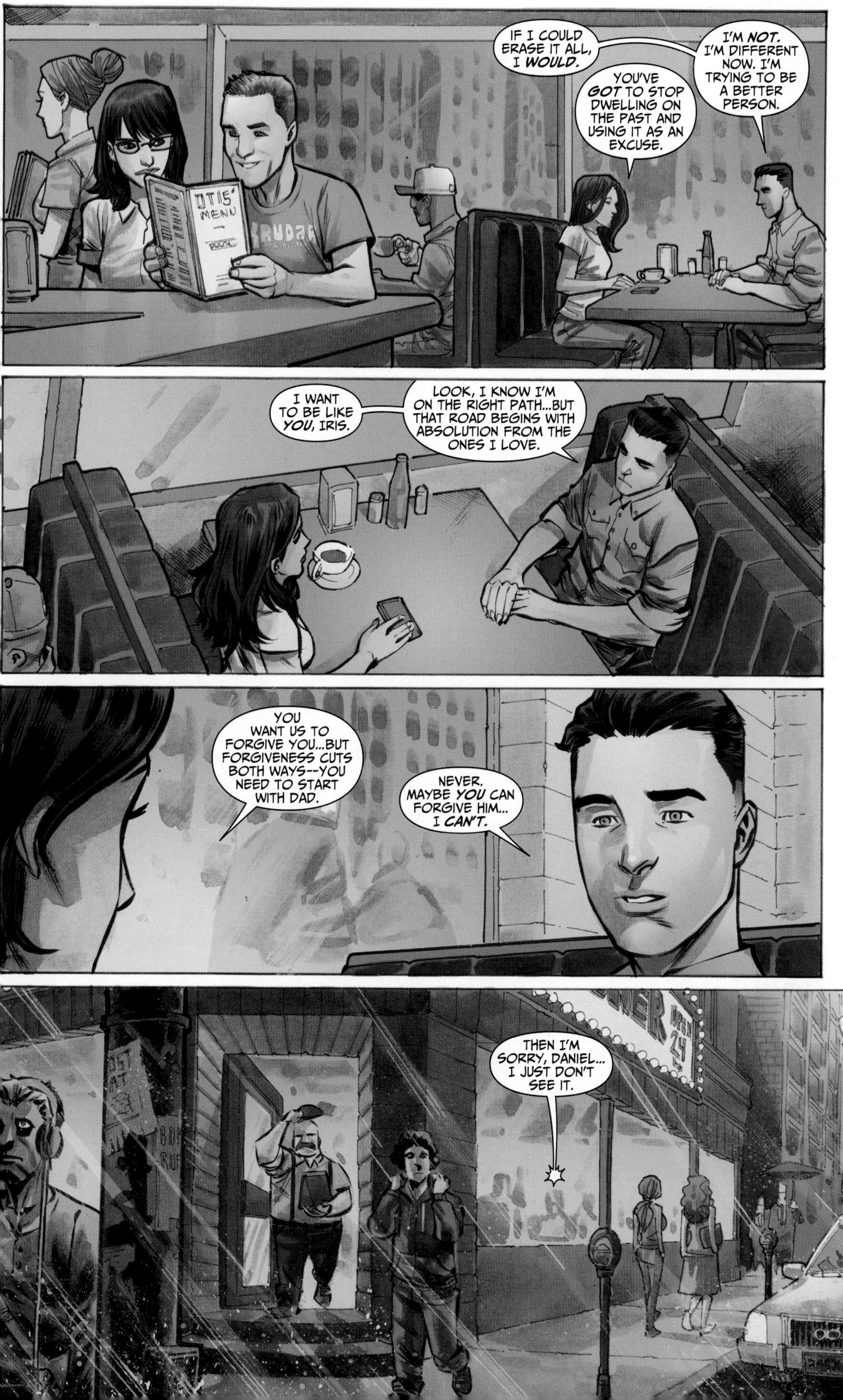
OTIS' MENU
IF I COULD ERASE IT ALL, I *WOULD.*
YOU'VE *GOT* TO STOP DWELLING ON THE PAST AND USING IT AS AN EXCUSE.
I'M *NOT.* I'M DIFFERENT NOW. I'M TRYING TO BE A BETTER PERSON.
I WANT TO BE LIKE *YOU*, IRIS.
LOOK, I KNOW I'M ON THE RIGHT PATH...BUT THAT ROAD BEGINS WITH ABSOLUTION FROM THE ONES I LOVE.
YOU WANT US TO FORGIVE YOU...BUT FORGIVENESS CUTS BOTH WAYS--YOU NEED TO START WITH DAD.
NEVER. MAYBE *YOU* CAN FORGIVE HIM... I *CAN'T.*
THEN I'M SORRY, DANIEL... I JUST DON'T SEE IT.

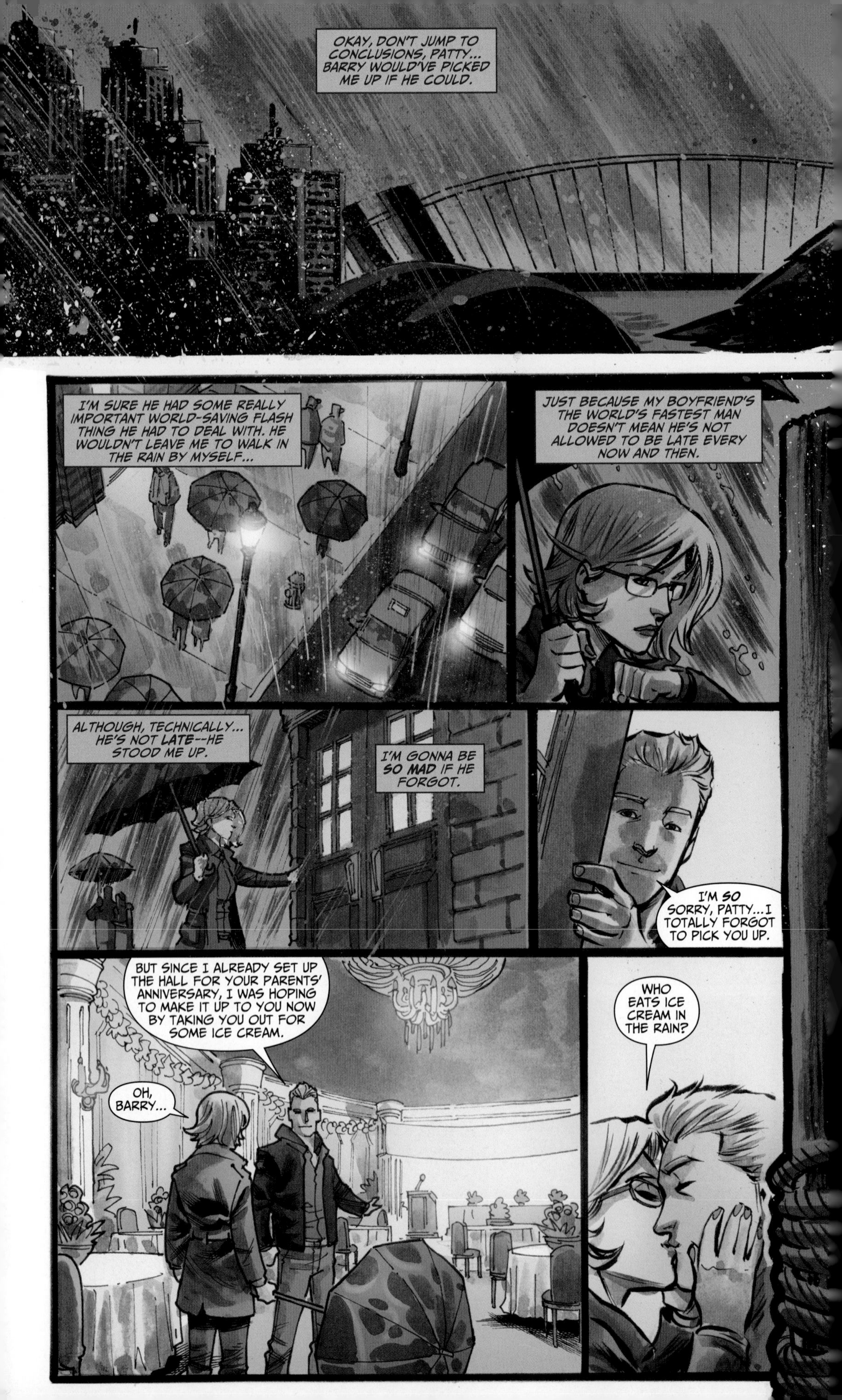

OKAY, DON'T JUMP TO CONCLUSIONS, PATTY... BARRY WOULD'VE PICKED ME UP IF HE COULD.
I'M SURE HE HAD SOME REALLY IMPORTANT WORLD-SAVING FLASH THING HE HAD TO DEAL WITH. HE WOULDN'T LEAVE ME TO WALK IN THE RAIN BY MYSELF...
JUST BECAUSE MY BOYFRIEND'S THE WORLD'S FASTEST MAN DOESN'T MEAN HE'S NOT ALLOWED TO BE LATE EVERY NOW AND THEN.
ALTHOUGH, TECHNICALLY... HE'S NOT LATE--HE STOOD ME UP.
I'M GONNA BE SO MAD IF HE FORGOT.
I'M SO SORRY, PATTY...I TOTALLY FORGOT TO PICK YOU UP.
BUT SINCE I ALREADY SET UP THE HALL FOR YOUR PARENTS' ANNIVERSARY, I WAS HOPING TO MAKE IT UP TO YOU NOW BY TAKING YOU OUT FOR SOME ICE CREAM.
OH, BARRY...
WHO EATS ICE CREAM IN THE RAIN?

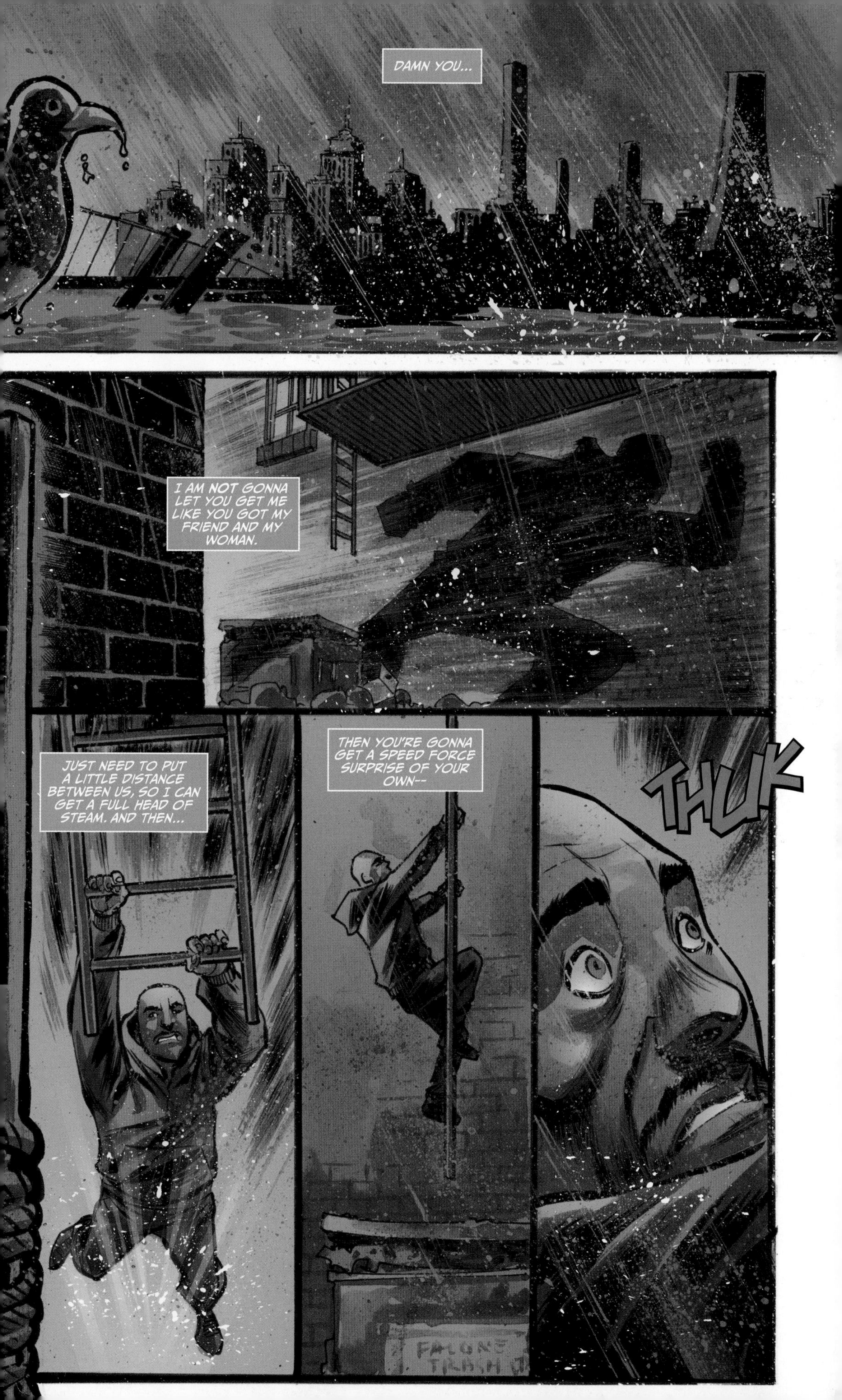
DAMN YOU...
I AM NOT GONNA LET YOU GET ME LIKE YOU GOT MY FRIEND AND MY WOMAN.
JUST NEED TO PUT A LITTLE DISTANCE BETWEEN US, SO I CAN GET A FULL HEAD OF STEAM. AND THEN...
THEN YOU'RE GONNA GET A SPEED FORCE SURPRISE OF YOUR OWN--
THUK

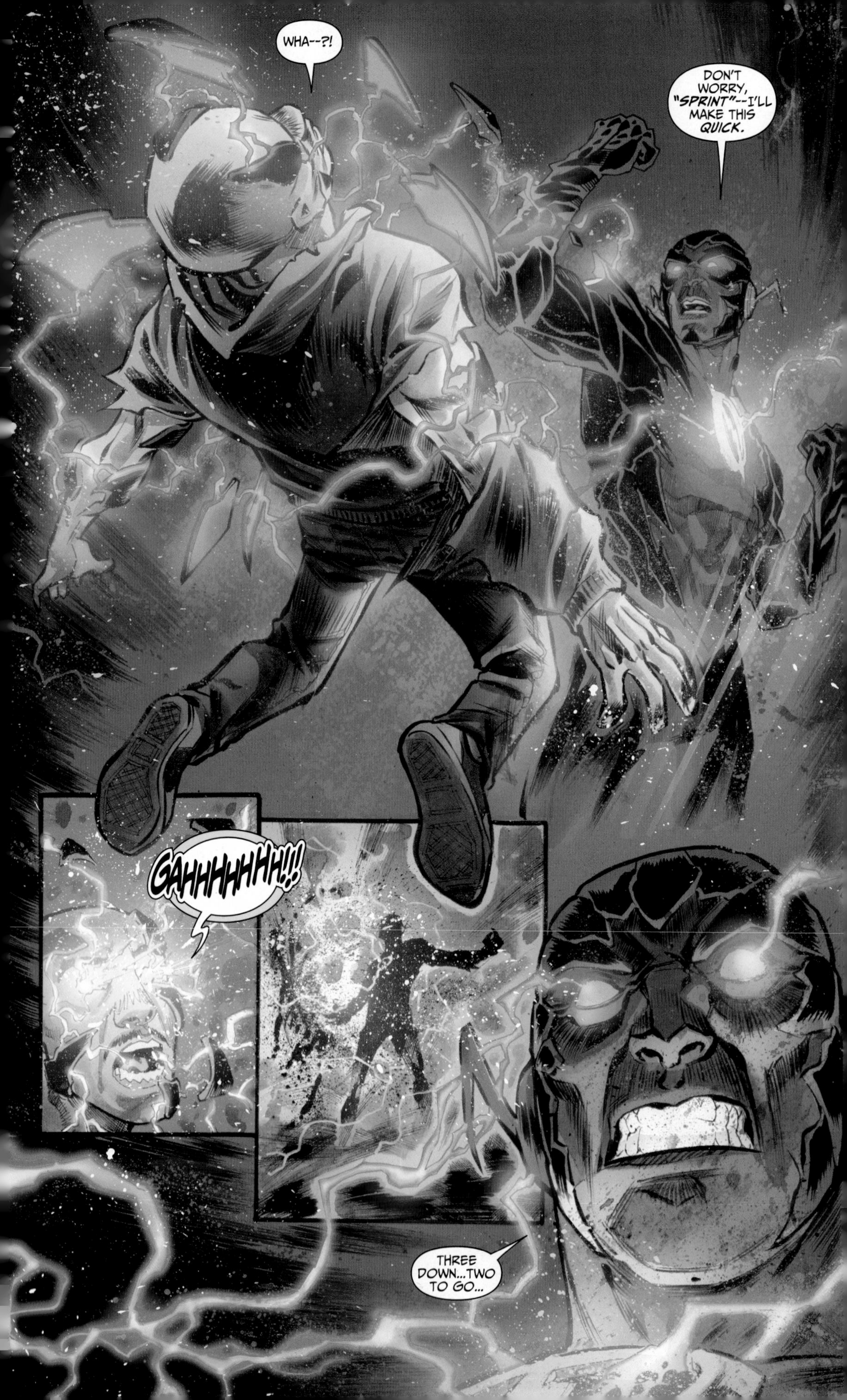
WHA--?!
DON'T WORRY, "SPRINT"--I'LL MAKE THIS QUICK.
GAHHHHHH!!!
THREE DOWN...TWO TO GO...

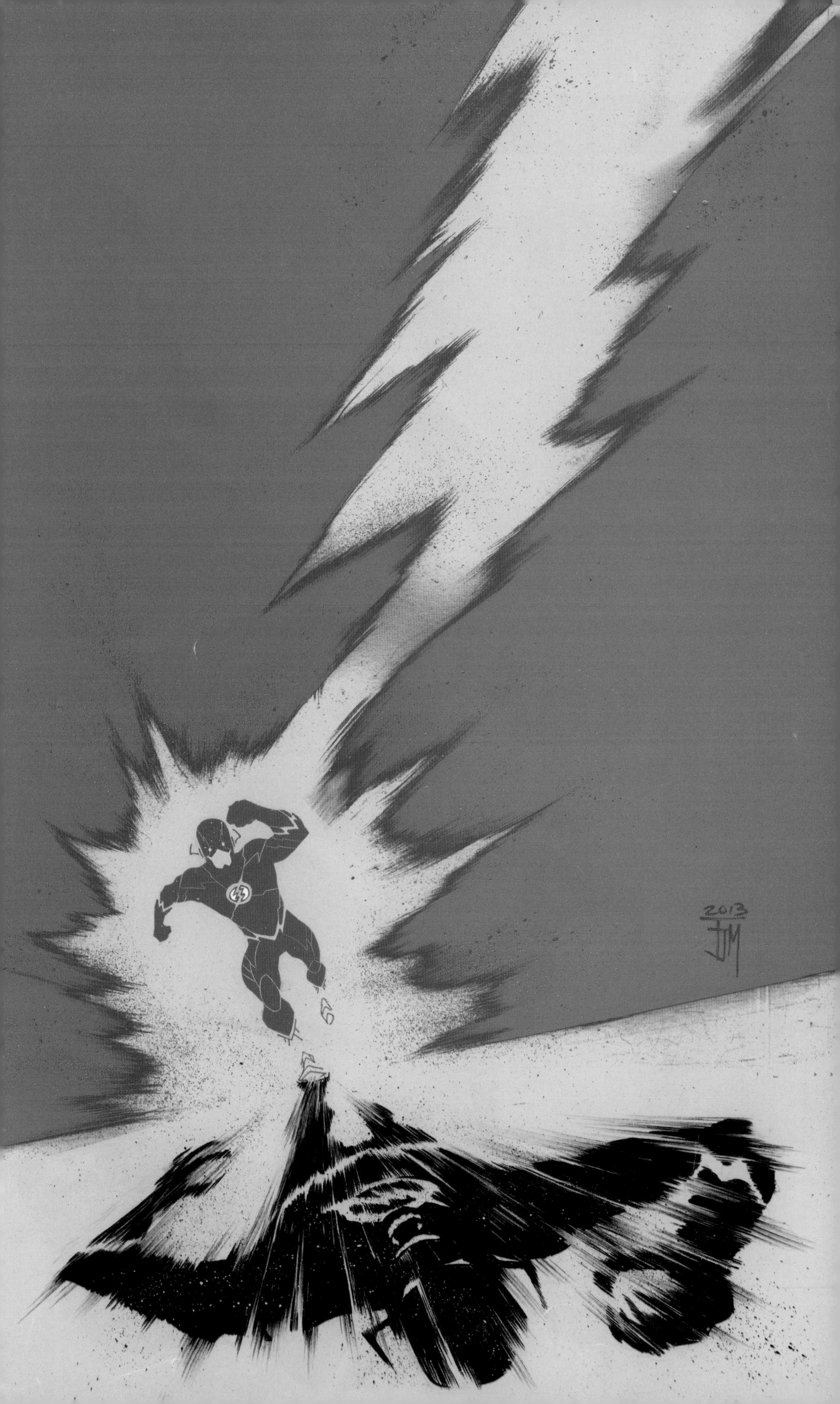

FRANCIS MANAPUL & BRIAN BUCCELLATO writers FRANCIS MANAPUL artist

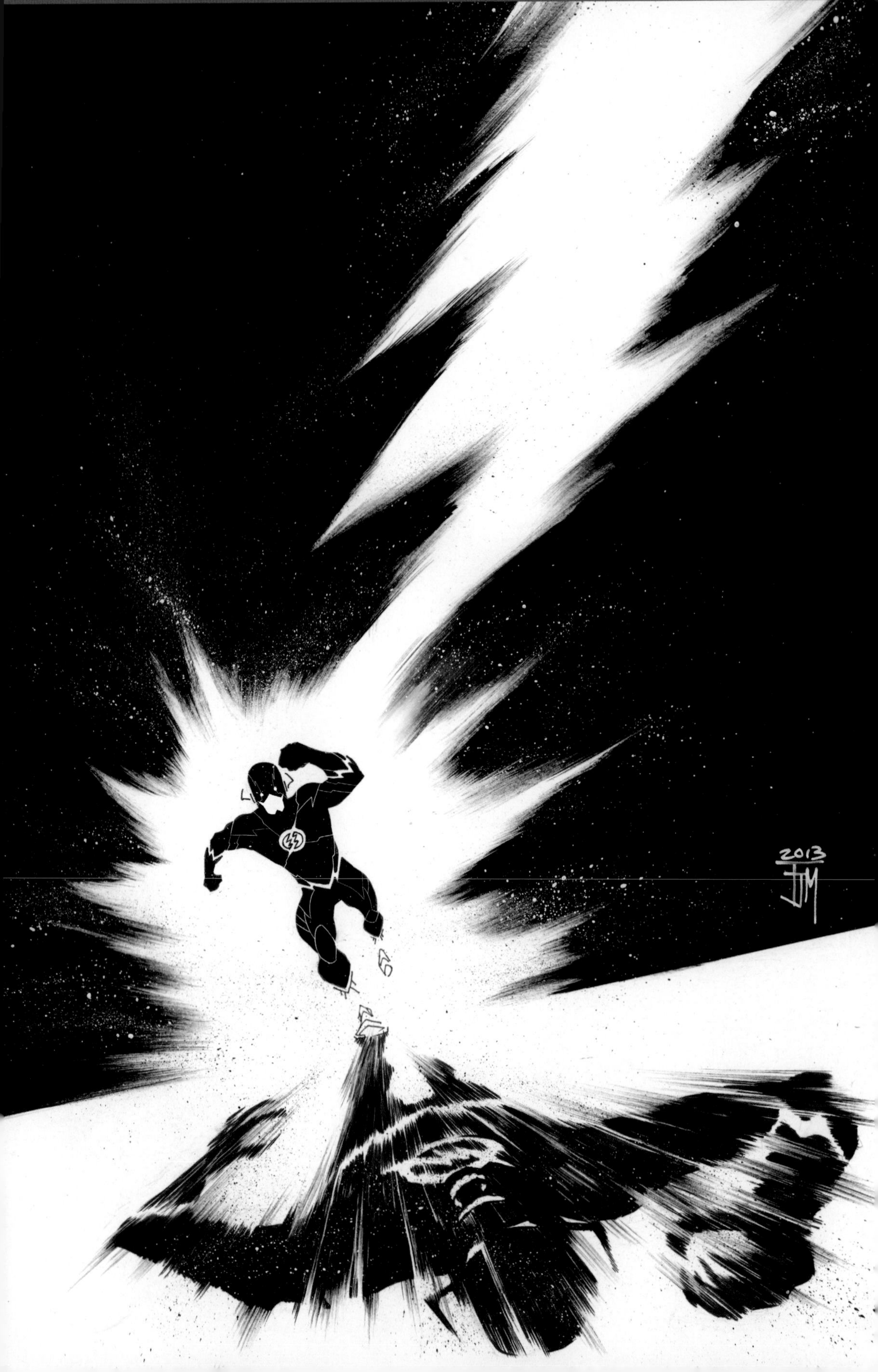
2013

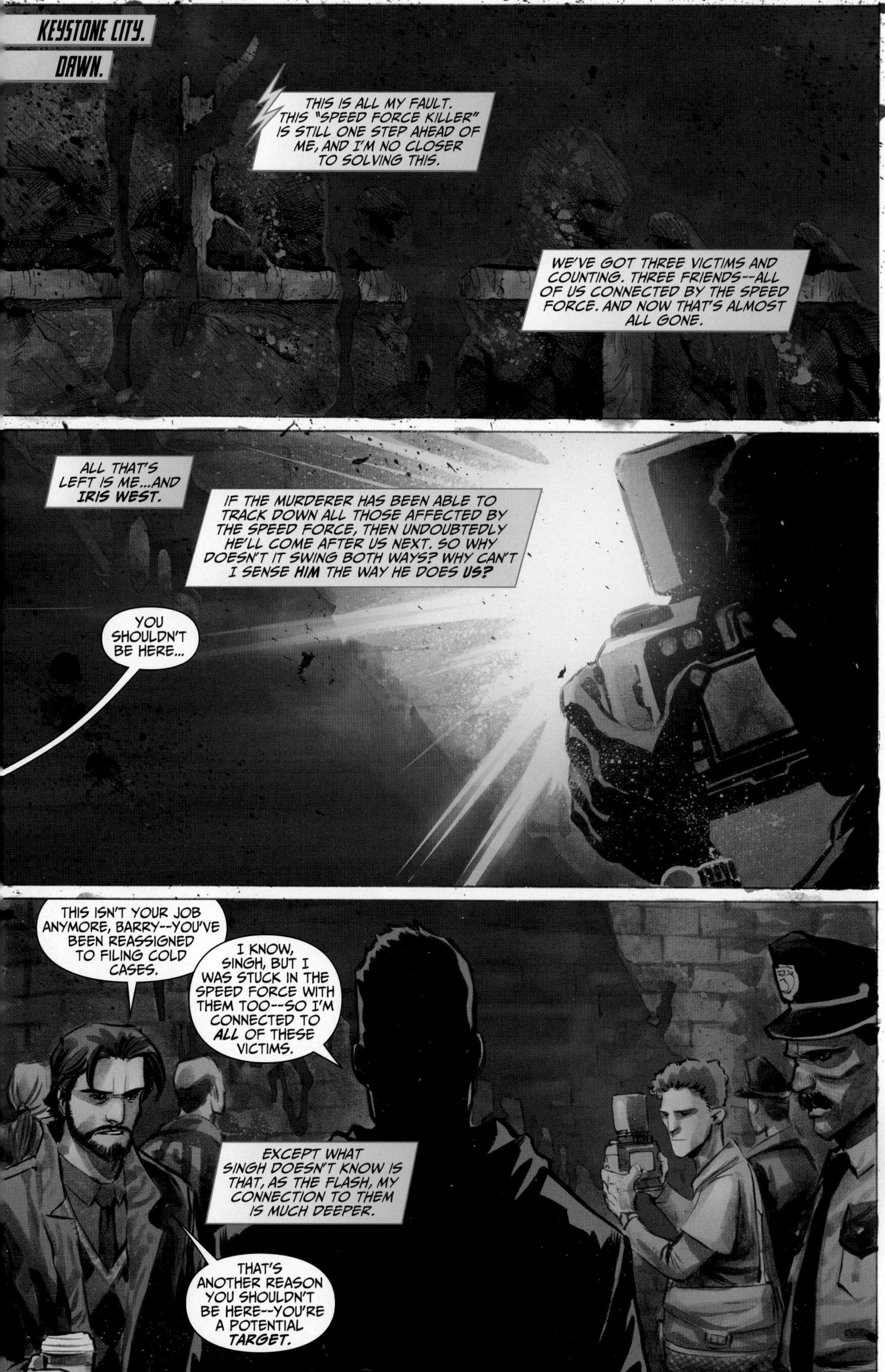
KEYSTONE CITY.
DAWN.
THIS IS ALL MY FAULT. THIS "SPEED FORCE KILLER" IS STILL ONE STEP AHEAD OF ME, AND I'M NO CLOSER TO SOLVING THIS.
WE'VE GOT THREE VICTIMS AND COUNTING. THREE FRIENDS--ALL OF US CONNECTED BY THE SPEED FORCE. AND NOW THAT'S ALMOST ALL GONE.
ALL THAT'S LEFT IS ME...AND IRIS WEST.
IF THE MURDERER HAS BEEN ABLE TO TRACK DOWN ALL THOSE AFFECTED BY THE SPEED FORCE, THEN UNDOUBTEDLY HE'LL COME AFTER US NEXT. SO WHY DOESN'T IT SWING BOTH WAYS? WHY CAN'T I SENSE HIM THE WAY HE DOES US?
YOU SHOULDN'T BE HERE...
THIS ISN'T YOUR JOB ANYMORE, BARRY--YOU'VE BEEN REASSIGNED TO FILING COLD CASES.
I KNOW, SINGH, BUT I WAS STUCK IN THE SPEED FORCE WITH THEM TOO--SO I'M CONNECTED TO ALL OF THESE VICTIMS.
EXCEPT WHAT SINGH DOESN'T KNOW IS THAT, AS THE FLASH, MY CONNECTION TO THEM IS MUCH DEEPER.
THAT'S ANOTHER REASON YOU SHOULDN'T BE HERE--YOU'RE A POTENTIAL TARGET.

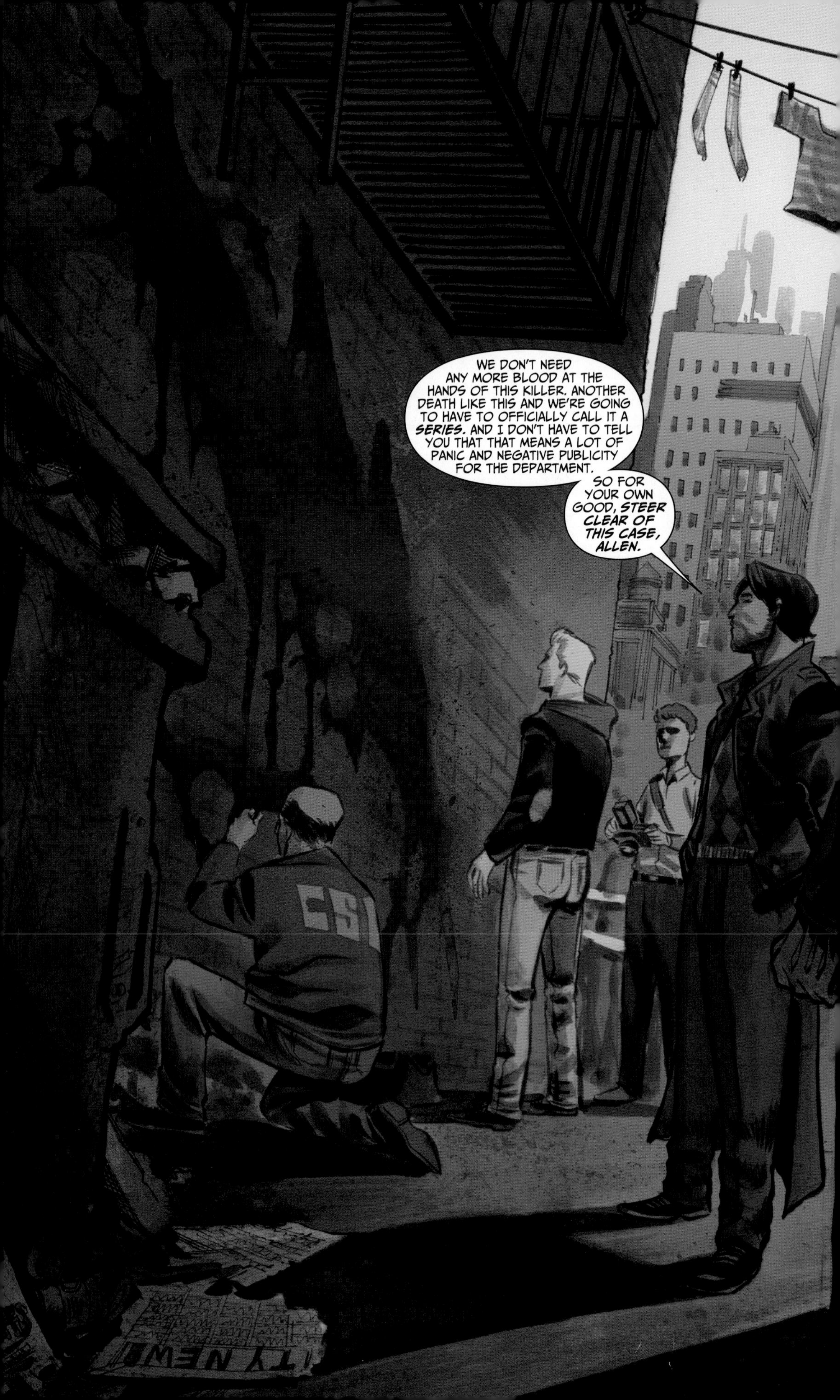
WE DON'T NEED ANY MORE BLOOD AT THE HANDS OF THIS KILLER. ANOTHER DEATH LIKE THIS AND WE'RE GOING TO HAVE TO OFFICIALLY CALL IT A *SERIES.* AND I DON'T HAVE TO TELL YOU THAT THAT MEANS A LOT OF PANIC AND NEGATIVE PUBLICITY FOR THE DEPARTMENT.
SO FOR YOUR OWN GOOD, *STEER CLEAR OF THIS CASE, ALLEN.*
CSI

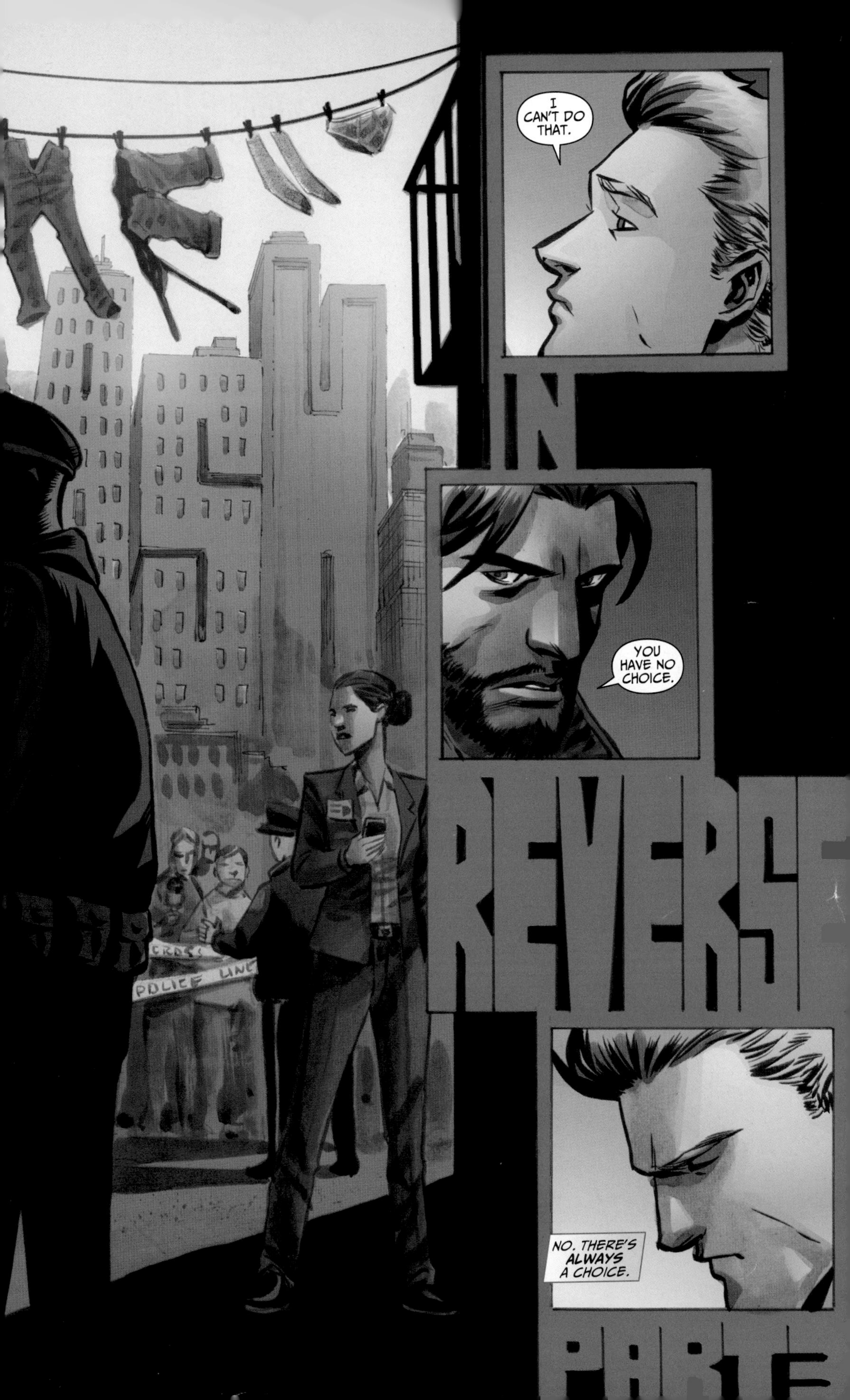

I CAN'T DO THAT.
IN
YOU HAVE NO CHOICE.
REVERSE
NO. THERE'S **ALWAYS** A CHOICE.
POLICE LINE

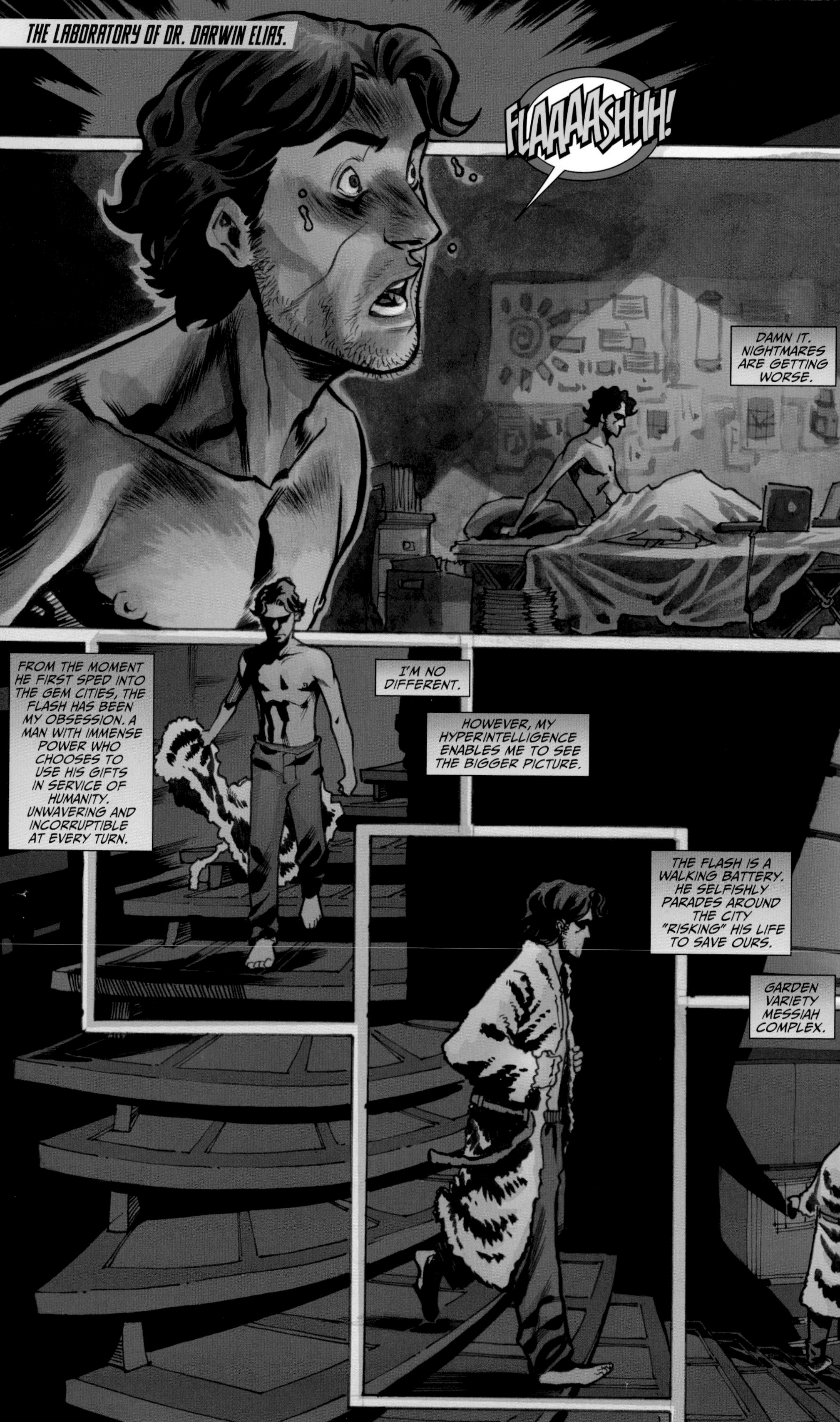
THE LABORATORY OF DR. DARWIN ELIAS.
FLAAAASHHH!
DAMN IT. NIGHTMARES ARE GETTING WORSE.
FROM THE MOMENT HE FIRST SPED INTO THE GEM CITIES, THE FLASH HAS BEEN MY OBSESSION. A MAN WITH IMMENSE POWER WHO CHOOSES TO USE HIS GIFTS IN SERVICE OF HUMANITY. UNWAVERING AND INCORRUPTIBLE AT EVERY TURN.
I'M NO DIFFERENT.
HOWEVER, MY HYPERINTELLIGENCE ENABLES ME TO SEE THE BIGGER PICTURE.
THE FLASH IS A WALKING BATTERY. HE SELFISHLY PARADES AROUND THE CITY "RISKING" HIS LIFE TO SAVE OURS.
GARDEN VARIETY MESSIAH COMPLEX.

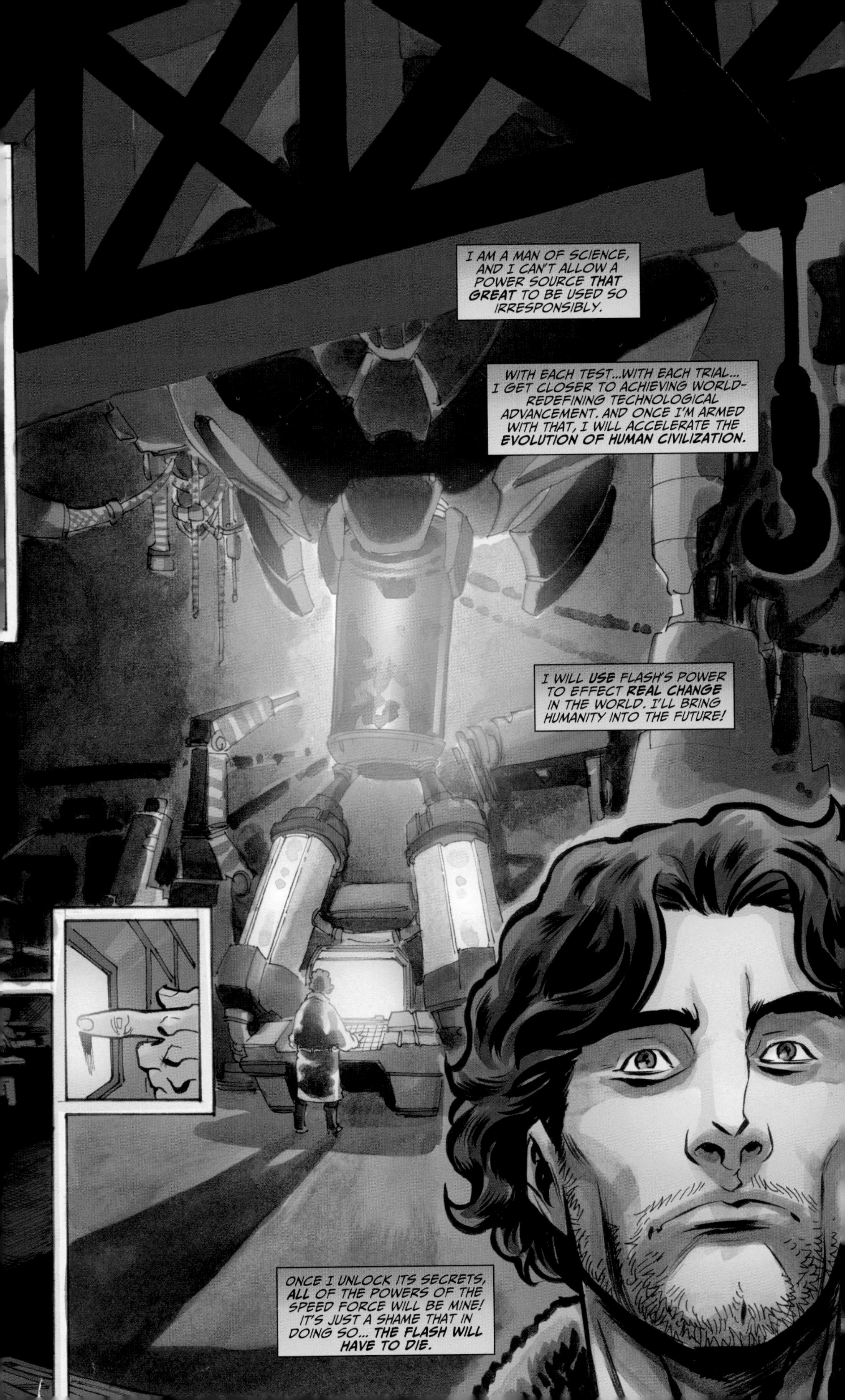
I AM A MAN OF SCIENCE, AND I CAN'T ALLOW A POWER SOURCE THAT GREAT TO BE USED SO IRRESPONSIBLY.
WITH EACH TEST...WITH EACH TRIAL... I GET CLOSER TO ACHIEVING WORLD-REDEFINING TECHNOLOGICAL ADVANCEMENT. AND ONCE I'M ARMED WITH THAT, I WILL ACCELERATE THE EVOLUTION OF HUMAN CIVILIZATION.
I WILL USE FLASH'S POWER TO EFFECT REAL CHANGE IN THE WORLD. I'LL BRING HUMANITY INTO THE FUTURE!
ONCE I UNLOCK ITS SECRETS, ALL OF THE POWERS OF THE SPEED FORCE WILL BE MINE! IT'S JUST A SHAME THAT IN DOING SO... THE FLASH WILL HAVE TO DIE.

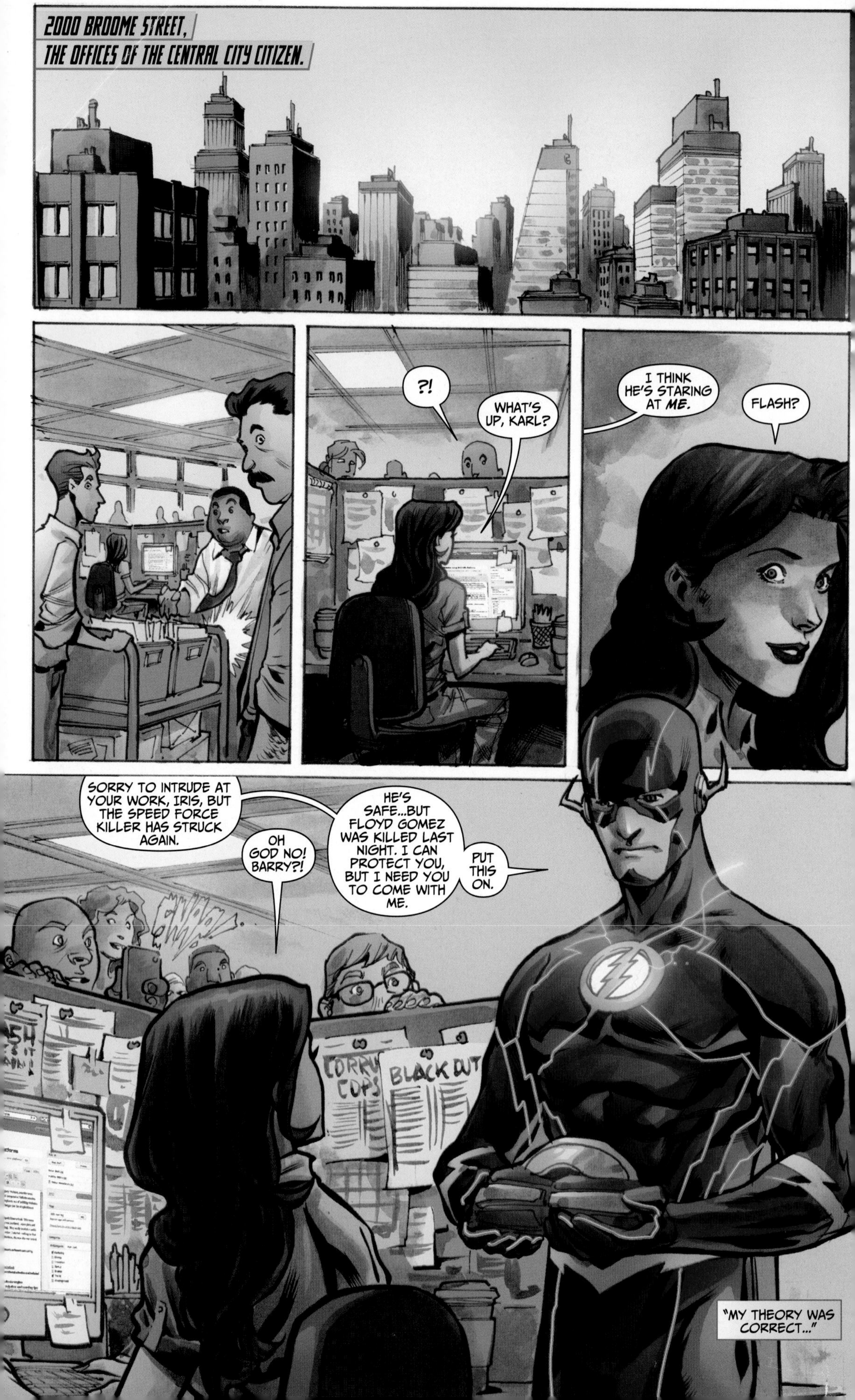
2000 BROOME STREET,
THE OFFICES OF THE CENTRAL CITY CITIZEN.
?!
WHAT'S UP, KARL?
I THINK HE'S STARING AT ME.
FLASH?
SORRY TO INTRUDE AT YOUR WORK, IRIS, BUT THE SPEED FORCE KILLER HAS STRUCK AGAIN.
OH GOD NO! BARRY?!
HE'S SAFE...BUT FLOYD GOMEZ WAS KILLED LAST NIGHT. I CAN PROTECT YOU, BUT I NEED YOU TO COME WITH ME.
PUT THIS ON.
BLACK OUT
"MY THEORY WAS CORRECT..."

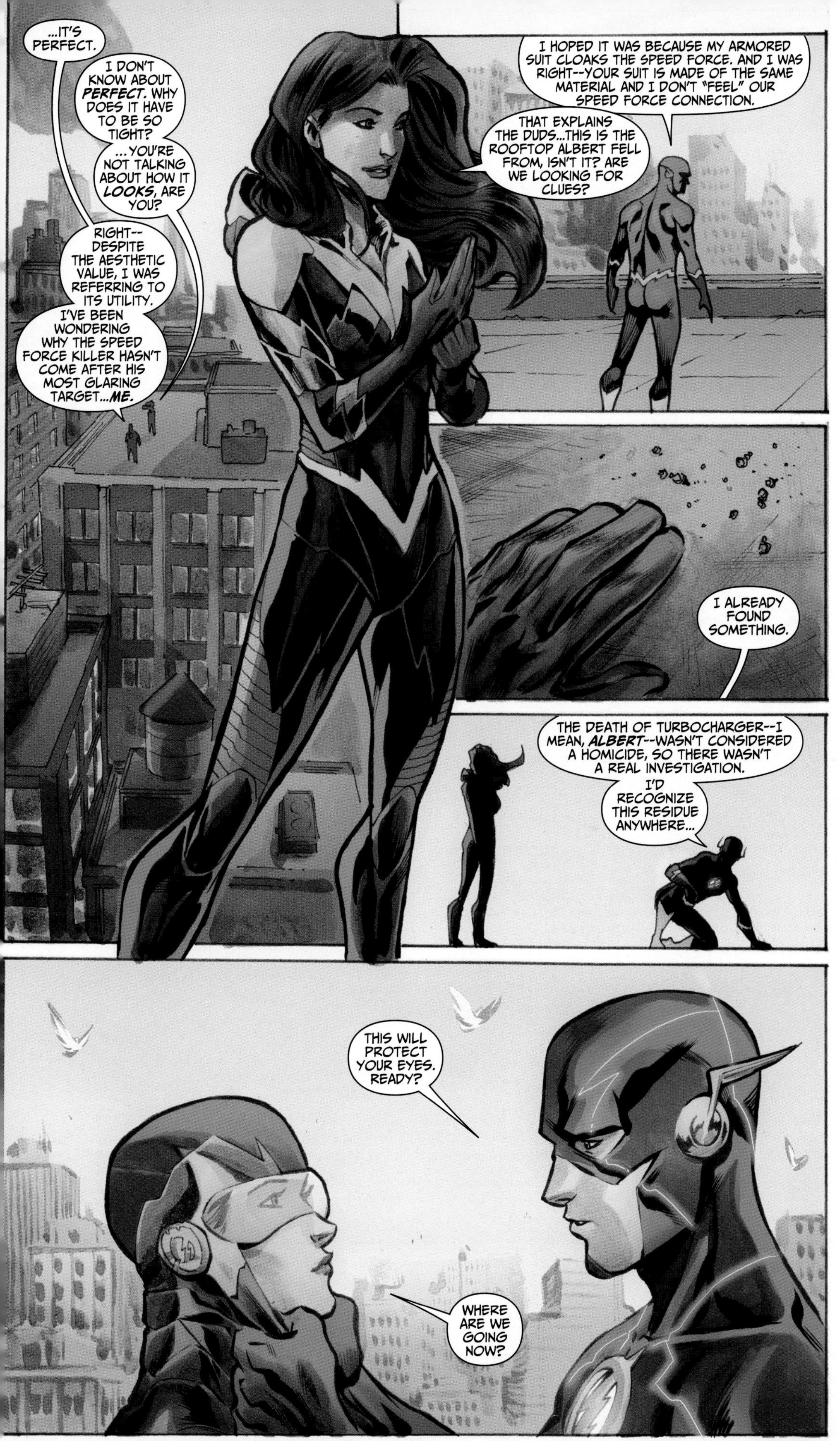
...IT'S PERFECT.
I DON'T KNOW ABOUT **PERFECT.** WHY DOES IT HAVE TO BE SO TIGHT?
...YOU'RE NOT TALKING ABOUT HOW IT **LOOKS**, ARE YOU?
RIGHT--DESPITE THE AESTHETIC VALUE, I WAS REFERRING TO ITS UTILITY.
I'VE BEEN WONDERING WHY THE SPEED FORCE KILLER HASN'T COME AFTER HIS MOST GLARING TARGET...**ME.**
I HOPED IT WAS BECAUSE MY ARMORED SUIT CLOAKS THE SPEED FORCE. AND I WAS RIGHT--YOUR SUIT IS MADE OF THE SAME MATERIAL AND I DON'T "FEEL" OUR SPEED FORCE CONNECTION.
THAT EXPLAINS THE DUDS...THIS IS THE ROOFTOP ALBERT FELL FROM, ISN'T IT? ARE WE LOOKING FOR CLUES?
I ALREADY FOUND SOMETHING.
THE DEATH OF TURBOCHARGER--I MEAN, **ALBERT**--WASN'T CONSIDERED A HOMICIDE, SO THERE WASN'T A REAL INVESTIGATION.
I'D RECOGNIZE THIS RESIDUE ANYWHERE...
THIS WILL PROTECT YOUR EYES. READY?
WHERE ARE WE GOING NOW?

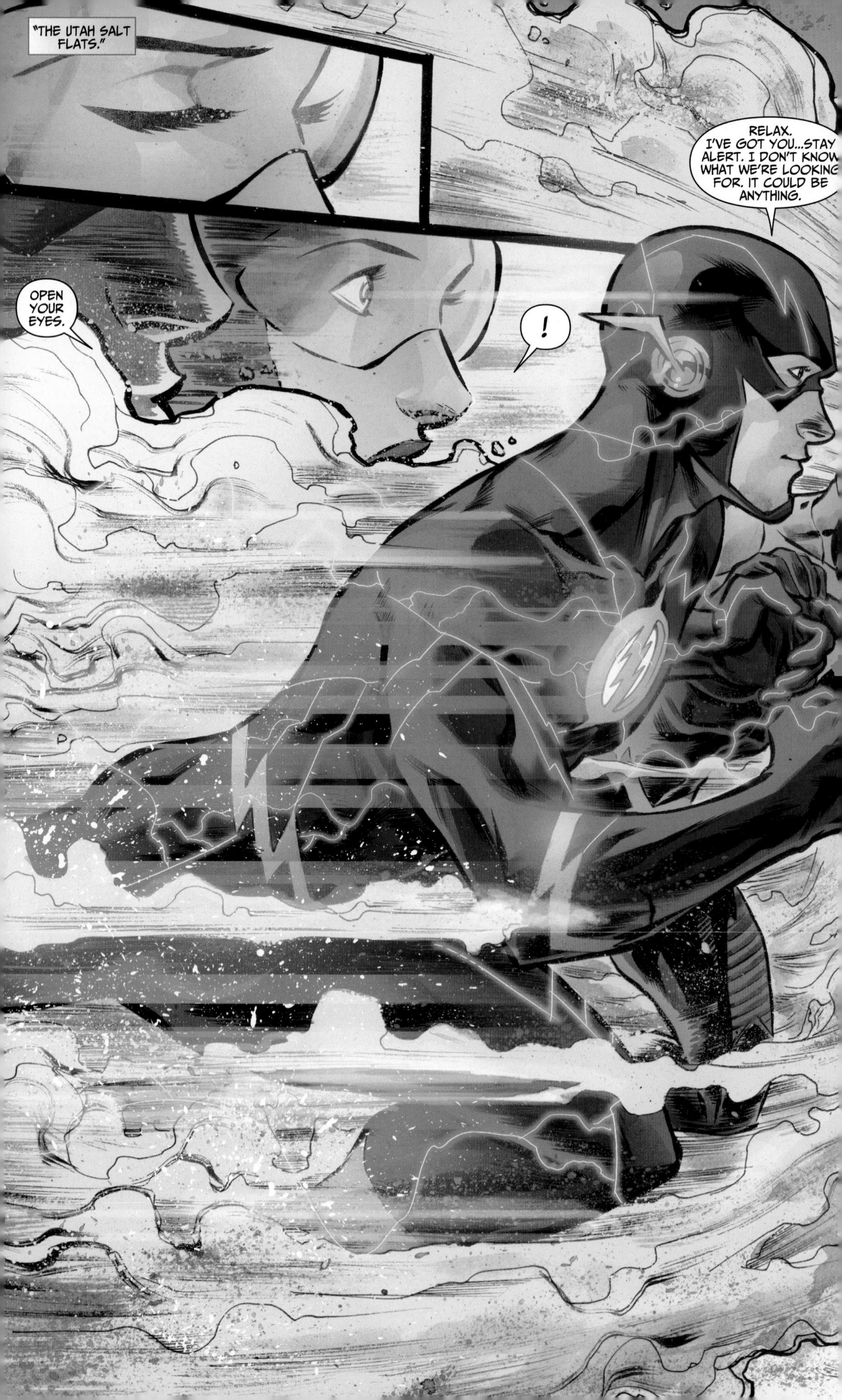
"THE UTAH SALT FLATS."
OPEN YOUR EYES.
!
RELAX. I'VE GOT YOU...STAY ALERT. I DON'T KNOW WHAT WE'RE LOOKING FOR. IT COULD BE ANYTHING.

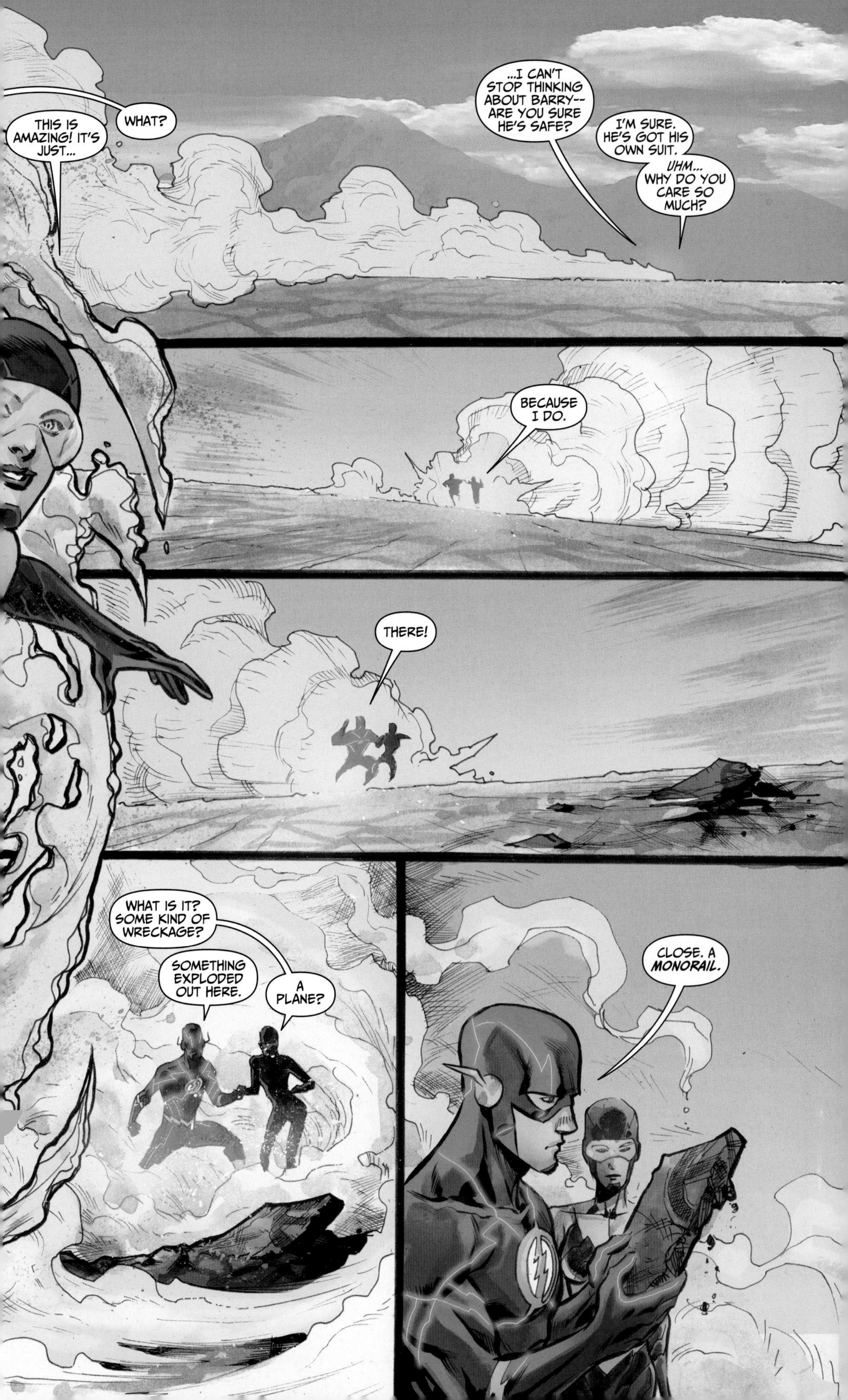
THIS IS AMAZING! IT'S JUST...
WHAT?
...I CAN'T STOP THINKING ABOUT BARRY-- ARE YOU SURE HE'S SAFE?
I'M SURE. HE'S GOT HIS OWN SUIT.
UHM... WHY DO YOU CARE SO MUCH?
BECAUSE I DO.
THERE!
WHAT IS IT? SOME KIND OF WRECKAGE?
SOMETHING EXPLODED OUT HERE.
A PLANE?
CLOSE. A MONORAIL.

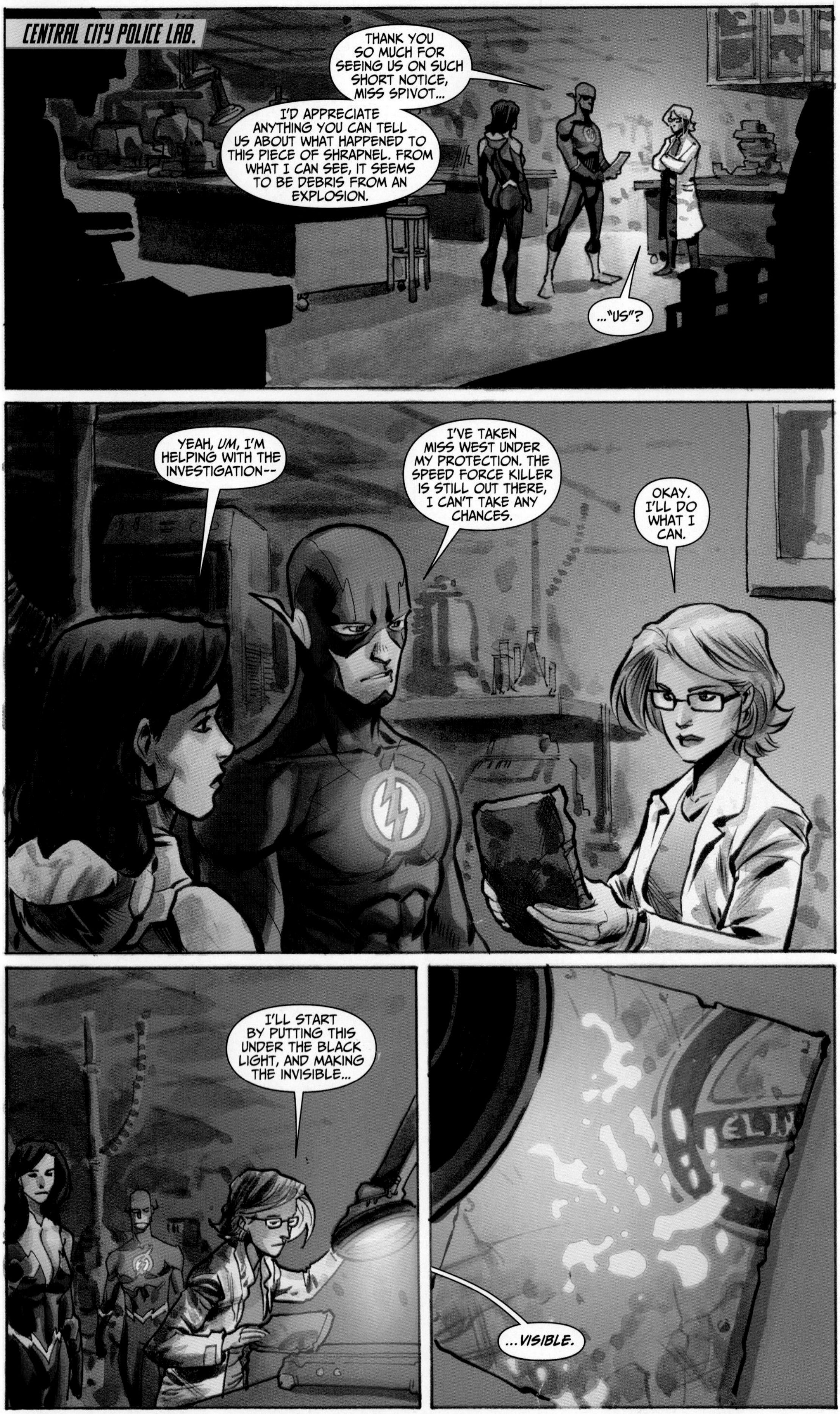

CENTRAL CITY POLICE LAB.
THANK YOU SO MUCH FOR SEEING US ON SUCH SHORT NOTICE, MISS SPIVOT...
I'D APPRECIATE ANYTHING YOU CAN TELL US ABOUT WHAT HAPPENED TO THIS PIECE OF SHRAPNEL. FROM WHAT I CAN SEE, IT SEEMS TO BE DEBRIS FROM AN EXPLOSION.
..."US"?
YEAH, UM, I'M HELPING WITH THE INVESTIGATION--
I'VE TAKEN MISS WEST UNDER MY PROTECTION. THE SPEED FORCE KILLER IS STILL OUT THERE, I CAN'T TAKE ANY CHANCES.
OKAY. I'LL DO WHAT I CAN.
I'LL START BY PUTTING THIS UNDER THE BLACK LIGHT, AND MAKING THE INVISIBLE...
...VISIBLE.

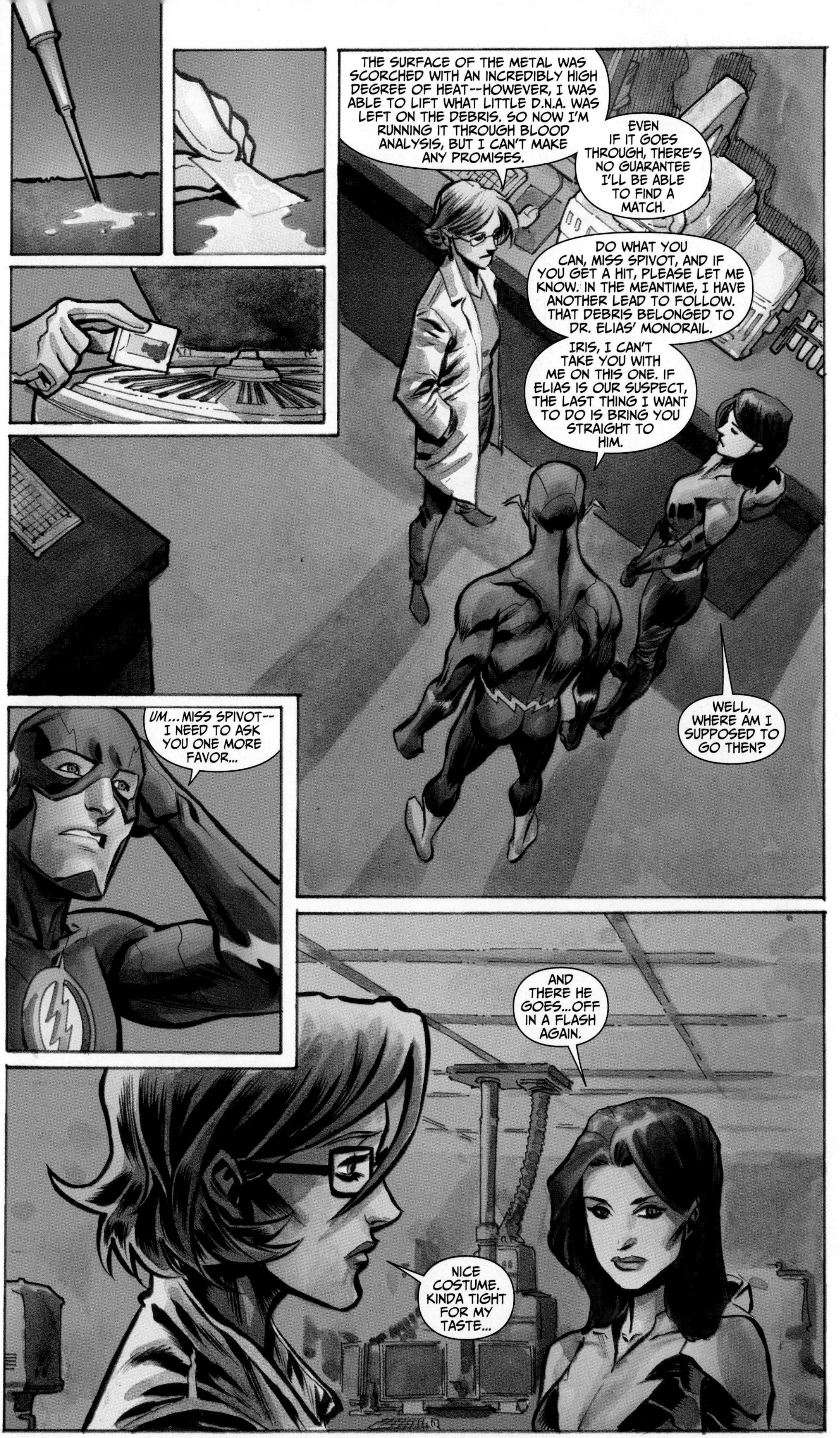
THE SURFACE OF THE METAL WAS SCORCHED WITH AN INCREDIBLY HIGH DEGREE OF HEAT--HOWEVER, I WAS ABLE TO LIFT WHAT LITTLE D.N.A. WAS LEFT ON THE DEBRIS. SO NOW I'M RUNNING IT THROUGH BLOOD ANALYSIS, BUT I CAN'T MAKE ANY PROMISES.
EVEN IF IT GOES THROUGH, THERE'S NO GUARANTEE I'LL BE ABLE TO FIND A MATCH.
DO WHAT YOU CAN, MISS SPIVOT, AND IF YOU GET A HIT, PLEASE LET ME KNOW. IN THE MEANTIME, I HAVE ANOTHER LEAD TO FOLLOW. THAT DEBRIS BELONGED TO DR. ELIAS' MONORAIL.
IRIS, I CAN'T TAKE YOU WITH ME ON THIS ONE. IF ELIAS IS OUR SUSPECT, THE LAST THING I WANT TO DO IS BRING YOU STRAIGHT TO HIM.
WELL, WHERE AM I SUPPOSED TO GO THEN?
UM...MISS SPIVOT--I NEED TO ASK YOU ONE MORE FAVOR...
AND THERE HE GOES...OFF IN A FLASH AGAIN.
NICE COSTUME. KINDA TIGHT FOR MY TASTE...

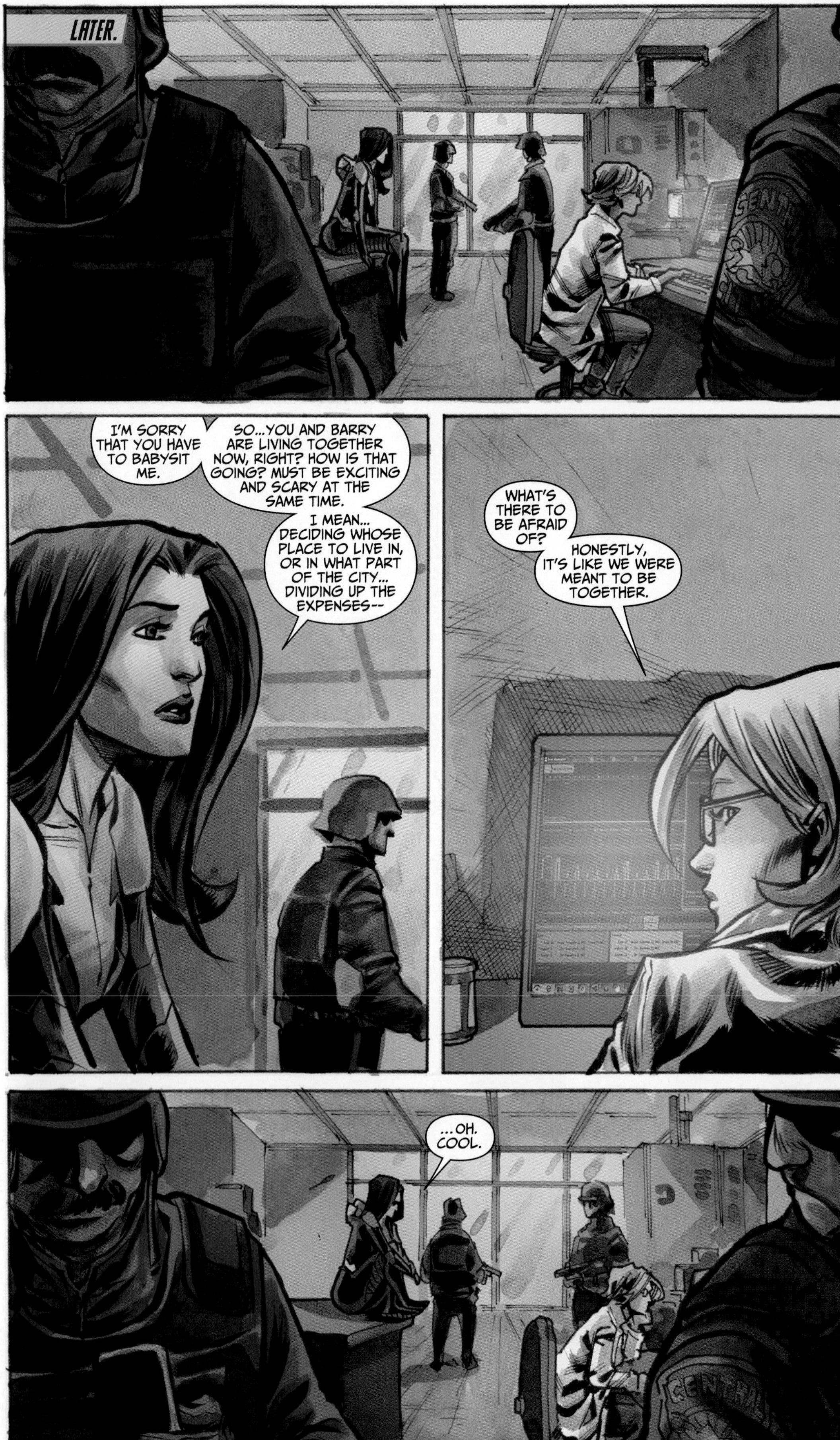
LATER.
I'M SORRY THAT YOU HAVE TO BABYSIT ME.
SO...YOU AND BARRY ARE LIVING TOGETHER NOW, RIGHT? HOW IS THAT GOING? MUST BE EXCITING AND SCARY AT THE SAME TIME.
I MEAN... DECIDING WHOSE PLACE TO LIVE IN, OR IN WHAT PART OF THE CITY... DIVIDING UP THE EXPENSES--
WHAT'S THERE TO BE AFRAID OF?
HONESTLY, IT'S LIKE WE WERE MEANT TO BE TOGETHER.
...OH. COOL.

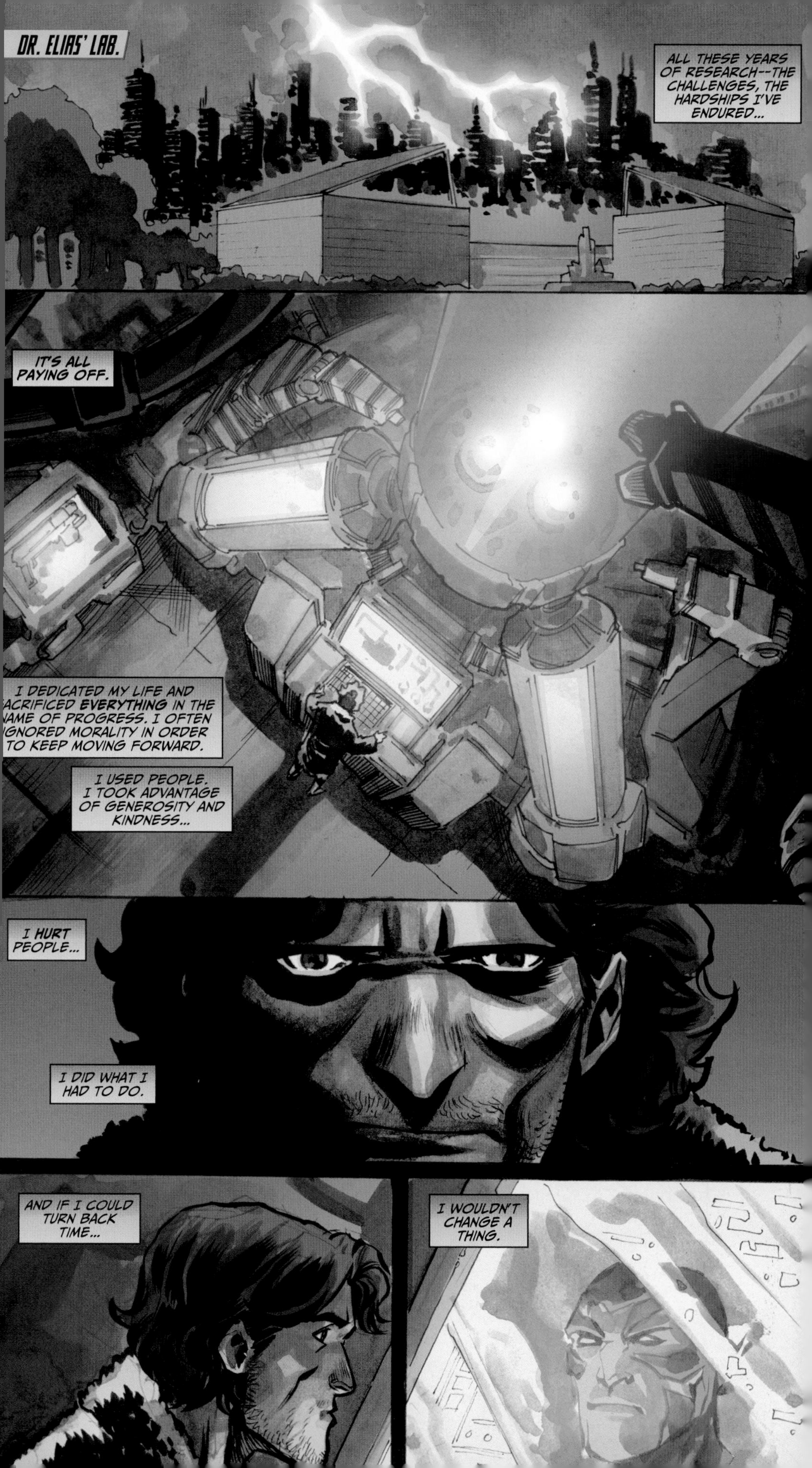

DR. ELIAS' LAB.
ALL THESE YEARS OF RESEARCH--THE CHALLENGES, THE HARDSHIPS I'VE ENDURED...
IT'S ALL PAYING OFF.
I DEDICATED MY LIFE AND SACRIFICED EVERYTHING IN THE NAME OF PROGRESS. I OFTEN IGNORED MORALITY IN ORDER TO KEEP MOVING FORWARD.
I USED PEOPLE. I TOOK ADVANTAGE OF GENEROSITY AND KINDNESS...
I HURT PEOPLE...
I DID WHAT I HAD TO DO.
AND IF I COULD TURN BACK TIME...
I WOULDN'T CHANGE A THING.

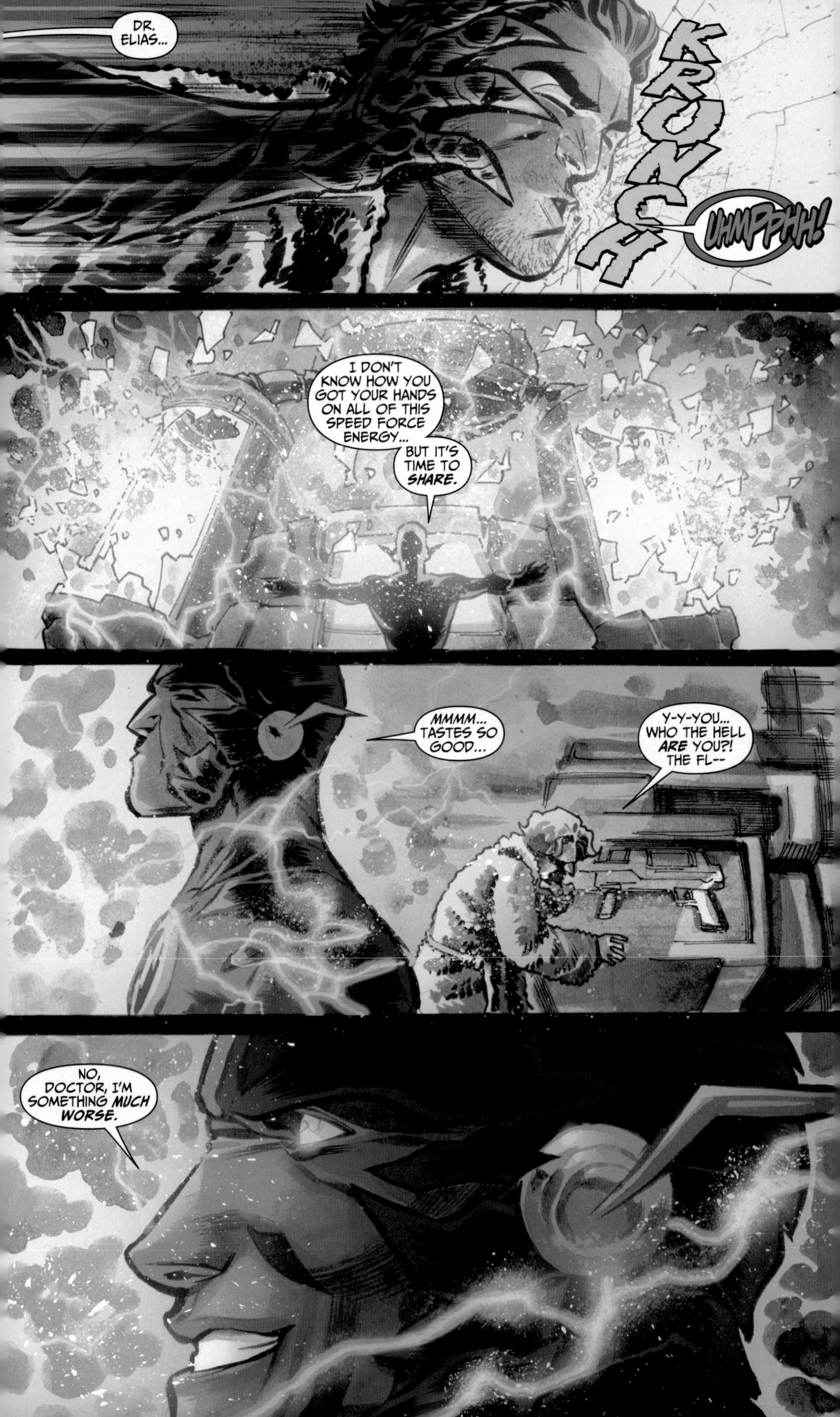
DR. ELIAS...
KRONCH
UHMPPHH!
I DON'T KNOW HOW YOU GOT YOUR HANDS ON ALL OF THIS SPEED FORCE ENERGY... BUT IT'S TIME TO SHARE.
MMMM... TASTES SO GOOD...
Y-Y-YOU... WHO THE HELL ARE YOU?! THE FL--
NO, DOCTOR, I'M SOMETHING MUCH WORSE.

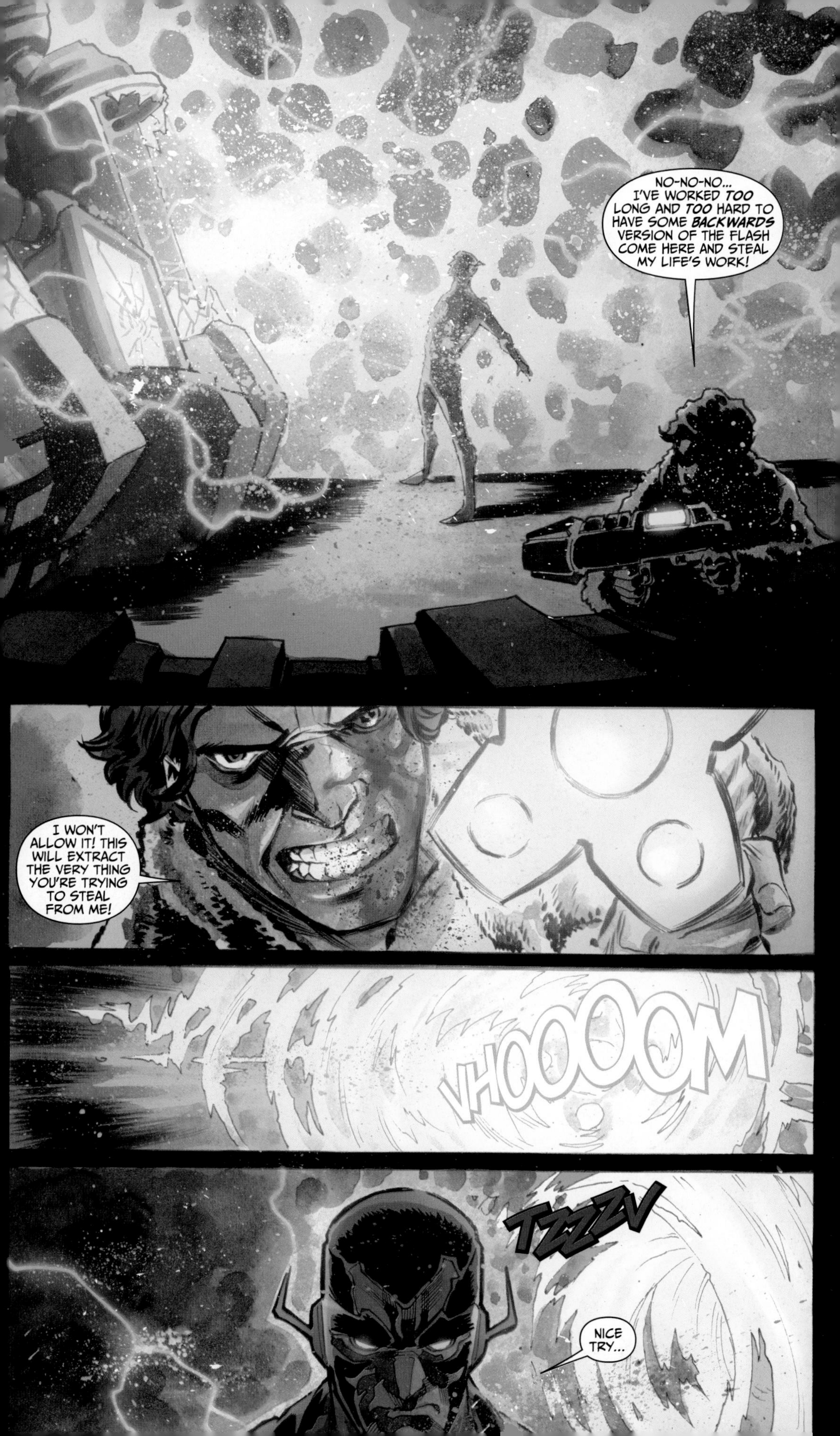
NO-NO-NO... I'VE WORKED TOO LONG AND TOO HARD TO HAVE SOME BACKWARDS VERSION OF THE FLASH COME HERE AND STEAL MY LIFE'S WORK!
I WON'T ALLOW IT! THIS WILL EXTRACT THE VERY THING YOU'RE TRYING TO STEAL FROM ME!
VHOOOOM
TZZZV
NICE TRY...

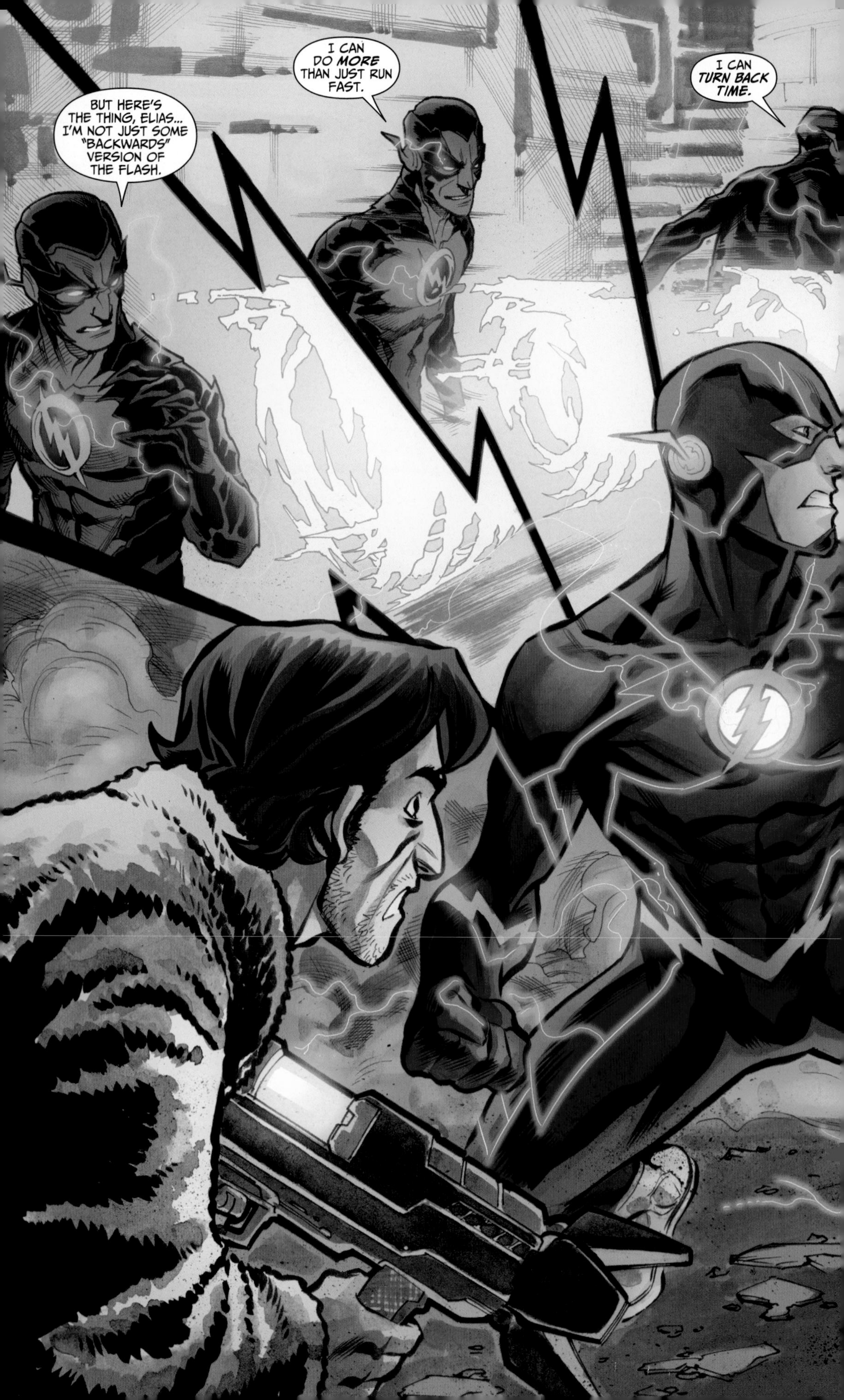
BUT HERE'S THE THING, ELIAS... I'M NOT JUST SOME "BACKWARDS" VERSION OF THE FLASH.
I CAN DO MORE THAN JUST RUN FAST.
I CAN TURN BACK TIME.

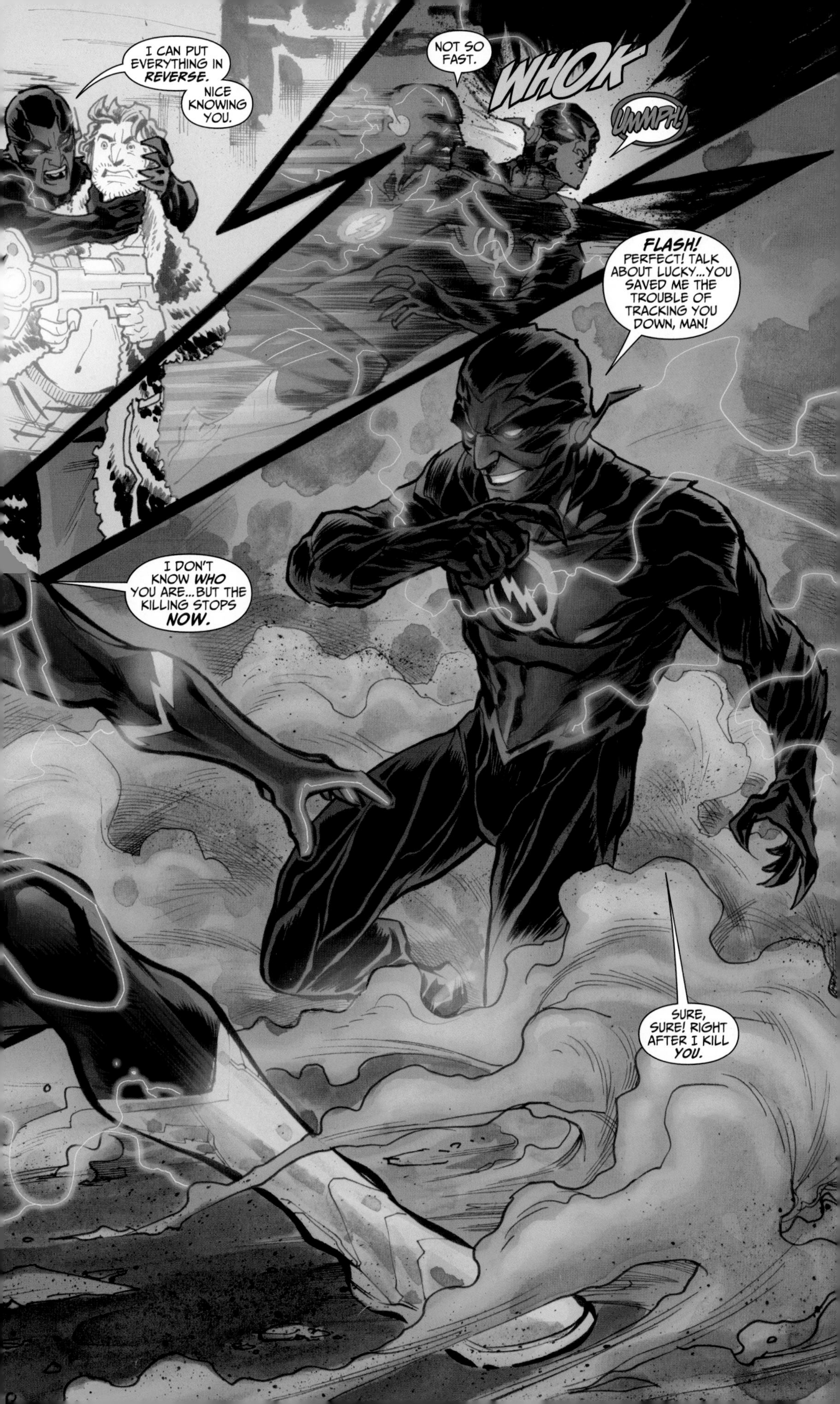
I CAN PUT EVERYTHING IN REVERSE.
NICE KNOWING YOU.
NOT SO FAST.
WHOK
UMMPH!
FLASH! PERFECT! TALK ABOUT LUCKY...YOU SAVED ME THE TROUBLE OF TRACKING YOU DOWN, MAN!
I DON'T KNOW WHO YOU ARE...BUT THE KILLING STOPS NOW.
SURE, SURE! RIGHT AFTER I KILL YOU.

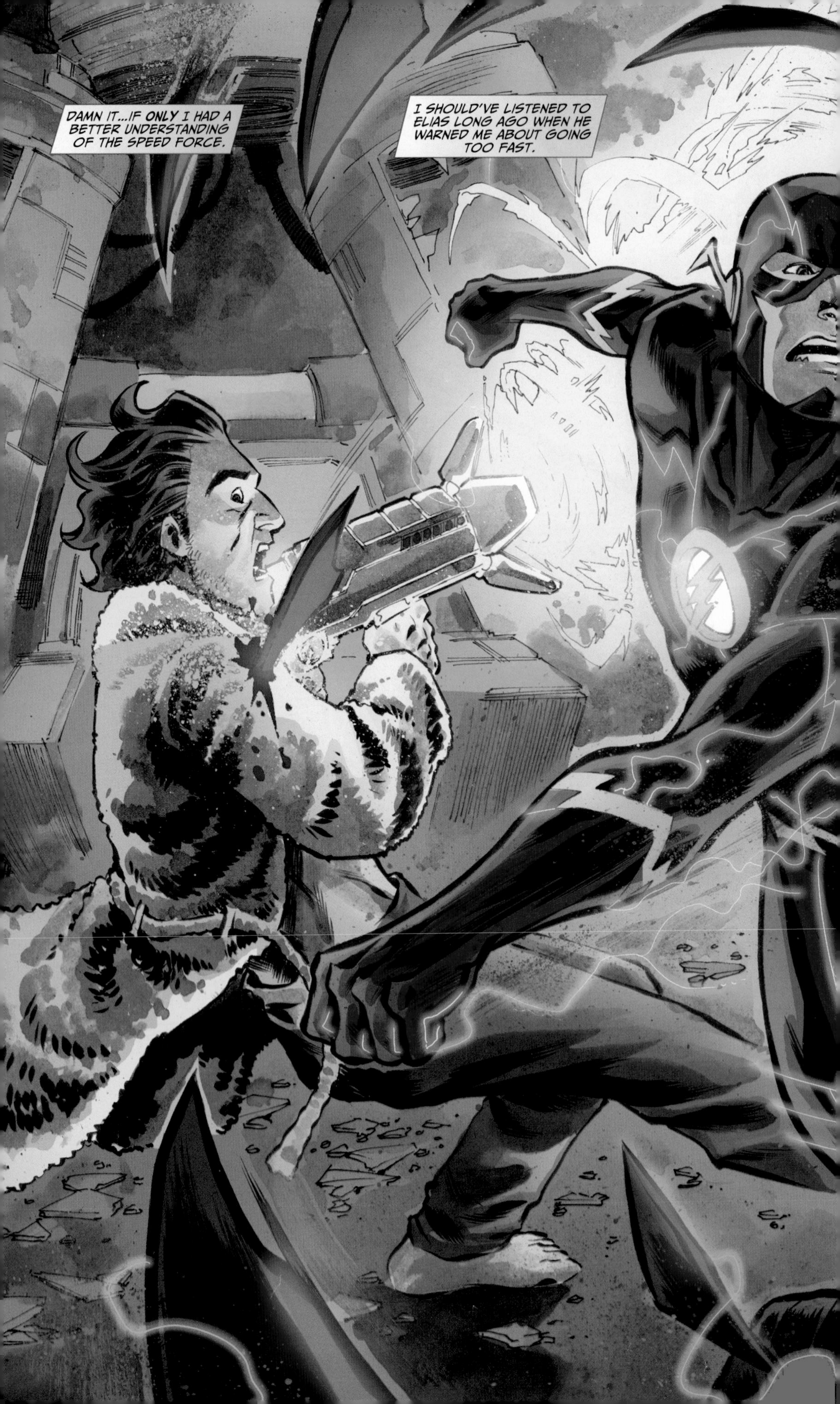
DAMN IT...IF ONLY I HAD A BETTER UNDERSTANDING OF THE SPEED FORCE.
I SHOULD'VE LISTENED TO ELIAS LONG AGO WHEN HE WARNED ME ABOUT GOING TOO FAST.

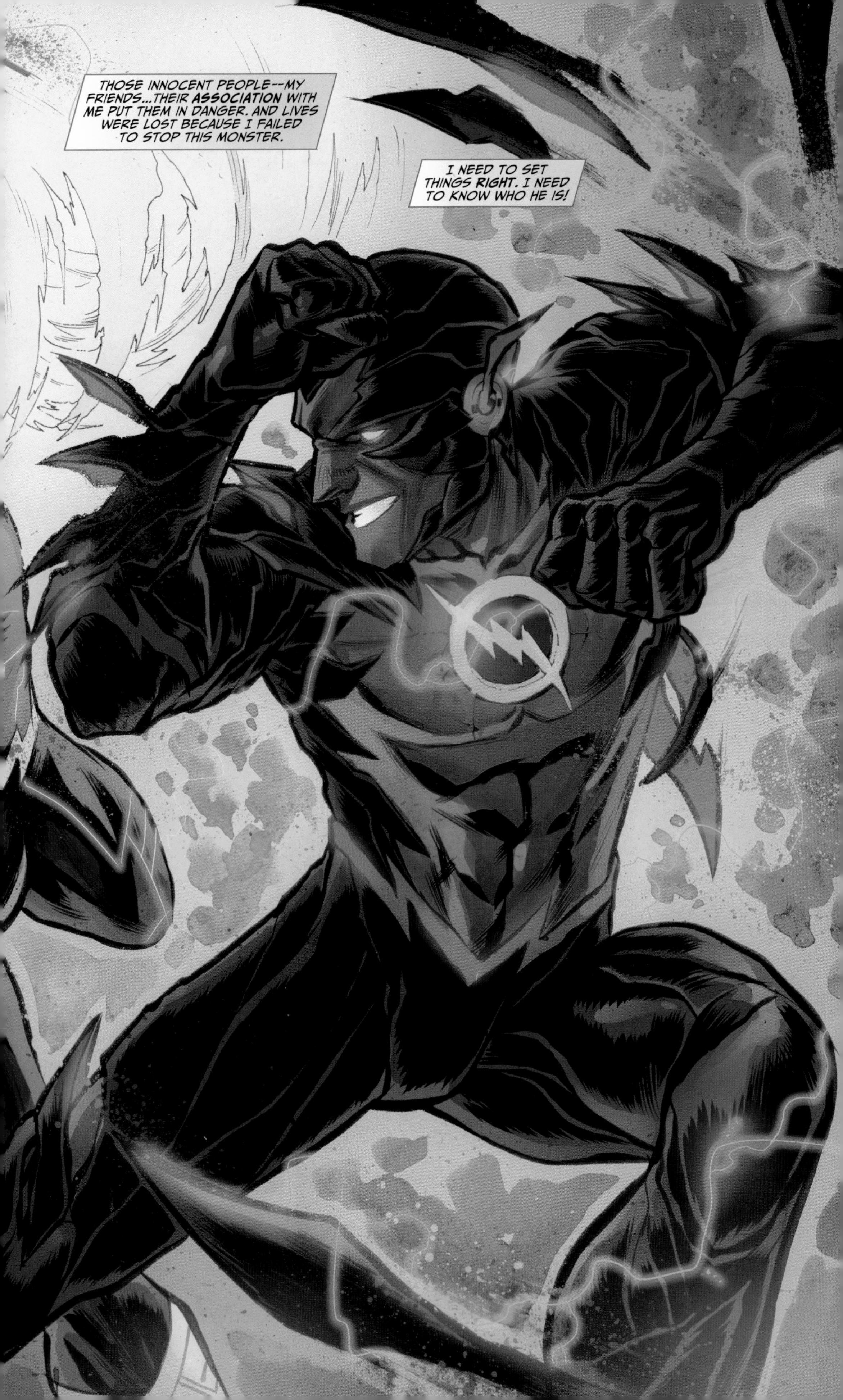
THOSE INNOCENT PEOPLE--MY FRIENDS...THEIR ASSOCIATION WITH ME PUT THEM IN DANGER. AND LIVES WERE LOST BECAUSE I FAILED TO STOP THIS MONSTER.
I NEED TO SET THINGS RIGHT. I NEED TO KNOW WHO HE IS!

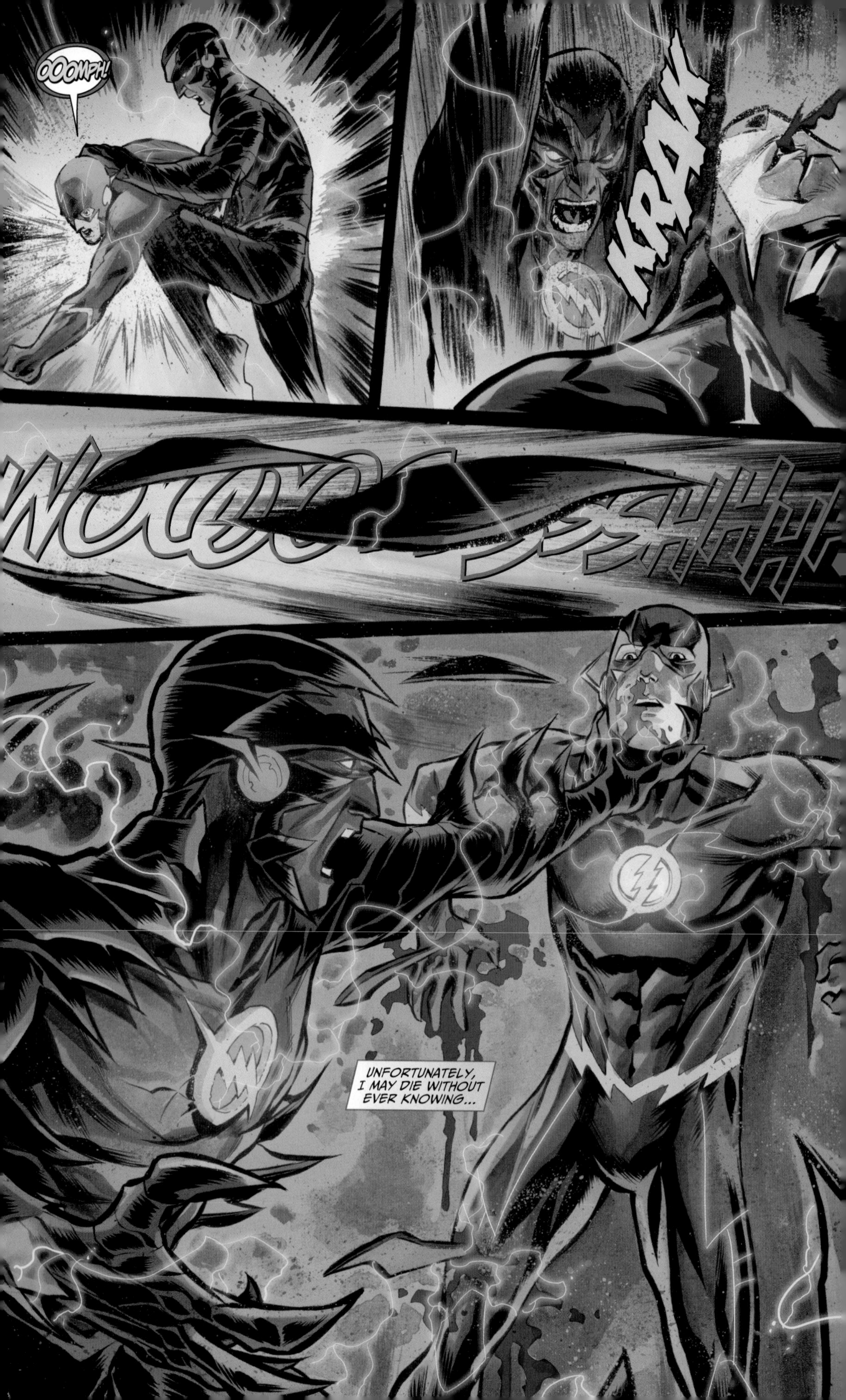
OOOMPH!
KRAK
WOOOOSSSHHH!
UNFORTUNATELY, I MAY DIE WITHOUT EVER KNOWING...

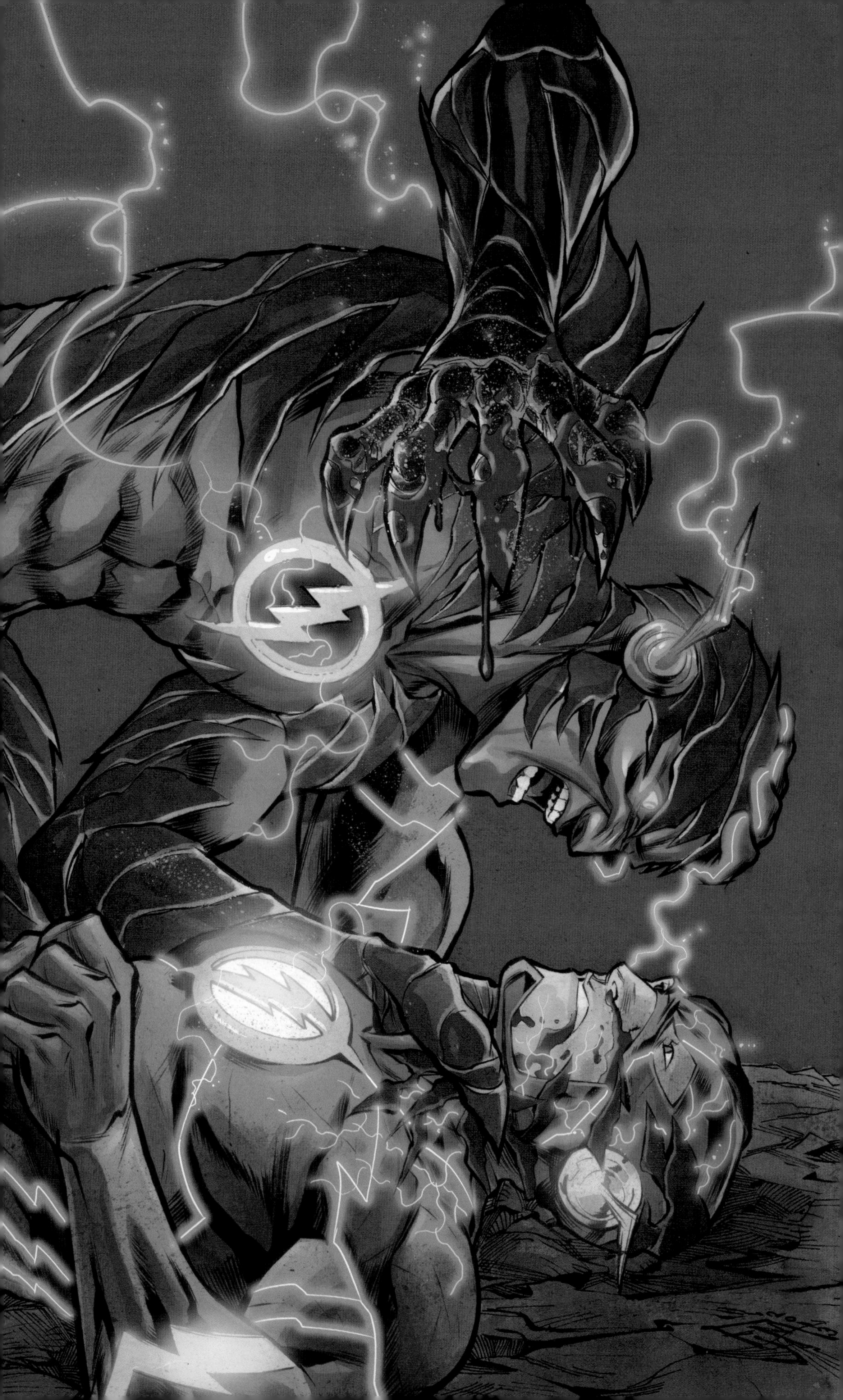

FRANCIS MANAPUL & BRIAN BUCCELLATO writers FRANCIS MANAPUL artist

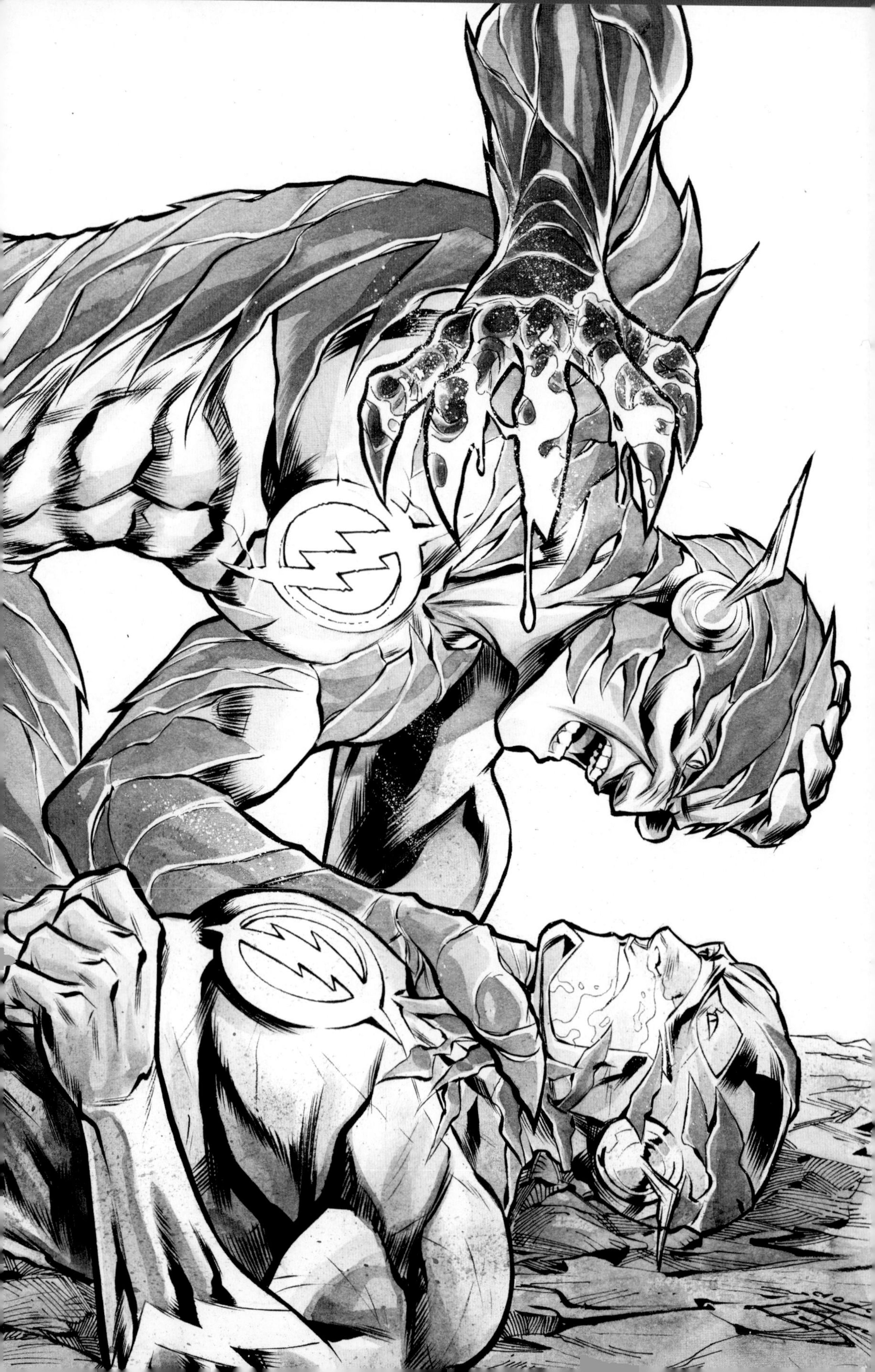

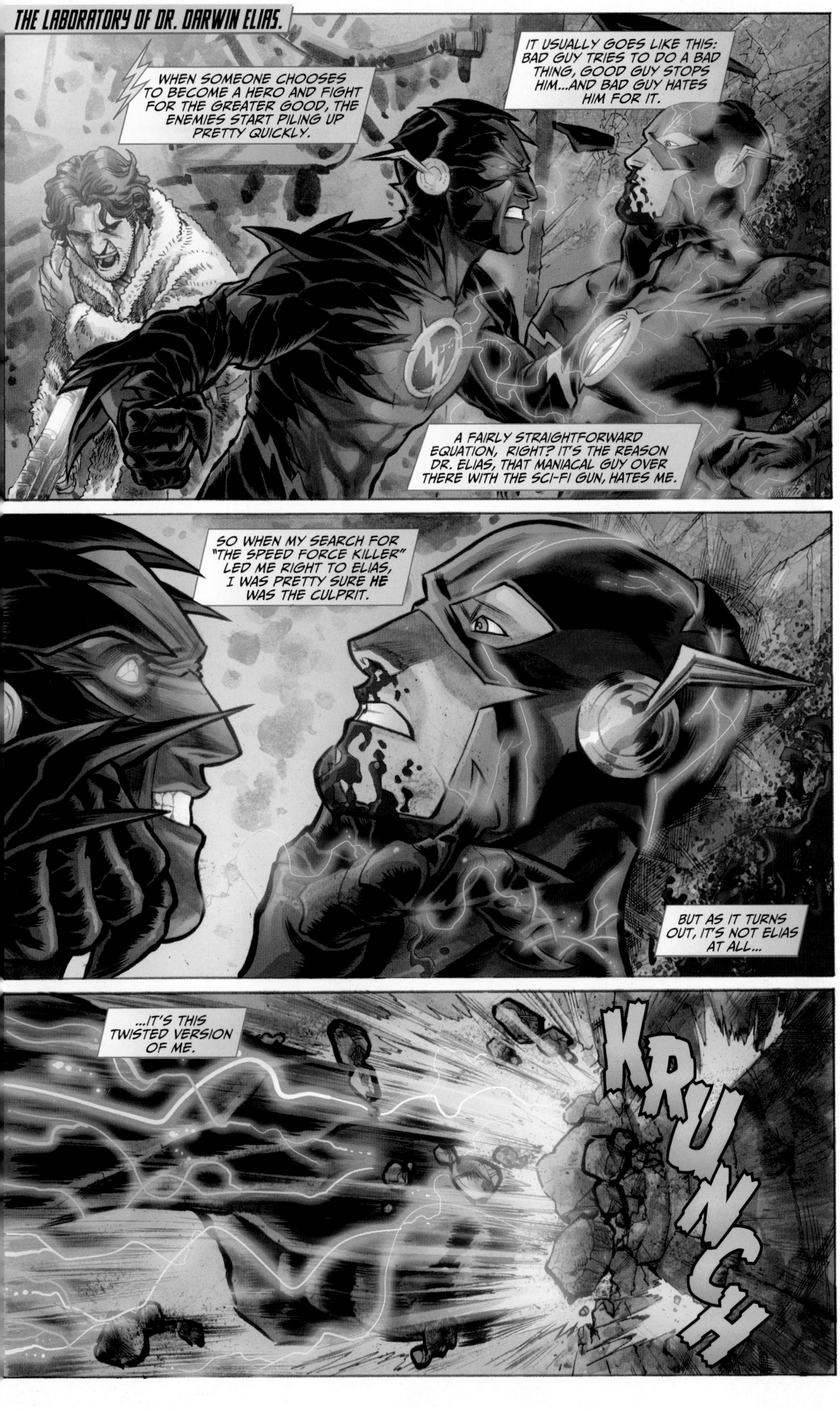
THE LABORATORY OF DR. DARWIN ELIAS.
WHEN SOMEONE CHOOSES TO BECOME A HERO AND FIGHT FOR THE GREATER GOOD, THE ENEMIES START PILING UP PRETTY QUICKLY.
IT USUALLY GOES LIKE THIS: BAD GUY TRIES TO DO A BAD THING, GOOD GUY STOPS HIM...AND BAD GUY HATES HIM FOR IT.
A FAIRLY STRAIGHTFORWARD EQUATION, RIGHT? IT'S THE REASON DR. ELIAS, THAT MANIACAL GUY OVER THERE WITH THE SCI-FI GUN, HATES ME.
SO WHEN MY SEARCH FOR "THE SPEED FORCE KILLER" LED ME RIGHT TO ELIAS, I WAS PRETTY SURE HE WAS THE CULPRIT.
BUT AS IT TURNS OUT, IT'S NOT ELIAS AT ALL...
...IT'S THIS TWISTED VERSION OF ME.
KRUNCH

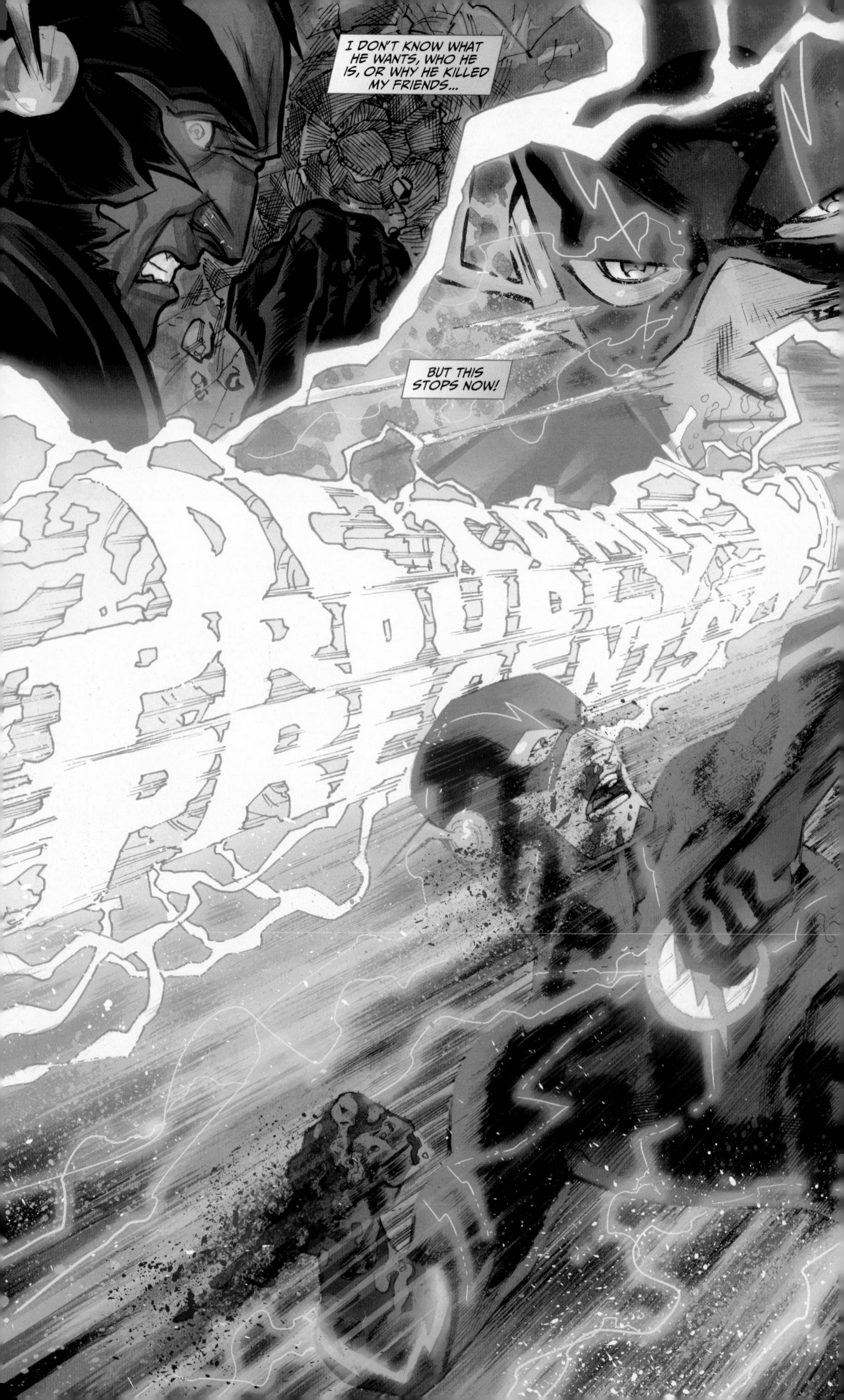
I DON'T KNOW WHAT HE WANTS, WHO HE IS, OR WHY HE KILLED MY FRIENDS...
BUT THIS STOPS NOW!

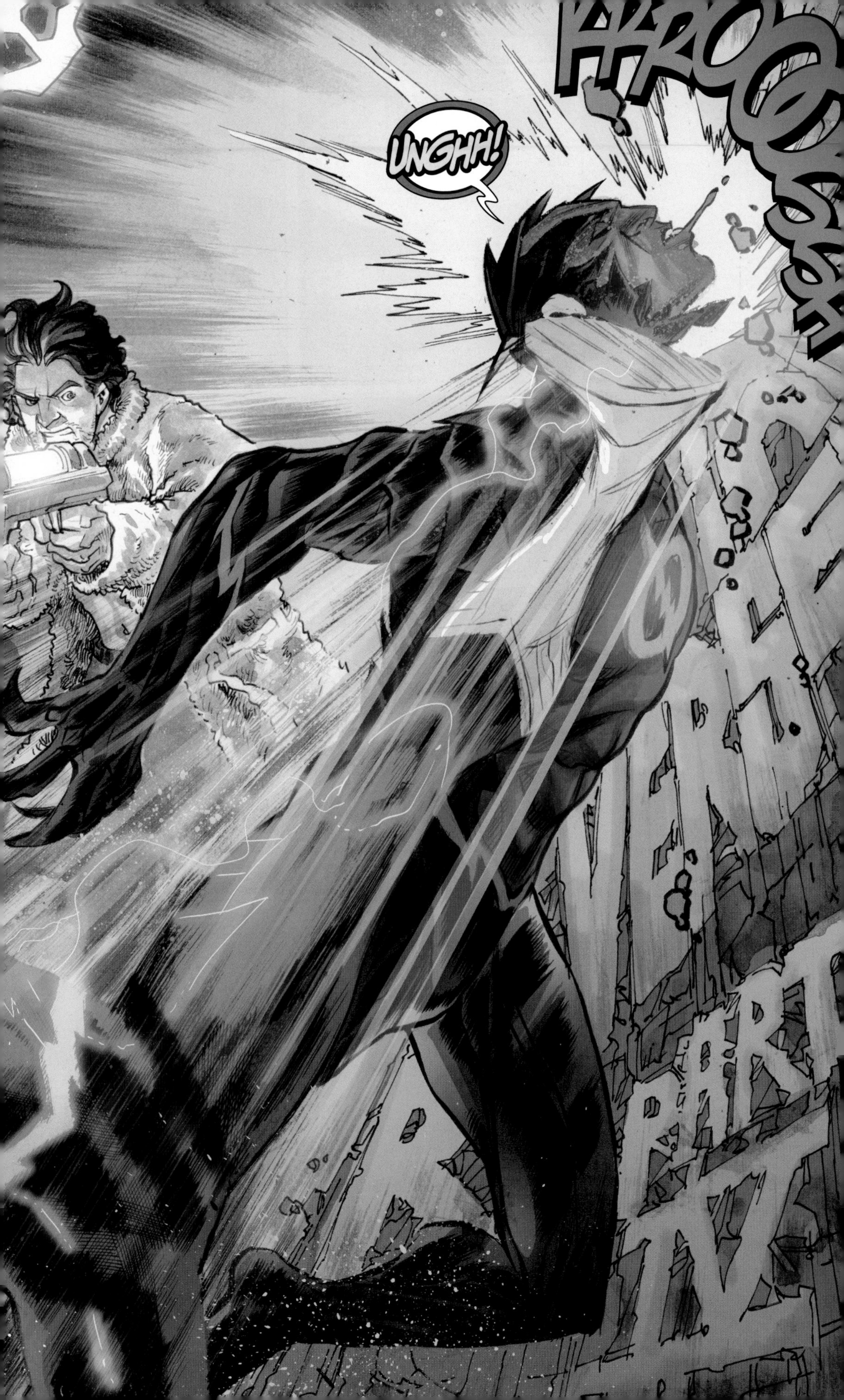
UNGHH!

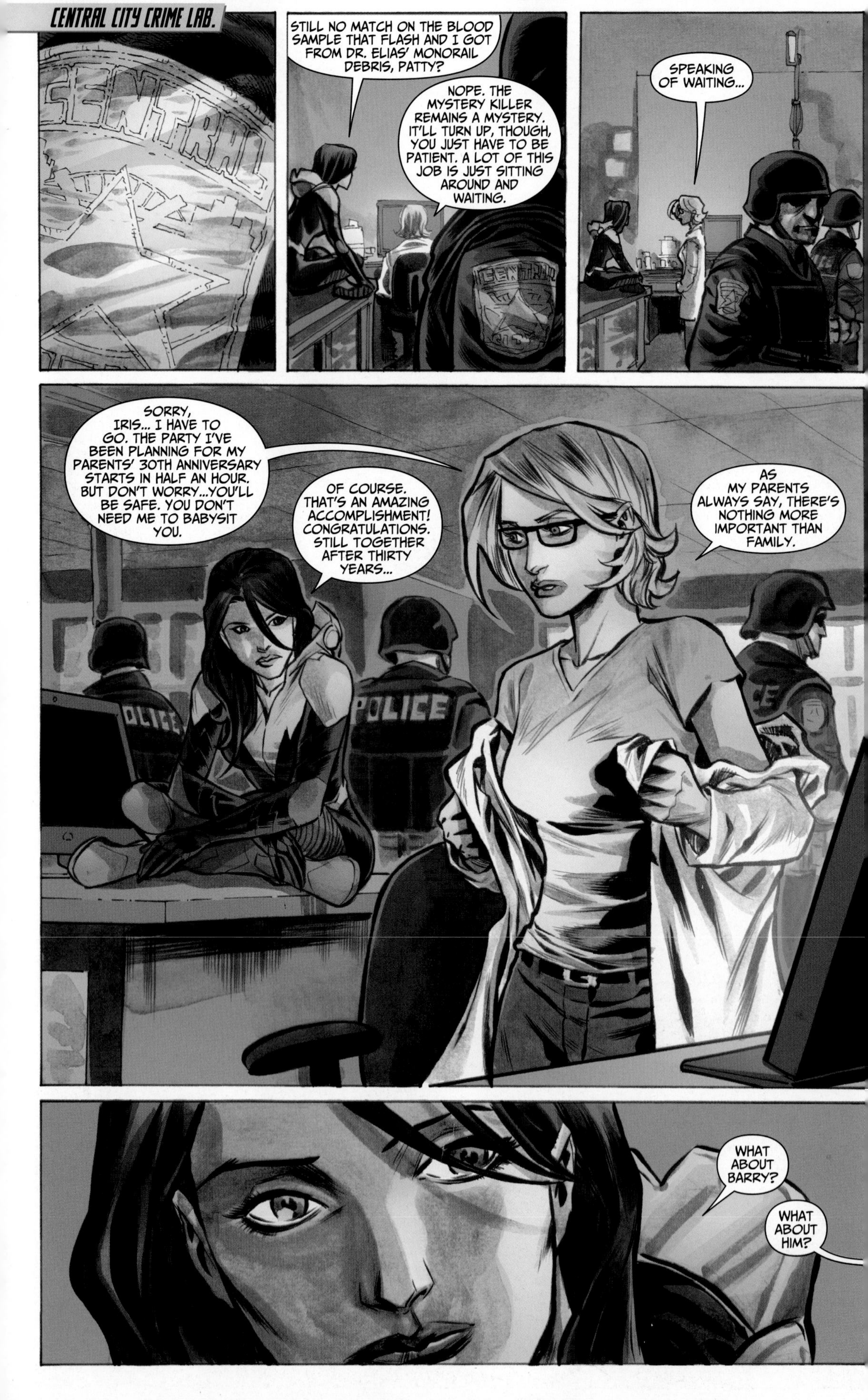
CENTRAL CITY CRIME LAB.
STILL NO MATCH ON THE BLOOD SAMPLE THAT FLASH AND I GOT FROM DR. ELIAS' MONORAIL DEBRIS, PATTY?
NOPE. THE MYSTERY KILLER REMAINS A MYSTERY. IT'LL TURN UP, THOUGH, YOU JUST HAVE TO BE PATIENT. A LOT OF THIS JOB IS JUST SITTING AROUND AND WAITING.
SPEAKING OF WAITING...
SORRY, IRIS... I HAVE TO GO. THE PARTY I'VE BEEN PLANNING FOR MY PARENTS' 30TH ANNIVERSARY STARTS IN HALF AN HOUR. BUT DON'T WORRY...YOU'LL BE SAFE. YOU DON'T NEED ME TO BABYSIT YOU.
OF COURSE. THAT'S AN AMAZING ACCOMPLISHMENT! CONGRATULATIONS. STILL TOGETHER AFTER THIRTY YEARS...
AS MY PARENTS ALWAYS SAY, THERE'S NOTHING MORE IMPORTANT THAN FAMILY.
WHAT ABOUT BARRY?
WHAT ABOUT HIM?

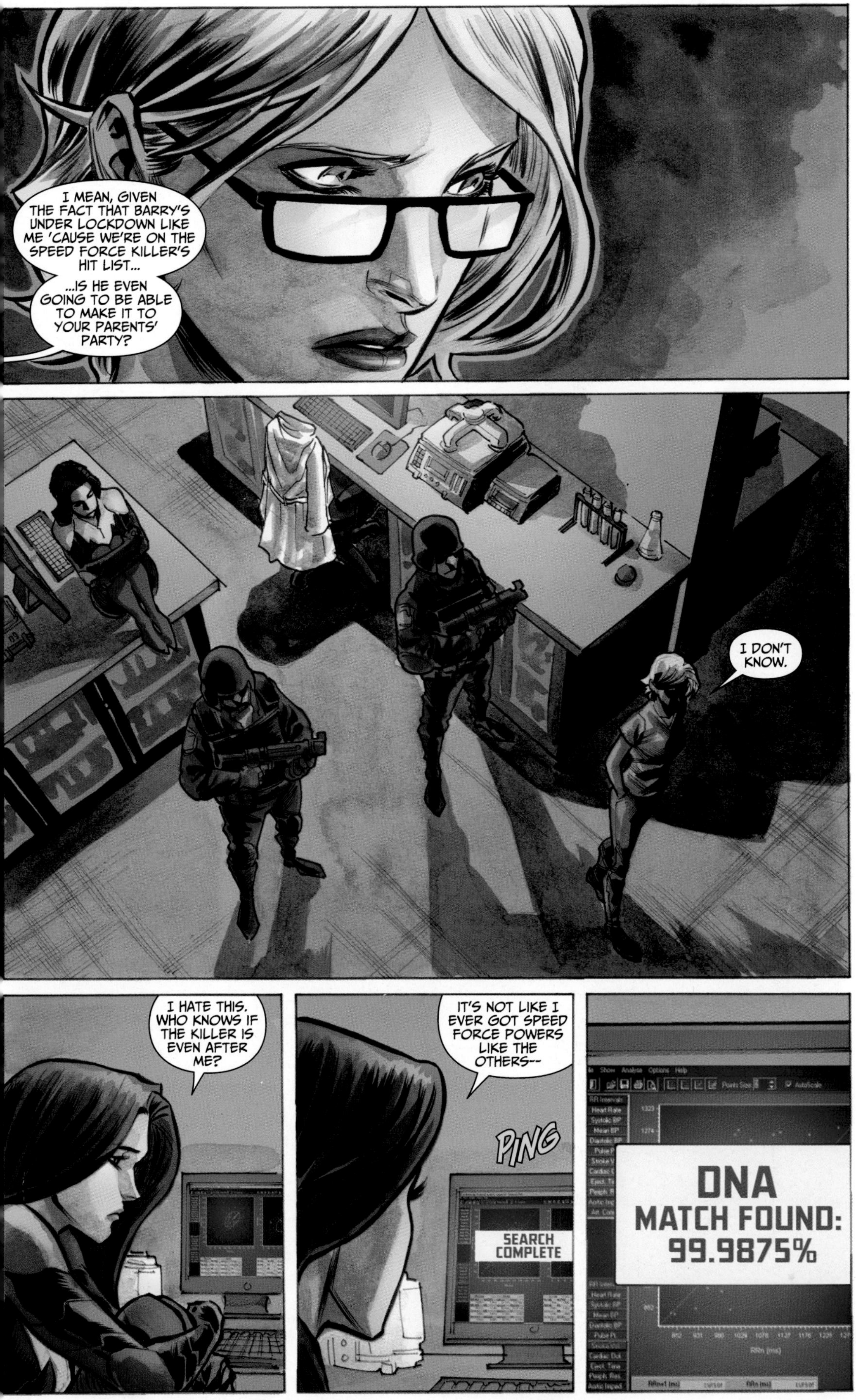
I MEAN, GIVEN THE FACT THAT BARRY'S UNDER LOCKDOWN LIKE ME 'CAUSE WE'RE ON THE SPEED FORCE KILLER'S HIT LIST...
...IS HE EVEN GOING TO BE ABLE TO MAKE IT TO YOUR PARENTS' PARTY?
I DON'T KNOW.
I HATE THIS. WHO KNOWS IF THE KILLER IS EVEN AFTER ME?
IT'S NOT LIKE I EVER GOT SPEED FORCE POWERS LIKE THE OTHERS--
PING
SEARCH COMPLETE
DNA
MATCH FOUND:
99.9875%

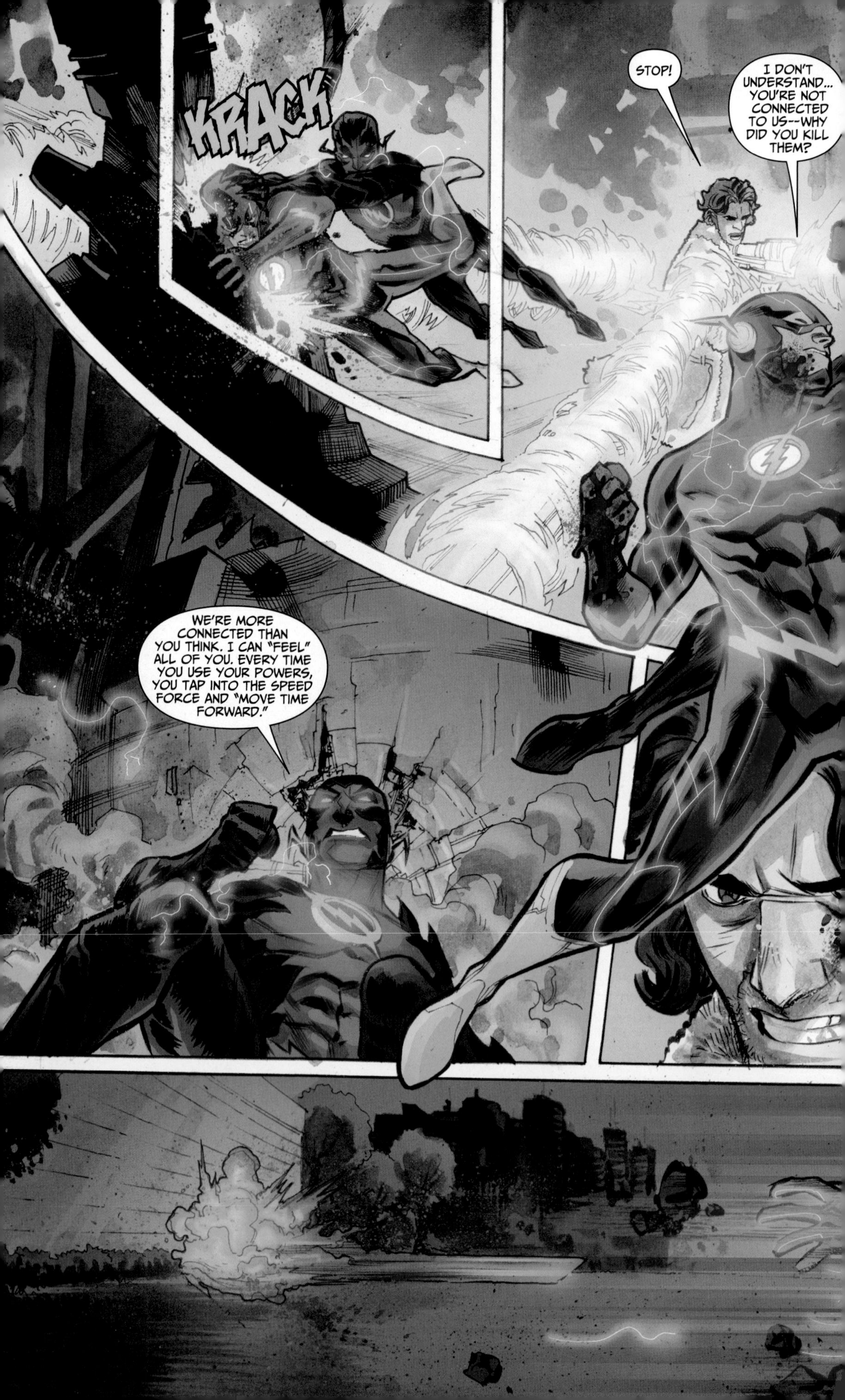
KRACK
STOP!
I DON'T UNDERSTAND... YOU'RE NOT CONNECTED TO US--WHY DID YOU KILL THEM?
WE'RE MORE CONNECTED THAN YOU THINK. I CAN "FEEL" ALL OF YOU. EVERY TIME YOU USE YOUR POWERS, YOU TAP INTO THE SPEED FORCE AND "MOVE TIME FORWARD."

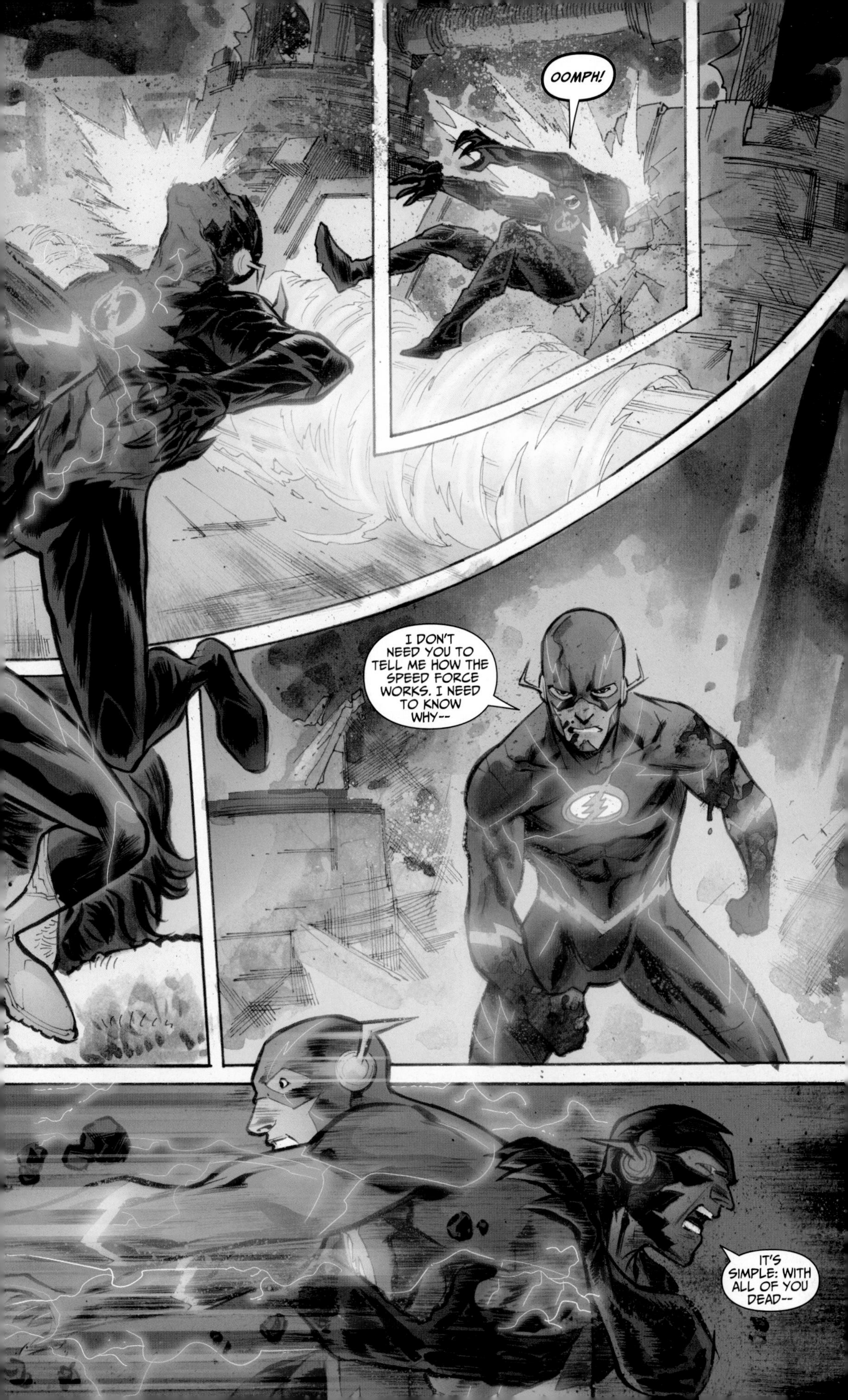
OOMPH!
I DON'T NEED YOU TO TELL ME HOW THE SPEED FORCE WORKS. I NEED TO KNOW WHY--
IT'S SIMPLE: WITH ALL OF YOU DEAD--

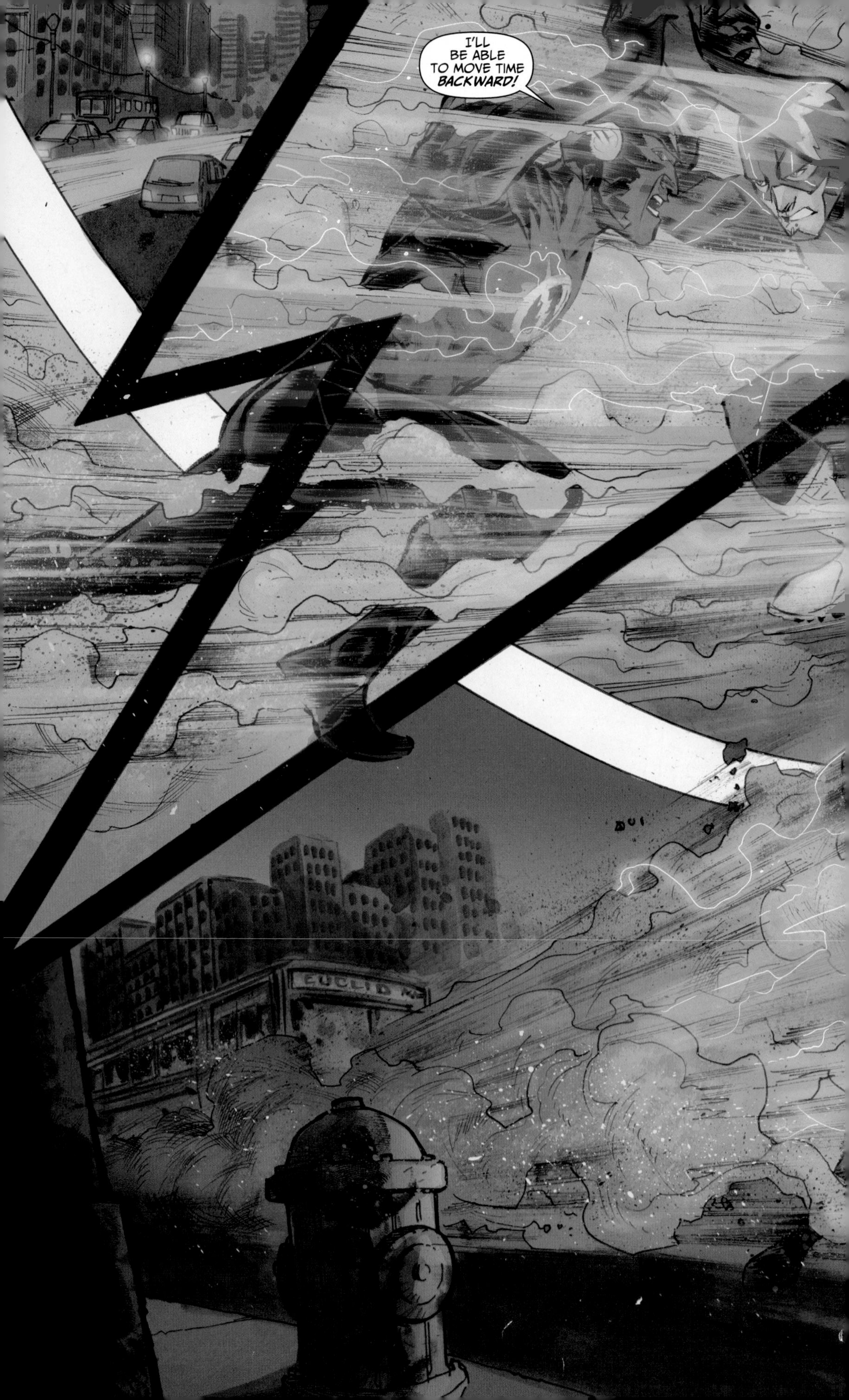
I'LL BE ABLE TO MOVE TIME *BACKWARD!*

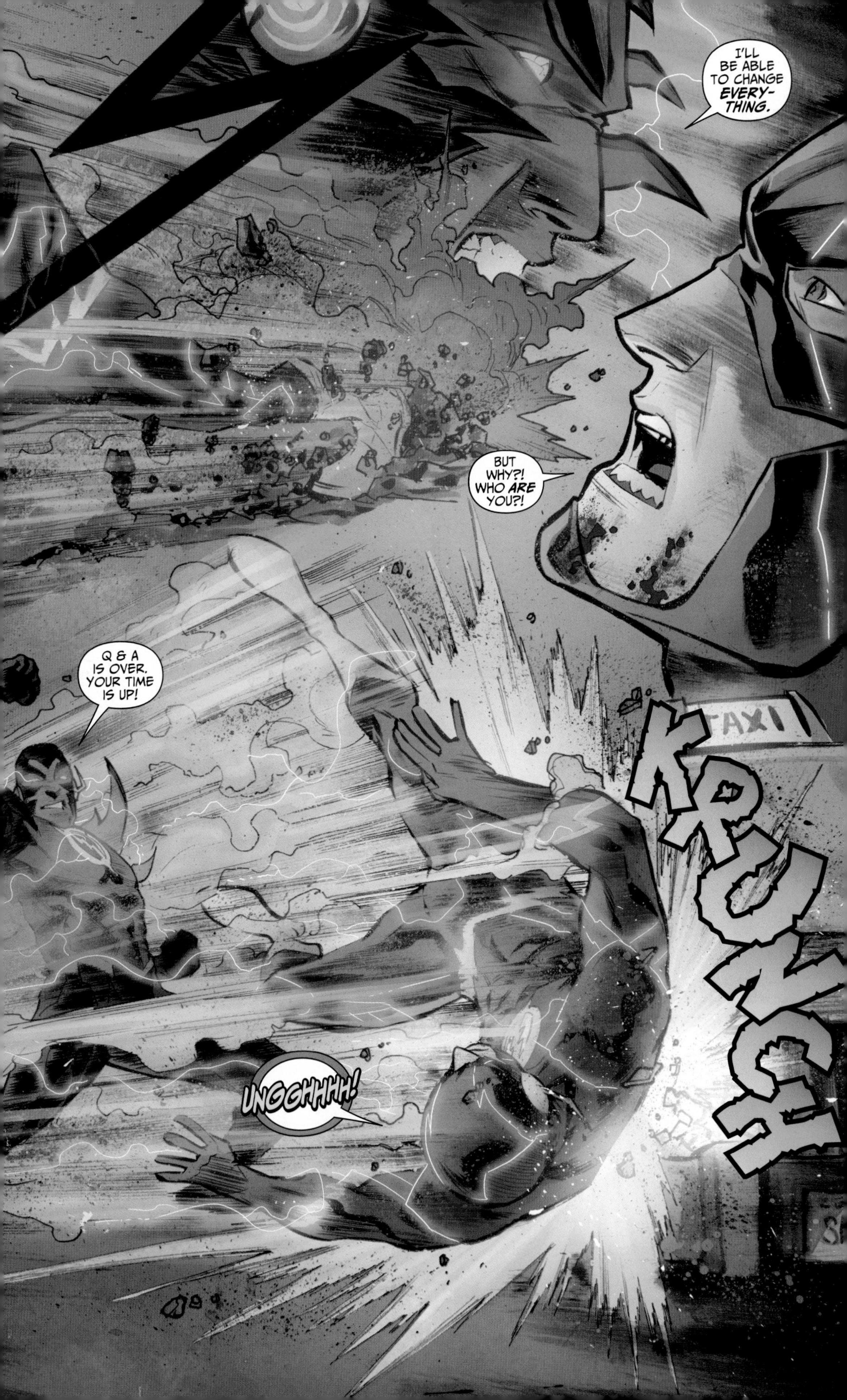
I'LL BE ABLE TO CHANGE EVERY-THING.
BUT WHY?! WHO ARE YOU?!
Q & A IS OVER. YOUR TIME IS UP!
TAXI
KRUNCH
UNGGHHHH!

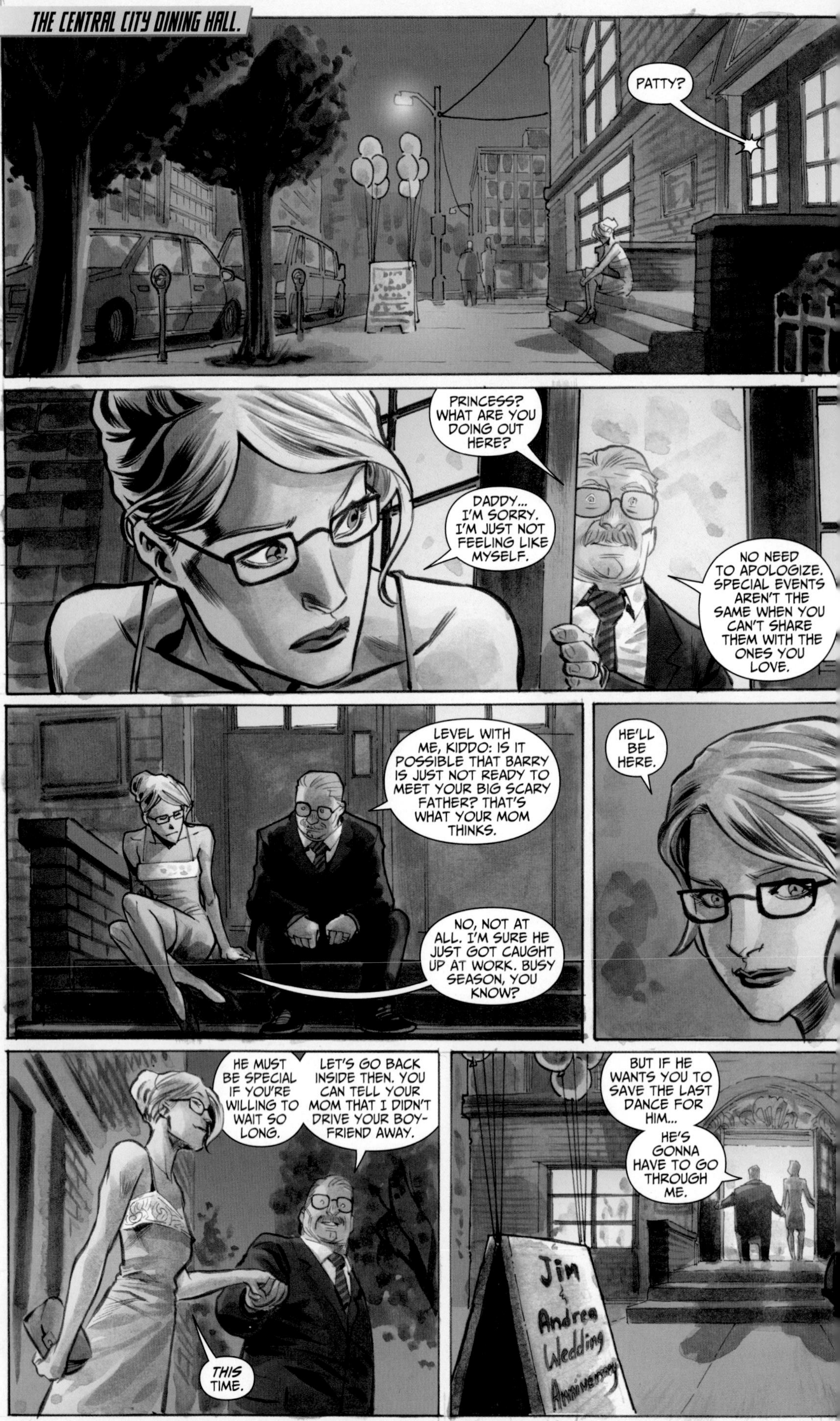
THE CENTRAL CITY DINING HALL.
PATTY?
PRINCESS? WHAT ARE YOU DOING OUT HERE?
DADDY... I'M SORRY. I'M JUST NOT FEELING LIKE MYSELF.
NO NEED TO APOLOGIZE. SPECIAL EVENTS AREN'T THE SAME WHEN YOU CAN'T SHARE THEM WITH THE ONES YOU LOVE.
LEVEL WITH ME, KIDDO: IS IT POSSIBLE THAT BARRY IS JUST NOT READY TO MEET YOUR BIG SCARY FATHER? THAT'S WHAT YOUR MOM THINKS.
NO, NOT AT ALL. I'M SURE HE JUST GOT CAUGHT UP AT WORK. BUSY SEASON, YOU KNOW?
HE'LL BE HERE.
HE MUST BE SPECIAL IF YOU'RE WILLING TO WAIT SO LONG.
LET'S GO BACK INSIDE THEN. YOU CAN TELL YOUR MOM THAT I DIDN'T DRIVE YOUR BOY-FRIEND AWAY.
THIS TIME.
BUT IF HE WANTS YOU TO SAVE THE LAST DANCE FOR HIM...
HE'S GONNA HAVE TO GO THROUGH ME.
Jim & Andrea Wedding Anniversary

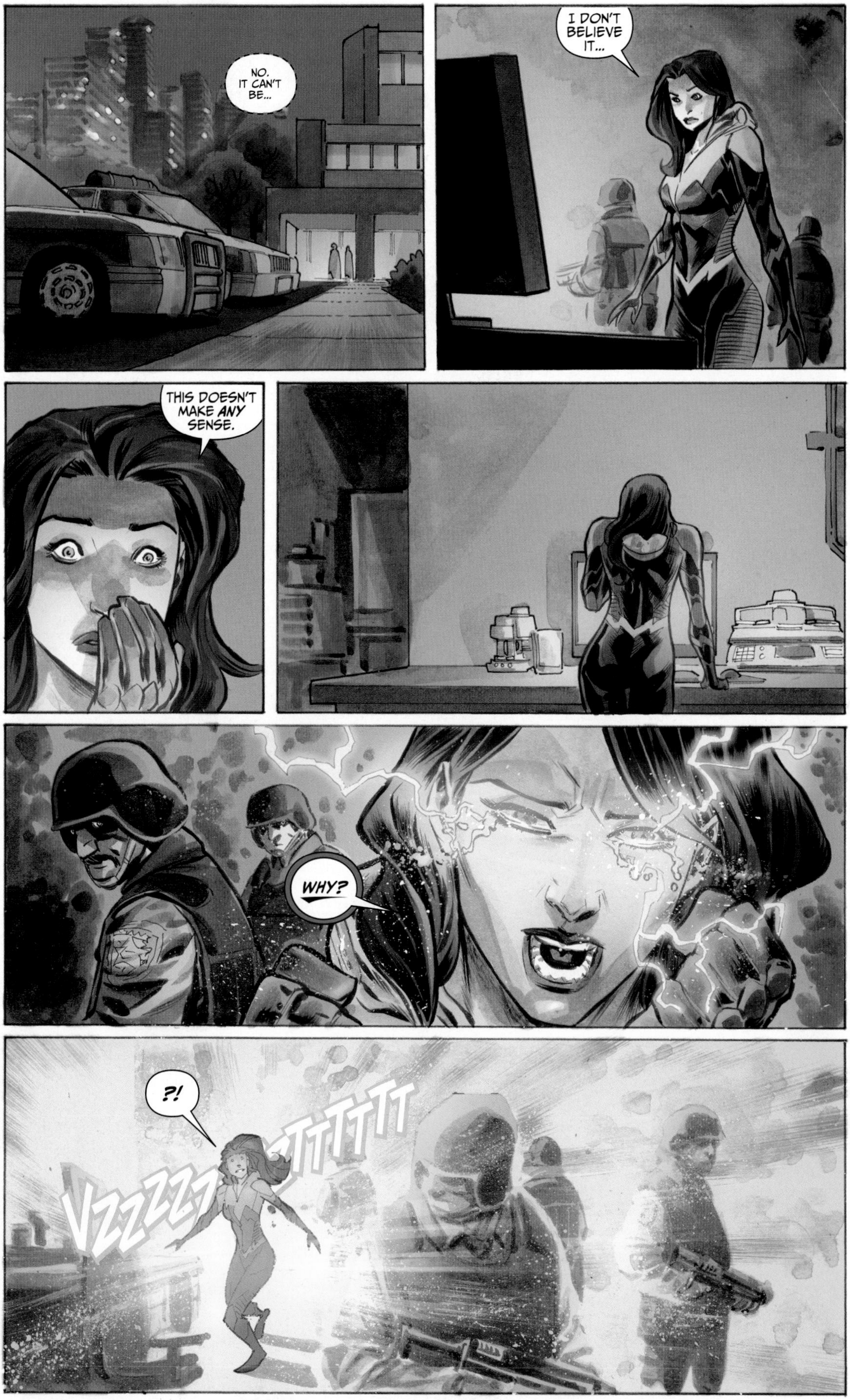

NO. IT CAN'T BE...
I DON'T BELIEVE IT...
THIS DOESN'T MAKE ANY SENSE.
WHY?
?!
VZZZZZTTTTTTT

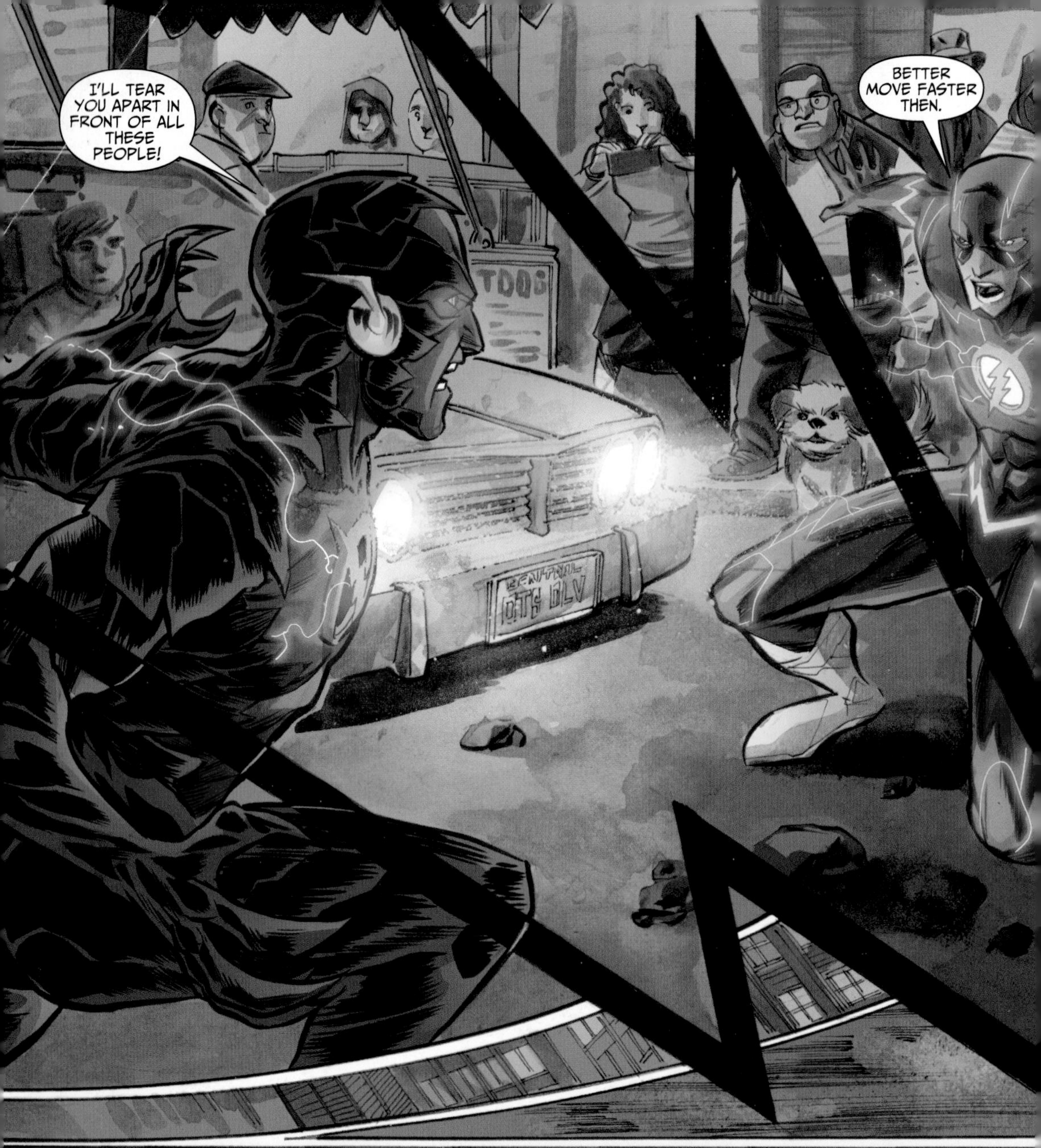
I'LL TEAR YOU APART IN FRONT OF ALL THESE PEOPLE!
BETTER MOVE FASTER THEN.

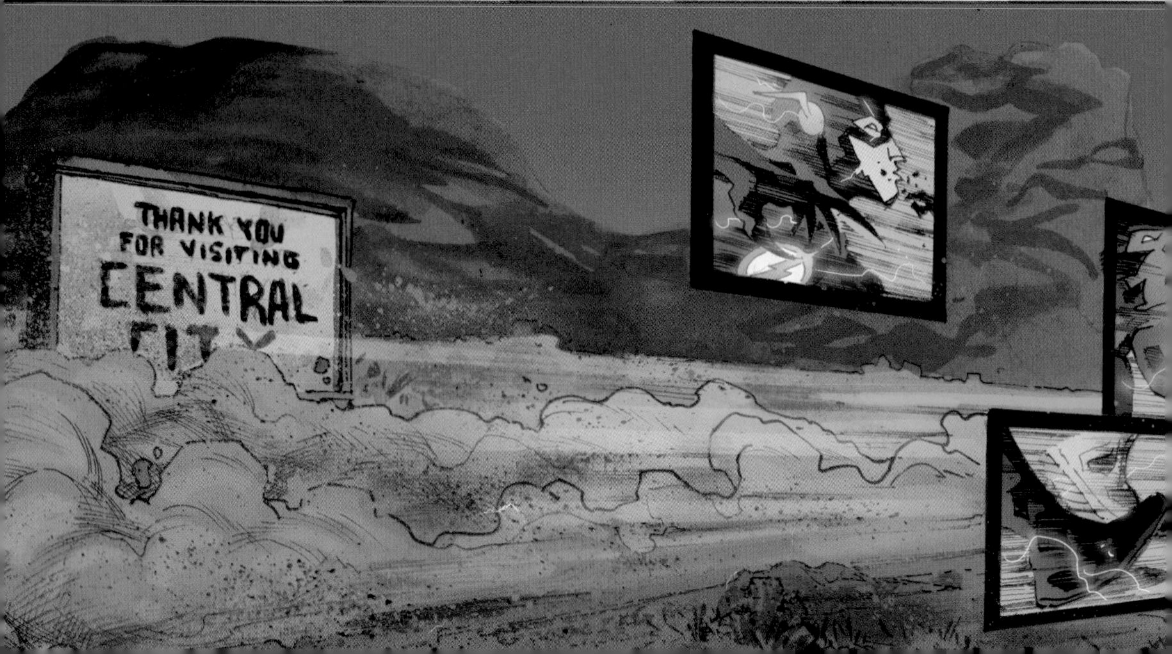
THANK YOU FOR VISITING CENTRAL

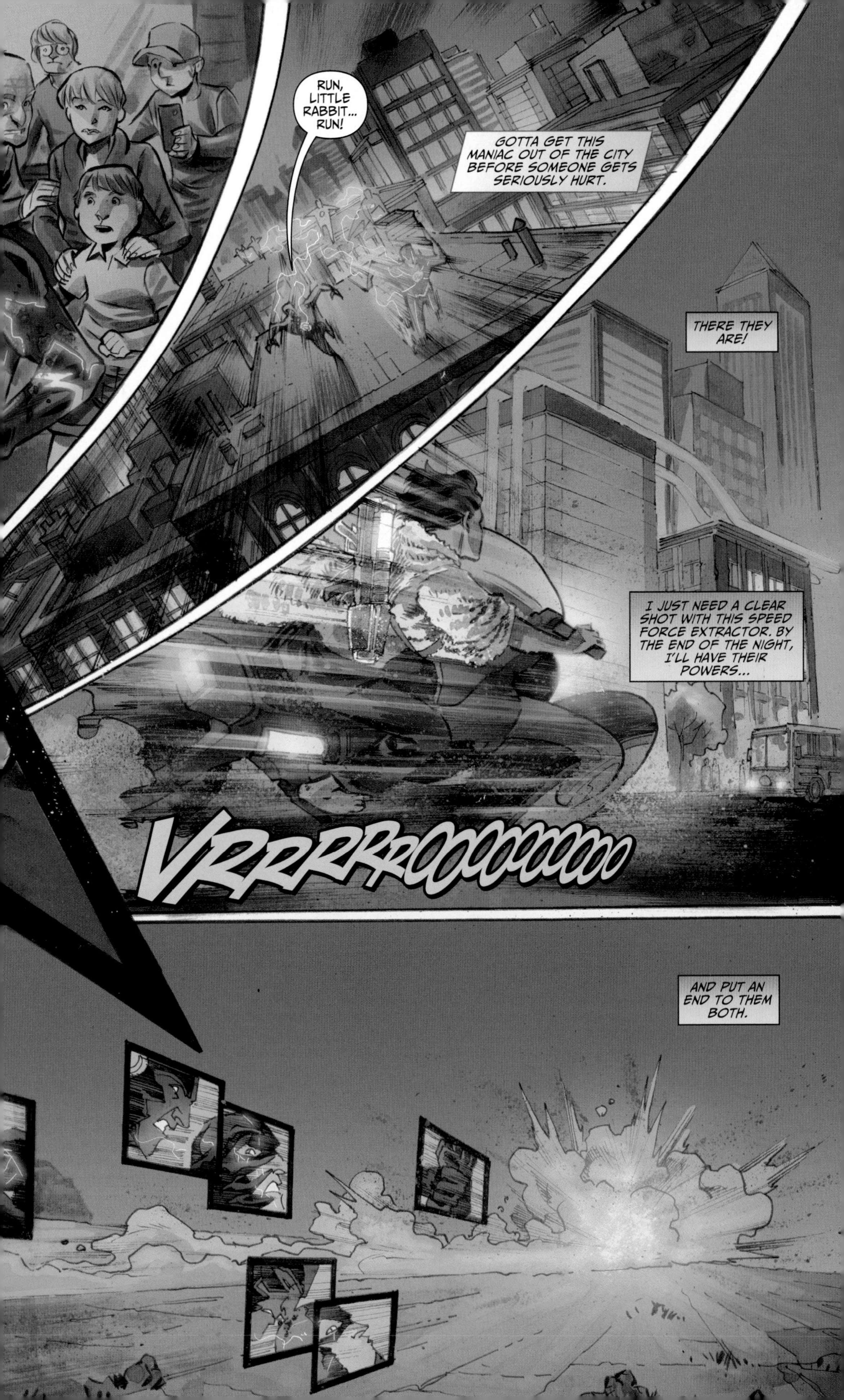
RUN, LITTLE RABBIT... RUN!
GOTTA GET THIS MANIAC OUT OF THE CITY BEFORE SOMEONE GETS SERIOUSLY HURT.
THERE THEY ARE!
I JUST NEED A CLEAR SHOT WITH THIS SPEED FORCE EXTRACTOR. BY THE END OF THE NIGHT, I'LL HAVE THEIR POWERS...
VRRRRROOOOOOOOOOO
AND PUT AN END TO THEM BOTH.

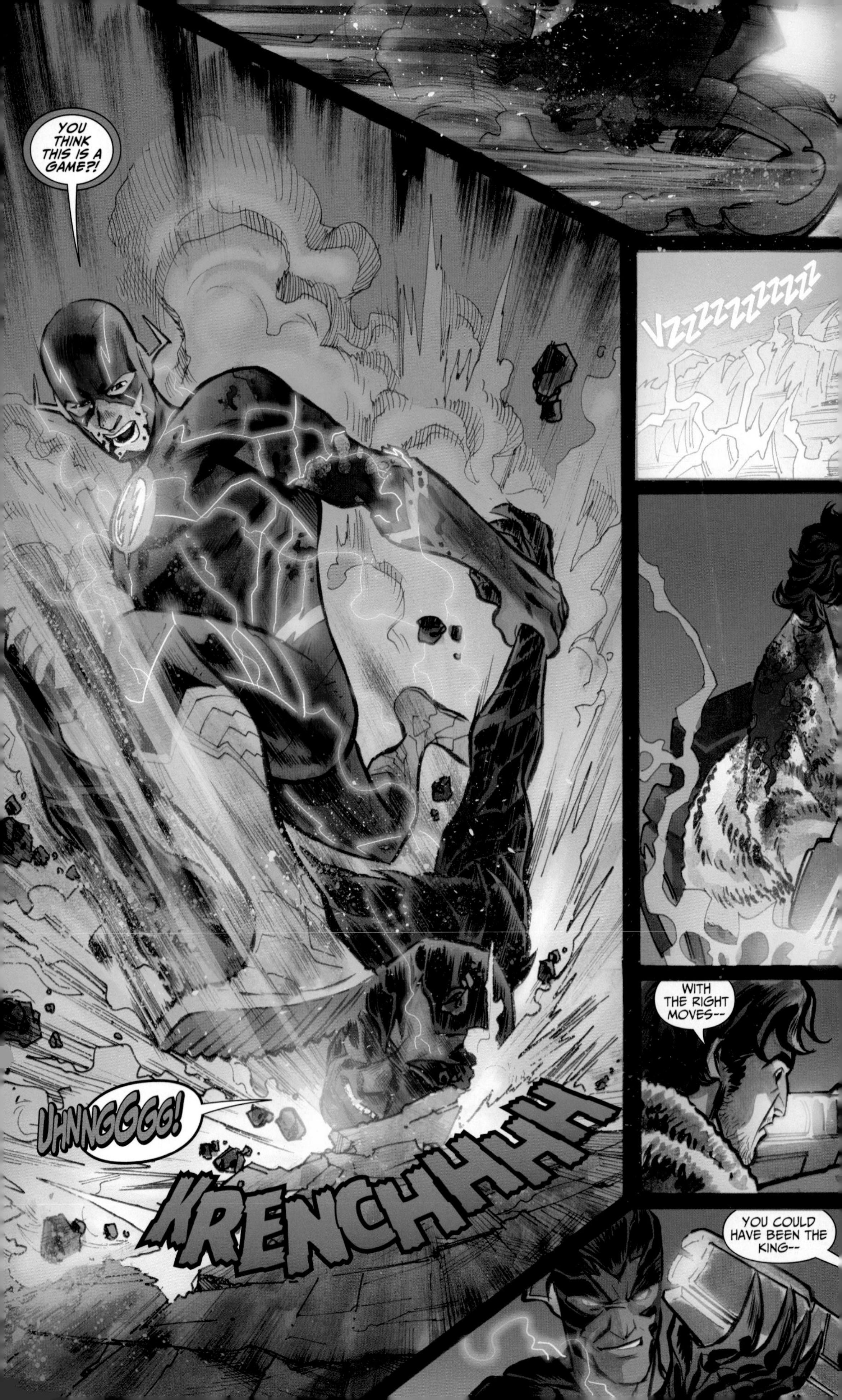
YOU THINK THIS IS A GAME?!
VZZZZZZZZZZ
WITH THE RIGHT MOVES--
UHNNGGGG!
KRENCHHHH
YOU COULD HAVE BEEN THE KING--

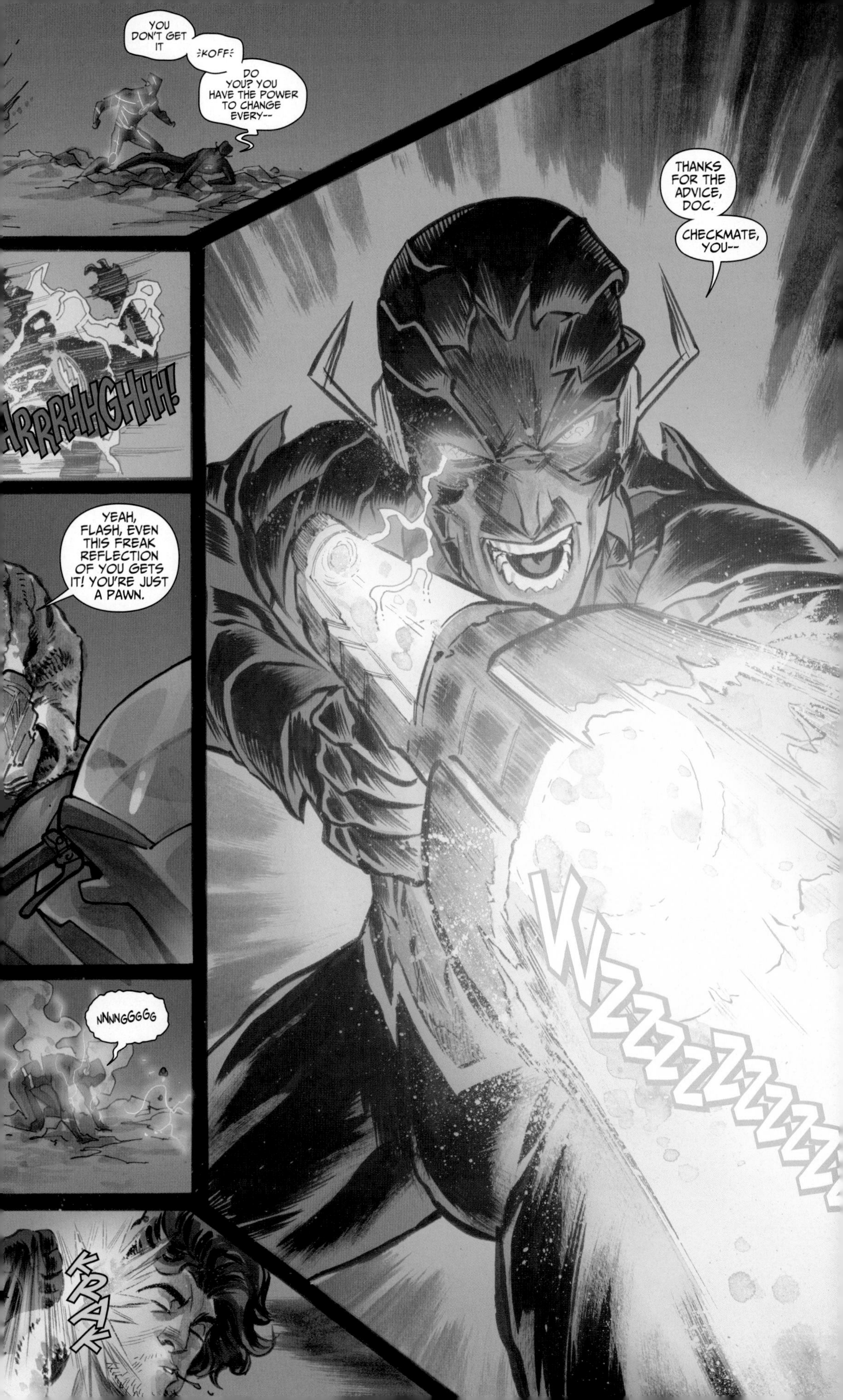

YOU DON'T GET IT
KOFF
DO YOU? YOU HAVE THE POWER TO CHANGE EVERY--
THANKS FOR THE ADVICE, DOC.
CHECKMATE, YOU--
ARRRHHGHHH!
YEAH, FLASH, EVEN THIS FREAK REFLECTION OF YOU GETS IT! YOU'RE JUST A PAWN.
WZZZZZZZZ
NNNNGGGGG
KRAK

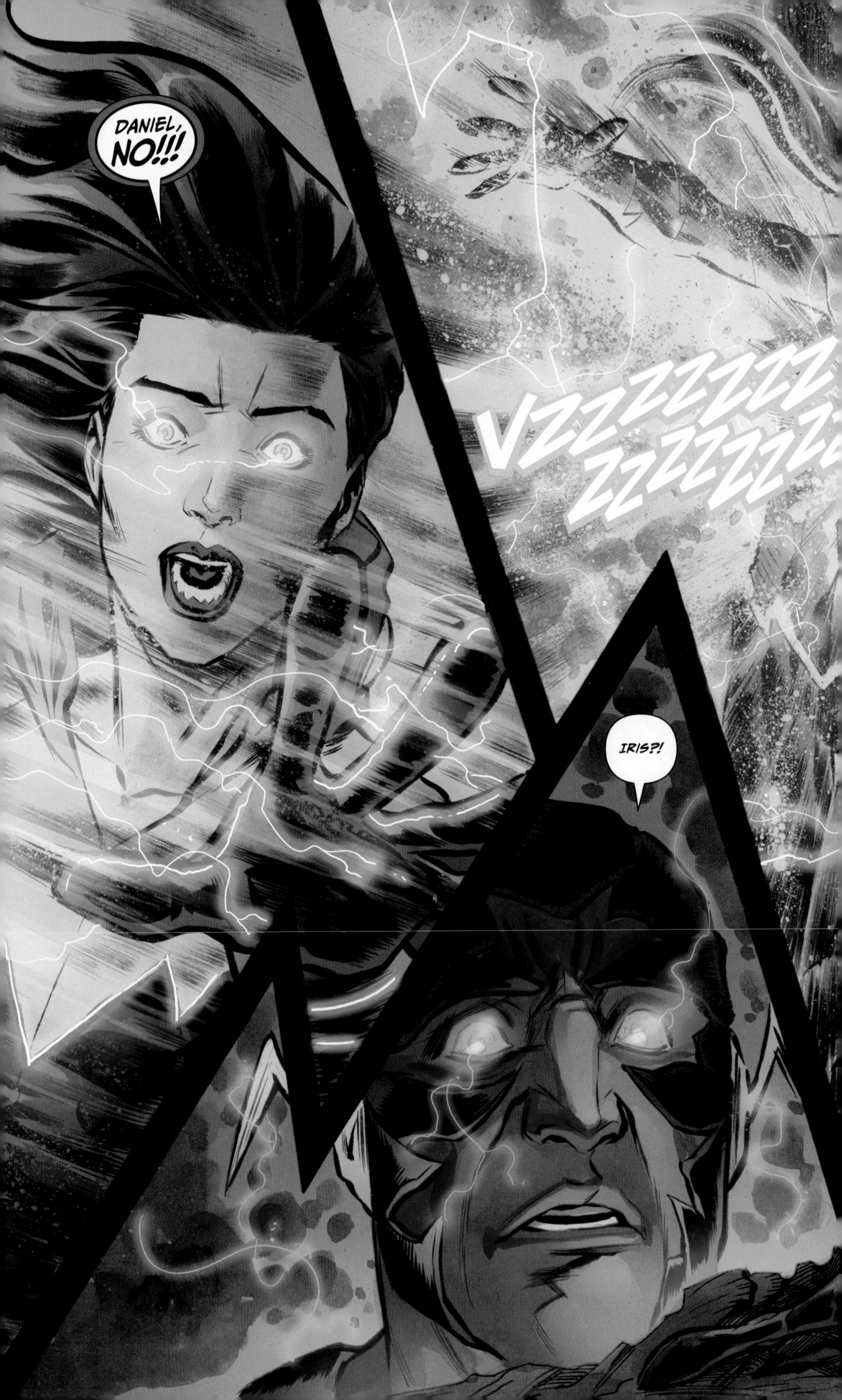
DANIEL, NO!!!
VZZZZZZZZ
ZZZZZZZZ
IRIS?!

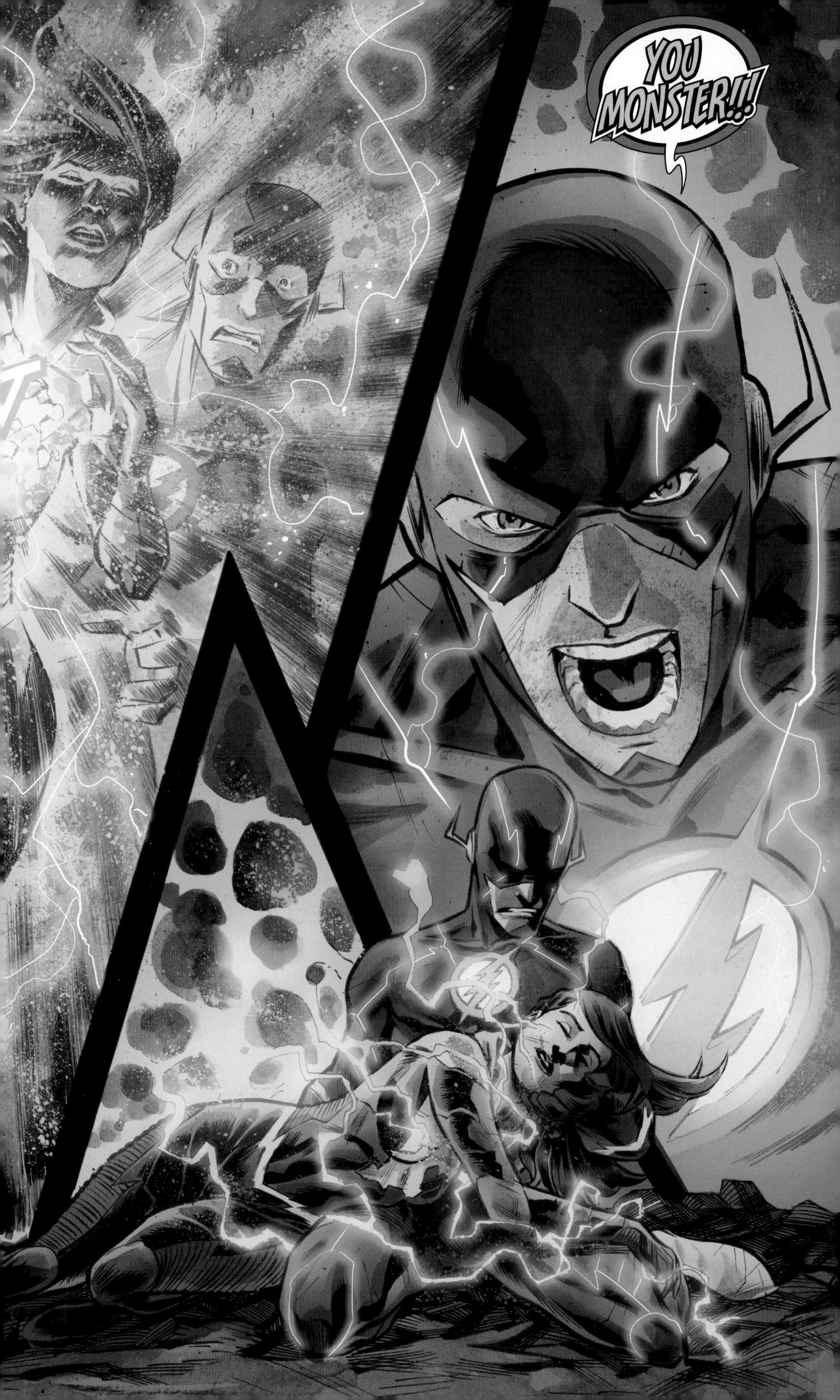
YOU MONSTER!!!

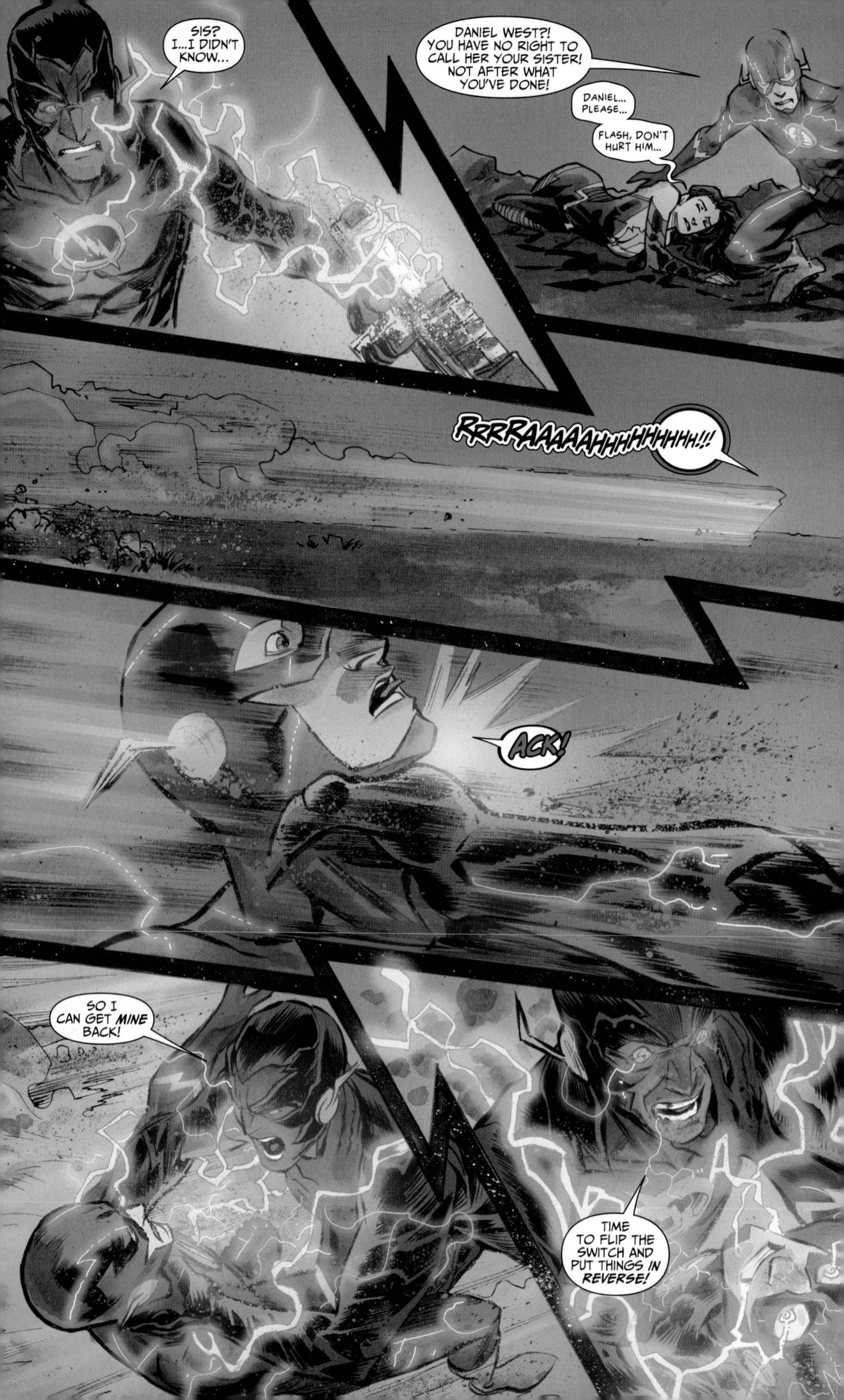
SIS? I...I DIDN'T KNOW...
DANIEL WEST?! YOU HAVE NO RIGHT TO CALL HER YOUR SISTER! NOT AFTER WHAT YOU'VE DONE!
DANIEL... PLEASE...
FLASH, DON'T HURT HIM...
RRRRAAAAAHHHHHHHH!!!
ACK!
SO I CAN GET *MINE* BACK!
TIME TO FLIP THE SWITCH AND PUT THINGS *IN REVERSE!*

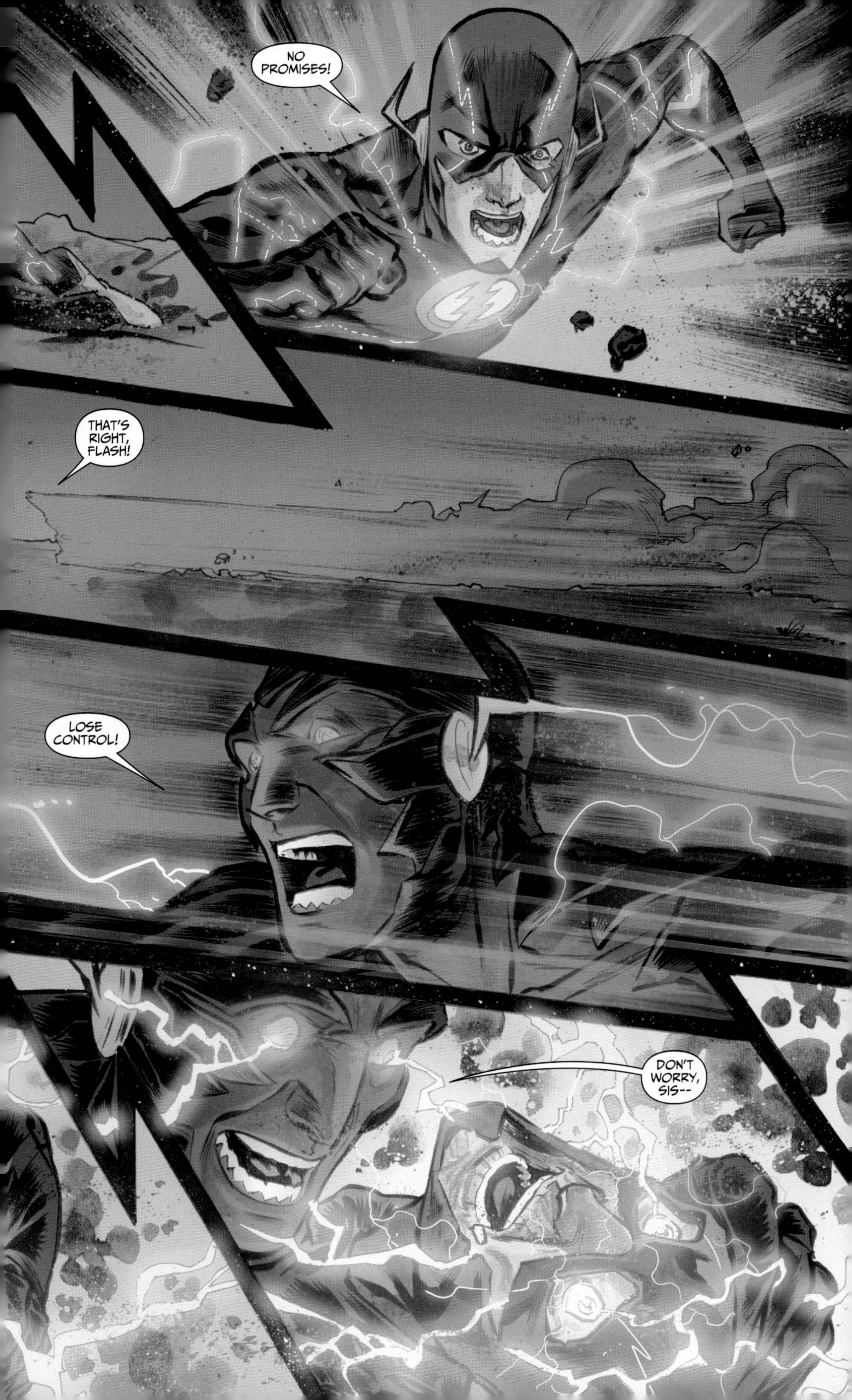
NO PROMISES!
THAT'S RIGHT, FLASH!
LOSE CONTROL!
DON'T WORRY, SIS--

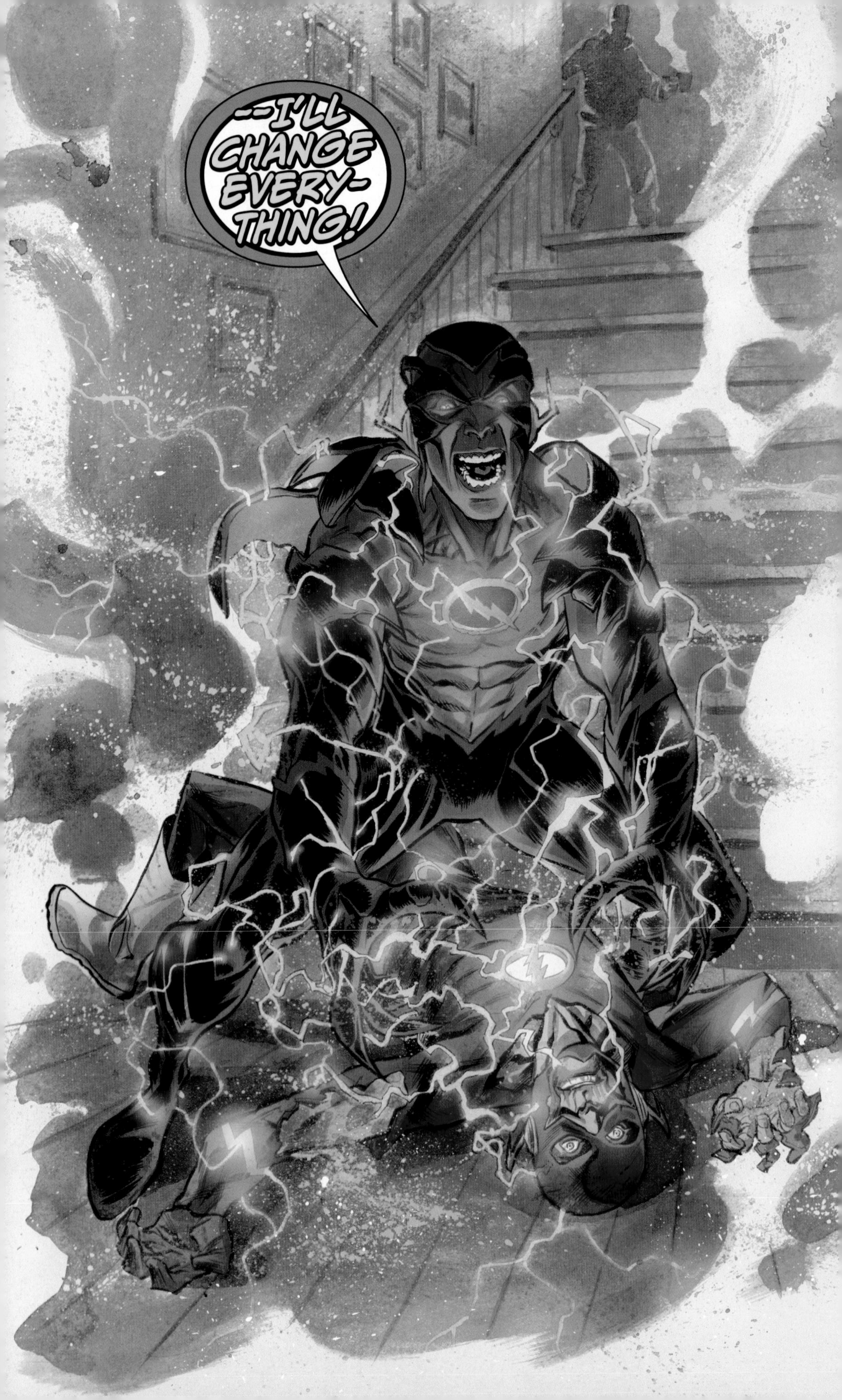
--I'LL CHANGE EVERY-THING!

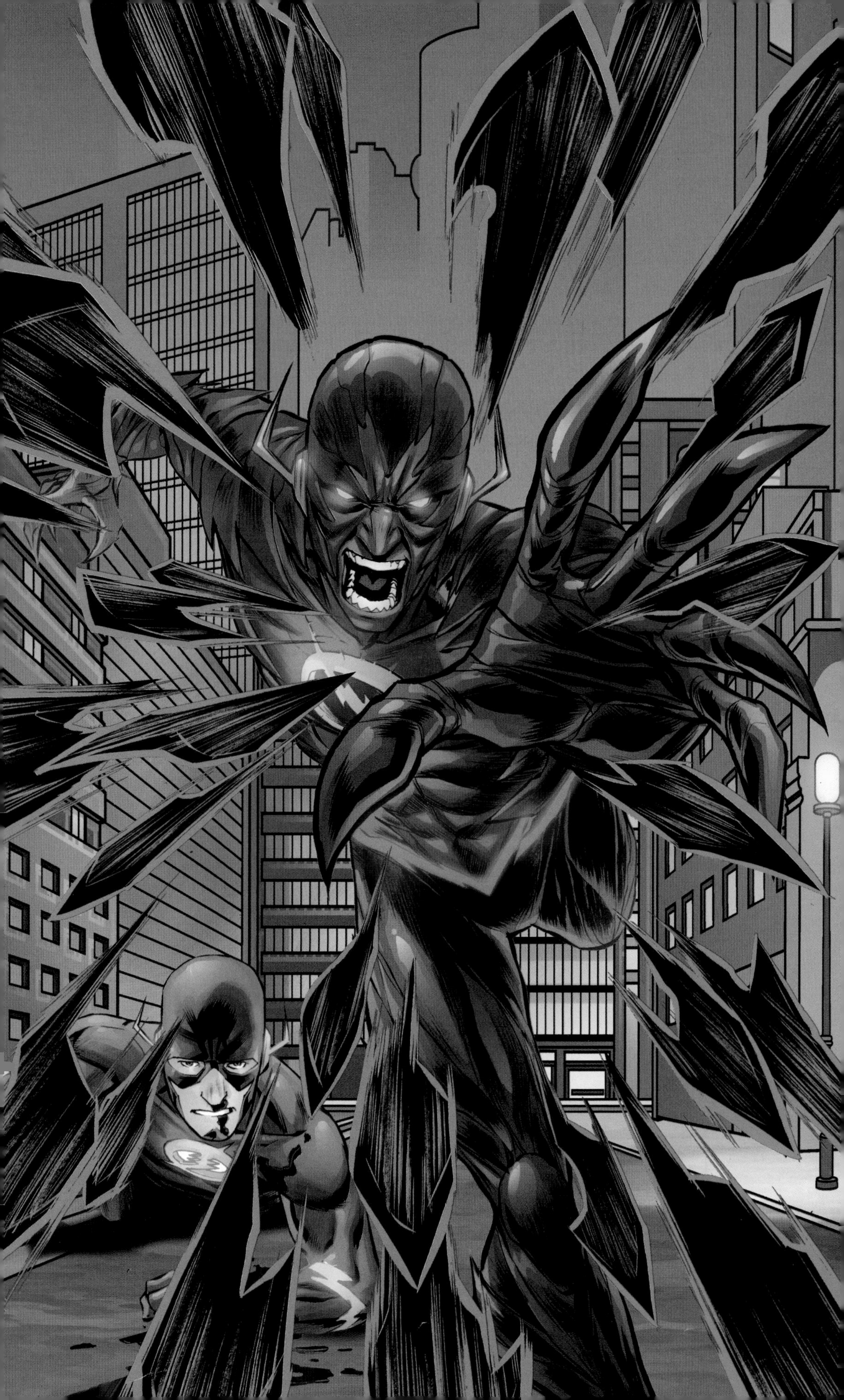

FRANCIS MANAPUL & BRIAN BUCCELLATO writers SCOTT HEPBURN artist

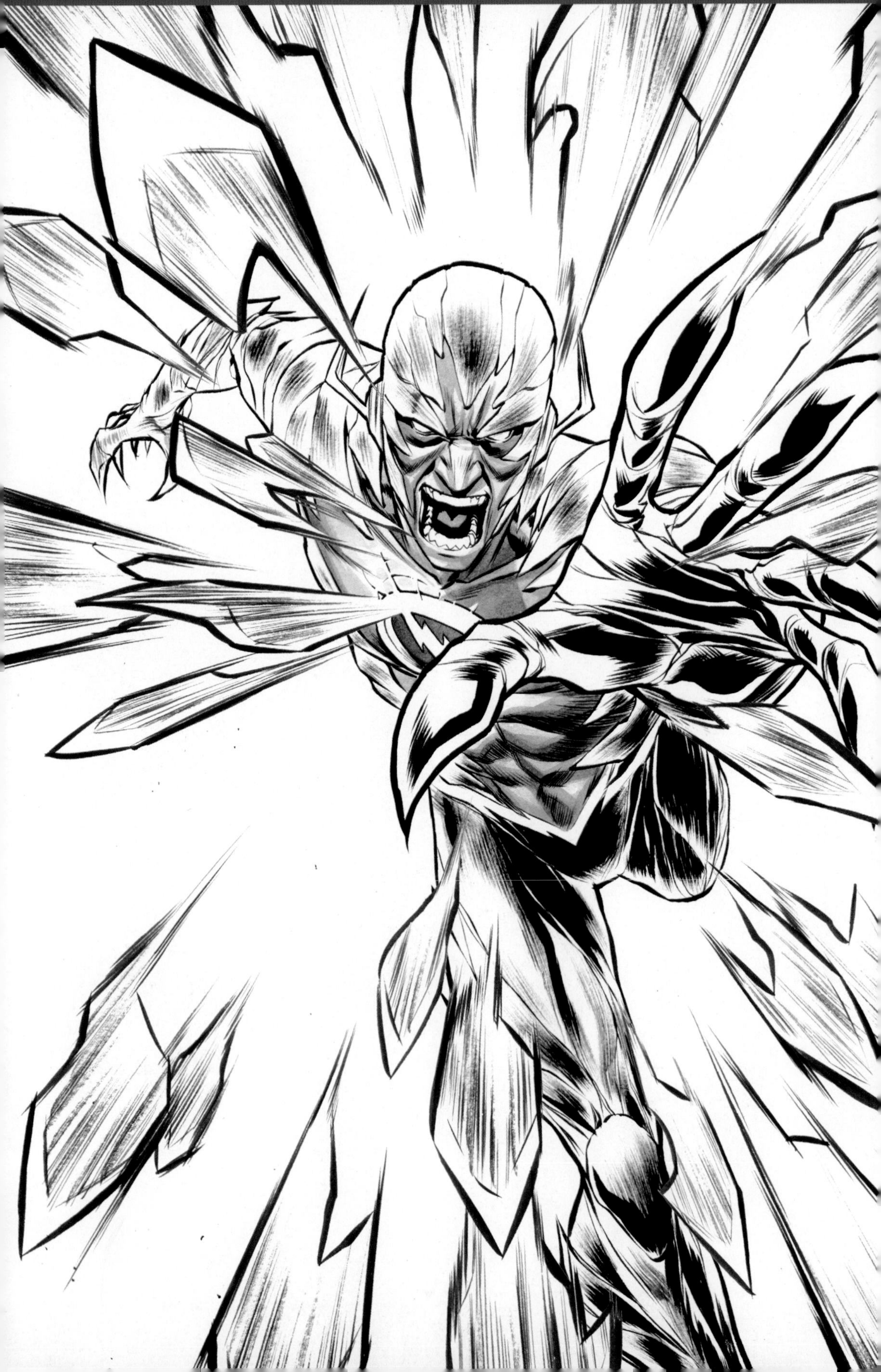

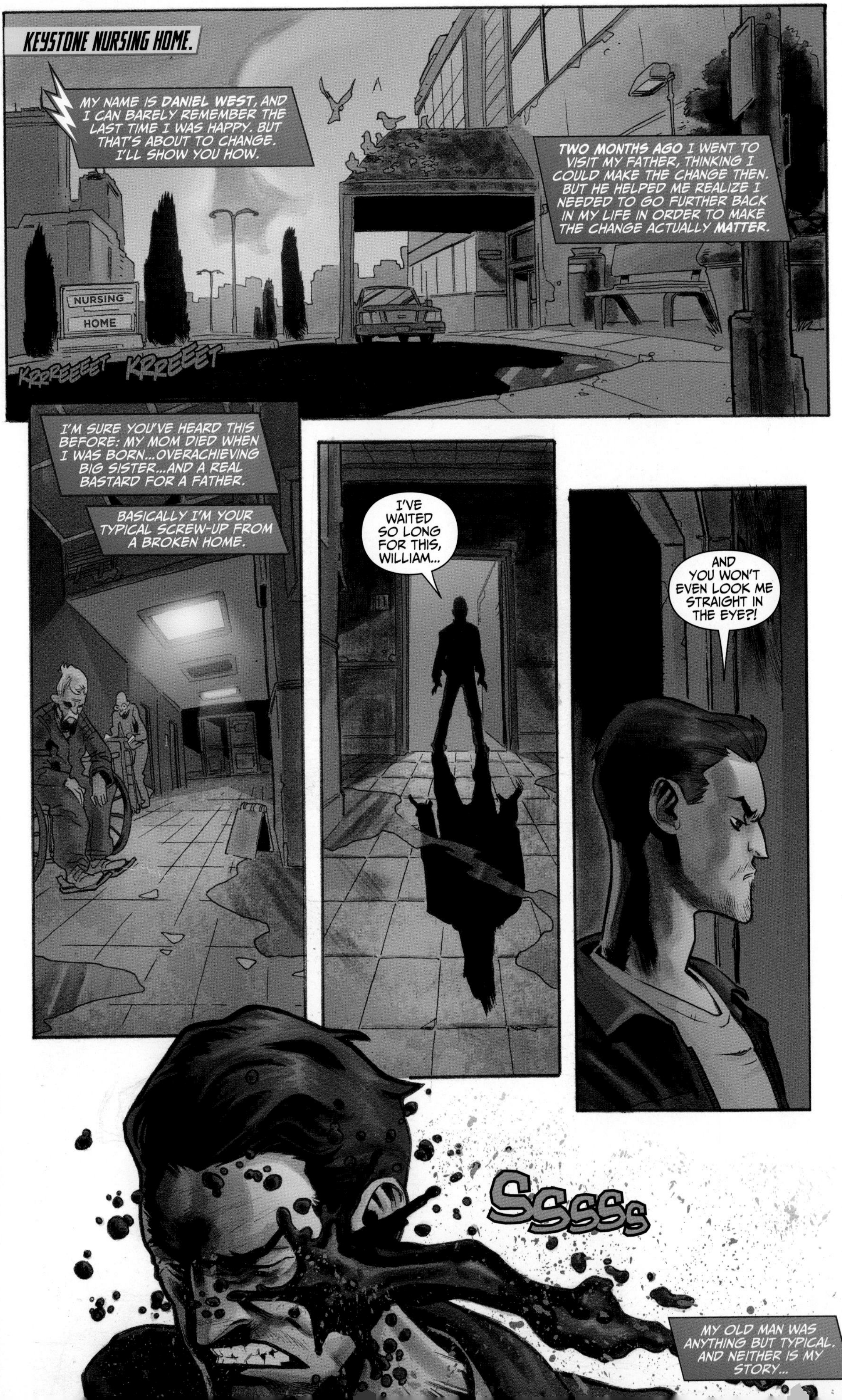
KEYSTONE NURSING HOME.
MY NAME IS DANIEL WEST, AND I CAN BARELY REMEMBER THE LAST TIME I WAS HAPPY. BUT THAT'S ABOUT TO CHANGE. I'LL SHOW YOU HOW.
TWO MONTHS AGO I WENT TO VISIT MY FATHER, THINKING I COULD MAKE THE CHANGE THEN. BUT HE HELPED ME REALIZE I NEEDED TO GO FURTHER BACK IN MY LIFE IN ORDER TO MAKE THE CHANGE ACTUALLY MATTER.
NURSING
HOME
KRRREEEET KRREEEET
I'M SURE YOU'VE HEARD THIS BEFORE: MY MOM DIED WHEN I WAS BORN...OVERACHIEVING BIG SISTER...AND A REAL BASTARD FOR A FATHER.
BASICALLY I'M YOUR TYPICAL SCREW-UP FROM A BROKEN HOME.
I'VE WAITED SO LONG FOR THIS, WILLIAM...
AND YOU WON'T EVEN LOOK ME STRAIGHT IN THE EYE?!
SSSSS
MY OLD MAN WAS ANYTHING BUT TYPICAL. AND NEITHER IS MY STORY...

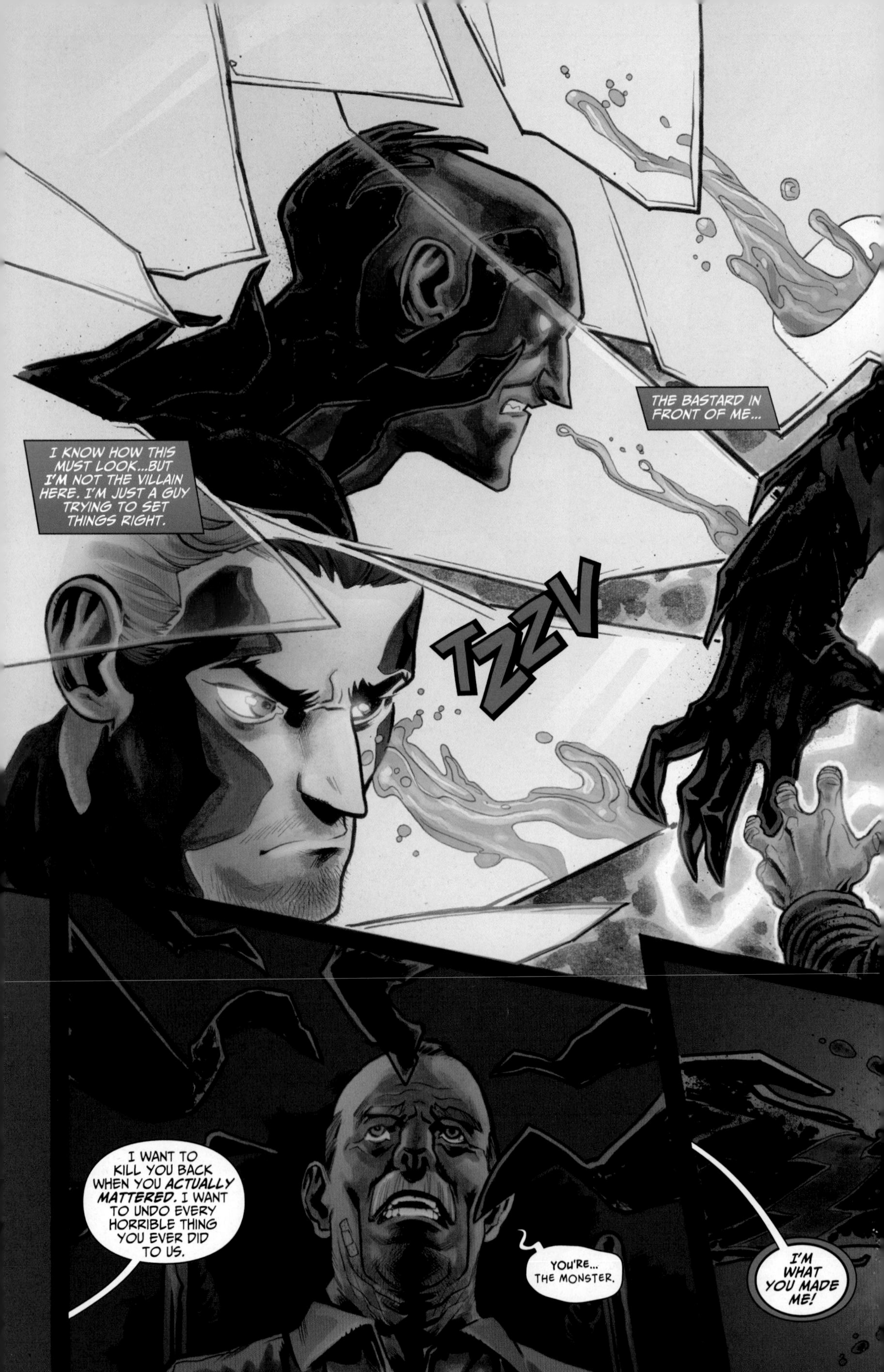
THE BASTARD IN FRONT OF ME...
I KNOW HOW THIS MUST LOOK...BUT I'M NOT THE VILLAIN HERE. I'M JUST A GUY TRYING TO SET THINGS RIGHT.
TZZV
I WANT TO KILL YOU BACK WHEN YOU ACTUALLY MATTERED. I WANT TO UNDO EVERY HORRIBLE THING YOU EVER DID TO US.
YOU'RE... THE MONSTER.
I'M WHAT YOU MADE ME!

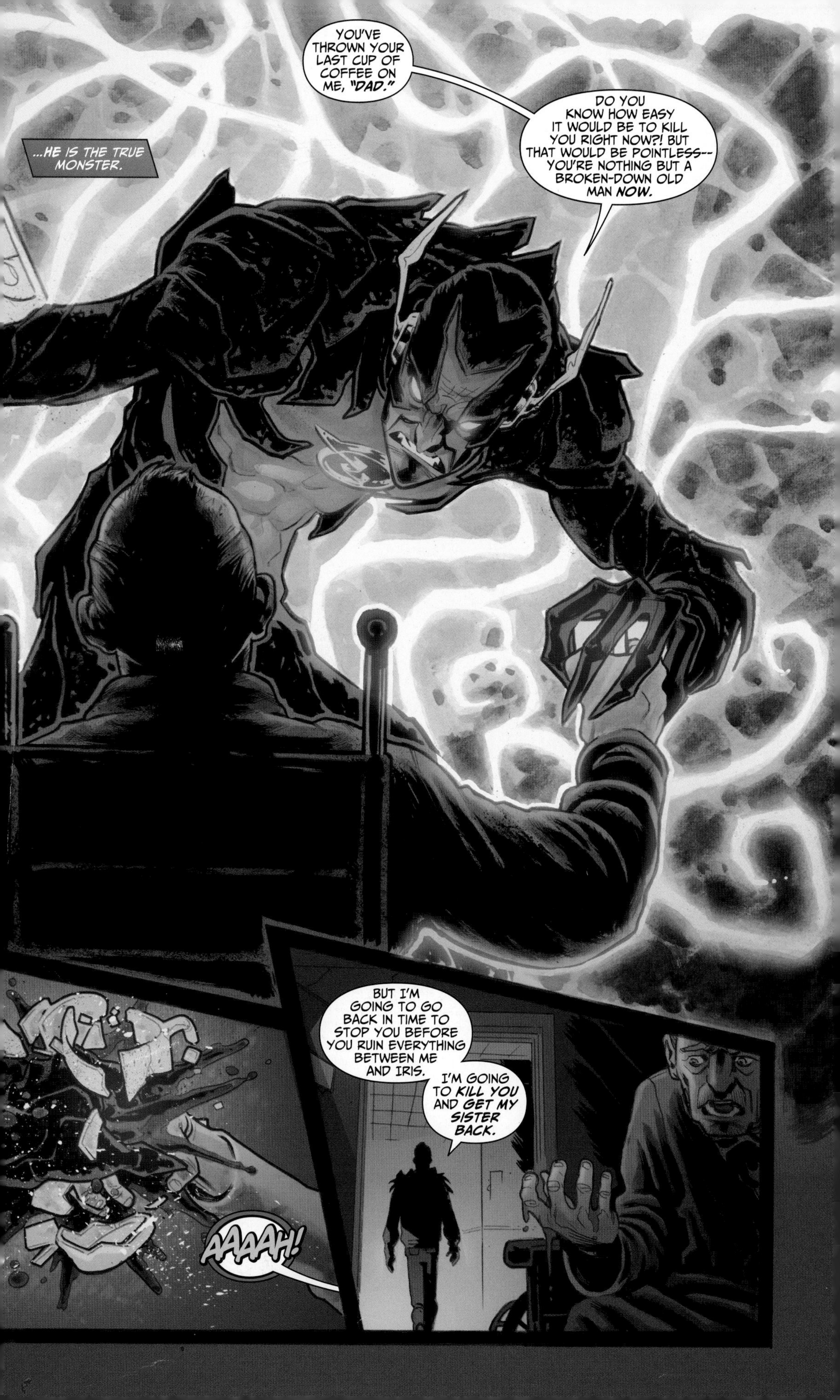
...HE IS THE TRUE MONSTER.
YOU'VE THROWN YOUR LAST CUP OF COFFEE ON ME, "DAD."
DO YOU KNOW HOW EASY IT WOULD BE TO KILL YOU RIGHT NOW?! BUT THAT WOULD BE POINTLESS-- YOU'RE NOTHING BUT A BROKEN-DOWN OLD MAN NOW.
AAAAH!
BUT I'M GOING TO GO BACK IN TIME TO STOP YOU BEFORE YOU RUIN EVERYTHING BETWEEN ME AND IRIS.
I'M GOING TO KILL YOU AND GET MY SISTER BACK.

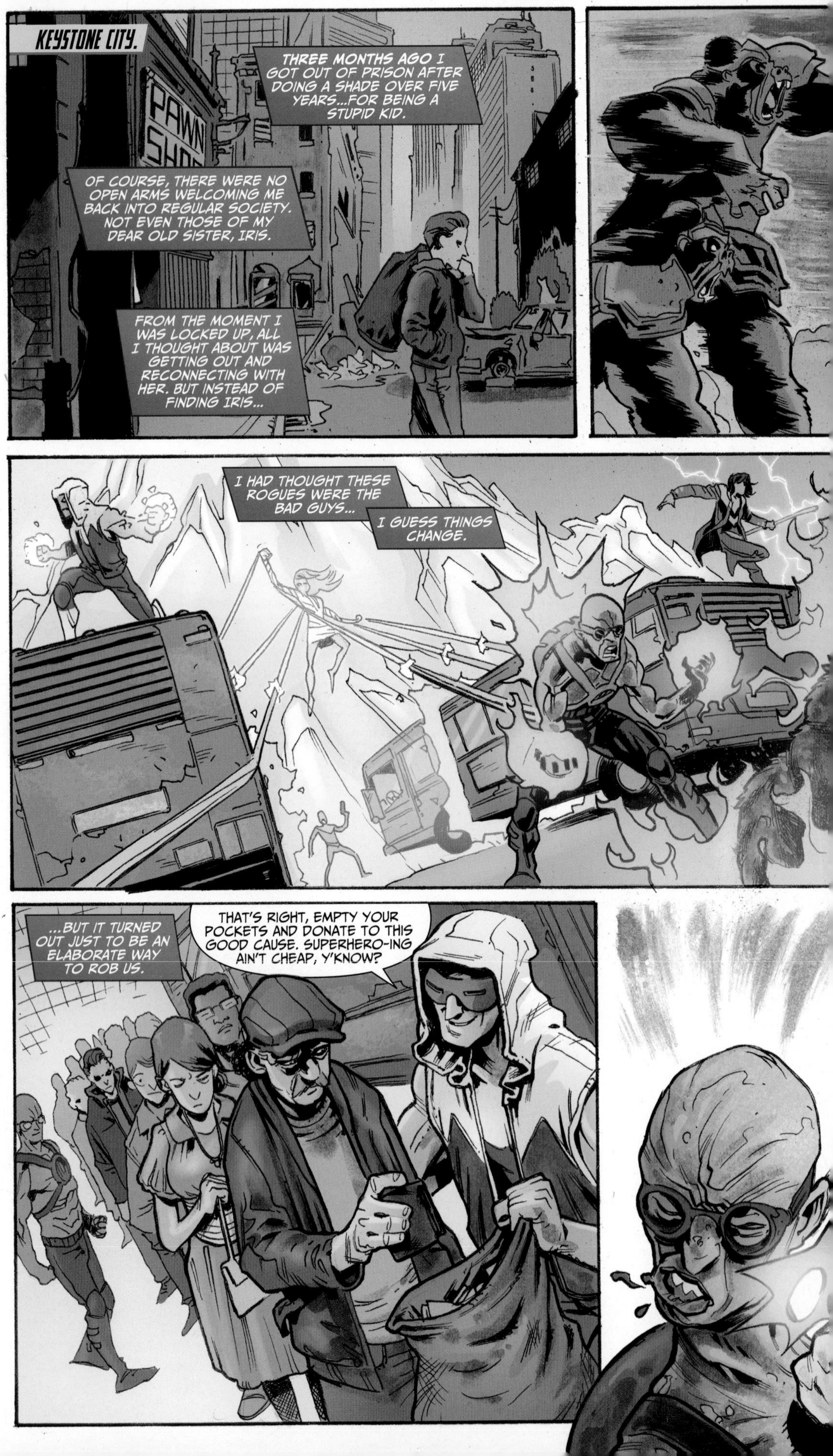
KEYSTONE CITY.
THREE MONTHS AGO I GOT OUT OF PRISON AFTER DOING A SHADE OVER FIVE YEARS...FOR BEING A STUPID KID.
PAWN SHOP
OF COURSE, THERE WERE NO OPEN ARMS WELCOMING ME BACK INTO REGULAR SOCIETY. NOT EVEN THOSE OF MY DEAR OLD SISTER, IRIS.
FROM THE MOMENT I WAS LOCKED UP, ALL I THOUGHT ABOUT WAS GETTING OUT AND RECONNECTING WITH HER. BUT INSTEAD OF FINDING IRIS...
I HAD THOUGHT THESE ROGUES WERE THE BAD GUYS...
I GUESS THINGS CHANGE.
...BUT IT TURNED OUT JUST TO BE AN ELABORATE WAY TO ROB US.
THAT'S RIGHT, EMPTY YOUR POCKETS AND DONATE TO THIS GOOD CAUSE. SUPERHERO-ING AIN'T CHEAP, Y'KNOW?

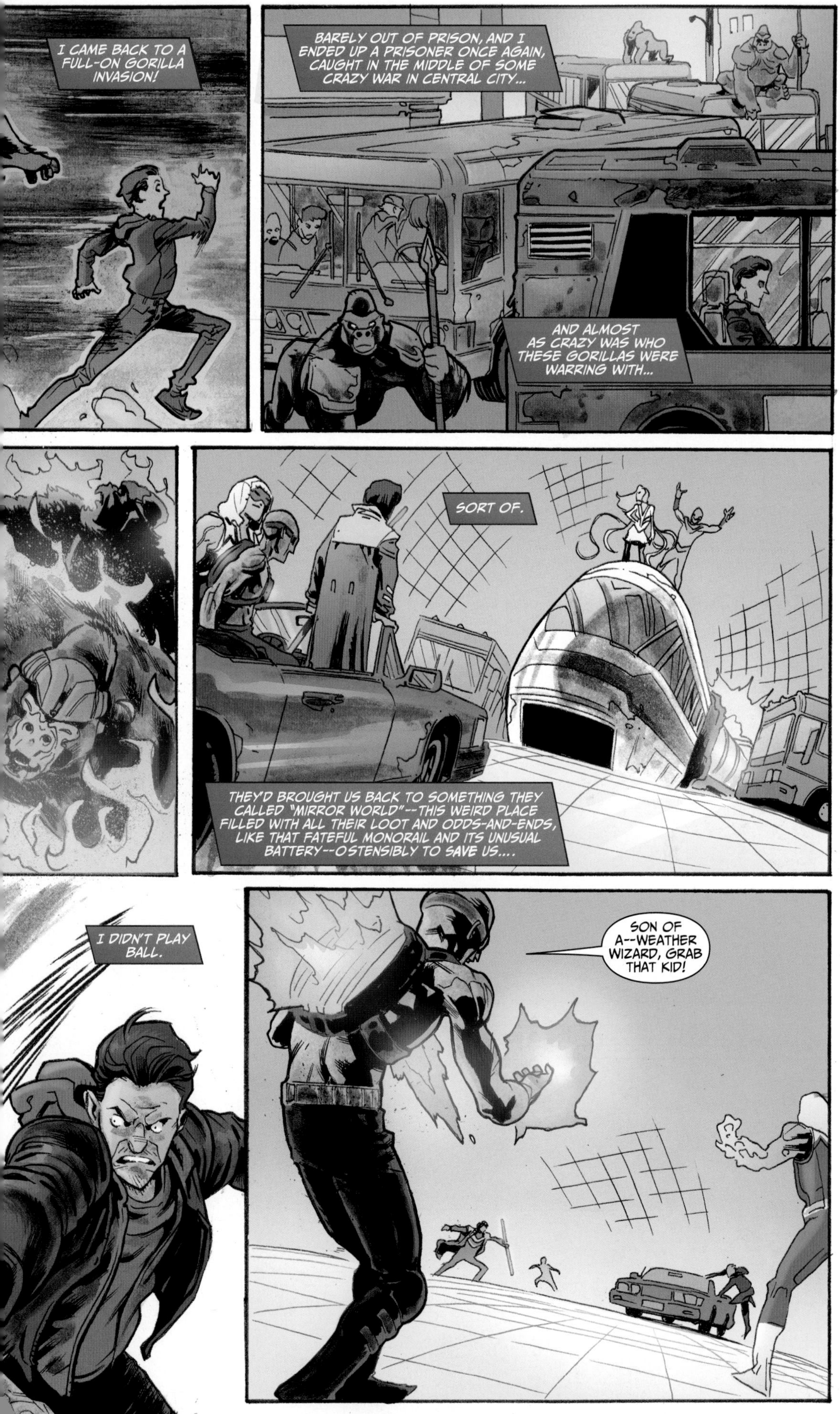
I CAME BACK TO A FULL-ON GORILLA INVASION!
BARELY OUT OF PRISON, AND I ENDED UP A PRISONER ONCE AGAIN, CAUGHT IN THE MIDDLE OF SOME CRAZY WAR IN CENTRAL CITY...
AND ALMOST AS CRAZY WAS WHO THESE GORILLAS WERE WARRING WITH...
SORT OF.
THEY'D BROUGHT US BACK TO SOMETHING THEY CALLED "MIRROR WORLD"--THIS WEIRD PLACE FILLED WITH ALL THEIR LOOT AND ODDS-AND-ENDS, LIKE THAT FATEFUL MONORAIL AND ITS UNUSUAL BATTERY--OSTENSIBLY TO SAVE US....
I DIDN'T PLAY BALL.
SON OF A--WEATHER WIZARD, GRAB THAT KID!

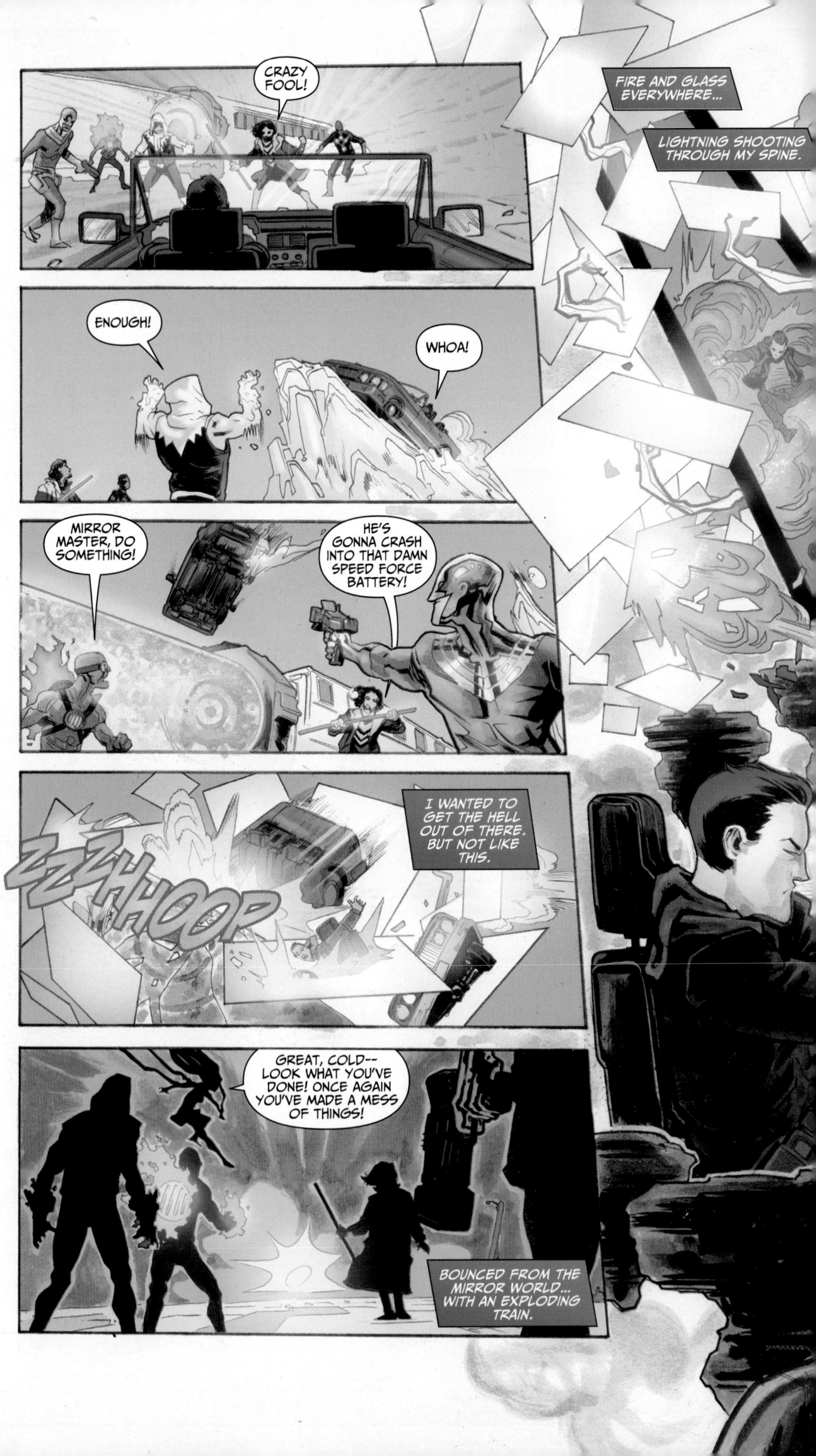

CRAZY FOOL!
FIRE AND GLASS EVERYWHERE...
LIGHTNING SHOOTING THROUGH MY SPINE.
ENOUGH!
WHOA!
MIRROR MASTER, DO SOMETHING!
HE'S GONNA CRASH INTO THAT DAMN SPEED FORCE BATTERY!
ZZZHHOOP
I WANTED TO GET THE HELL OUT OF THERE. BUT NOT LIKE THIS.
GREAT, COLD-- LOOK WHAT YOU'VE DONE! ONCE AGAIN YOU'VE MADE A MESS OF THINGS!
BOUNCED FROM THE MIRROR WORLD... WITH AN EXPLODING TRAIN.

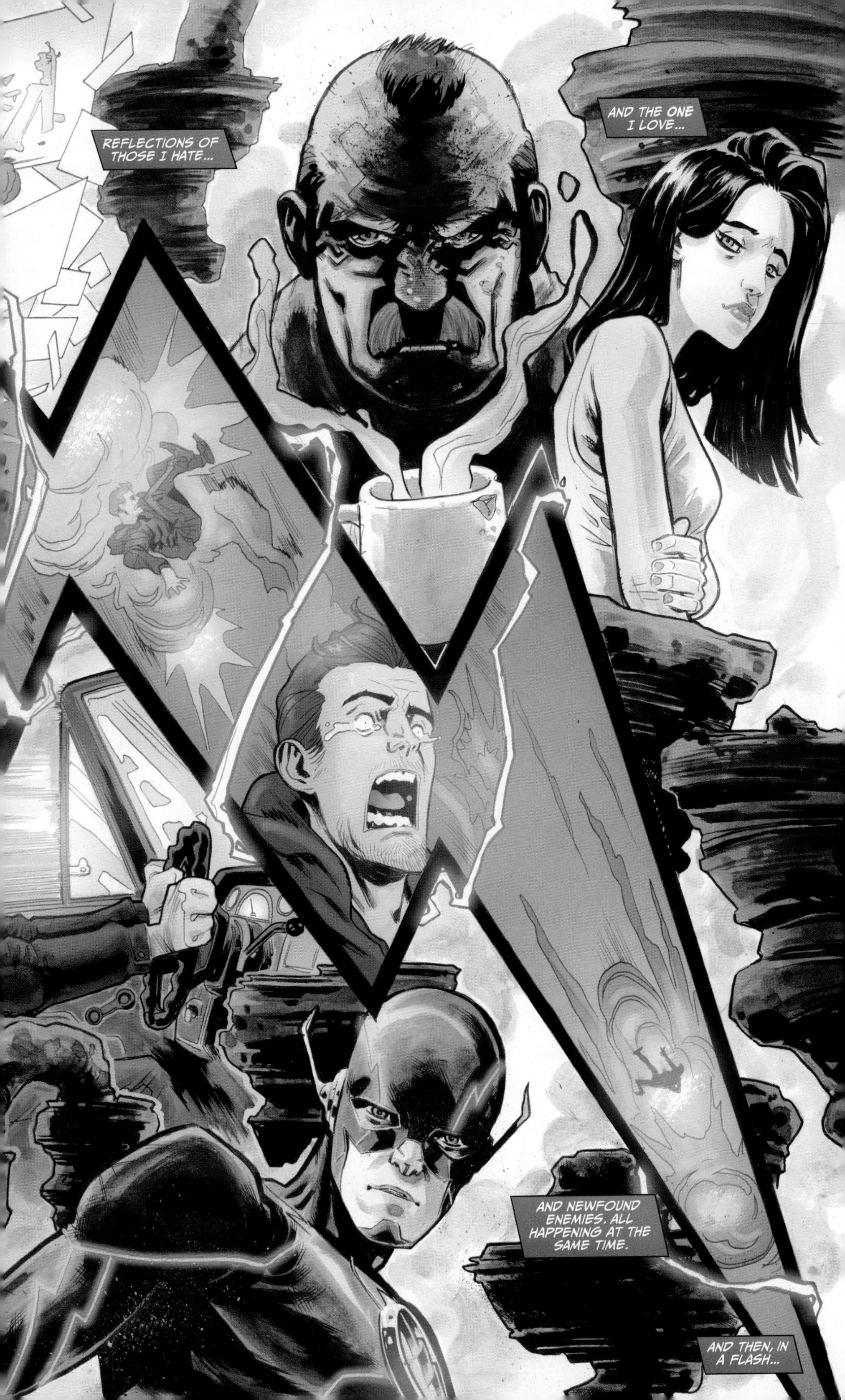
REFLECTIONS OF THOSE I HATE...
AND THE ONE I LOVE...
AND NEWFOUND ENEMIES. ALL HAPPENING AT THE SAME TIME.
AND THEN, IN A FLASH...

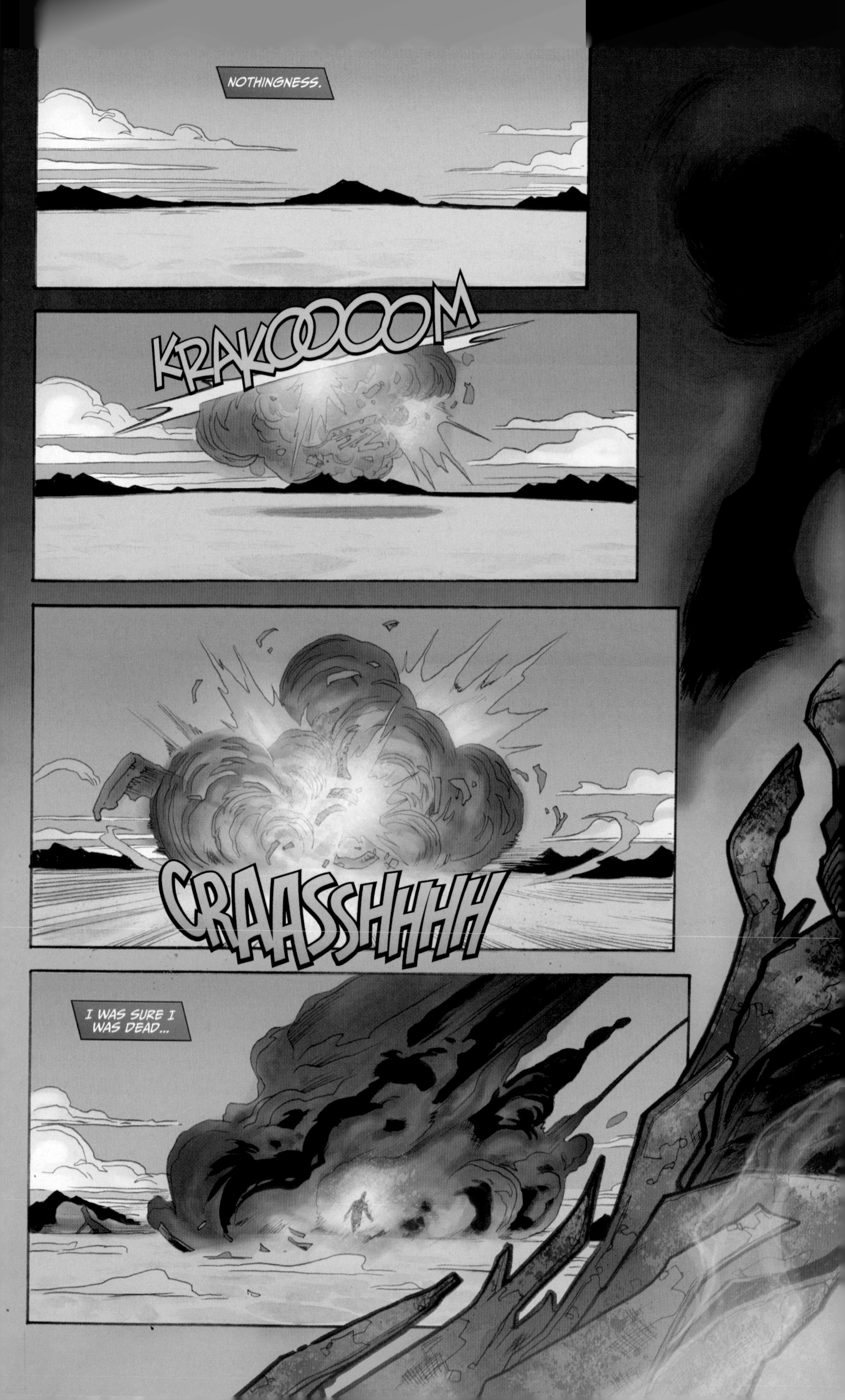
NOTHINGNESS.
KRAKOOOOOM
CRAASSHHHH
I WAS SURE I WAS DEAD...

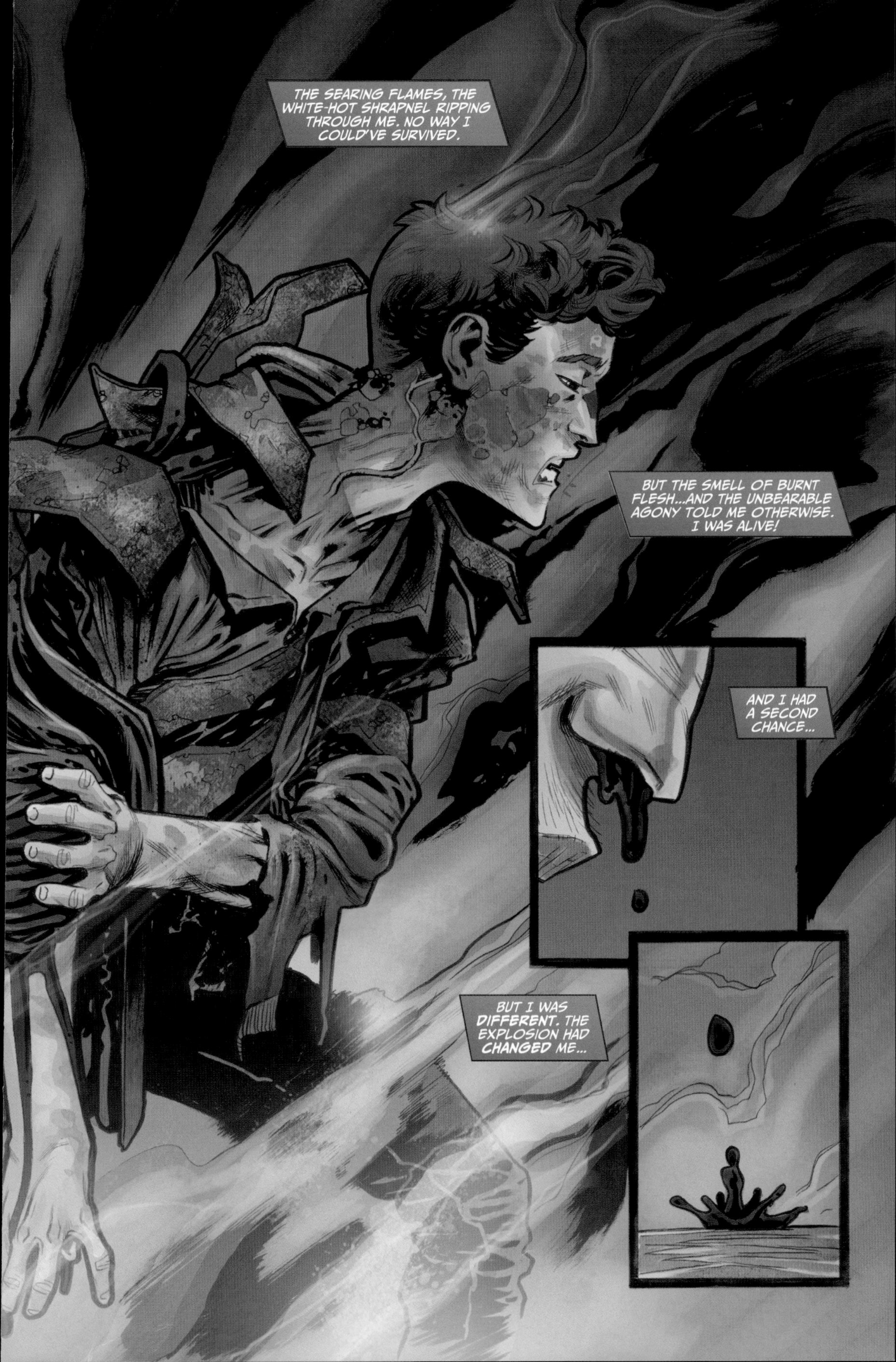
THE SEARING FLAMES, THE WHITE-HOT SHRAPNEL RIPPING THROUGH ME. NO WAY I COULD'VE SURVIVED.
BUT THE SMELL OF BURNT FLESH...AND THE UNBEARABLE AGONY TOLD ME OTHERWISE. I WAS ALIVE!
AND I HAD A SECOND CHANCE...
BUT I WAS DIFFERENT. THE EXPLOSION HAD CHANGED ME...

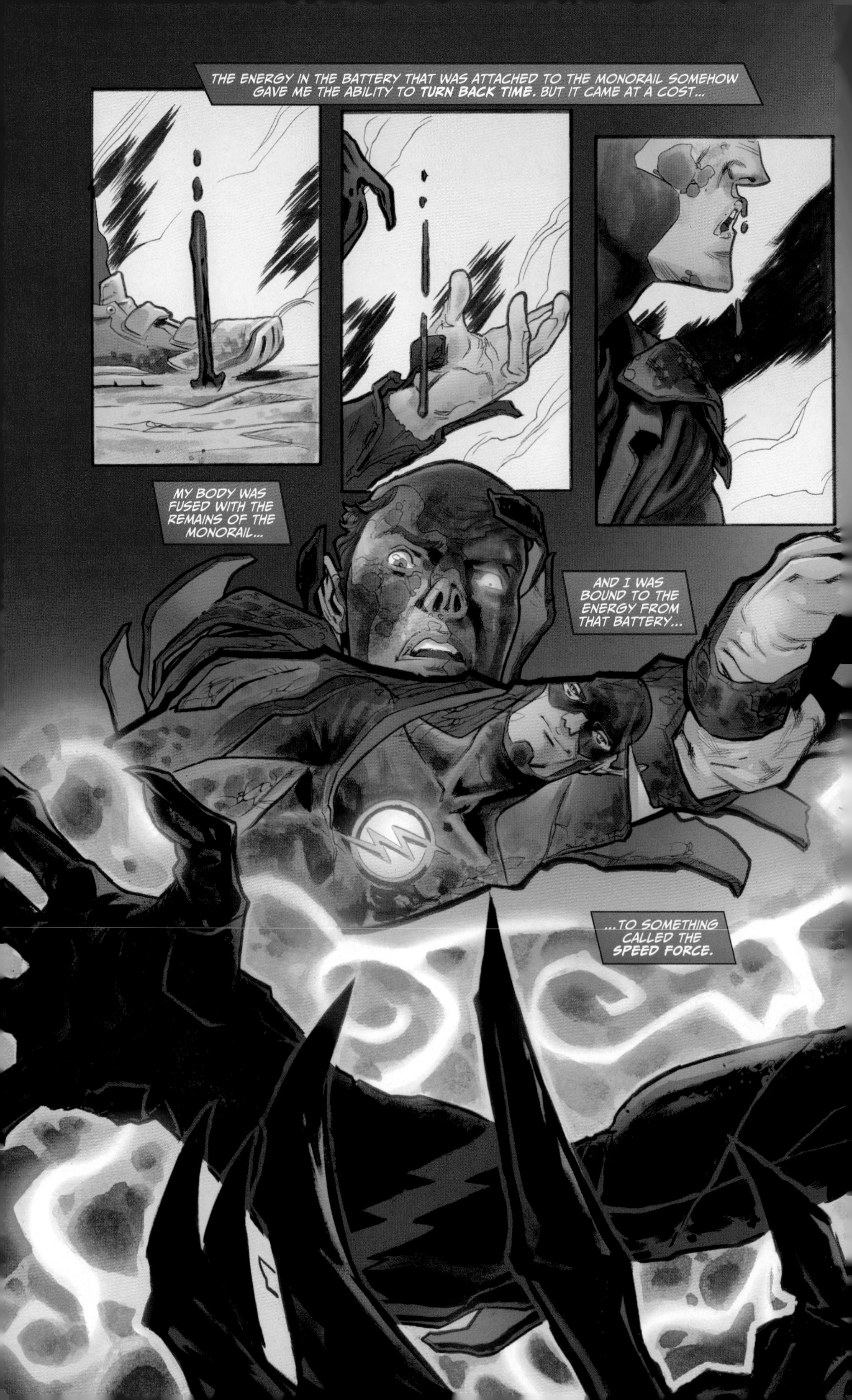
THE ENERGY IN THE BATTERY THAT WAS ATTACHED TO THE MONORAIL SOMEHOW GAVE ME THE ABILITY TO TURN BACK TIME. BUT IT CAME AT A COST...
MY BODY WAS FUSED WITH THE REMAINS OF THE MONORAIL...
AND I WAS BOUND TO THE ENERGY FROM THAT BATTERY...
...TO SOMETHING CALLED THE SPEED FORCE.

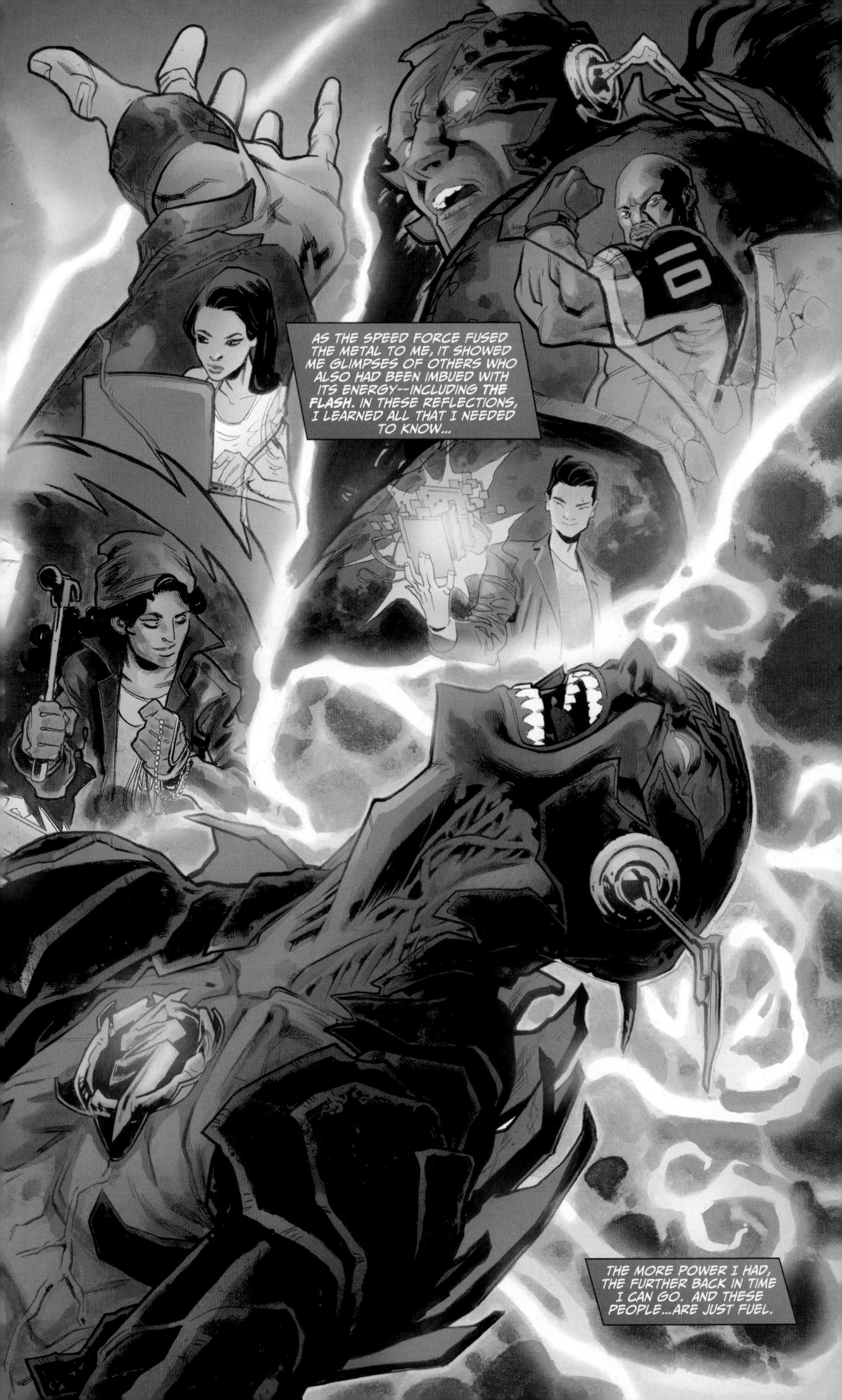
AS THE SPEED FORCE FUSED THE METAL TO ME, IT SHOWED ME GLIMPSES OF OTHERS WHO ALSO HAD BEEN IMBUED WITH ITS ENERGY--INCLUDING **THE FLASH.** IN THESE REFLECTIONS, I LEARNED ALL THAT I NEEDED TO KNOW...
THE MORE POWER I HAD, THE FURTHER BACK IN TIME I CAN GO. AND THESE PEOPLE...ARE JUST FUEL.

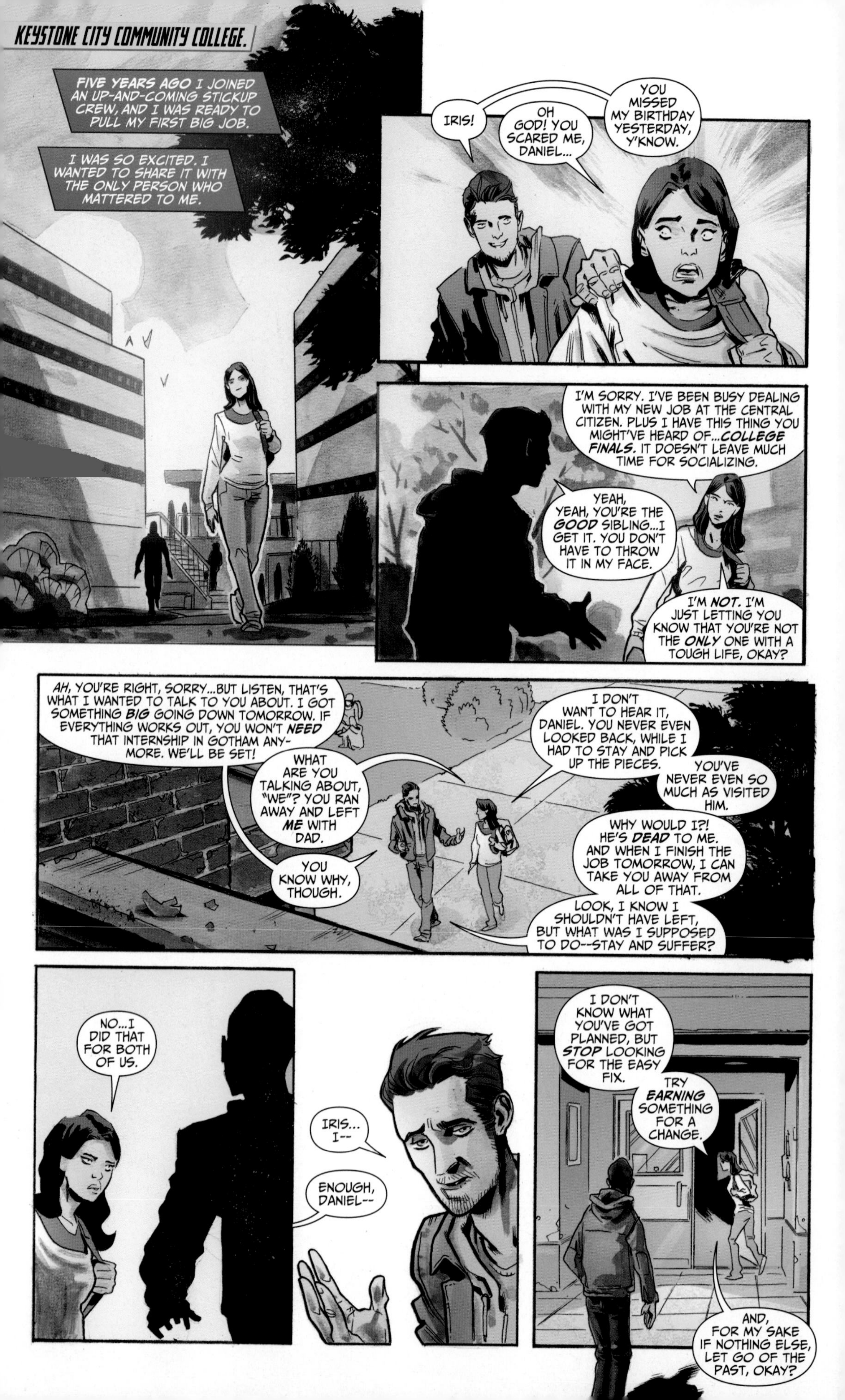
KEYSTONE CITY COMMUNITY COLLEGE.
FIVE YEARS AGO I JOINED AN UP-AND-COMING STICKUP CREW, AND I WAS READY TO PULL MY FIRST BIG JOB.
I WAS SO EXCITED. I WANTED TO SHARE IT WITH THE ONLY PERSON WHO MATTERED TO ME.
IRIS!
OH GOD! YOU SCARED ME, DANIEL...
YOU MISSED MY BIRTHDAY YESTERDAY, Y'KNOW.
I'M SORRY. I'VE BEEN BUSY DEALING WITH MY NEW JOB AT THE CENTRAL CITIZEN. PLUS I HAVE THIS THING YOU MIGHT'VE HEARD OF...COLLEGE FINALS. IT DOESN'T LEAVE MUCH TIME FOR SOCIALIZING.
YEAH, YEAH, YOU'RE THE GOOD SIBLING...I GET IT. YOU DON'T HAVE TO THROW IT IN MY FACE.
I'M NOT. I'M JUST LETTING YOU KNOW THAT YOU'RE NOT THE ONLY ONE WITH A TOUGH LIFE, OKAY?
AH, YOU'RE RIGHT, SORRY...BUT LISTEN, THAT'S WHAT I WANTED TO TALK TO YOU ABOUT. I GOT SOMETHING BIG GOING DOWN TOMORROW. IF EVERYTHING WORKS OUT, YOU WON'T NEED THAT INTERNSHIP IN GOTHAM ANY-MORE. WE'LL BE SET!
WHAT ARE YOU TALKING ABOUT, "WE"? YOU RAN AWAY AND LEFT ME WITH DAD.
YOU KNOW WHY, THOUGH.
I DON'T WANT TO HEAR IT, DANIEL. YOU NEVER EVEN LOOKED BACK, WHILE I HAD TO STAY AND PICK UP THE PIECES.
YOU'VE NEVER EVEN SO MUCH AS VISITED HIM.
WHY WOULD I?! HE'S DEAD TO ME. AND WHEN I FINISH THE JOB TOMORROW, I CAN TAKE YOU AWAY FROM ALL OF THAT.
LOOK, I KNOW I SHOULDN'T HAVE LEFT, BUT WHAT WAS I SUPPOSED TO DO--STAY AND SUFFER?
NO...I DID THAT FOR BOTH OF US.
IRIS... I--
ENOUGH, DANIEL--
I DON'T KNOW WHAT YOU'VE GOT PLANNED, BUT STOP LOOKING FOR THE EASY FIX.
TRY EARNING SOMETHING FOR A CHANGE.
AND, FOR MY SAKE IF NOTHING ELSE, LET GO OF THE PAST, OKAY?

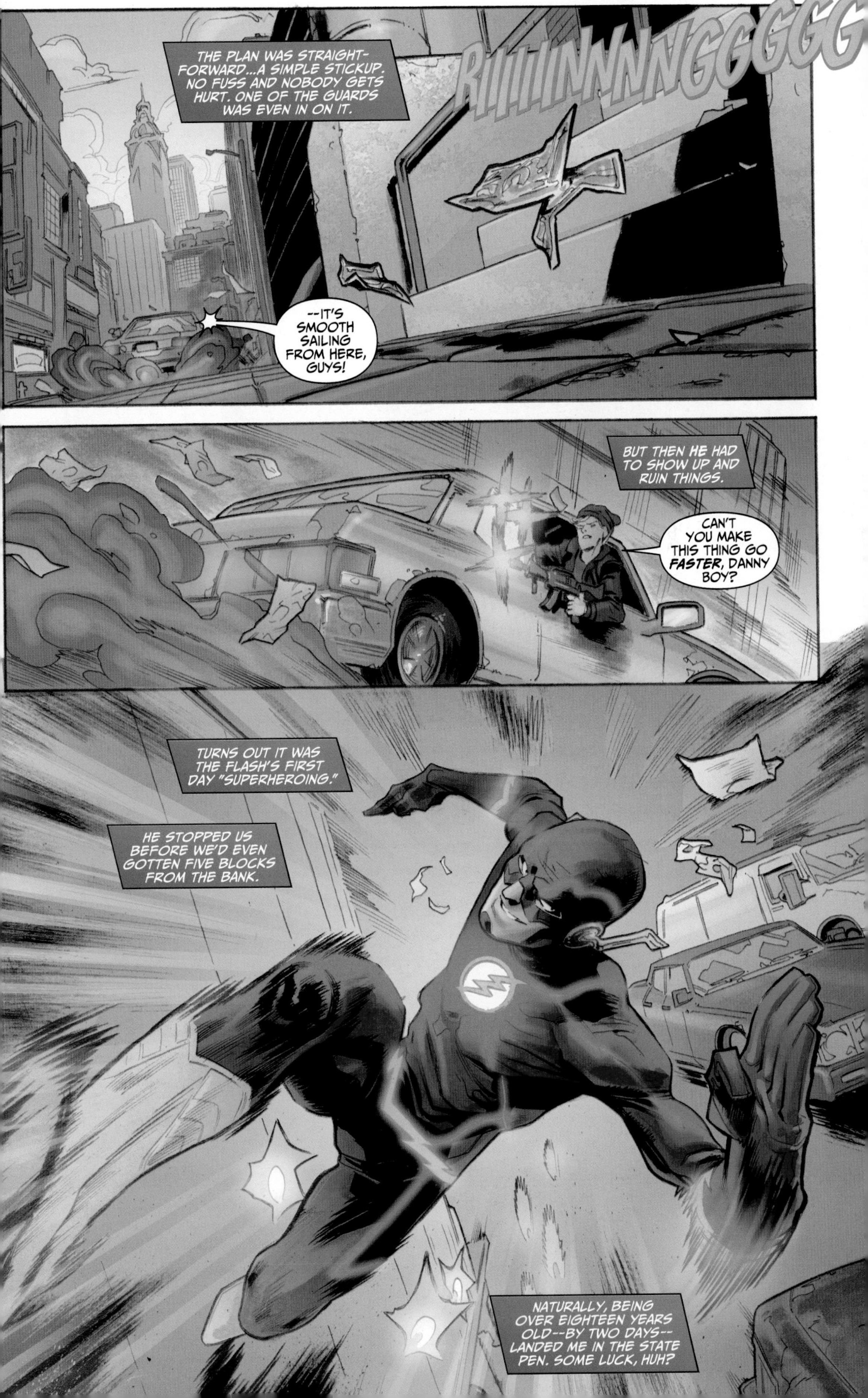
THE PLAN WAS STRAIGHT-FORWARD...A SIMPLE STICKUP. NO FUSS AND NOBODY GETS HURT. ONE OF THE GUARDS WAS EVEN IN ON IT.
RIIIIINNNNNGGGGG
--IT'S SMOOTH SAILING FROM HERE, GUYS!
BUT THEN HE HAD TO SHOW UP AND RUIN THINGS.
CAN'T YOU MAKE THIS THING GO FASTER, DANNY BOY?
TURNS OUT IT WAS THE FLASH'S FIRST DAY "SUPERHEROING."
HE STOPPED US BEFORE WE'D EVEN GOTTEN FIVE BLOCKS FROM THE BANK.
NATURALLY, BEING OVER EIGHTEEN YEARS OLD--BY TWO DAYS--LANDED ME IN THE STATE PEN. SOME LUCK, HUH?

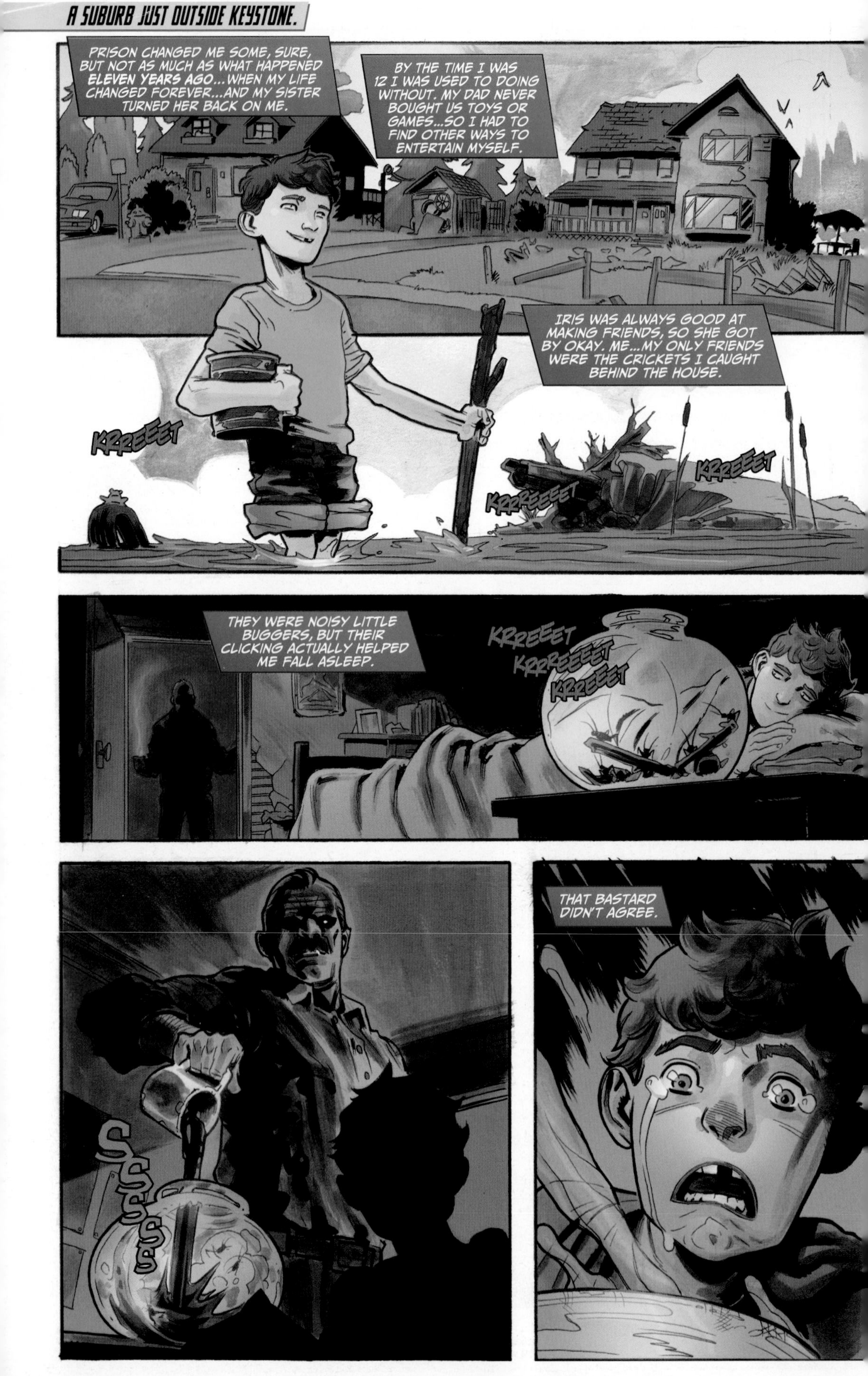
A SUBURB JUST OUTSIDE KEYSTONE.
PRISON CHANGED ME SOME, SURE, BUT NOT AS MUCH AS WHAT HAPPENED ELEVEN YEARS AGO...WHEN MY LIFE CHANGED FOREVER...AND MY SISTER TURNED HER BACK ON ME.
BY THE TIME I WAS 12 I WAS USED TO DOING WITHOUT. MY DAD NEVER BOUGHT US TOYS OR GAMES...SO I HAD TO FIND OTHER WAYS TO ENTERTAIN MYSELF.
IRIS WAS ALWAYS GOOD AT MAKING FRIENDS, SO SHE GOT BY OKAY. ME...MY ONLY FRIENDS WERE THE CRICKETS I CAUGHT BEHIND THE HOUSE.
KRREEEET
KRRREEEET
KRREEET
THEY WERE NOISY LITTLE BUGGERS, BUT THEIR CLICKING ACTUALLY HELPED ME FALL ASLEEP.
KRREEET
KRRREEEET
KRREEET
SSSSSS
THAT BASTARD DIDN'T AGREE.

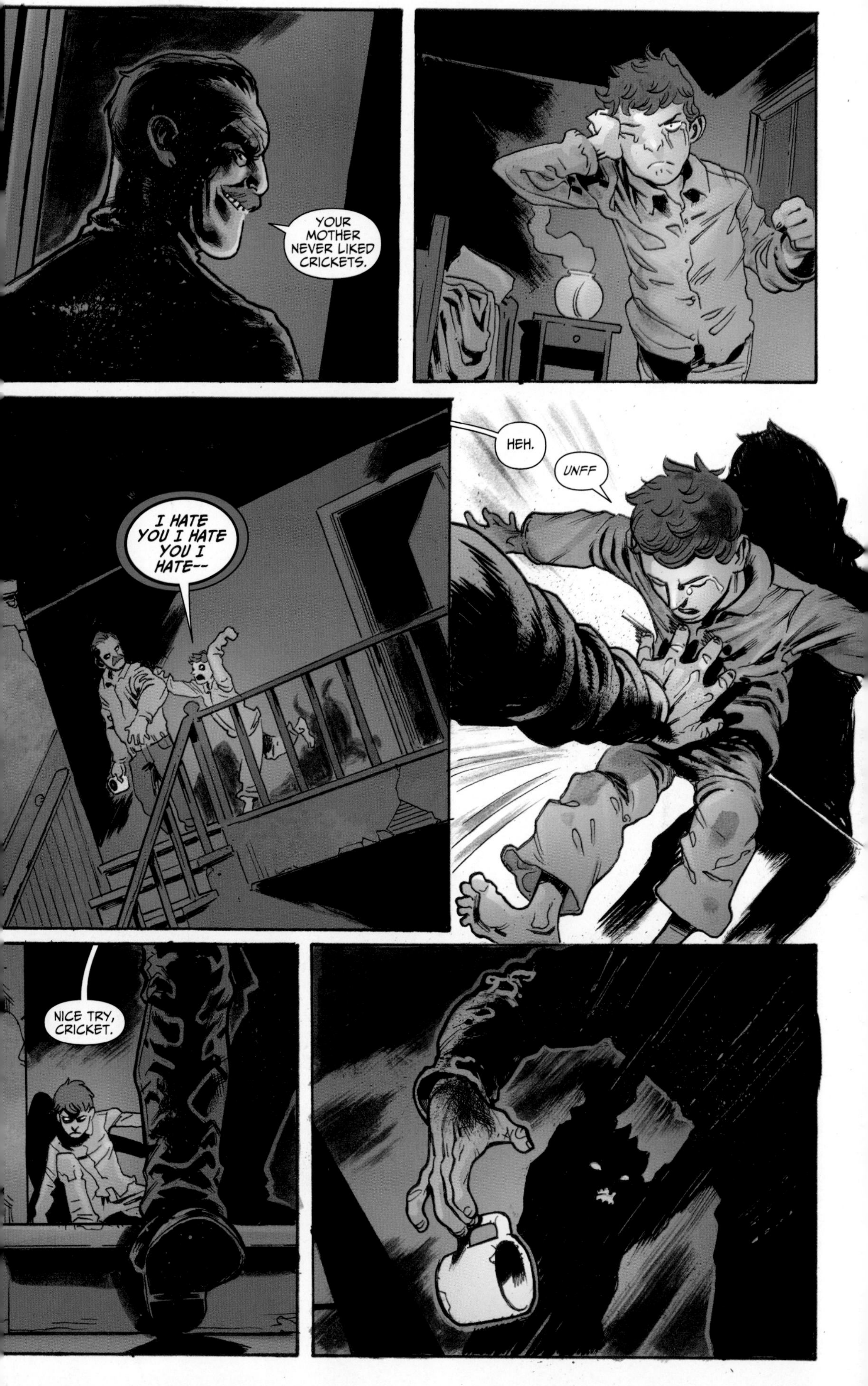
YOUR MOTHER NEVER LIKED CRICKETS.
I HATE YOU I HATE YOU I HATE--
HEH.
UNFF
NICE TRY, CRICKET.

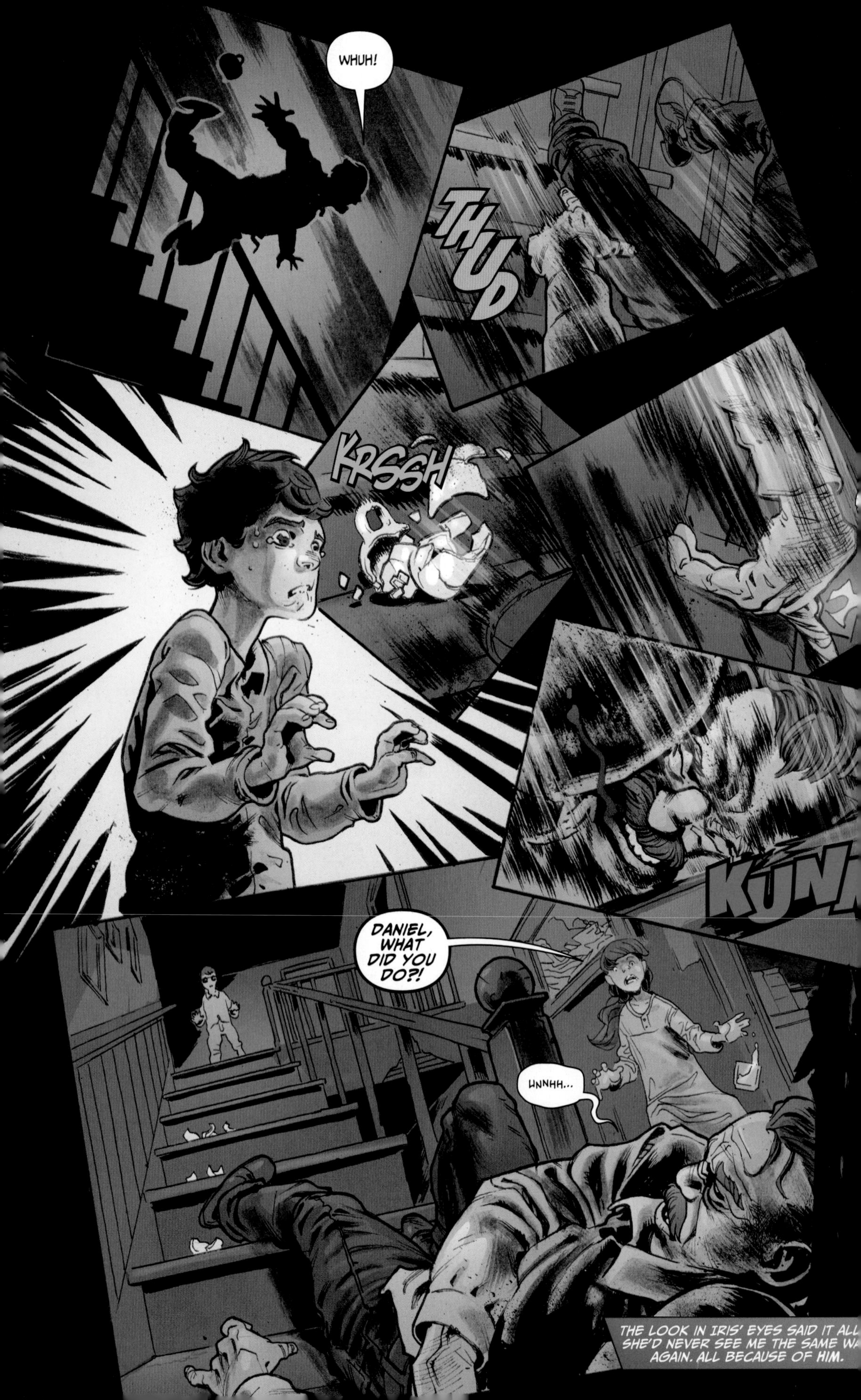
WHUH!
THUD
KRSSH
KUNN
DANIEL, WHAT DID YOU DO?!
UNNHH...
THE LOOK IN IRIS' EYES SAID IT ALL
SHE'D NEVER SEE ME THE SAME WA
AGAIN. ALL BECAUSE OF HIM.

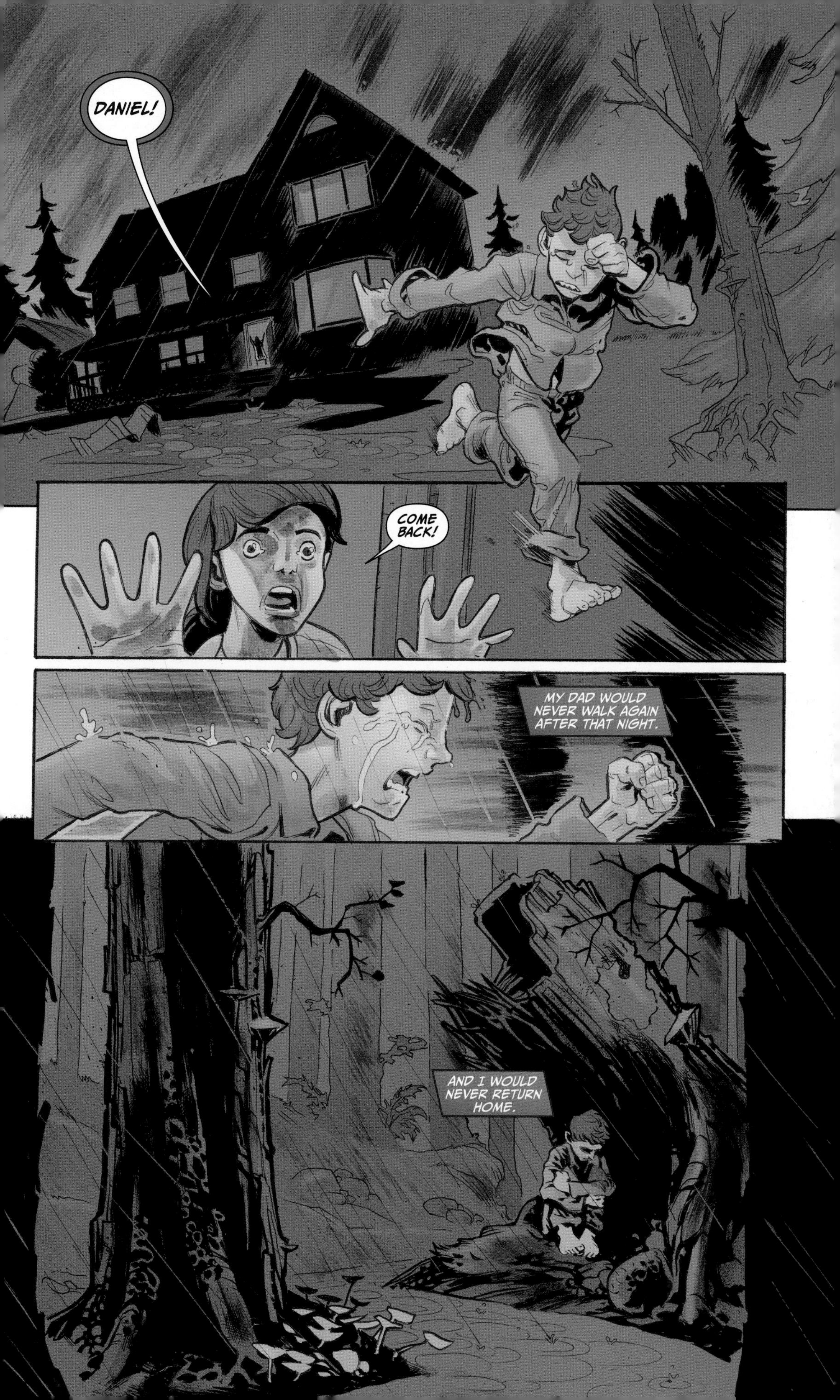
DANIEL!
COME BACK!
MY DAD WOULD NEVER WALK AGAIN AFTER THAT NIGHT.
AND I WOULD NEVER RETURN HOME.

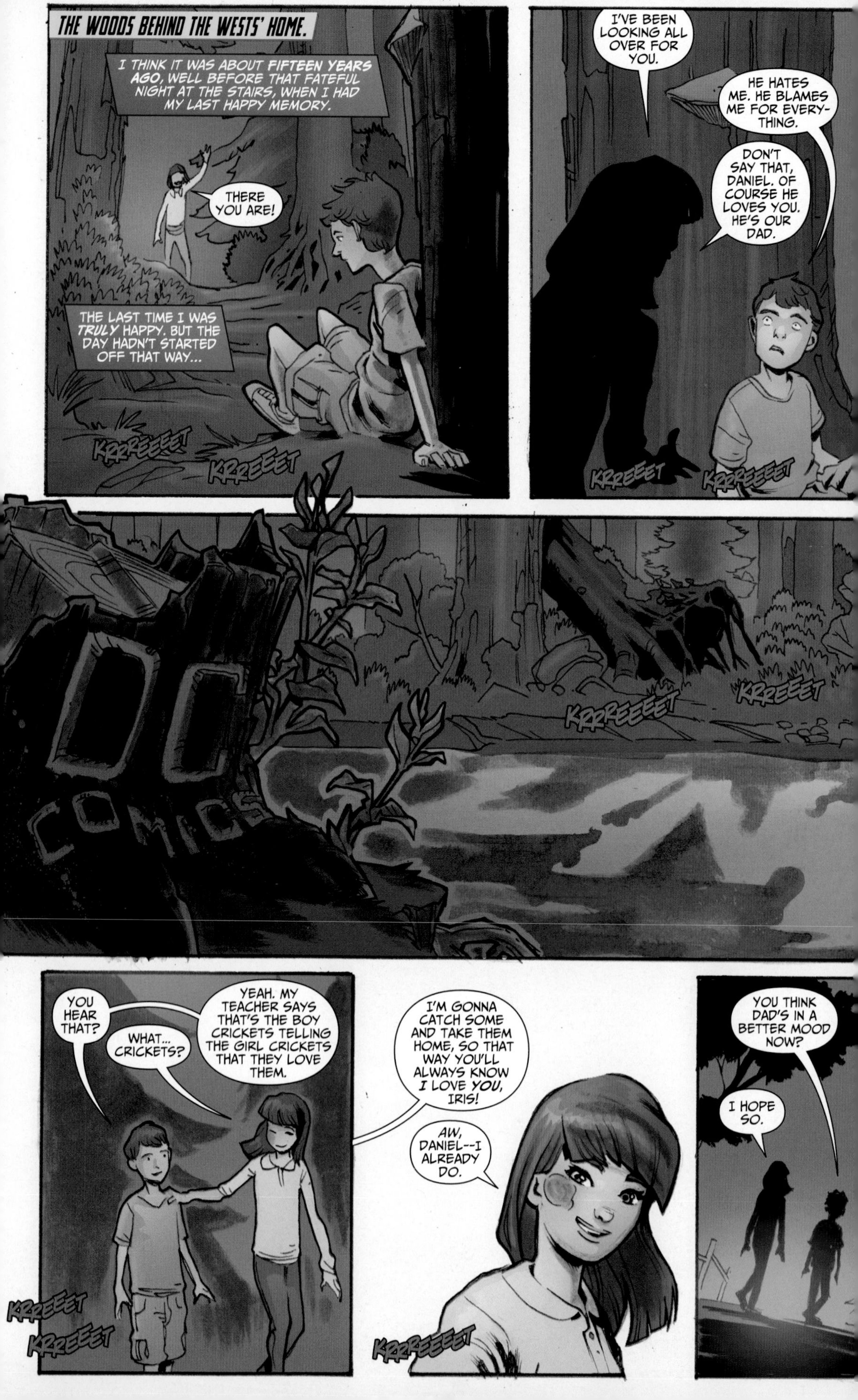
THE WOODS BEHIND THE WESTS' HOME.
I THINK IT WAS ABOUT FIFTEEN YEARS AGO, WELL BEFORE THAT FATEFUL NIGHT AT THE STAIRS, WHEN I HAD MY LAST HAPPY MEMORY.
THERE YOU ARE!
THE LAST TIME I WAS TRULY HAPPY. BUT THE DAY HADN'T STARTED OFF THAT WAY...
KRRREEEET
KRREEET
I'VE BEEN LOOKING ALL OVER FOR YOU.
HE HATES ME. HE BLAMES ME FOR EVERY-THING.
DON'T SAY THAT, DANIEL. OF COURSE HE LOVES YOU. HE'S OUR DAD.
KRREEET
KRRREEEET
KRRREEEET
KRREEET
YOU HEAR THAT?
WHAT... CRICKETS?
YEAH. MY TEACHER SAYS THAT'S THE BOY CRICKETS TELLING THE GIRL CRICKETS THAT THEY LOVE THEM.
KRREEET
KRREEET
I'M GONNA CATCH SOME AND TAKE THEM HOME, SO THAT WAY YOU'LL ALWAYS KNOW I LOVE YOU, IRIS!
AW, DANIEL--I ALREADY DO.
KRRREEEET
YOU THINK DAD'S IN A BETTER MOOD NOW?
I HOPE SO.

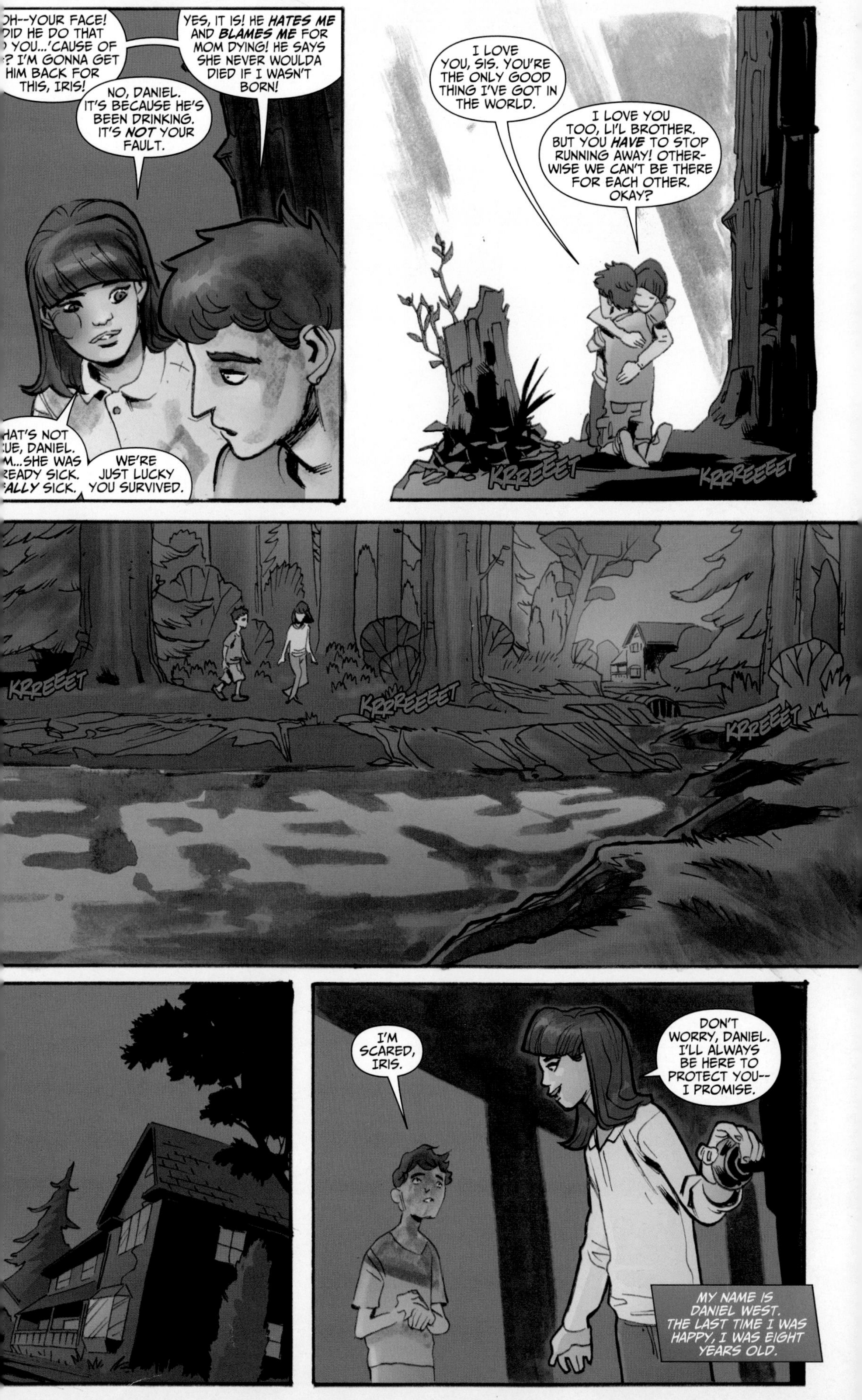

OH--YOUR FACE! DID HE DO THAT TO YOU...'CAUSE OF ME? I'M GONNA GET HIM BACK FOR THIS, IRIS!
NO, DANIEL. IT'S BECAUSE HE'S BEEN DRINKING. IT'S NOT YOUR FAULT.
YES, IT IS! HE HATES ME AND BLAMES ME FOR MOM DYING! HE SAYS SHE NEVER WOULDA DIED IF I WASN'T BORN!
THAT'S NOT TRUE, DANIEL. MOM...SHE WAS ALREADY SICK. REALLY SICK.
WE'RE JUST LUCKY YOU SURVIVED.
I LOVE YOU, SIS. YOU'RE THE ONLY GOOD THING I'VE GOT IN THE WORLD.
I LOVE YOU TOO, LI'L BROTHER. BUT YOU HAVE TO STOP RUNNING AWAY! OTHER-WISE WE CAN'T BE THERE FOR EACH OTHER. OKAY?
KRREEET
KRRREEEET
KRREEET
KRRREEEET
KRREEET
I'M SCARED, IRIS.
DON'T WORRY, DANIEL. I'LL ALWAYS BE HERE TO PROTECT YOU-- I PROMISE.
MY NAME IS DANIEL WEST. THE LAST TIME I WAS HAPPY, I WAS EIGHT YEARS OLD.

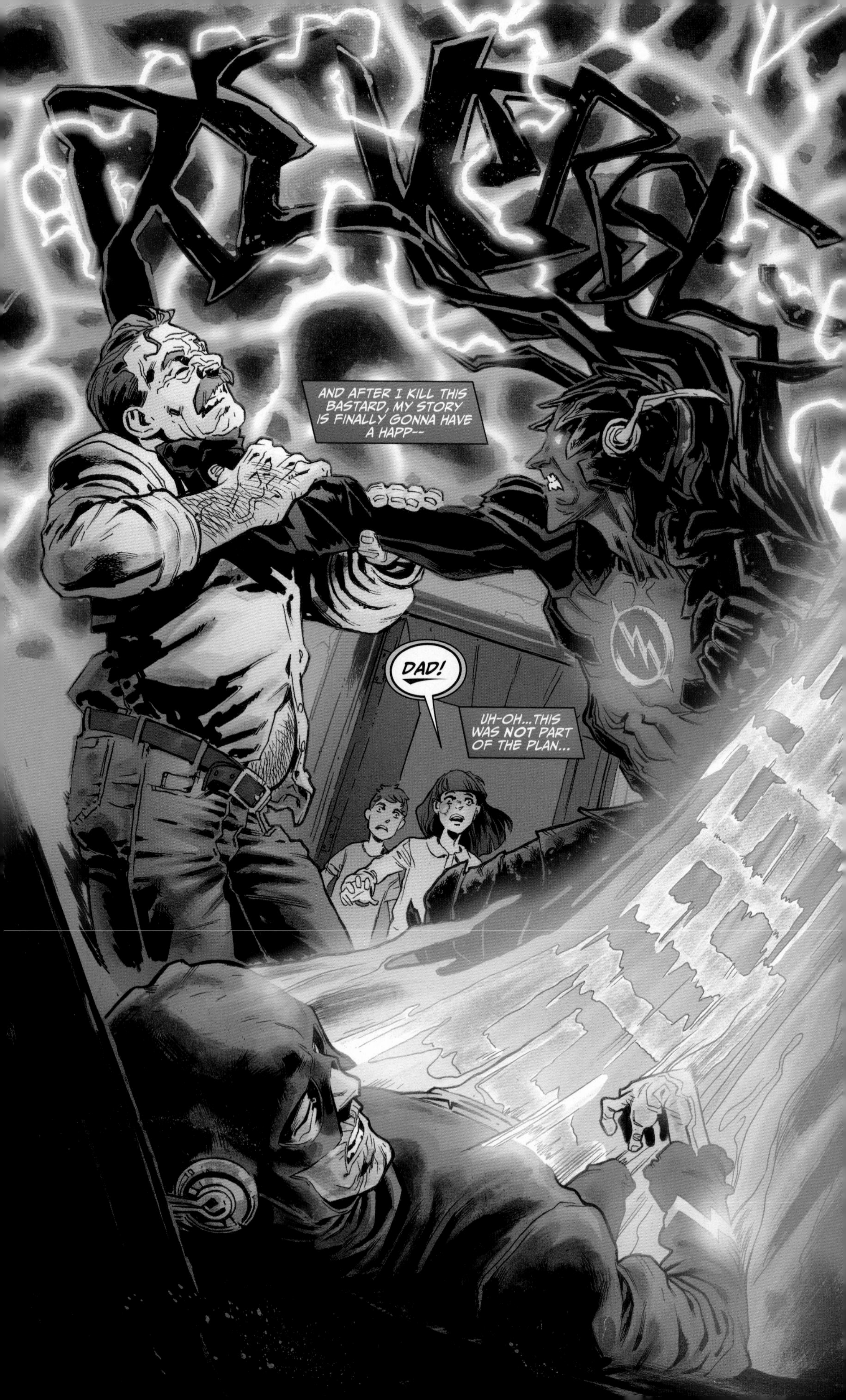
AND AFTER I KILL THIS BASTARD, MY STORY IS FINALLY GONNA HAVE A HAPP--
DAD!
UH-OH...THIS WAS NOT PART OF THE PLAN...

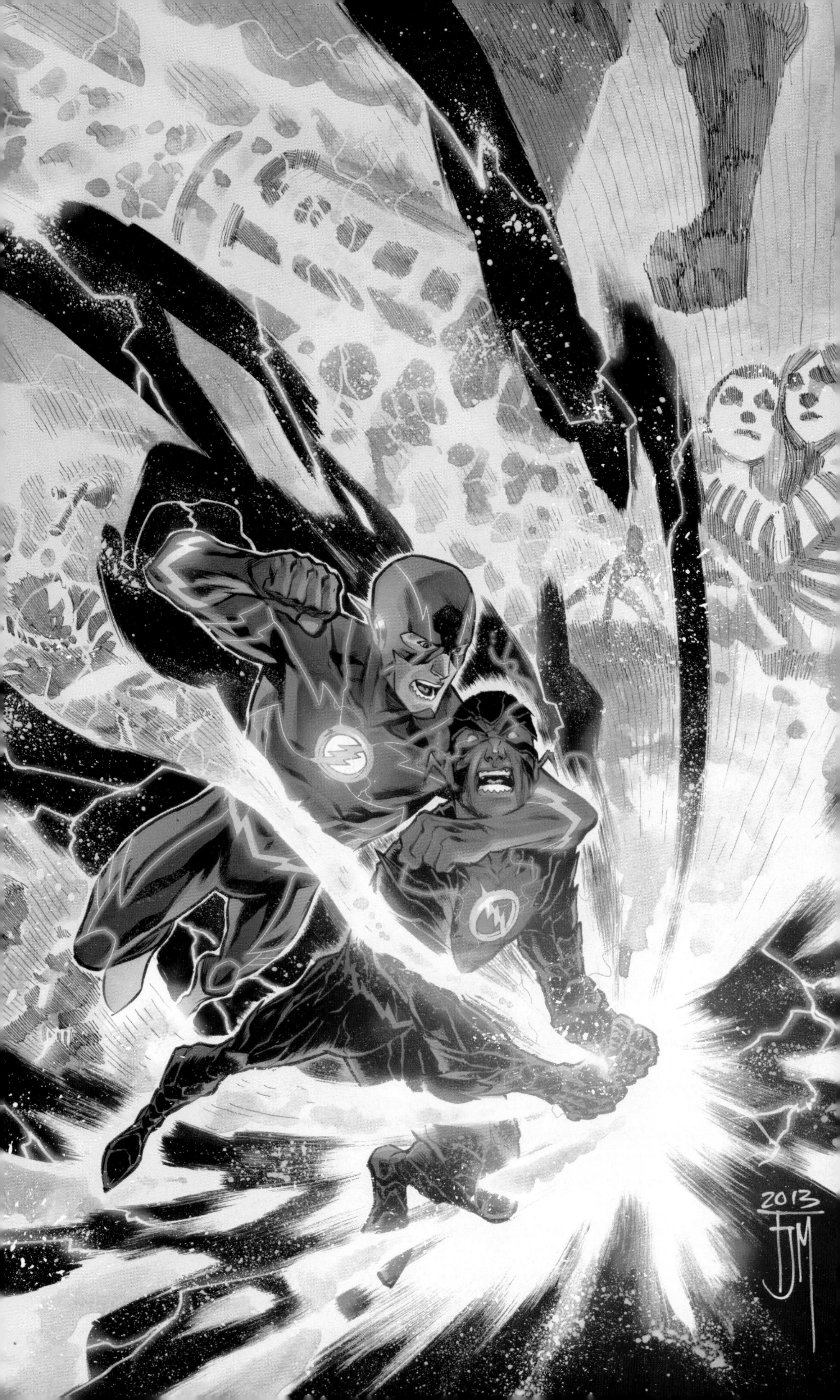
2013

FRANCIS MANAPUL & BRIAN BUCCELLATO writers **FRANCIS MANAPUL** artist

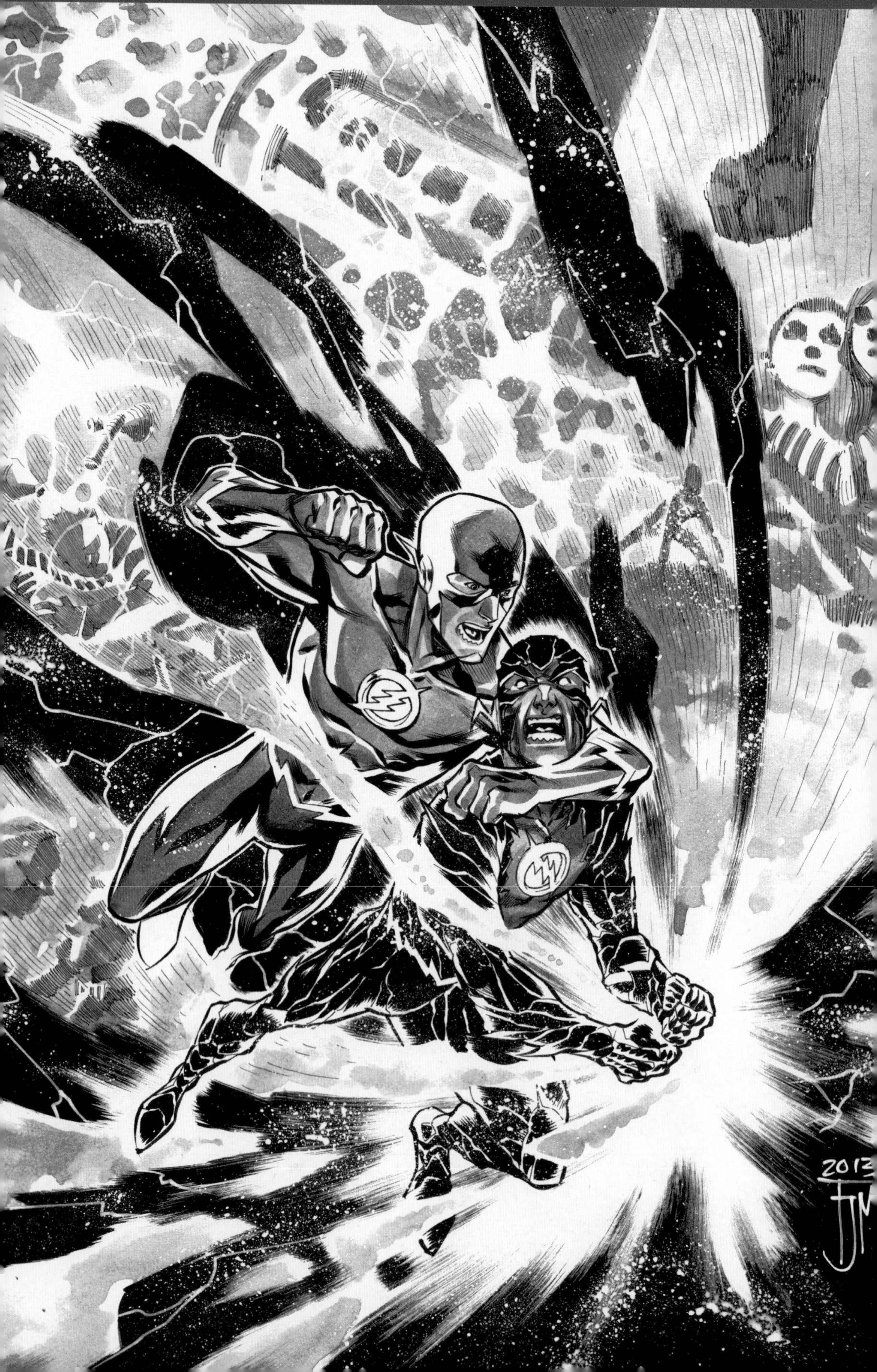

POWER IS A STRANGE THING. IT GIVES YOU THE ABILITY TO CHANGE THINGS, TO MAKE A DIFFERENCE. I GOT MINE FROM A PLACE CALLED THE SPEED FORCE. I USED IT TO SAVE PEOPLE'S LIVES...BUT AFTER A MISTAKE I MADE, INNOCENT PEOPLE, INCLUDING IRIS WEST, GOT TRAPPED INSIDE IT. WHEN I FINALLY RESCUED THEM, THEY CAME BACK DIFFERENT.

THEY MANIFESTED POWERS FROM THE SPEED FORCE, WHICH PUT A TARGET ON THEIR BACK. ONE BY ONE THEY WERE MURDERED-- ALL BUT IRIS.

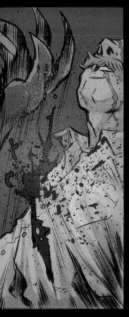

I FOLLOWED THE TRAIL OF THEIR KILLER. BUT WHEN I FOUND HIM, HE DRAGGED ME BACK IN TIME. I GUESS HE WANTED TO MAKE A DIFFERENCE TOO.

DC COMICS

GIVEN THE OPPORTUNITY... WHAT WOULD YOU CHANGE?

PROUDLY PRESENTS

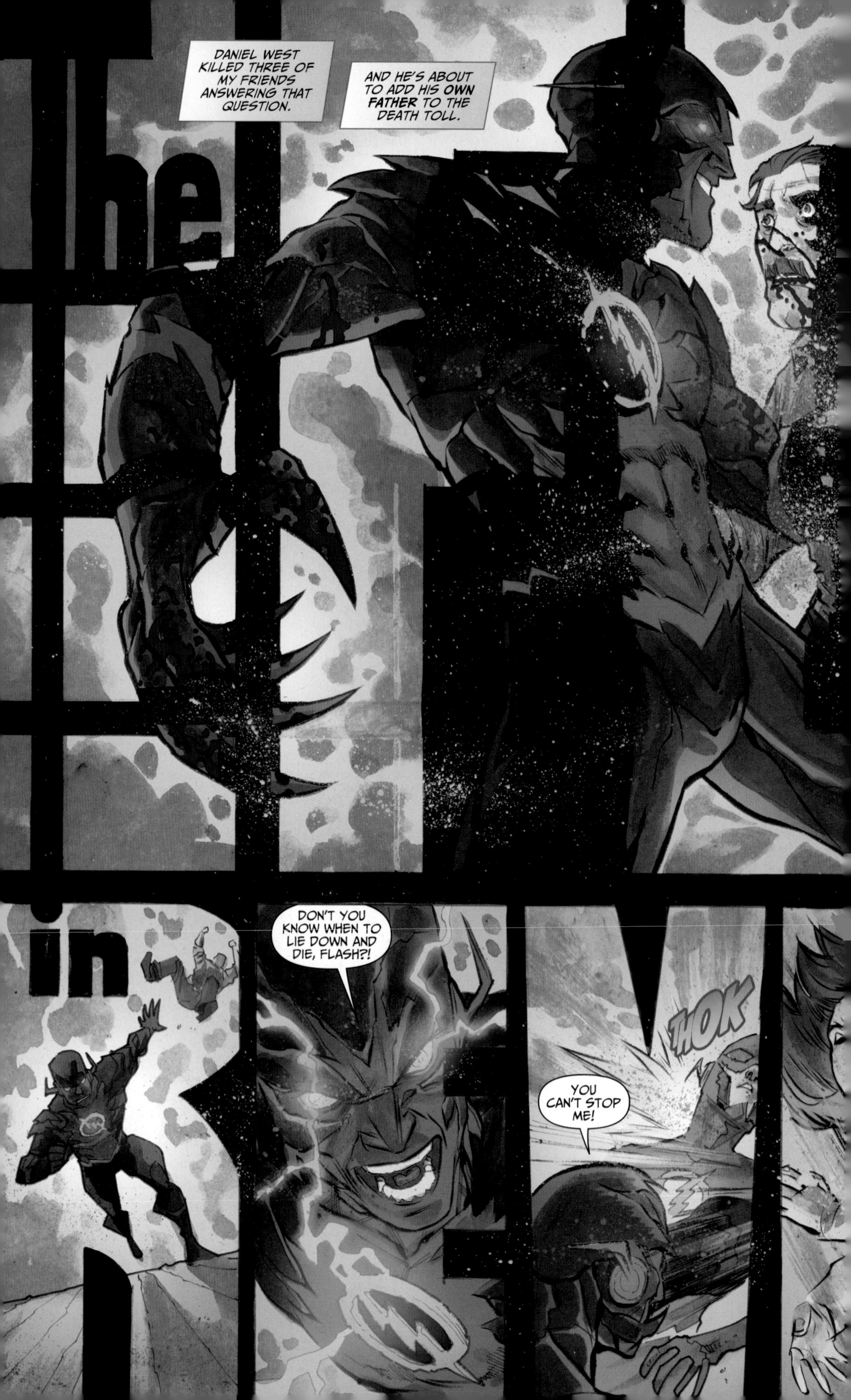

DANIEL WEST KILLED THREE OF MY FRIENDS ANSWERING THAT QUESTION.
AND HE'S ABOUT TO ADD HIS OWN FATHER TO THE DEATH TOLL.
DON'T YOU KNOW WHEN TO LIE DOWN AND DIE, FLASH?!
THOK
YOU CAN'T STOP ME!

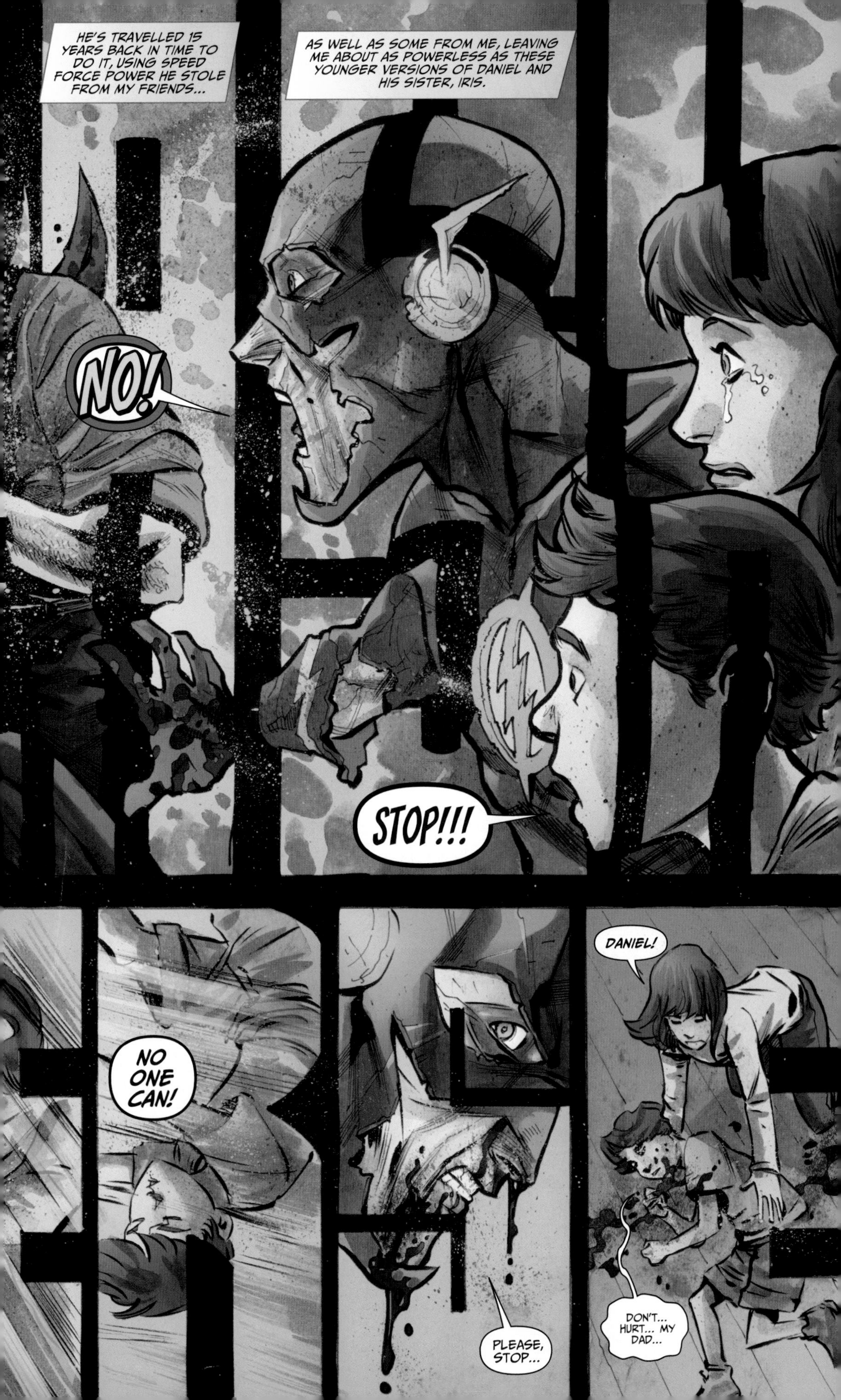
HE'S TRAVELLED 15 YEARS BACK IN TIME TO DO IT, USING SPEED FORCE POWER HE STOLE FROM MY FRIENDS...
AS WELL AS SOME FROM ME, LEAVING ME ABOUT AS POWERLESS AS THESE YOUNGER VERSIONS OF DANIEL AND HIS SISTER, IRIS.
NO!
STOP!!!
NO ONE CAN!
PLEASE, STOP...
DANIEL!
DON'T... HURT... MY DAD...

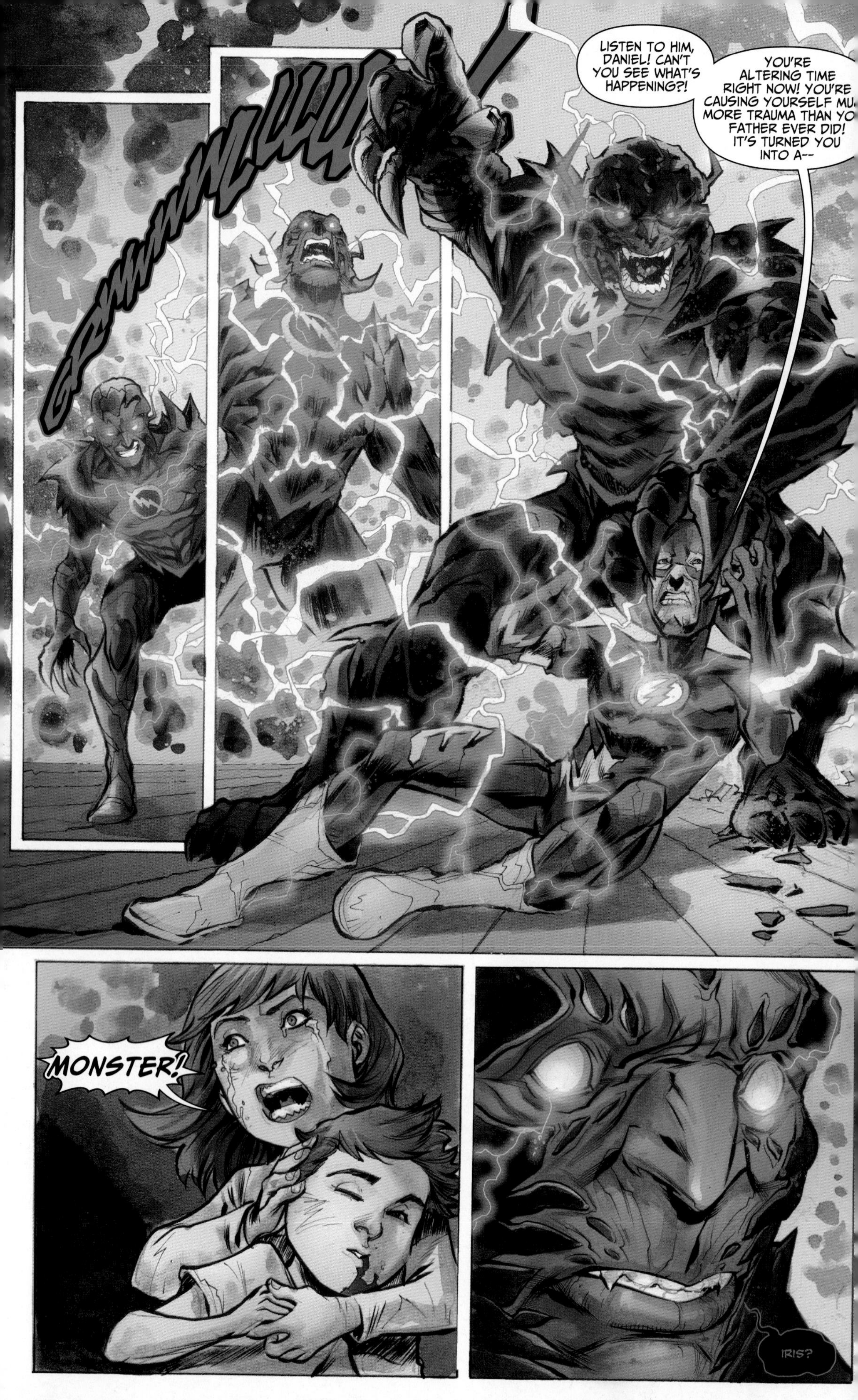
LISTEN TO HIM, DANIEL! CAN'T YOU SEE WHAT'S HAPPENING?!
YOU'RE ALTERING TIME RIGHT NOW! YOU'RE CAUSING YOURSELF MU MORE TRAUMA THAN YO FATHER EVER DID! IT'S TURNED YOU INTO A--
MONSTER!
IRIS?

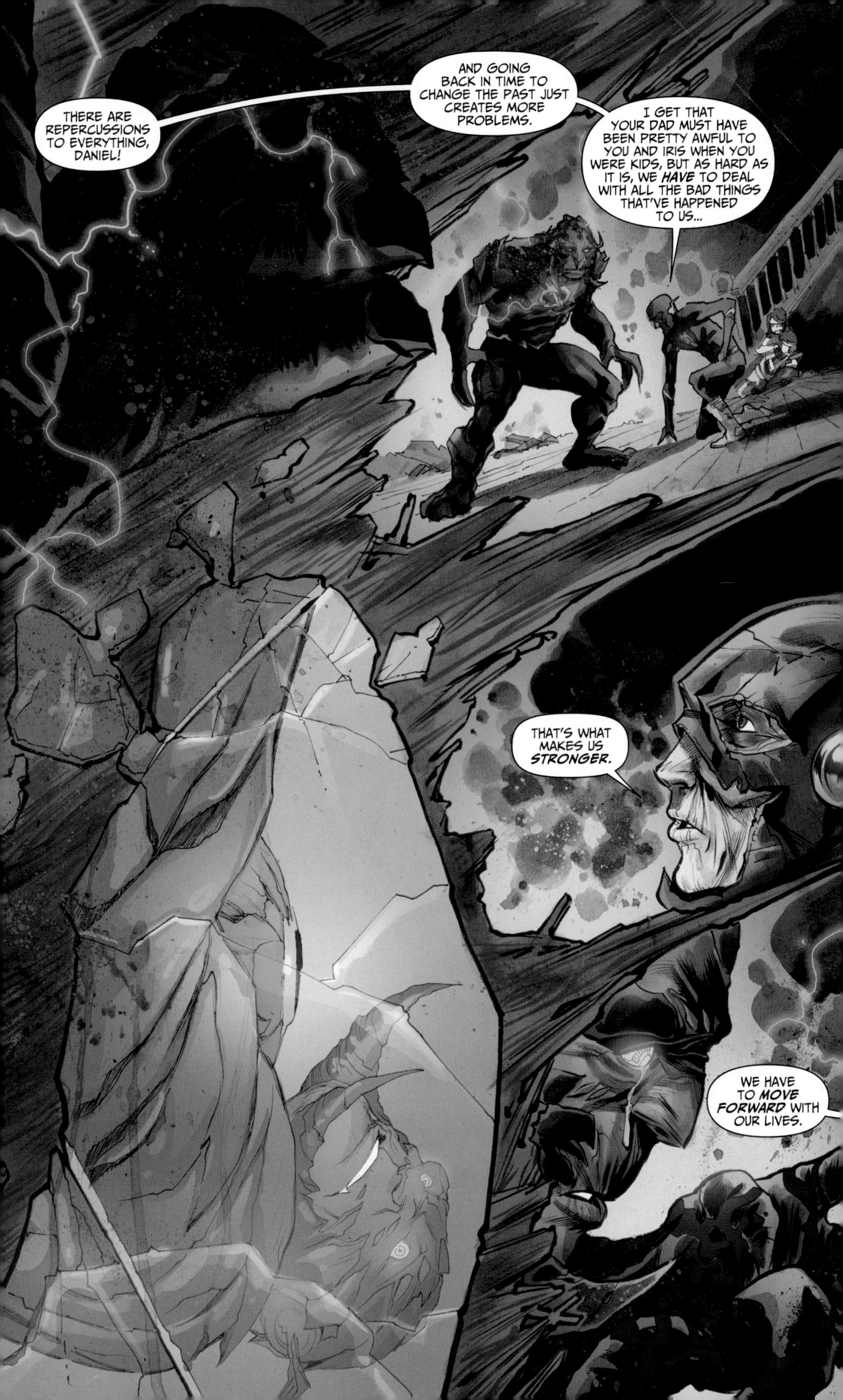
THERE ARE REPERCUSSIONS TO EVERYTHING, DANIEL!
AND GOING BACK IN TIME TO CHANGE THE PAST JUST CREATES MORE PROBLEMS.
I GET THAT YOUR DAD MUST HAVE BEEN PRETTY AWFUL TO YOU AND IRIS WHEN YOU WERE KIDS, BUT AS HARD AS IT IS, WE *HAVE* TO DEAL WITH ALL THE BAD THINGS THAT'VE HAPPENED TO US...
THAT'S WHAT MAKES US *STRONGER.*
WE HAVE TO *MOVE FORWARD* WITH OUR LIVES.

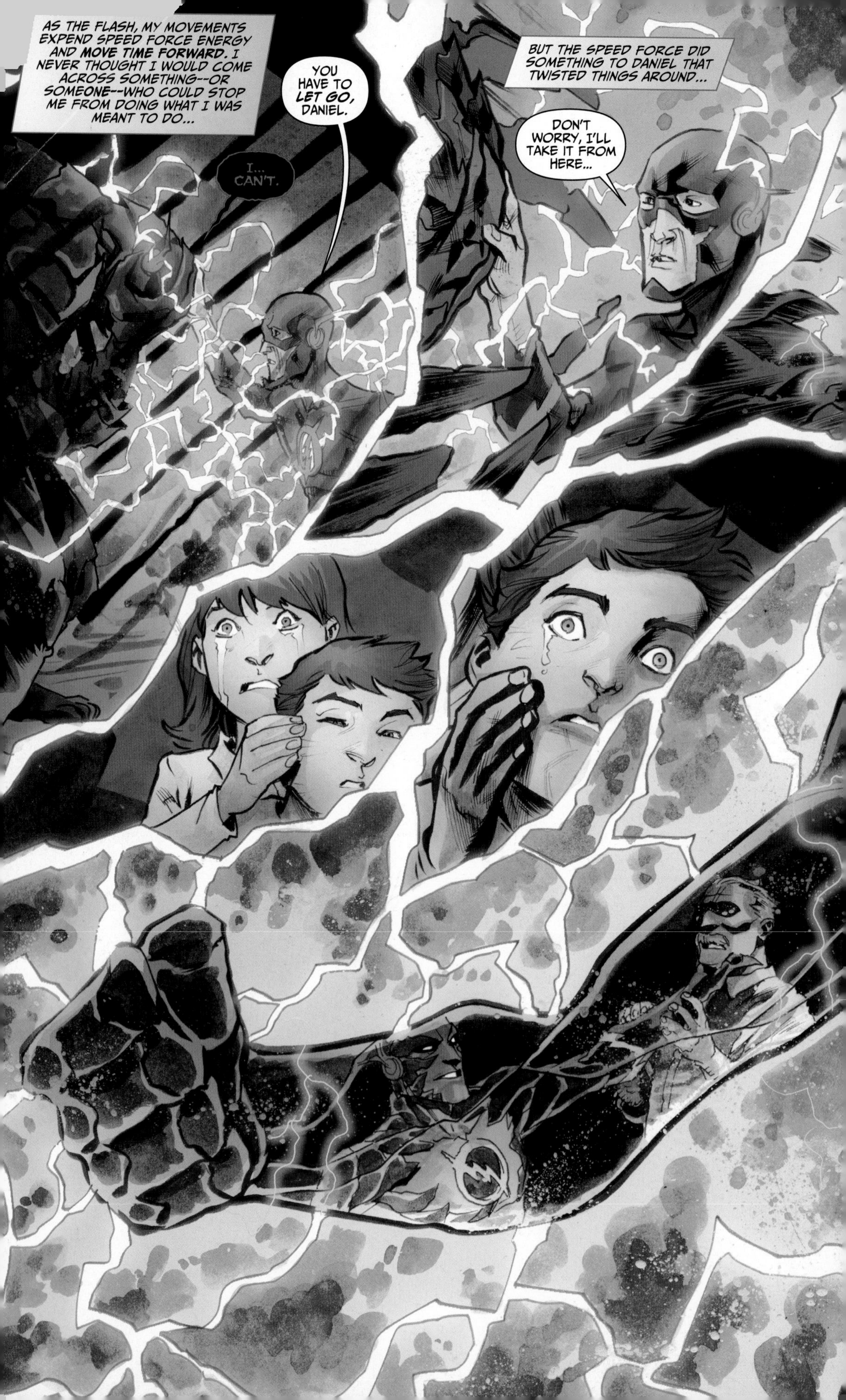
AS THE FLASH, MY MOVEMENTS EXPEND SPEED FORCE ENERGY AND MOVE TIME FORWARD. I NEVER THOUGHT I WOULD COME ACROSS SOMETHING--OR SOMEONE--WHO COULD STOP ME FROM DOING WHAT I WAS MEANT TO DO...
YOU HAVE TO LET GO, DANIEL.
I... CAN'T.
BUT THE SPEED FORCE DID SOMETHING TO DANIEL THAT TWISTED THINGS AROUND...
DON'T WORRY, I'LL TAKE IT FROM HERE...

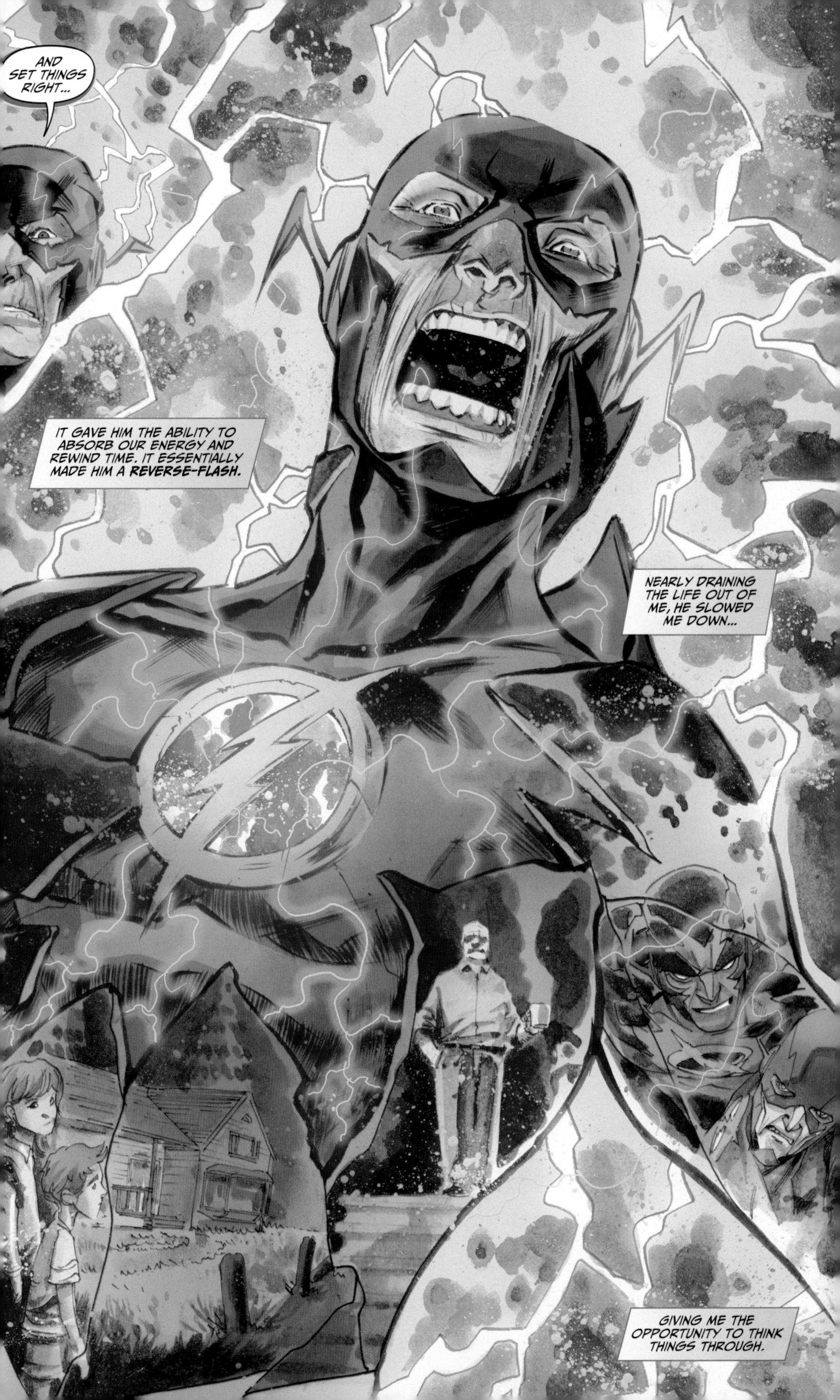
AND SET THINGS RIGHT...
IT GAVE HIM THE ABILITY TO ABSORB OUR ENERGY AND REWIND TIME. IT ESSENTIALLY MADE HIM A REVERSE-FLASH.
NEARLY DRAINING THE LIFE OUT OF ME, HE SLOWED ME DOWN...
GIVING ME THE OPPORTUNITY TO THINK THINGS THROUGH.

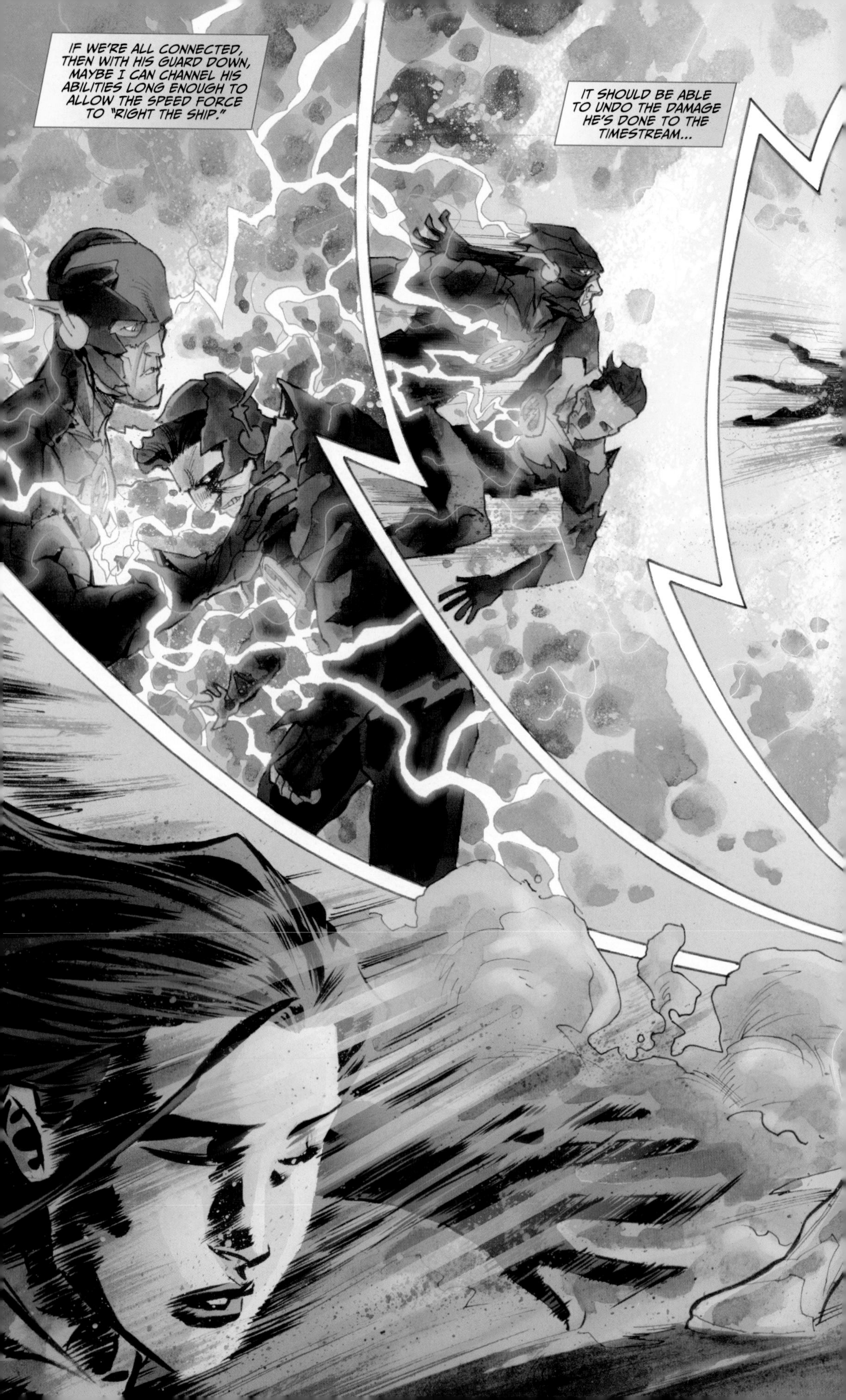
IF WE'RE ALL CONNECTED, THEN WITH HIS GUARD DOWN, MAYBE I CAN CHANNEL HIS ABILITIES LONG ENOUGH TO ALLOW THE SPEED FORCE TO "RIGHT THE SHIP."
IT SHOULD BE ABLE TO UNDO THE DAMAGE HE'S DONE TO THE TIMESTREAM...

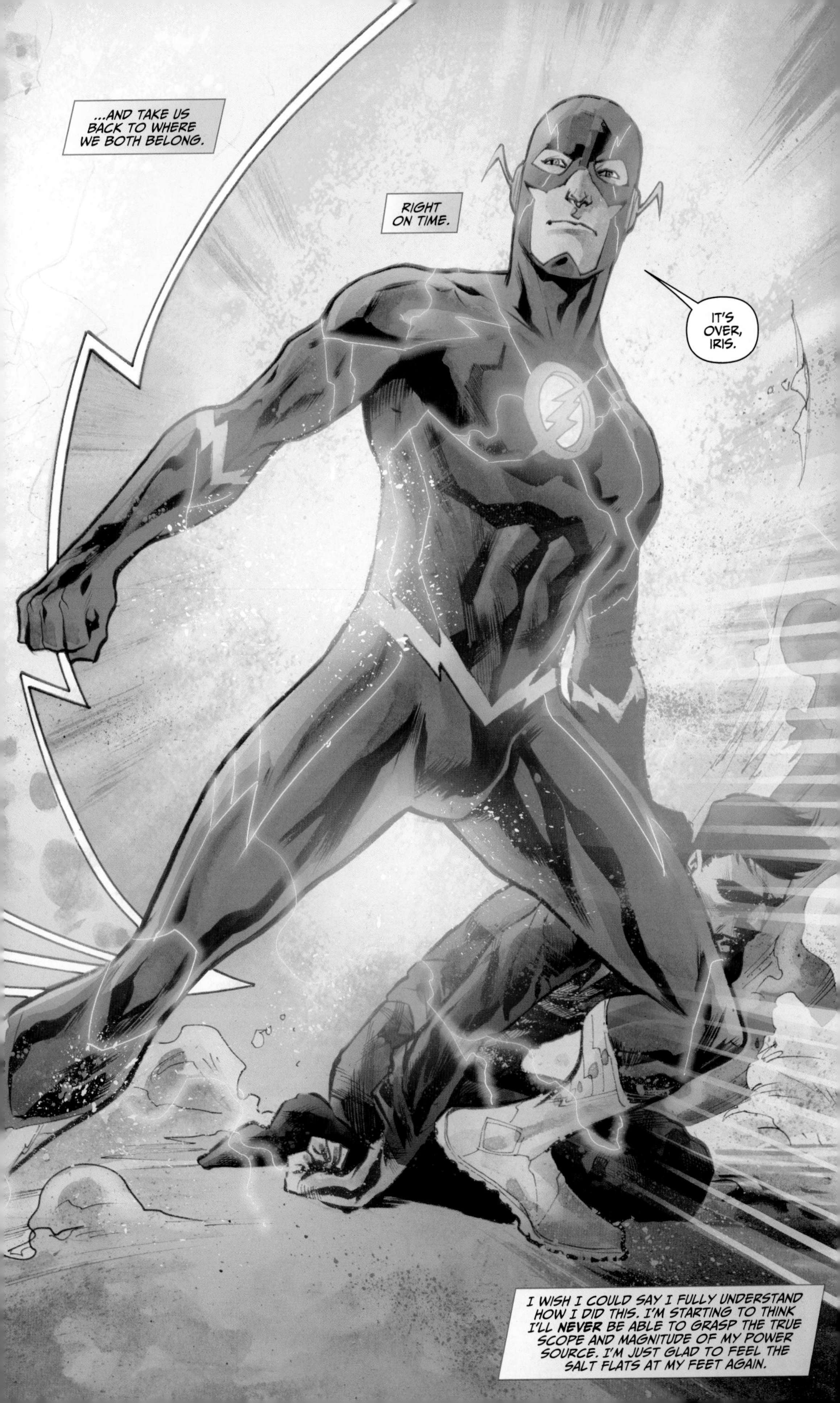
...AND TAKE US BACK TO WHERE WE BOTH BELONG.
RIGHT ON TIME.
IT'S OVER, IRIS.
I WISH I COULD SAY I FULLY UNDERSTAND HOW I DID THIS. I'M STARTING TO THINK I'LL NEVER BE ABLE TO GRASP THE TRUE SCOPE AND MAGNITUDE OF MY POWER SOURCE. I'M JUST GLAD TO FEEL THE SALT FLATS AT MY FEET AGAIN.

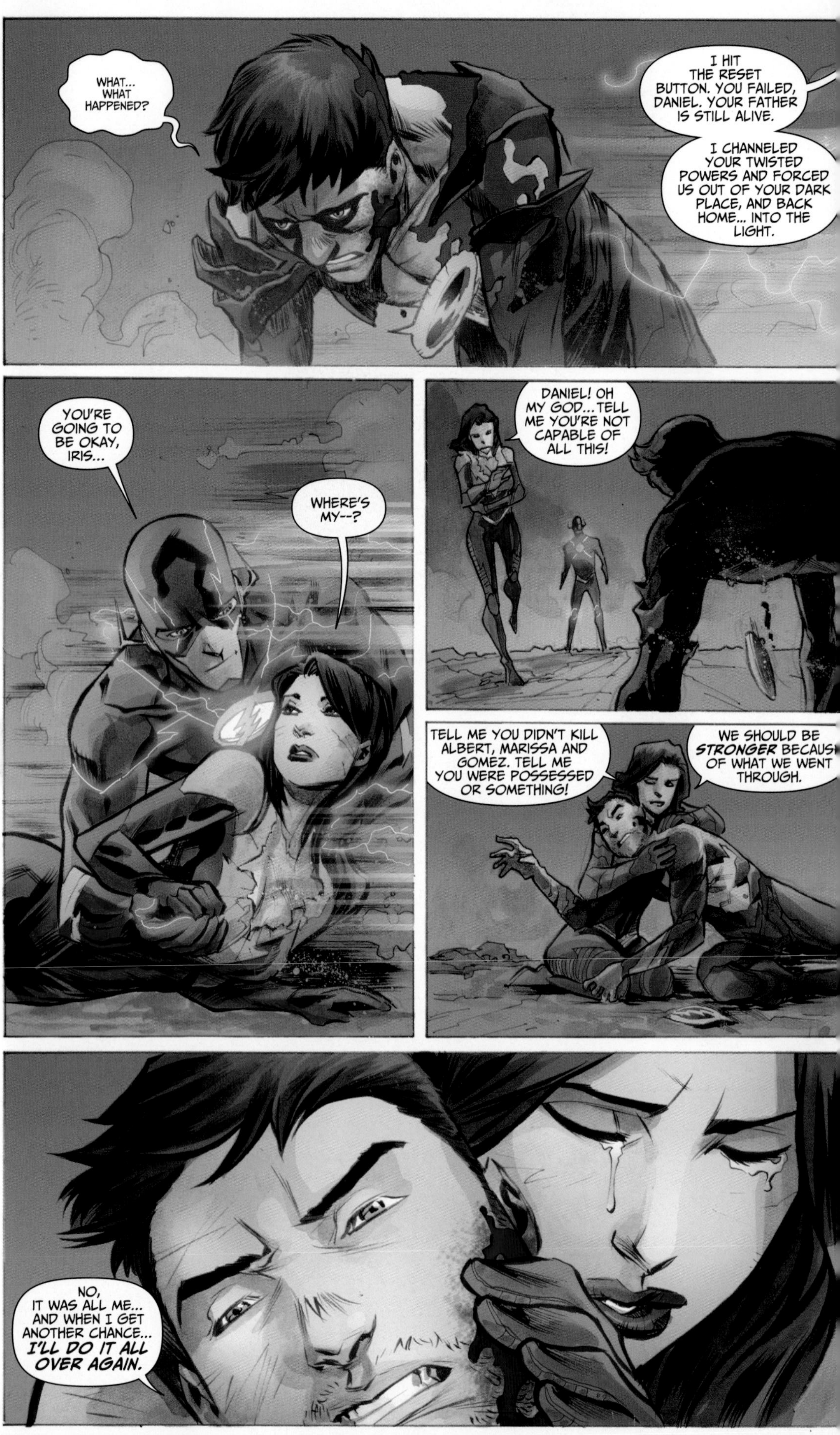
WHAT... WHAT HAPPENED?
I HIT THE RESET BUTTON. YOU FAILED, DANIEL. YOUR FATHER IS STILL ALIVE.
I CHANNELED YOUR TWISTED POWERS AND FORCED US OUT OF YOUR DARK PLACE, AND BACK HOME... INTO THE LIGHT.
YOU'RE GOING TO BE OKAY, IRIS...
WHERE'S MY--?
DANIEL! OH MY GOD...TELL ME YOU'RE NOT CAPABLE OF ALL THIS!
TELL ME YOU DIDN'T KILL ALBERT, MARISSA AND GOMEZ. TELL ME YOU WERE POSSESSED OR SOMETHING!
WE SHOULD BE *STRONGER* BECAUS OF WHAT WE WENT THROUGH.
NO, IT WAS ALL ME... AND WHEN I GET ANOTHER CHANCE... ***I'LL DO IT ALL OVER AGAIN.***

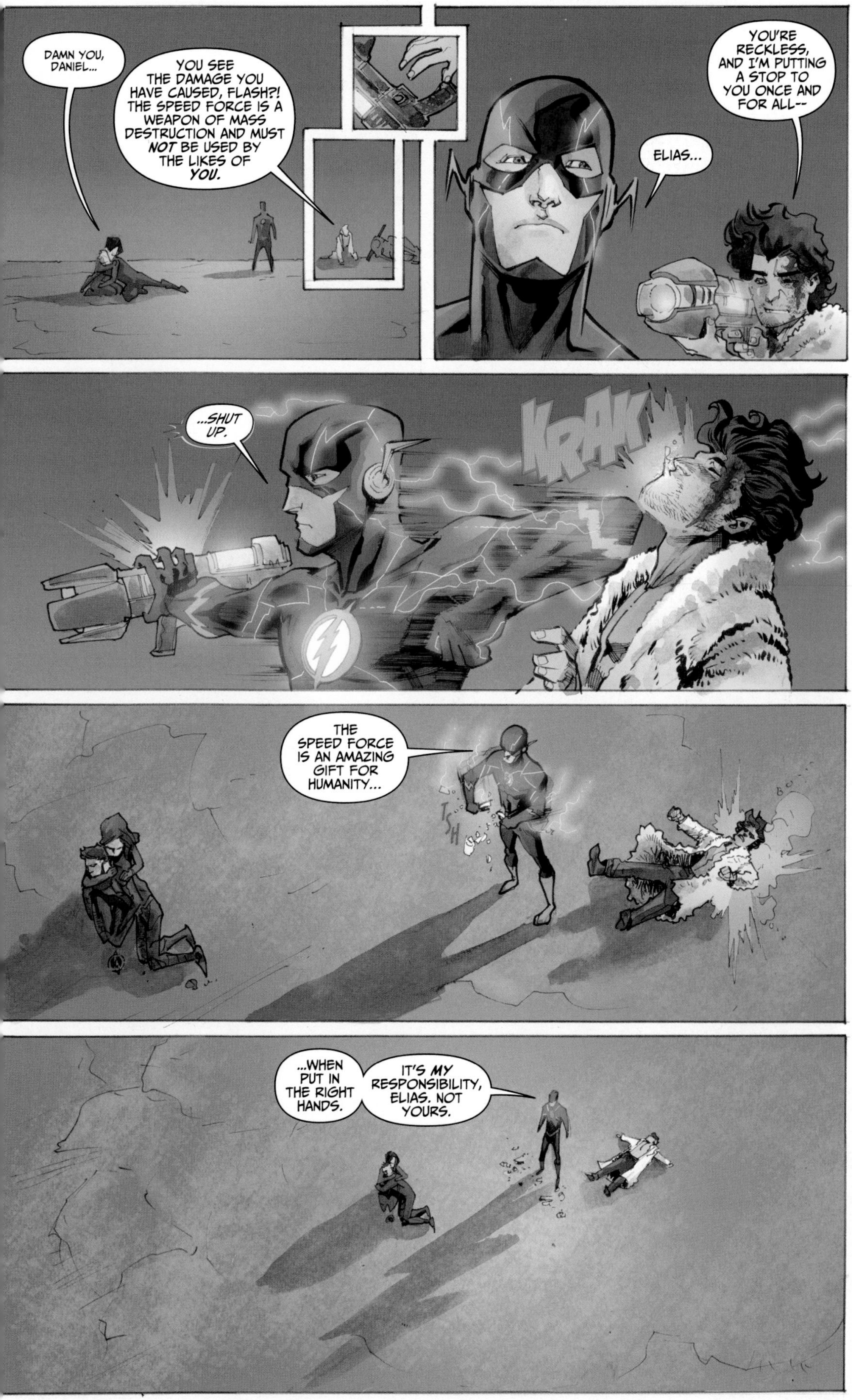
DAMN YOU, DANIEL...
YOU SEE THE DAMAGE YOU HAVE CAUSED, FLASH?! THE SPEED FORCE IS A WEAPON OF MASS DESTRUCTION AND MUST *NOT* BE USED BY THE LIKES OF *YOU.*
YOU'RE RECKLESS, AND I'M PUTTING A STOP TO YOU ONCE AND FOR ALL--
ELIAS...
...SHUT UP.
KRAK
THE SPEED FORCE IS AN AMAZING GIFT FOR HUMANITY...
TSH
...WHEN PUT IN THE RIGHT HANDS.
IT'S *MY* RESPONSIBILITY, ELIAS. NOT YOURS.

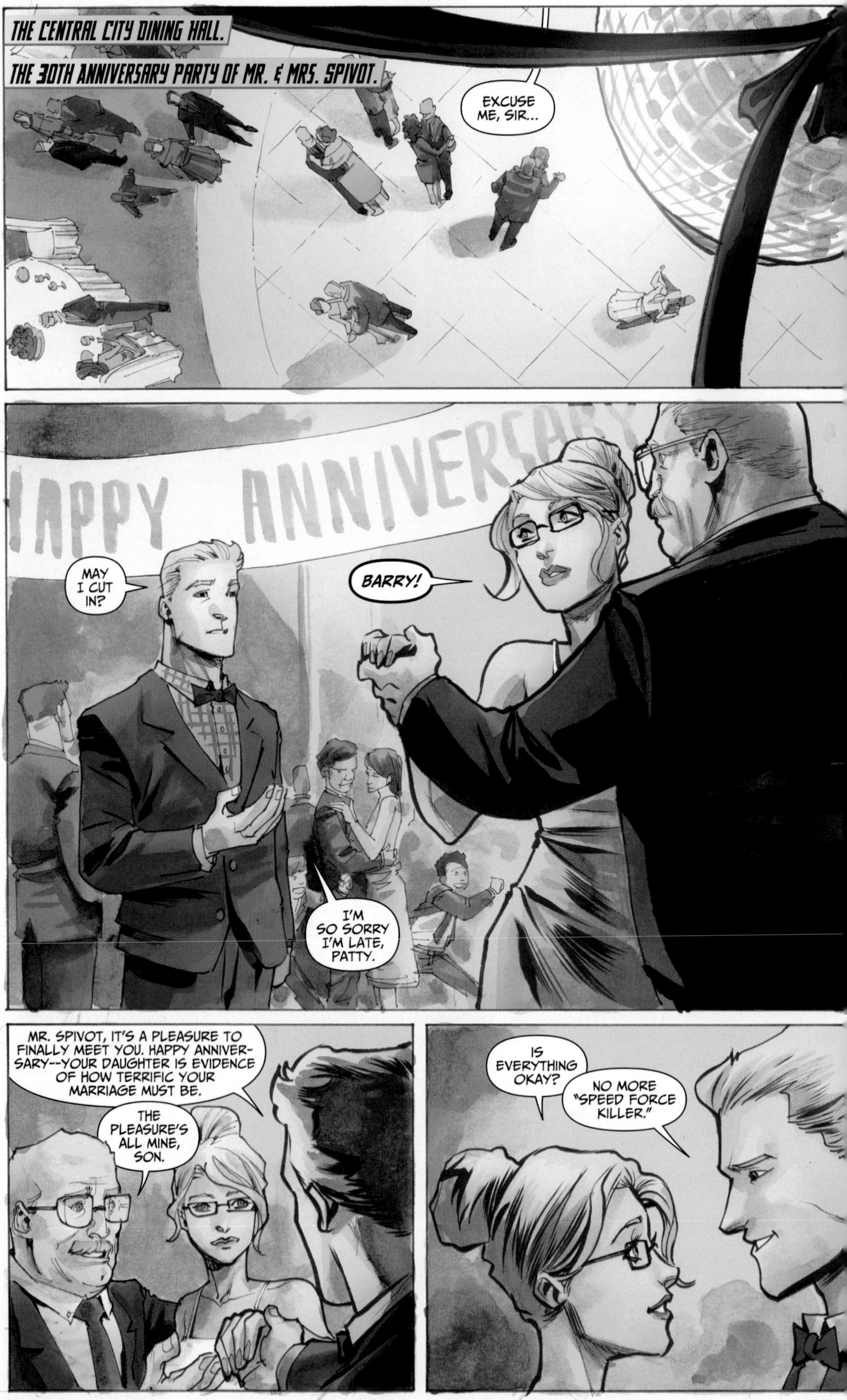

THE CENTRAL CITY DINING HALL.
THE 30TH ANNIVERSARY PARTY OF MR. & MRS. SPIVOT.
EXCUSE ME, SIR...
HAPPY ANNIVERSARY
MAY I CUT IN?
BARRY!
I'M SO SORRY I'M LATE, PATTY.
MR. SPIVOT, IT'S A PLEASURE TO FINALLY MEET YOU. HAPPY ANNIVER-SARY--YOUR DAUGHTER IS EVIDENCE OF HOW TERRIFIC YOUR MARRIAGE MUST BE.
THE PLEASURE'S ALL MINE, SON.
IS EVERYTHING OKAY?
NO MORE "SPEED FORCE KILLER."

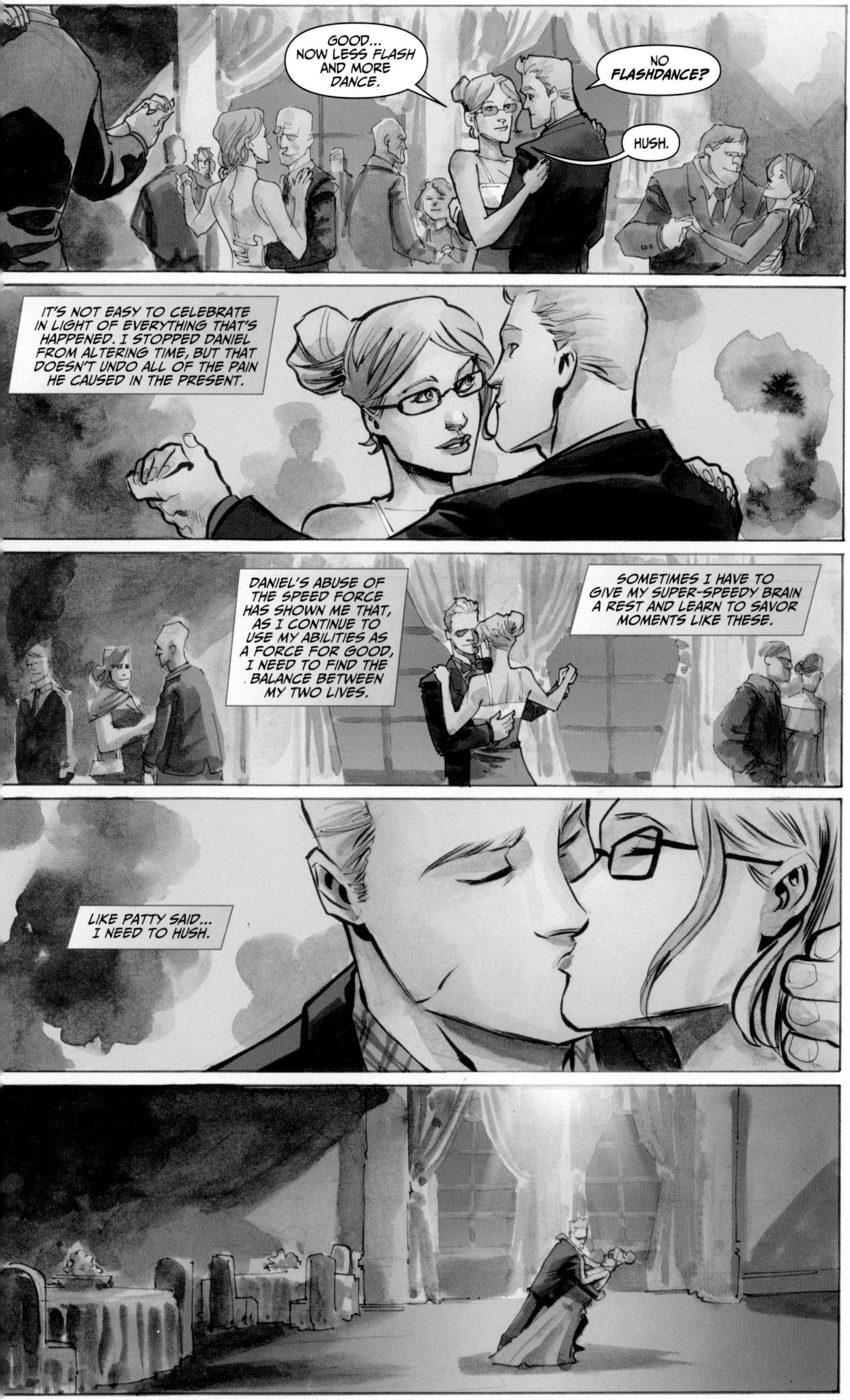
GOOD... NOW LESS FLASH AND MORE DANCE.
NO FLASHDANCE?
HUSH.
IT'S NOT EASY TO CELEBRATE IN LIGHT OF EVERYTHING THAT'S HAPPENED. I STOPPED DANIEL FROM ALTERING TIME, BUT THAT DOESN'T UNDO ALL OF THE PAIN HE CAUSED IN THE PRESENT.
DANIEL'S ABUSE OF THE SPEED FORCE HAS SHOWN ME THAT, AS I CONTINUE TO USE MY ABILITIES AS A FORCE FOR GOOD, I NEED TO FIND THE BALANCE BETWEEN MY TWO LIVES.
SOMETIMES I HAVE TO GIVE MY SUPER-SPEEDY BRAIN A REST AND LEARN TO SAVOR MOMENTS LIKE THESE.
LIKE PATTY SAID... I NEED TO HUSH.

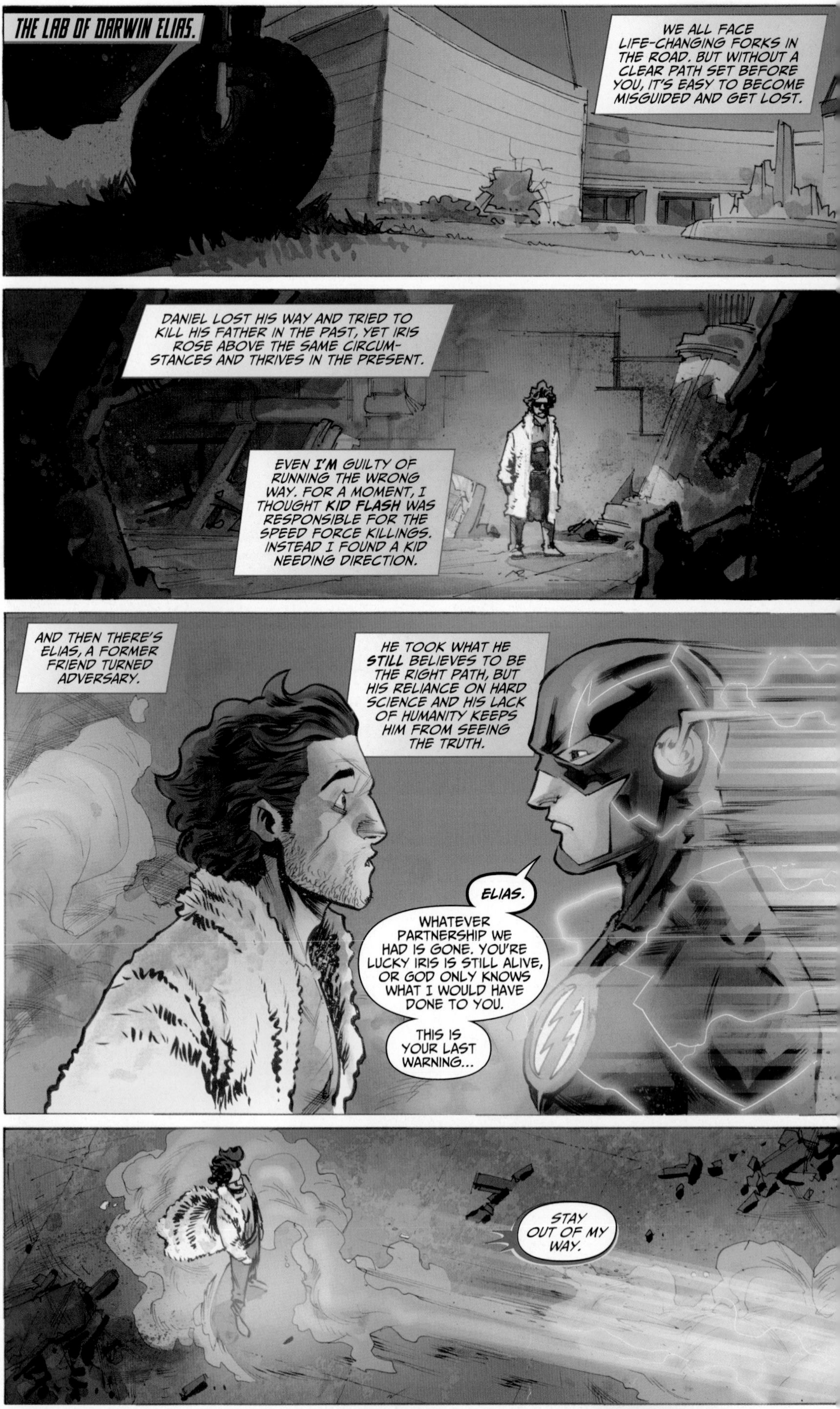
THE LAB OF DARWIN ELIAS.
WE ALL FACE LIFE-CHANGING FORKS IN THE ROAD. BUT WITHOUT A CLEAR PATH SET BEFORE YOU, IT'S EASY TO BECOME MISGUIDED AND GET LOST.
DANIEL LOST HIS WAY AND TRIED TO KILL HIS FATHER IN THE PAST, YET IRIS ROSE ABOVE THE SAME CIRCUM-STANCES AND THRIVES IN THE PRESENT.
EVEN I'M GUILTY OF RUNNING THE WRONG WAY. FOR A MOMENT, I THOUGHT KID FLASH WAS RESPONSIBLE FOR THE SPEED FORCE KILLINGS. INSTEAD I FOUND A KID NEEDING DIRECTION.
AND THEN THERE'S ELIAS, A FORMER FRIEND TURNED ADVERSARY.
HE TOOK WHAT HE STILL BELIEVES TO BE THE RIGHT PATH, BUT HIS RELIANCE ON HARD SCIENCE AND HIS LACK OF HUMANITY KEEPS HIM FROM SEEING THE TRUTH.
ELIAS.
WHATEVER PARTNERSHIP WE HAD IS GONE. YOU'RE LUCKY IRIS IS STILL ALIVE, OR GOD ONLY KNOWS WHAT I WOULD HAVE DONE TO YOU.
THIS IS YOUR LAST WARNING...
STAY OUT OF MY WAY.

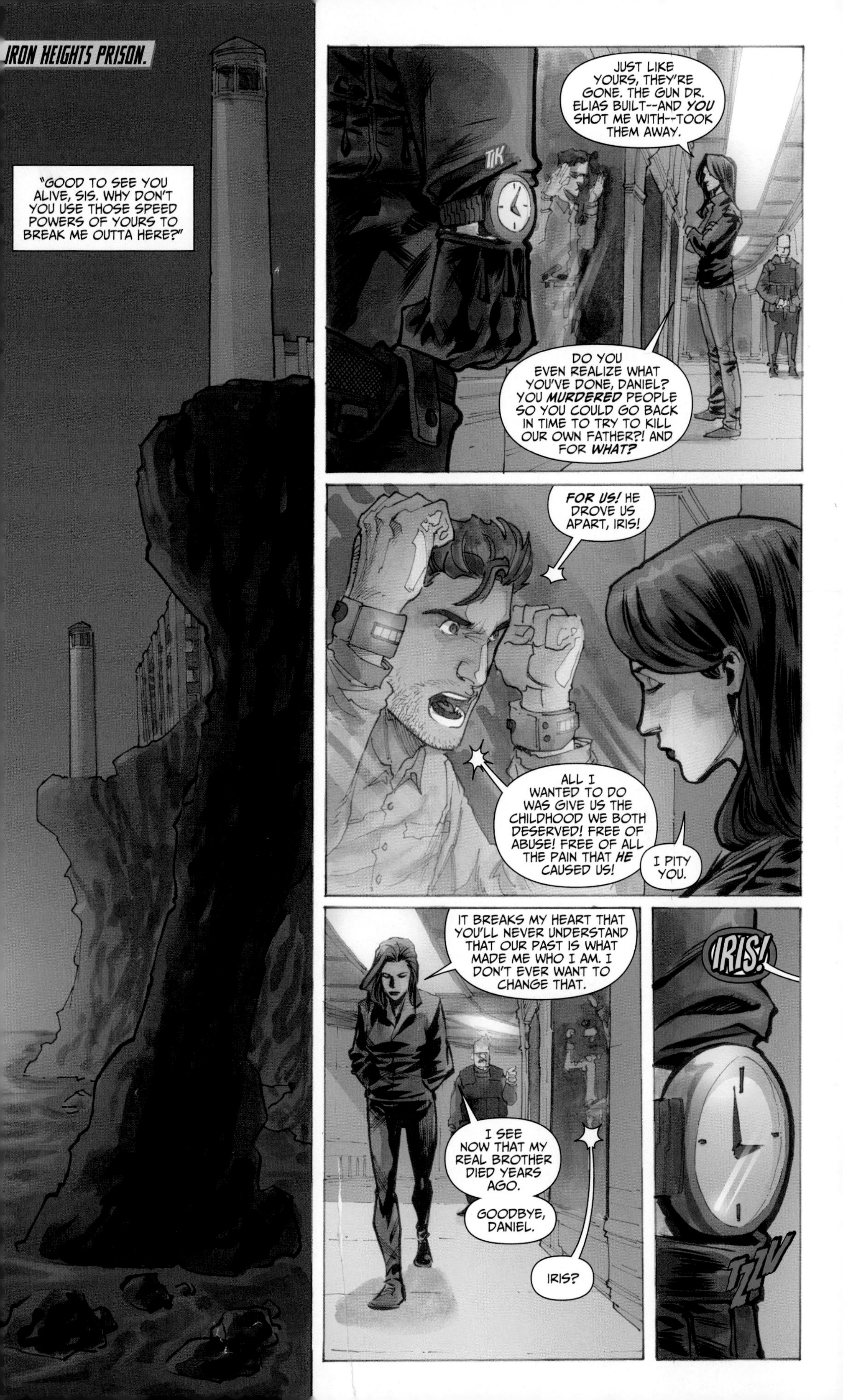
IRON HEIGHTS PRISON.
"GOOD TO SEE YOU ALIVE, SIS. WHY DON'T YOU USE THOSE SPEED POWERS OF YOURS TO BREAK ME OUTTA HERE?"
JUST LIKE YOURS, THEY'RE GONE. THE GUN DR. ELIAS BUILT--AND YOU SHOT ME WITH--TOOK THEM AWAY.
DO YOU EVEN REALIZE WHAT YOU'VE DONE, DANIEL? YOU MURDERED PEOPLE SO YOU COULD GO BACK IN TIME TO TRY TO KILL OUR OWN FATHER?! AND FOR WHAT?
FOR US! HE DROVE US APART, IRIS!
ALL I WANTED TO DO WAS GIVE US THE CHILDHOOD WE BOTH DESERVED! FREE OF ABUSE! FREE OF ALL THE PAIN THAT HE CAUSED US!
I PITY YOU.
IT BREAKS MY HEART THAT YOU'LL NEVER UNDERSTAND THAT OUR PAST IS WHAT MADE ME WHO I AM. I DON'T EVER WANT TO CHANGE THAT.
I SEE NOW THAT MY REAL BROTHER DIED YEARS AGO.
GOODBYE, DANIEL.
IRIS?
IRIS!
TZZV

I'VE SEEN AND DONE SO MANY THINGS SINCE I BECAME THE FLASH. WHEN I LOOK BACK, I CAN'T BELIEVE ALL THE CHALLENGES I'VE FACED.

MY ABILITIES HAVE GIVEN ME THE INCREDIBLE OPPORTUNITY TO MAKE A POSITIVE DIFFERENCE...

AND I WILL NEVER TAKE THAT RESPONSIBILITY LIGHTLY.

IT HAUNTS ME THAT REVERSE-FLASH PROVED WHAT I HAVE BEEN AFRAID TO ADMIT TO MYSELF--THAT WE HAVE THE POWER TO CHANGE THE PAST.

I'D LIKE TO THINK MY MOM WOULD BE PROUD OF THE WAY I'VE HANDLED IT ALL. I'D GIVE ALMOST **ANYTHING** TO SEE HER FACE ONE MORE TIME.

I COULD "FIX" EVERYTHING-- SAVE MY MOM, PROVE MY DAD INNOCENT, GET MY FAMILY BACK. SO WHAT'S STOPPING ME FROM HAVING IT ALL?

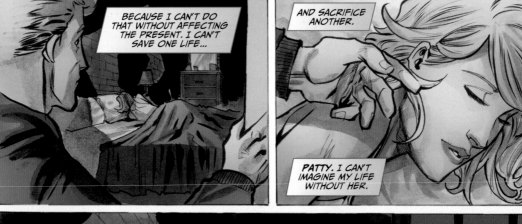

BECAUSE I CAN'T DO THAT WITHOUT AFFECTING THE PRESENT. I CAN'T SAVE ONE LIFE...

AND SACRIFICE ANOTHER.

PATTY. I CAN'T IMAGINE MY LIFE WITHOUT HER.

AS TEMPTING AS IT IS, I CAN **NEVER** GO BACK TO CHANGE THE PAST.

I MUST LOOK AHEAD AND CHANGE WHAT I CAN IN THE PRESENT.

I HAVE A CASE TO REOPEN.

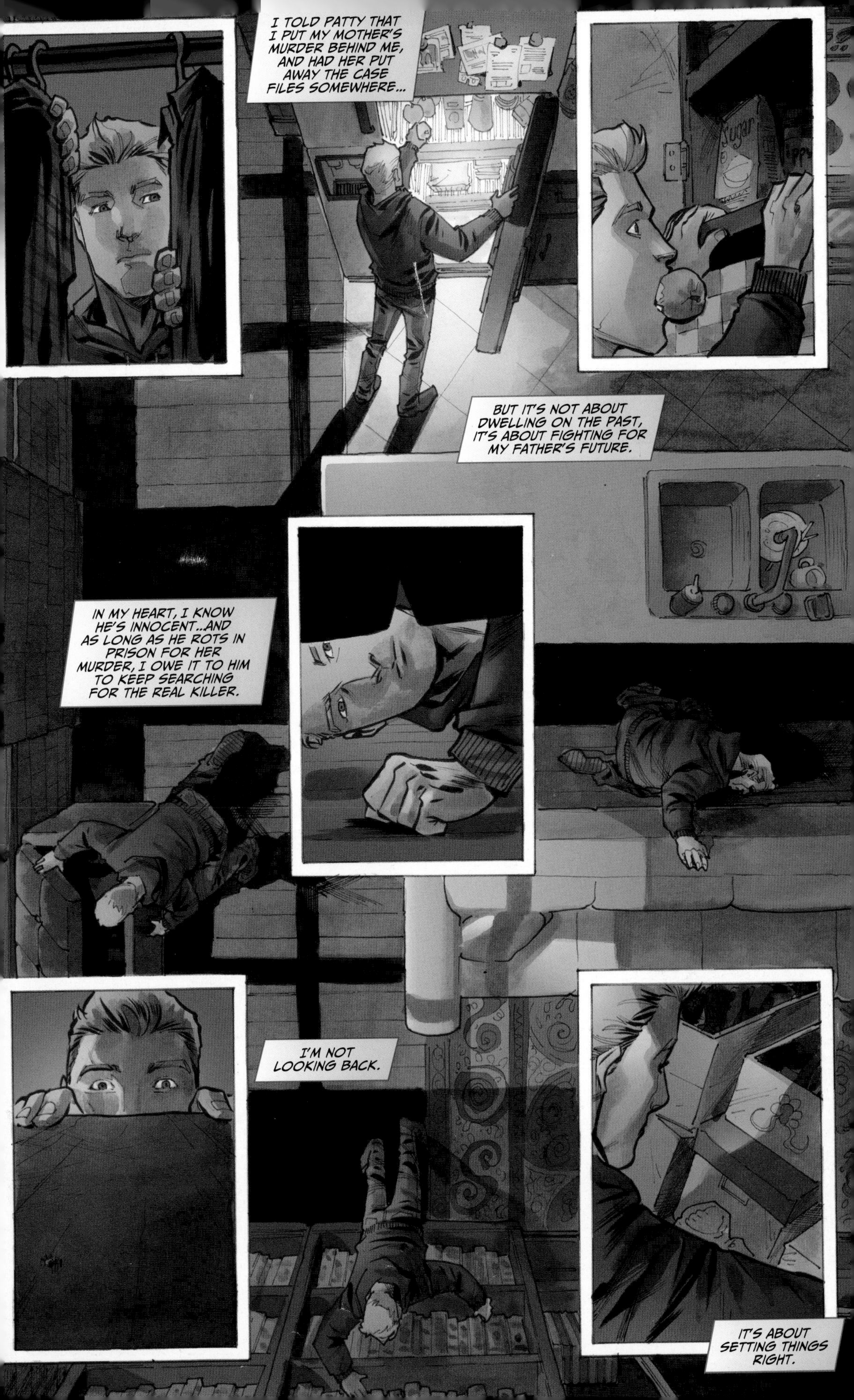

I TOLD PATTY THAT I PUT MY MOTHER'S MURDER BEHIND ME, AND HAD HER PUT AWAY THE CASE FILES SOMEWHERE...
Sugar
BUT IT'S NOT ABOUT DWELLING ON THE PAST, IT'S ABOUT FIGHTING FOR MY FATHER'S FUTURE.
IN MY HEART, I KNOW HE'S INNOCENT...AND AS LONG AS HE ROTS IN PRISON FOR HER MURDER, I OWE IT TO HIM TO KEEP SEARCHING FOR THE REAL KILLER.
I'M NOT LOOKING BACK.
IT'S ABOUT SETTING THINGS RIGHT.

BARRY?

AND ALTHOUGH SOME- TIMES WHEN YOU TRY TO SET THINGS RIGHT...YOU RISK LETTING OTHER PEOPLE DOWN...

IF YOU'RE NOT MOVING, YOU'RE NOT LIVING.

...YOU MUST NOT LET THAT KEEP YOU FROM MOVING FORWARD.

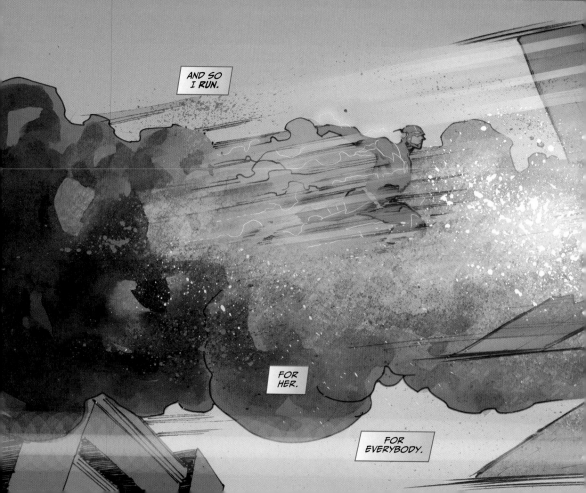

AND SO I RUN.

FOR HER.

FOR EVERYBODY.

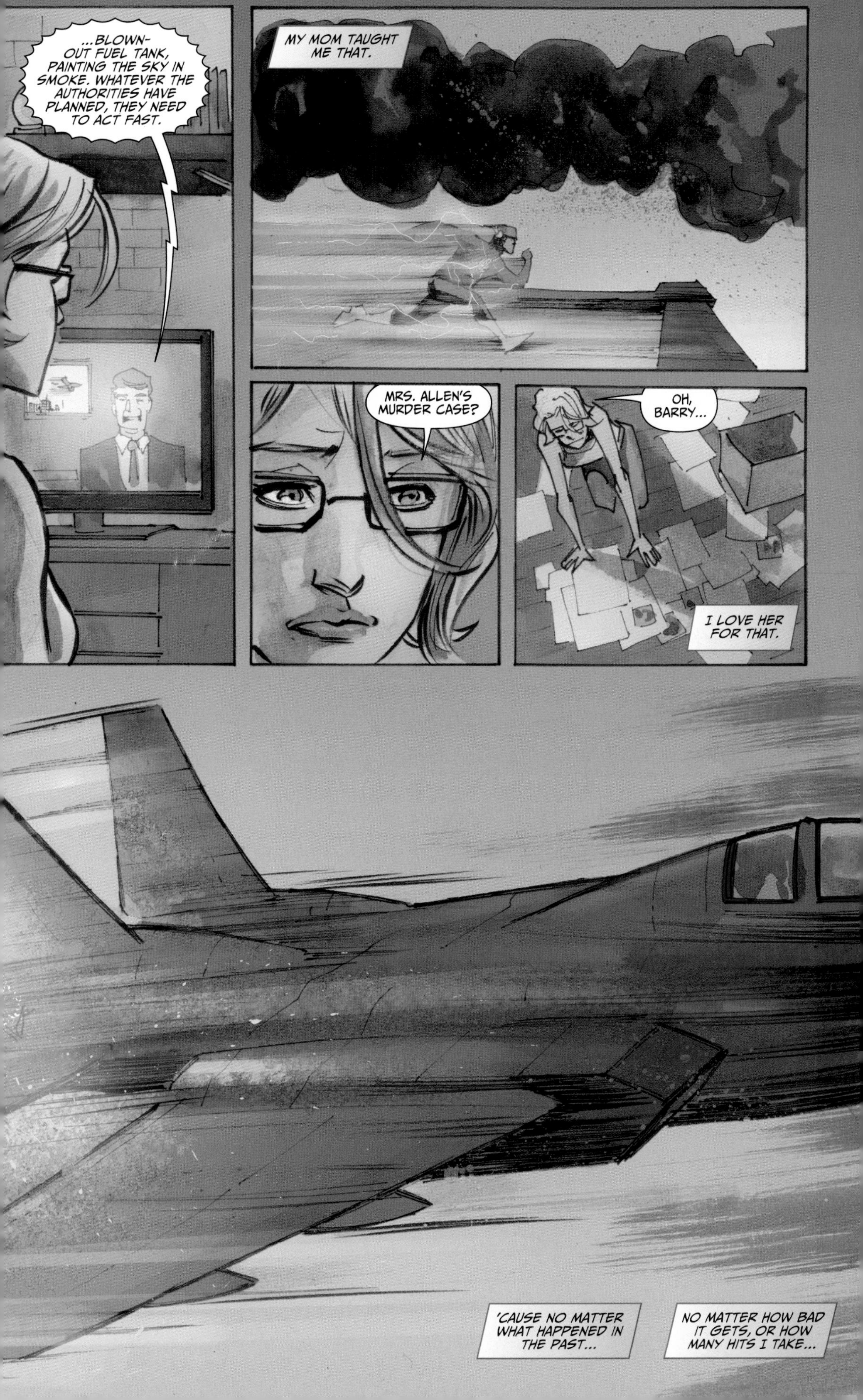
...BLOWN-OUT FUEL TANK, PAINTING THE SKY IN SMOKE. WHATEVER THE AUTHORITIES HAVE PLANNED, THEY NEED TO ACT FAST.
MY MOM TAUGHT ME THAT.
MRS. ALLEN'S MURDER CASE?
OH, BARRY...
I LOVE HER FOR THAT.
'CAUSE NO MATTER WHAT HAPPENED IN THE PAST...
NO MATTER HOW BAD IT GETS, OR HOW MANY HITS I TAKE...

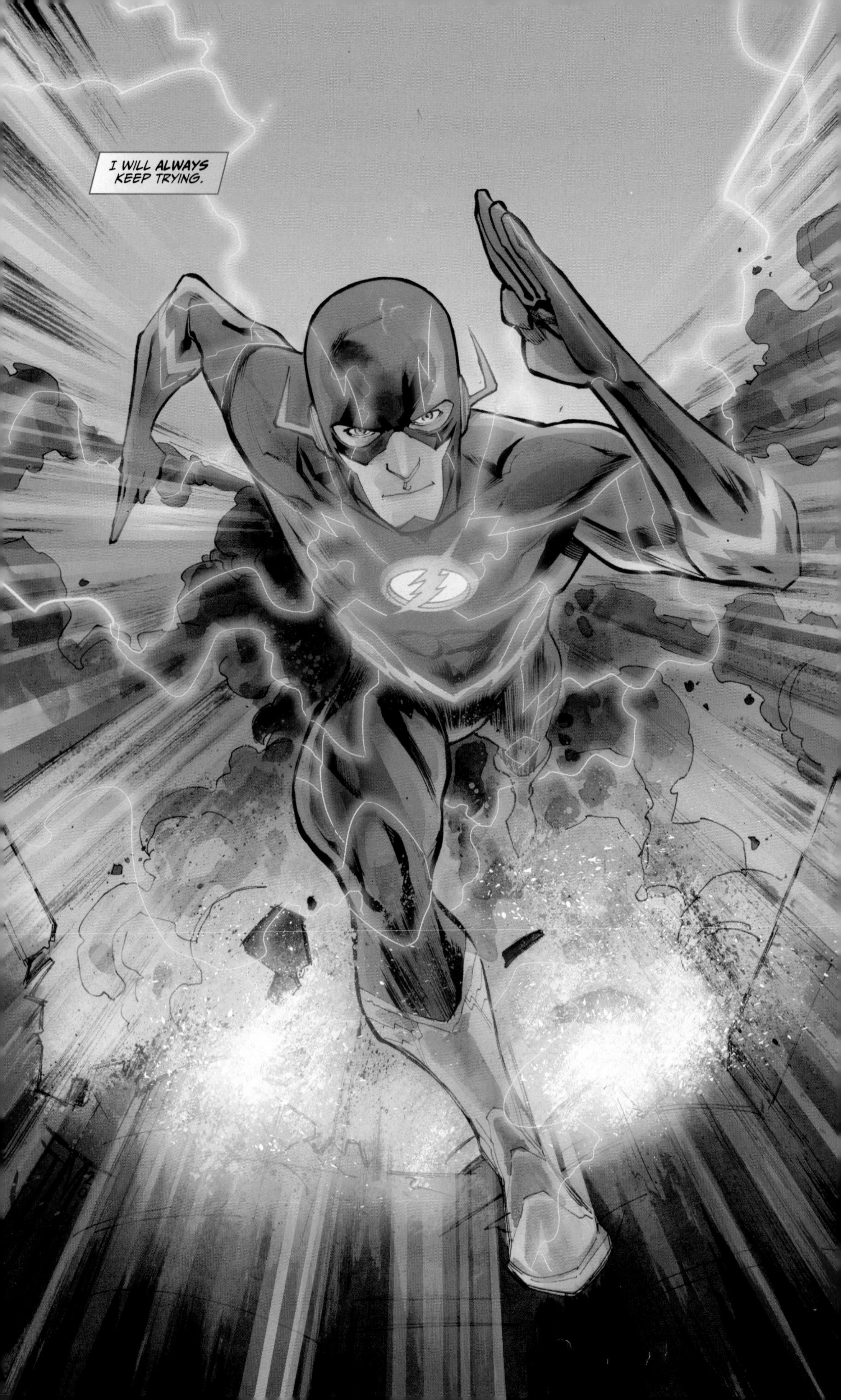
I WILL ALWAYS KEEP TRYING.

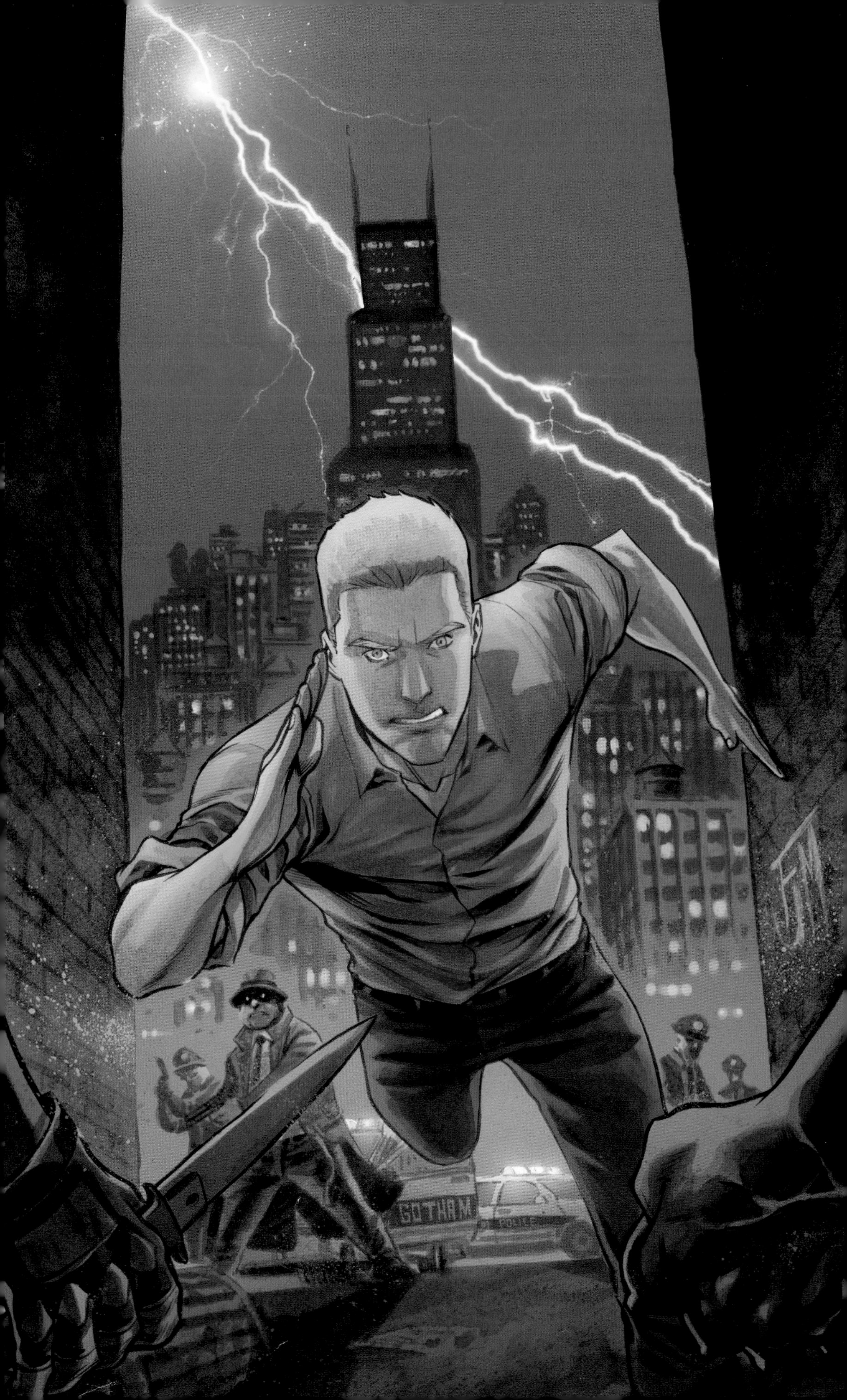
GOTHAM
POLICE

FRANCIS MANAPUL & BRIAN BUCCELLATO writers CHRIS SPROUSE, FRANCIS MANAPUL pencillers
KARL STORY, KEITH CHAMPAGNE, FRANCIS MANAPUL inkers

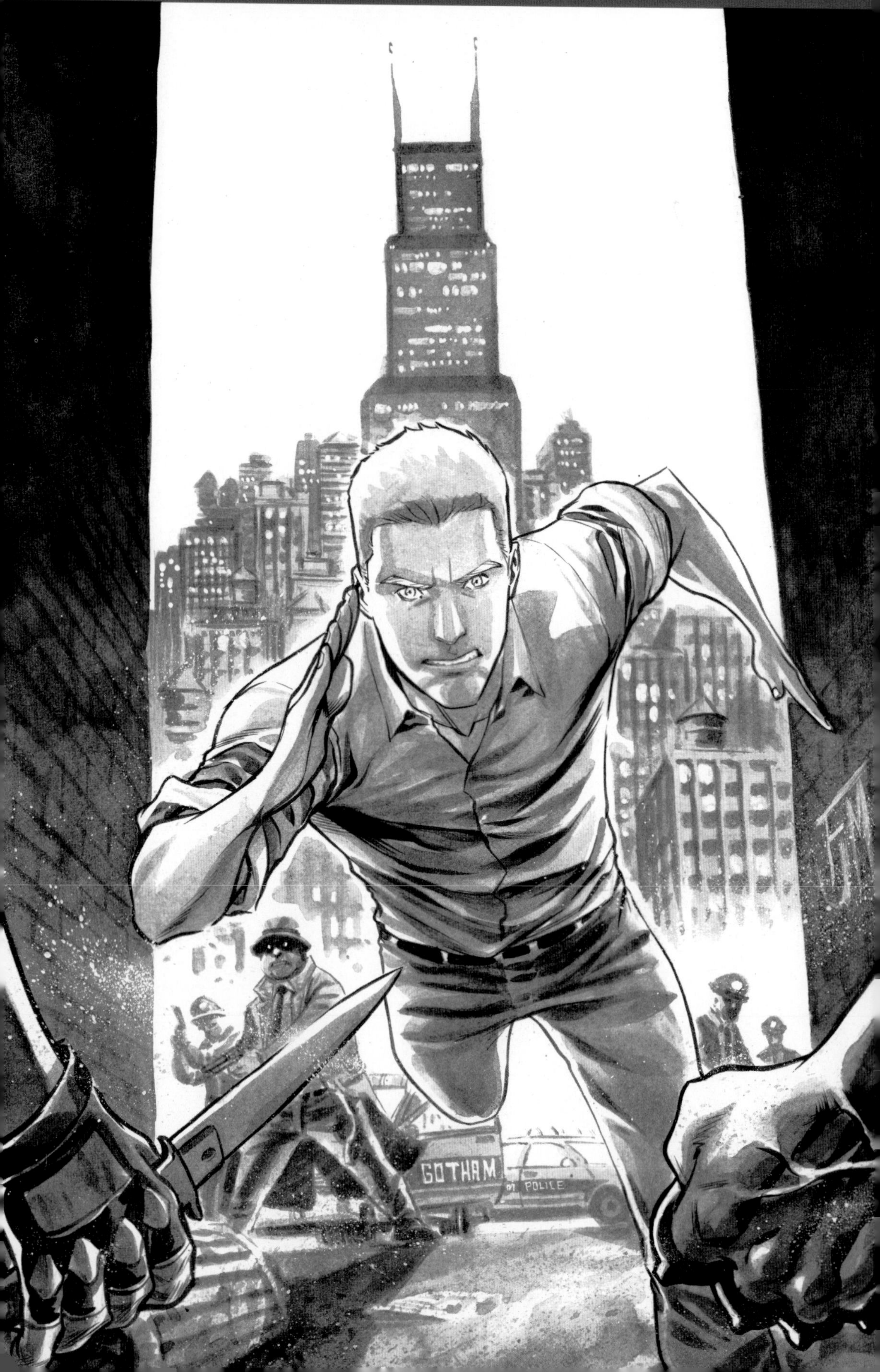
GOTHAM
POLICE

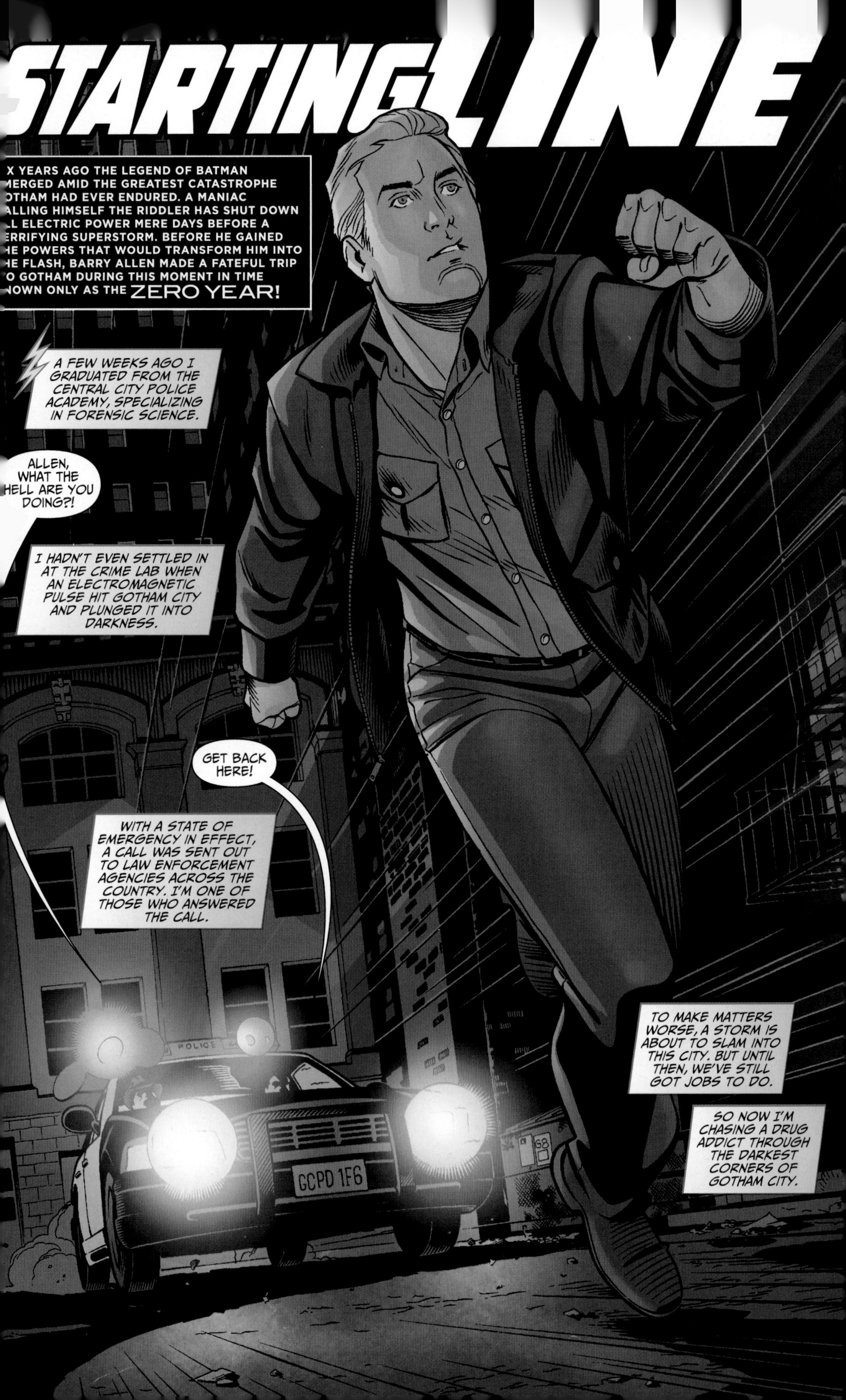
STARTING LINE
X YEARS AGO THE LEGEND OF BATMAN ERGED AMID THE GREATEST CATASTROPHE OTHAM HAD EVER ENDURED. A MANIAC ALLING HIMSELF THE RIDDLER HAS SHUT DOWN L ELECTRIC POWER MERE DAYS BEFORE A ERRIFYING SUPERSTORM. BEFORE HE GAINED HE POWERS THAT WOULD TRANSFORM HIM INTO HE FLASH, BARRY ALLEN MADE A FATEFUL TRIP O GOTHAM DURING THIS MOMENT IN TIME NOWN ONLY AS THE ZERO YEAR!
A FEW WEEKS AGO I GRADUATED FROM THE CENTRAL CITY POLICE ACADEMY, SPECIALIZING IN FORENSIC SCIENCE.
ALLEN, WHAT THE HELL ARE YOU DOING?!
I HADN'T EVEN SETTLED IN AT THE CRIME LAB WHEN AN ELECTROMAGNETIC PULSE HIT GOTHAM CITY AND PLUNGED IT INTO DARKNESS.
GET BACK HERE!
WITH A STATE OF EMERGENCY IN EFFECT, A CALL WAS SENT OUT TO LAW ENFORCEMENT AGENCIES ACROSS THE COUNTRY. I'M ONE OF THOSE WHO ANSWERED THE CALL.
POLICE
GCPD 1F6
TO MAKE MATTERS WORSE, A STORM IS ABOUT TO SLAM INTO THIS CITY. BUT UNTIL THEN, WE'VE STILL GOT JOBS TO DO.
SO NOW I'M CHASING A DRUG ADDICT THROUGH THE DARKEST CORNERS OF GOTHAM CITY.

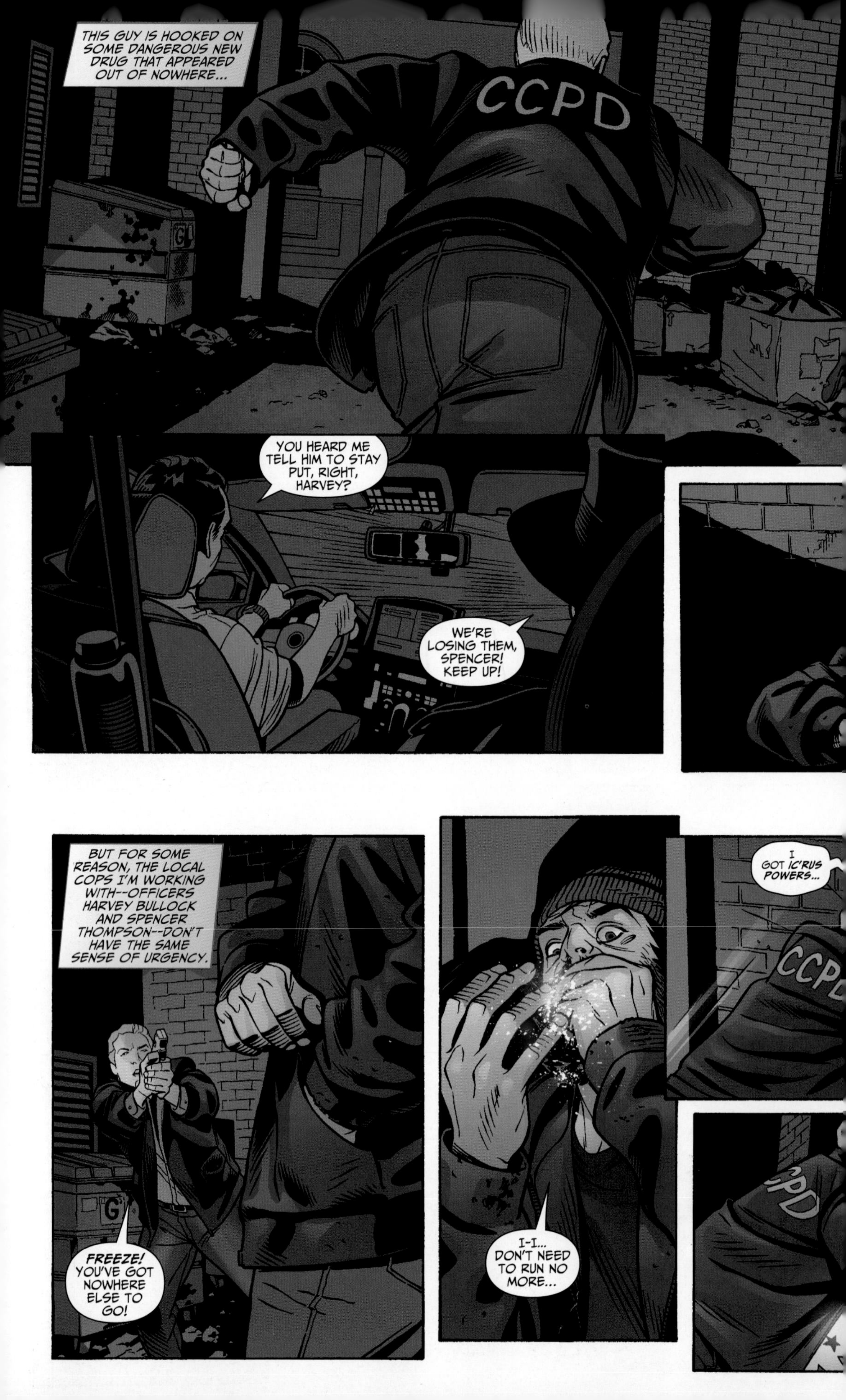
THIS GUY IS HOOKED ON SOME DANGEROUS NEW DRUG THAT APPEARED OUT OF NOWHERE...
CCPD
YOU HEARD ME TELL HIM TO STAY PUT, RIGHT, HARVEY?
WE'RE LOSING THEM, SPENCER! KEEP UP!
BUT FOR SOME REASON, THE LOCAL COPS I'M WORKING WITH--OFFICERS HARVEY BULLOCK AND SPENCER THOMPSON--DON'T HAVE THE SAME SENSE OF URGENCY.
FREEZE! YOU'VE GOT NOWHERE ELSE TO GO!
I-I... DON'T NEED TO RUN NO MORE...
I GOT IC'RUS POWERS...
CCPD
CCPD

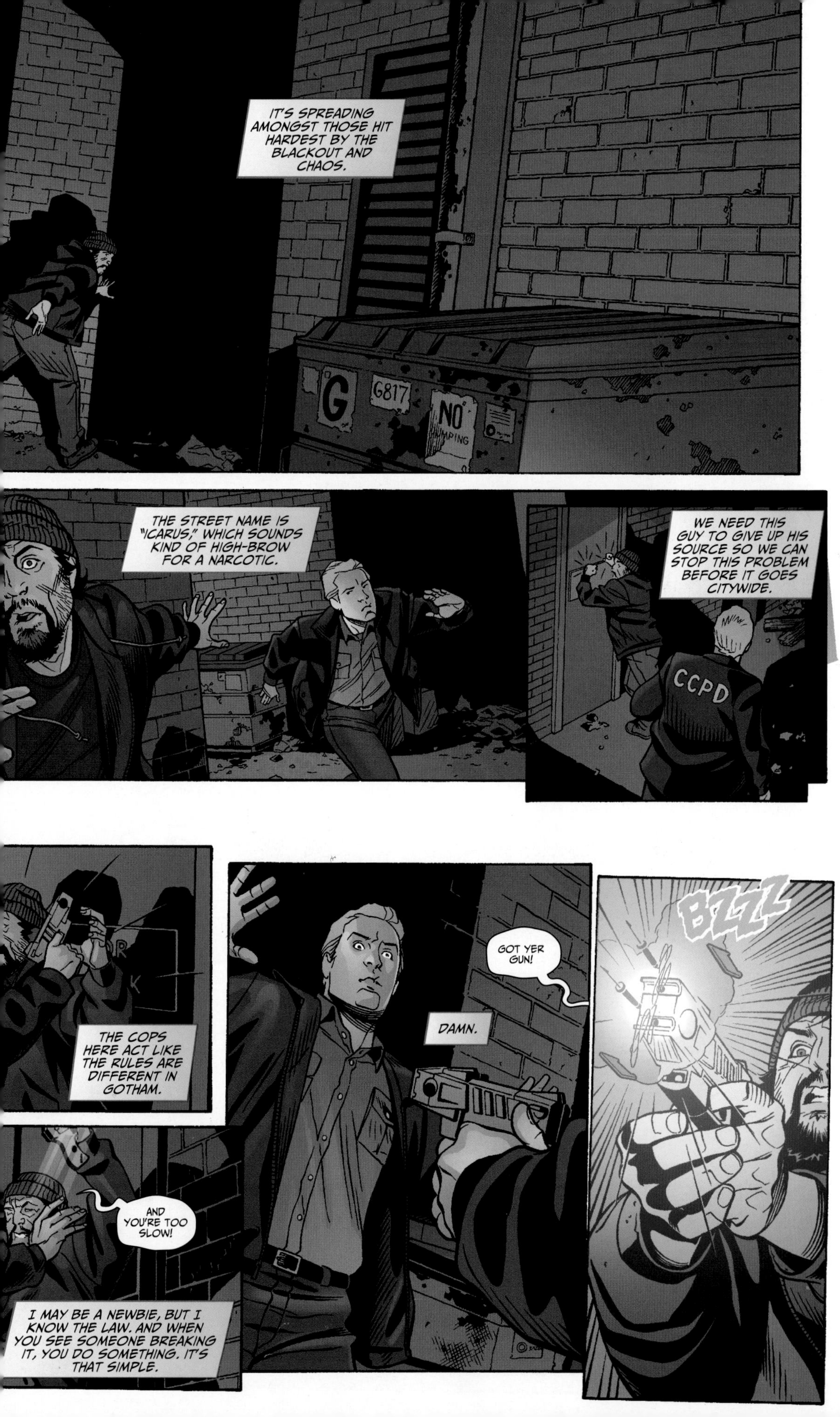
IT'S SPREADING AMONGST THOSE HIT HARDEST BY THE BLACKOUT AND CHAOS.
G
G817
NO
THE STREET NAME IS "ICARUS," WHICH SOUNDS KIND OF HIGH-BROW FOR A NARCOTIC.
WE NEED THIS GUY TO GIVE UP HIS SOURCE SO WE CAN STOP THIS PROBLEM BEFORE IT GOES CITYWIDE.
CCPD
THE COPS HERE ACT LIKE THE RULES ARE DIFFERENT IN GOTHAM.
AND YOU'RE TOO SLOW!
I MAY BE A NEWBIE, BUT I KNOW THE LAW. AND WHEN YOU SEE SOMEONE BREAKING IT, YOU DO SOMETHING. IT'S THAT SIMPLE.
GOT YER GUN!
DAMN.
BZZZ

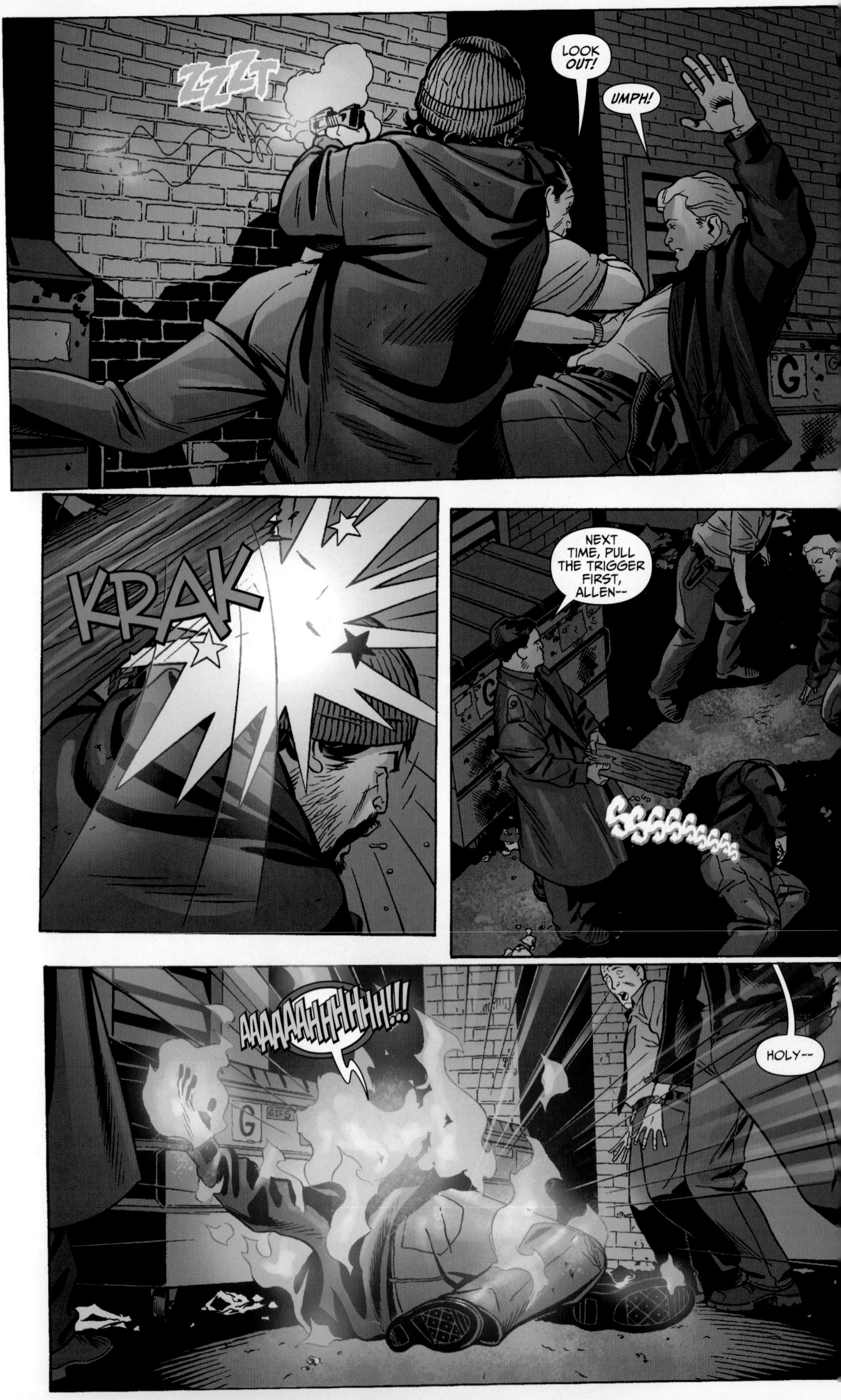
ZZZT
LOOK OUT!
UMPH!
KRAK
NEXT TIME, PULL THE TRIGGER FIRST, ALLEN--
SSSSSSSSSS
AAAAAAHHHHHH!!!
HOLY--

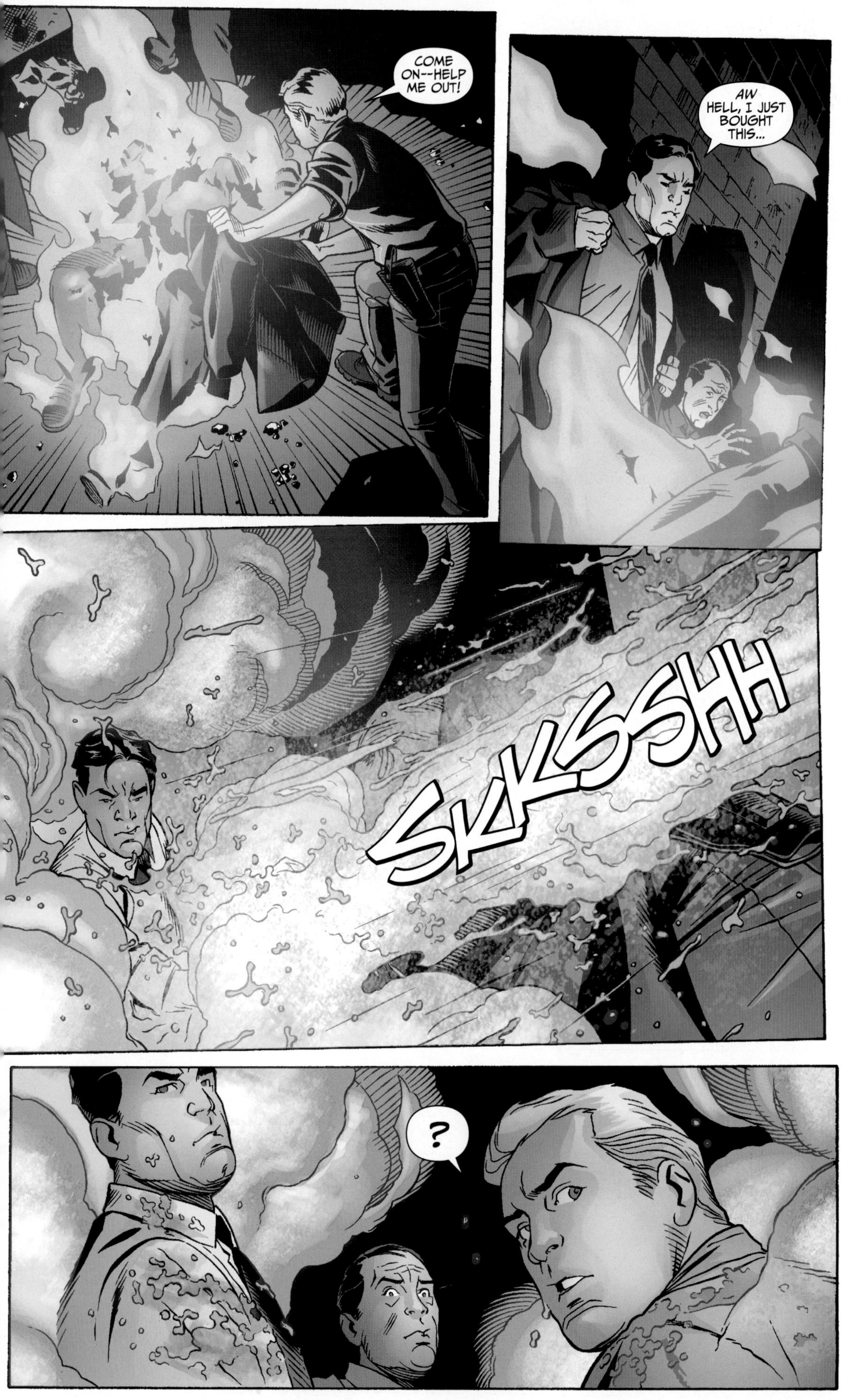

COME ON--HELP ME OUT!
AW HELL, I JUST BOUGHT THIS...
SKKSSHH
?

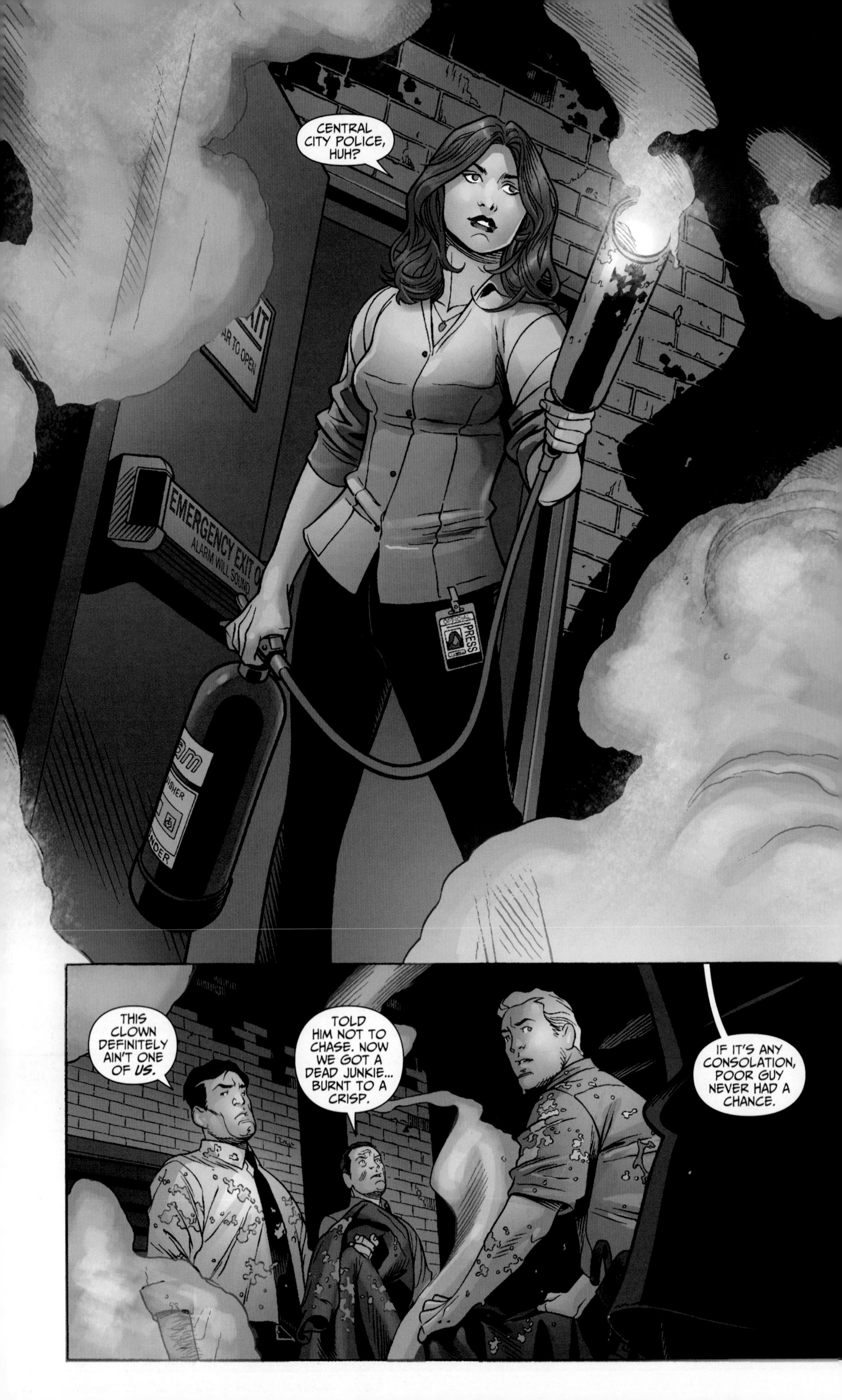
CENTRAL CITY POLICE, HUH?
EXIT
BAR TO OPEN
EMERGENCY EXIT ONLY
ALARM WILL SOUND
OFFICIAL PRESS
THIS CLOWN DEFINITELY AIN'T ONE OF US.
TOLD HIM NOT TO CHASE. NOW WE GOT A DEAD JUNKIE... BURNT TO A CRISP.
IF IT'S ANY CONSOLATION, POOR GUY NEVER HAD A CHANCE.

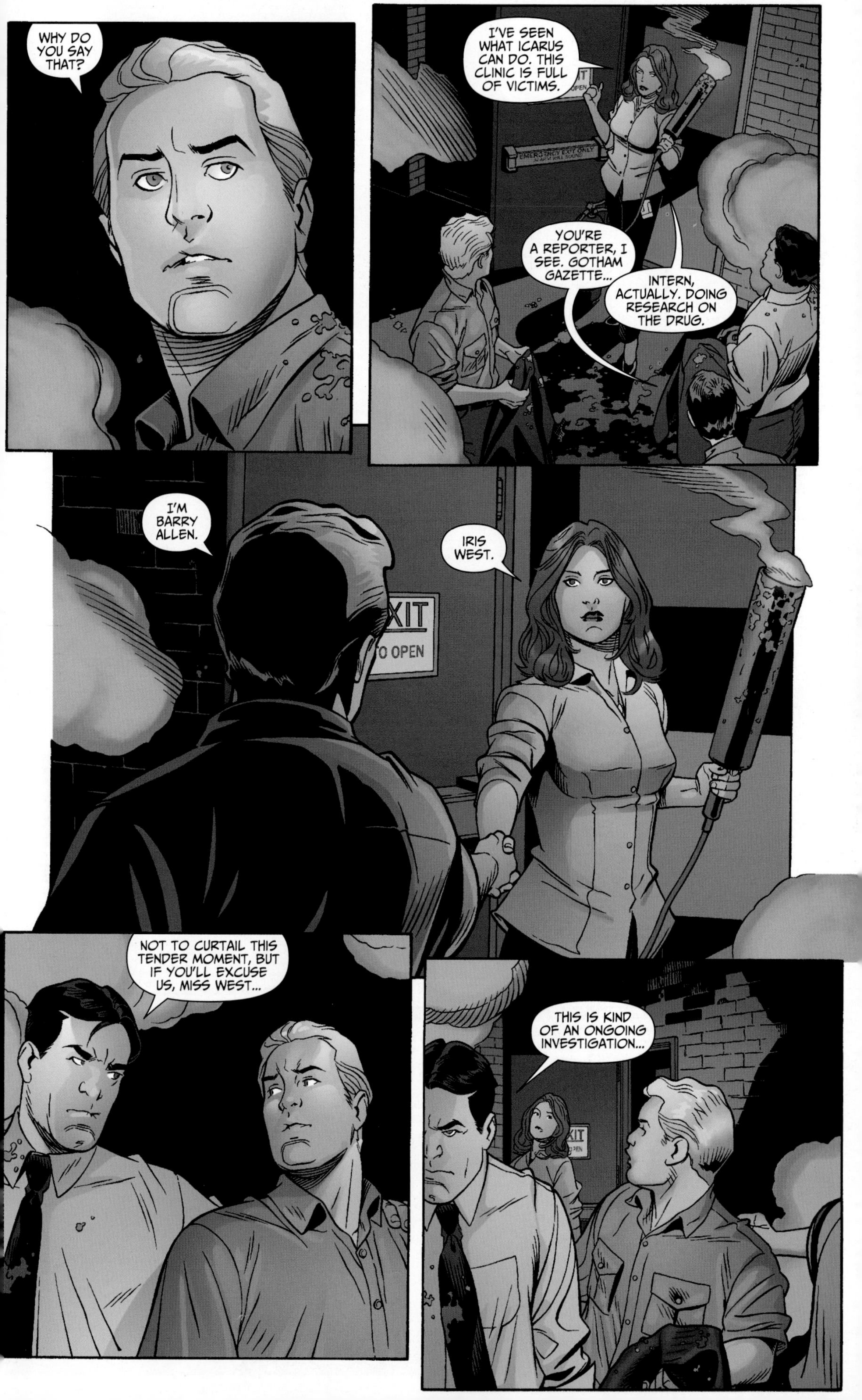
WHY DO YOU SAY THAT?
I'VE SEEN WHAT ICARUS CAN DO. THIS CLINIC IS FULL OF VICTIMS.
EMERGENCY EXIT ONLY
YOU'RE A REPORTER, I SEE. GOTHAM GAZETTE...
INTERN, ACTUALLY. DOING RESEARCH ON THE DRUG.
I'M BARRY ALLEN.
IRIS WEST.
XIT
TO OPEN
NOT TO CURTAIL THIS TENDER MOMENT, BUT IF YOU'LL EXCUSE US, MISS WEST...
THIS IS KIND OF AN ONGOING INVESTIGATION...

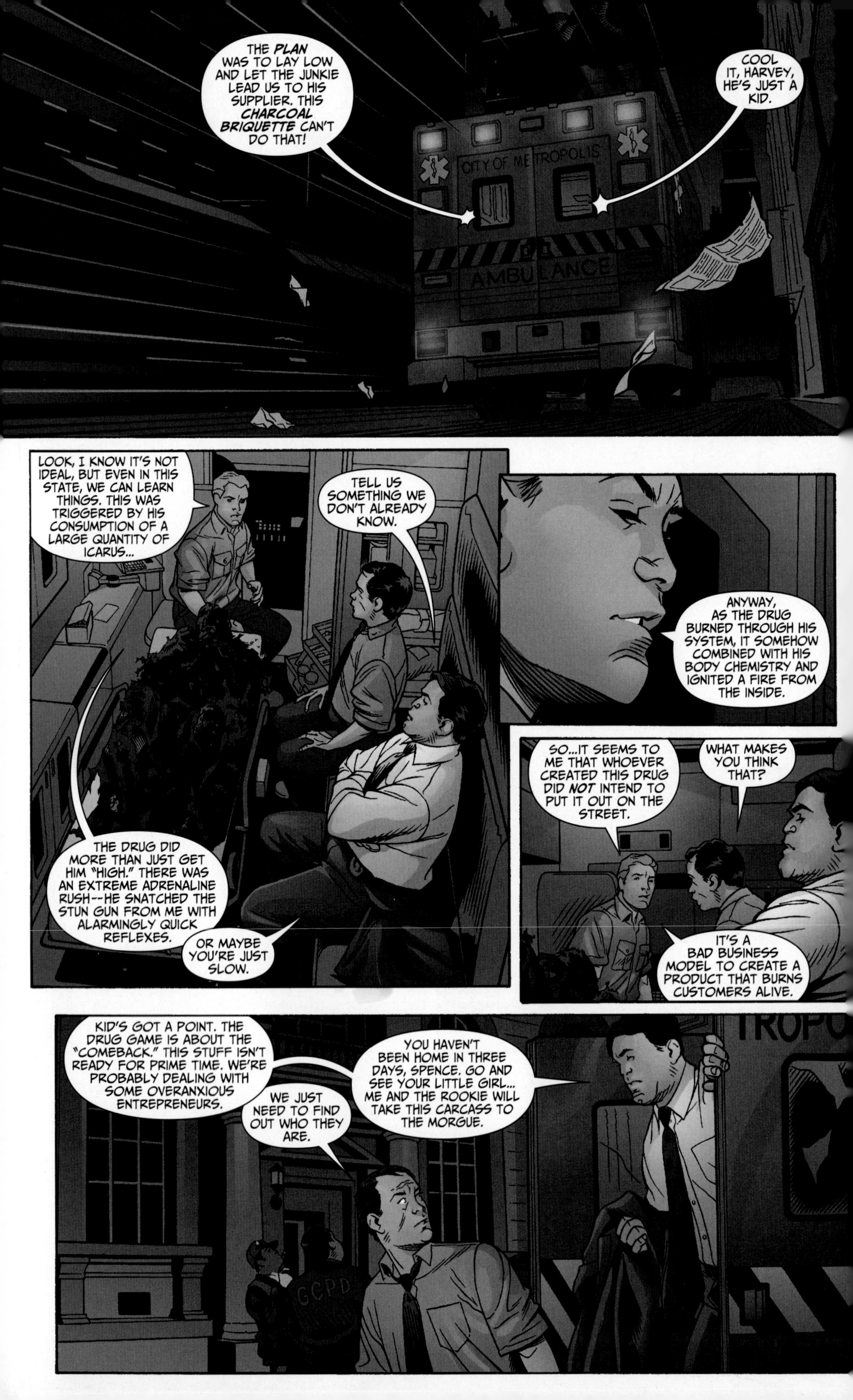
THE *PLAN* WAS TO LAY LOW AND LET THE JUNKIE LEAD US TO HIS SUPPLIER. THIS *CHARCOAL BRIQUETTE* CAN'T DO THAT!
COOL IT, HARVEY, HE'S JUST A KID.
CITY OF METROPOLIS
AMBULANCE
LOOK, I KNOW IT'S NOT IDEAL, BUT EVEN IN THIS STATE, WE CAN LEARN THINGS. THIS WAS TRIGGERED BY HIS CONSUMPTION OF A LARGE QUANTITY OF ICARUS...
TELL US SOMETHING WE DON'T ALREADY KNOW.
THE DRUG DID MORE THAN JUST GET HIM "HIGH." THERE WAS AN EXTREME ADRENALINE RUSH--HE SNATCHED THE STUN GUN FROM ME WITH ALARMINGLY QUICK REFLEXES.
OR MAYBE YOU'RE JUST SLOW.
ANYWAY, AS THE DRUG BURNED THROUGH HIS SYSTEM, IT SOMEHOW COMBINED WITH HIS BODY CHEMISTRY AND IGNITED A FIRE FROM THE INSIDE.
SO...IT SEEMS TO ME THAT WHOEVER CREATED THIS DRUG DID *NOT* INTEND TO PUT IT OUT ON THE STREET.
WHAT MAKES YOU THINK THAT?
IT'S A BAD BUSINESS MODEL TO CREATE A PRODUCT THAT BURNS CUSTOMERS ALIVE.
KID'S GOT A POINT. THE DRUG GAME IS ABOUT THE "COMEBACK." THIS STUFF ISN'T READY FOR PRIME TIME. WE'RE PROBABLY DEALING WITH SOME OVERANXIOUS ENTREPRENEURS.
WE JUST NEED TO FIND OUT WHO THEY ARE.
YOU HAVEN'T BEEN HOME IN THREE DAYS, SPENCE. GO AND SEE YOUR LITTLE GIRL... ME AND THE ROOKIE WILL TAKE THIS CARCASS TO THE MORGUE.
GCPD

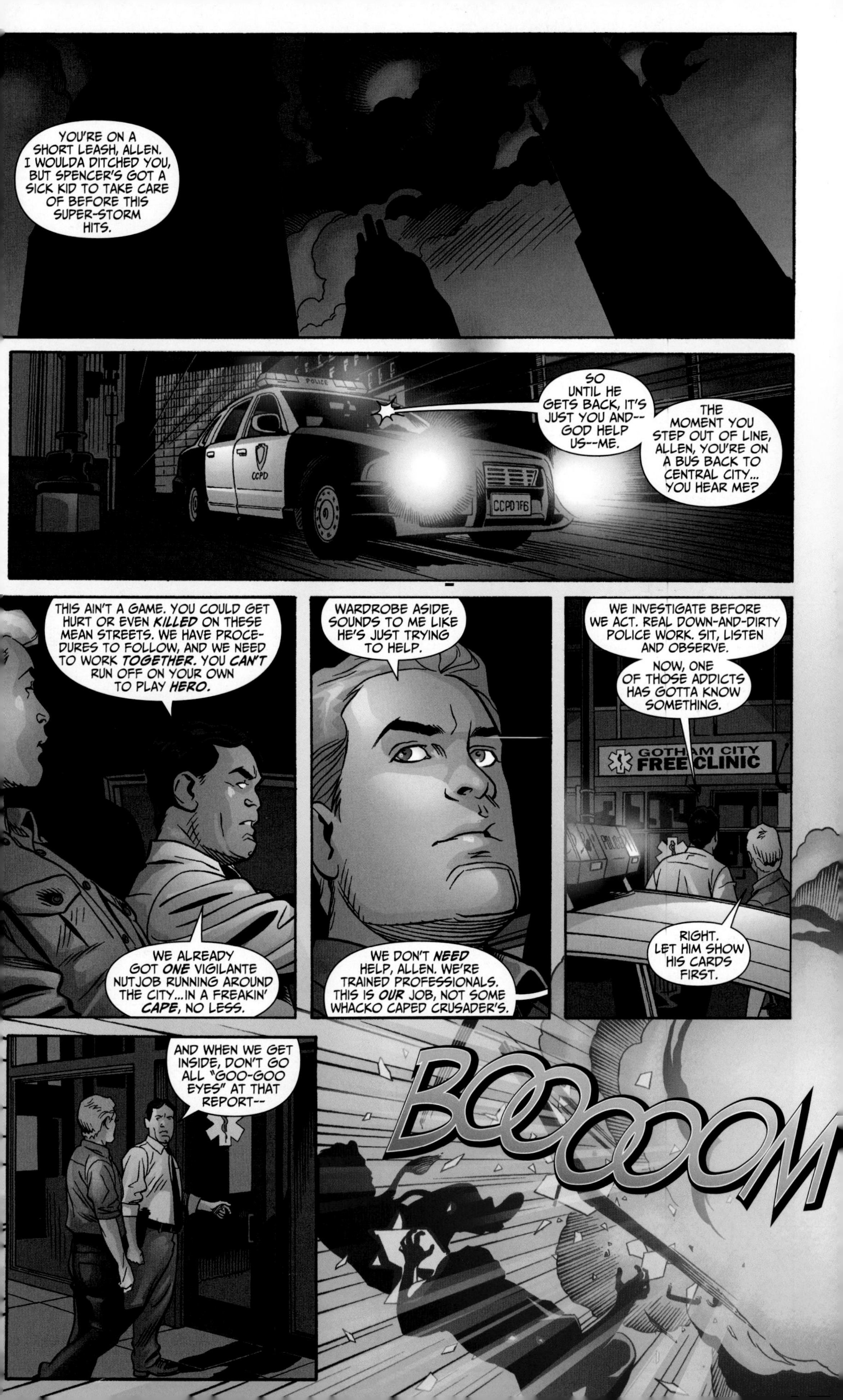

YOU'RE ON A SHORT LEASH, ALLEN. I WOULDA DITCHED YOU, BUT SPENCER'S GOT A SICK KID TO TAKE CARE OF BEFORE THIS SUPER-STORM HITS.
POLICE
CCPD
CCPD 7F6
SO UNTIL HE GETS BACK, IT'S JUST YOU AND--GOD HELP US--ME.
THE MOMENT YOU STEP OUT OF LINE, ALLEN, YOU'RE ON A BUS BACK TO CENTRAL CITY... YOU HEAR ME?
THIS AIN'T A GAME. YOU COULD GET HURT OR EVEN *KILLED* ON THESE MEAN STREETS. WE HAVE PROCEDURES TO FOLLOW, AND WE NEED TO WORK *TOGETHER*. YOU *CAN'T* RUN OFF ON YOUR OWN TO PLAY *HERO*.
WE ALREADY GOT *ONE* VIGILANTE NUTJOB RUNNING AROUND THE CITY...IN A FREAKIN' *CAPE*, NO LESS.
WARDROBE ASIDE, SOUNDS TO ME LIKE HE'S JUST TRYING TO HELP.
WE DON'T *NEED* HELP, ALLEN. WE'RE TRAINED PROFESSIONALS. THIS IS *OUR* JOB, NOT SOME WHACKO CAPED CRUSADER'S.
WE INVESTIGATE BEFORE WE ACT. REAL DOWN-AND-DIRTY POLICE WORK. SIT, LISTEN AND OBSERVE.
NOW, ONE OF THOSE ADDICTS HAS GOTTA KNOW SOMETHING.
GOTHAM CITY FREE CLINIC
RIGHT. LET HIM SHOW HIS CARDS FIRST.
AND WHEN WE GET INSIDE, DON'T GO ALL "GOO-GOO EYES" AT THAT REPORT--
BOOOOOM

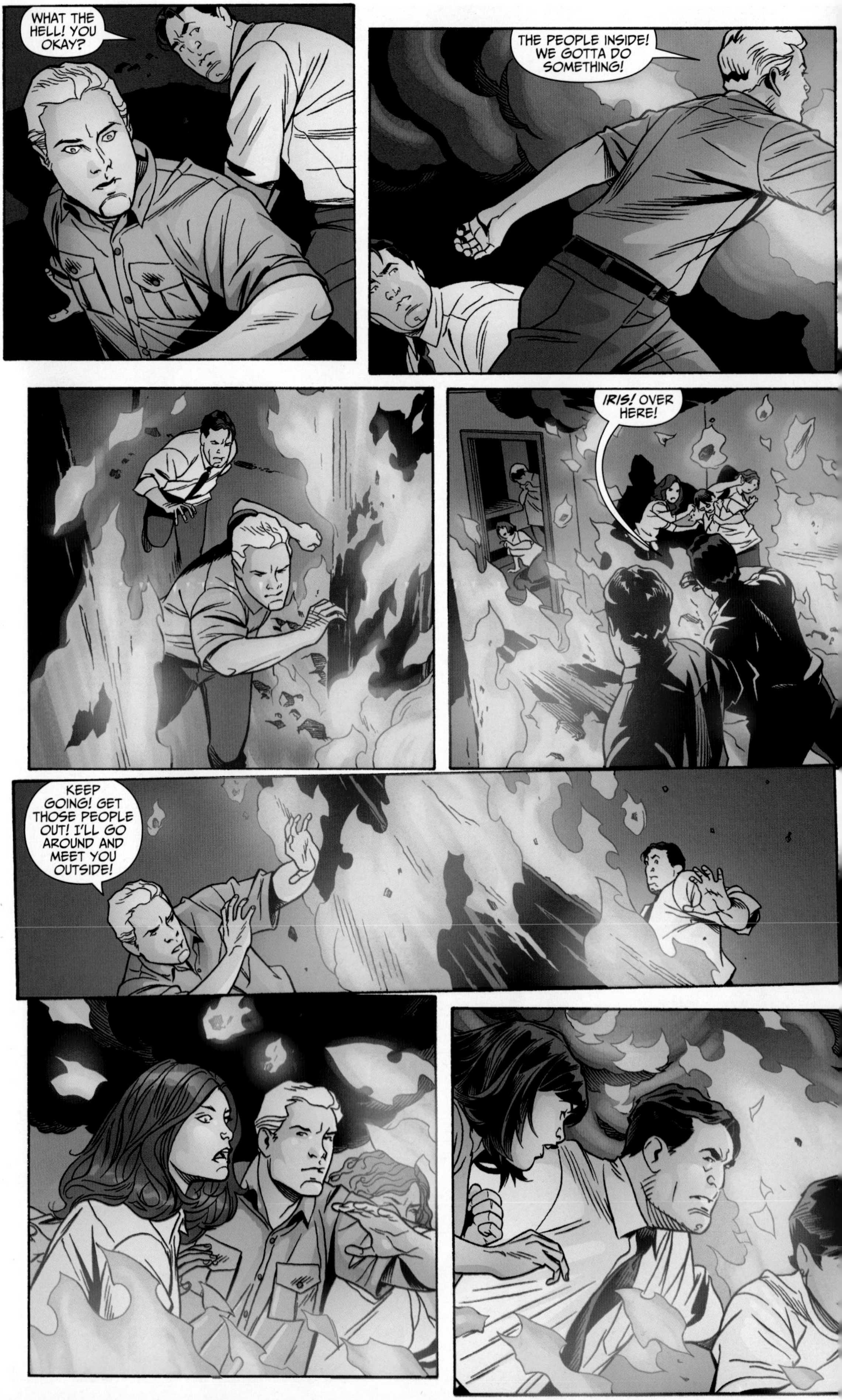
WHAT THE HELL! YOU OKAY?
THE PEOPLE INSIDE! WE GOTTA DO SOMETHING!
IRIS! OVER HERE!
KEEP GOING! GET THOSE PEOPLE OUT! I'LL GO AROUND AND MEET YOU OUTSIDE!

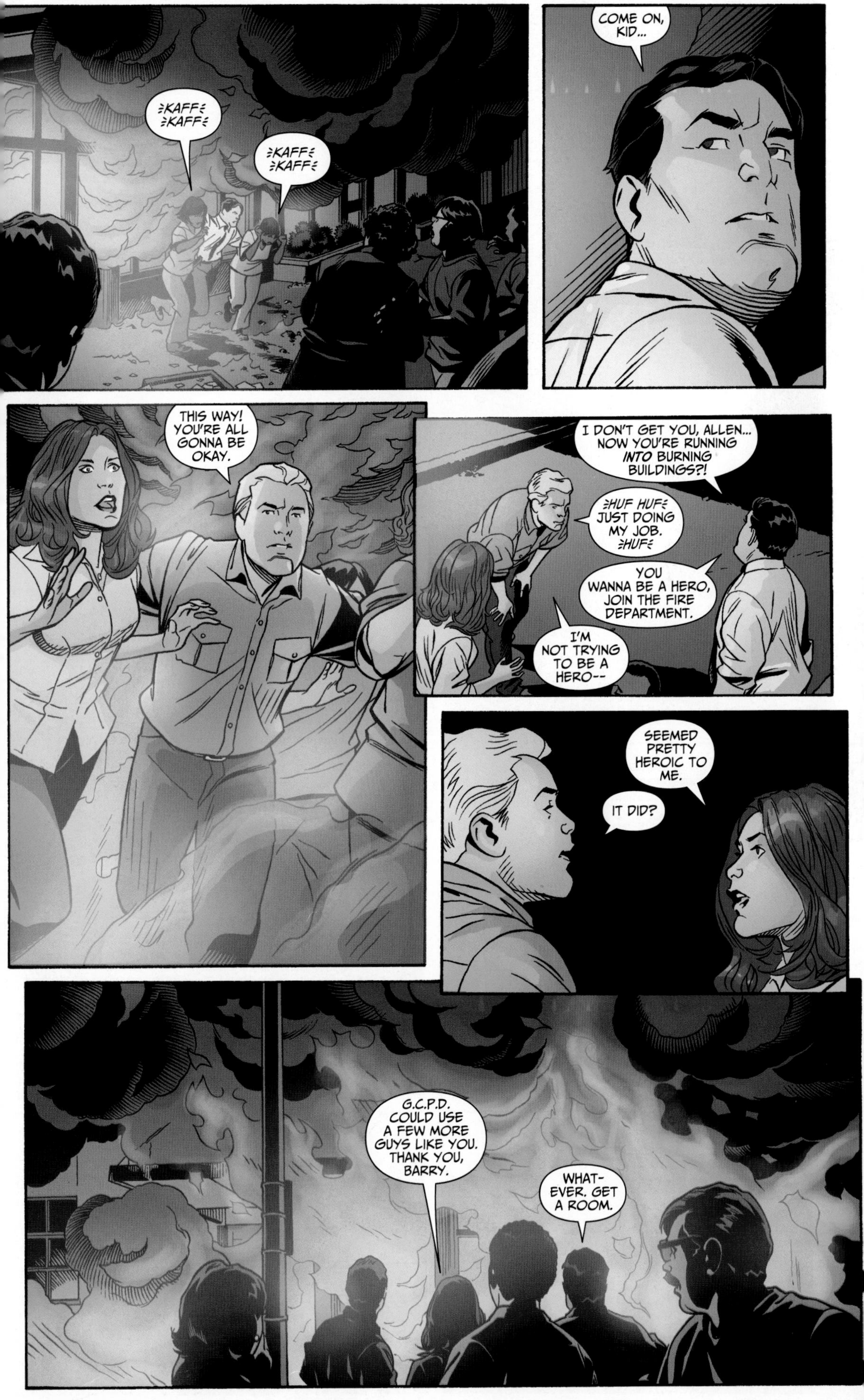

KAFF KAFF
KAFF KAFF
COME ON, KID...
THIS WAY! YOU'RE ALL GONNA BE OKAY.
I DON'T GET YOU, ALLEN... NOW YOU'RE RUNNING INTO BURNING BUILDINGS?!
HUF HUF JUST DOING MY JOB. HUF
YOU WANNA BE A HERO, JOIN THE FIRE DEPARTMENT.
I'M NOT TRYING TO BE A HERO--
SEEMED PRETTY HEROIC TO ME.
IT DID?
G.C.P.D. COULD USE A FEW MORE GUYS LIKE YOU. THANK YOU, BARRY.
WHAT-EVER. GET A ROOM.

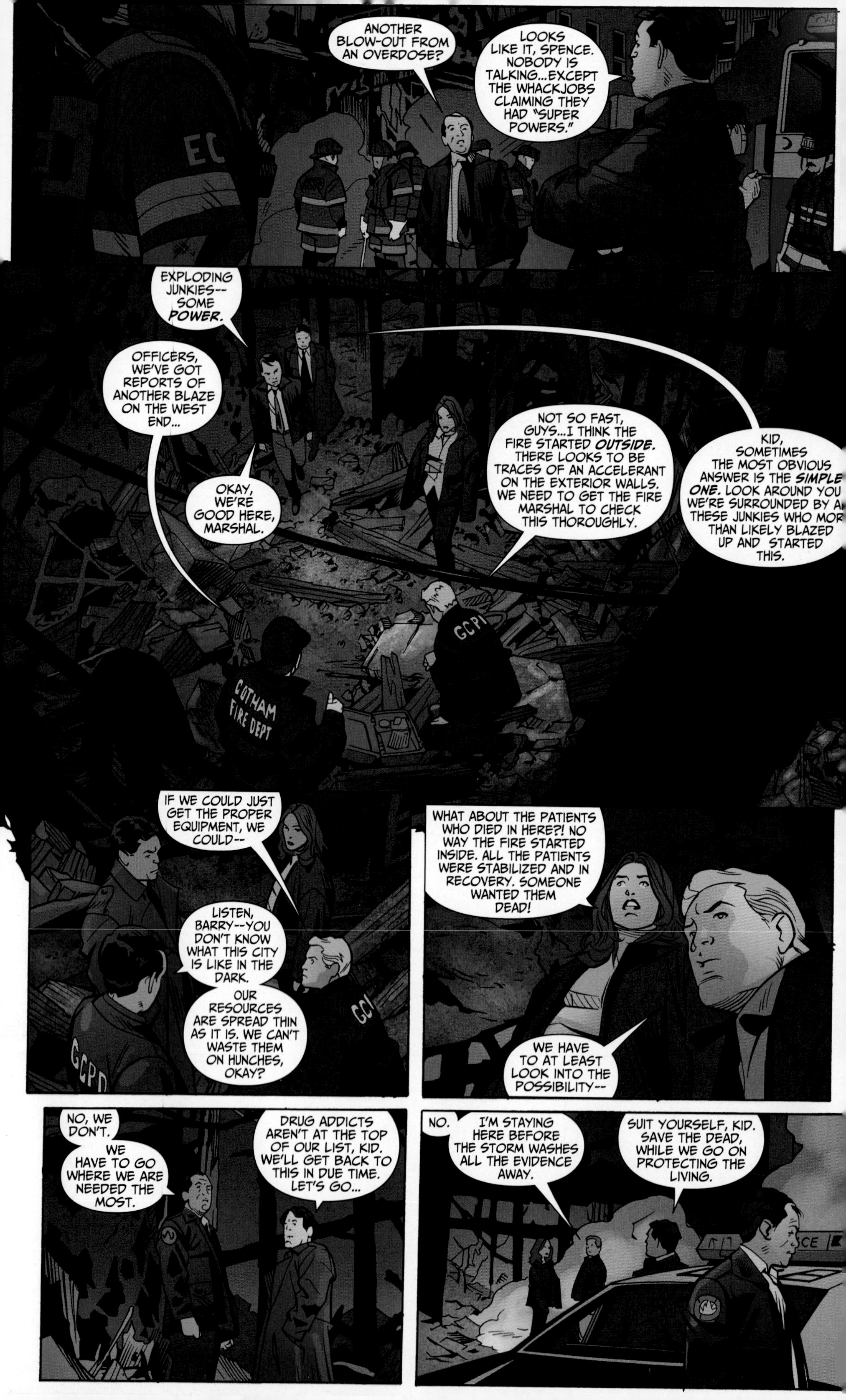
ANOTHER BLOW-OUT FROM AN OVERDOSE?
LOOKS LIKE IT, SPENCE. NOBODY IS TALKING...EXCEPT THE WHACKJOBS CLAIMING THEY HAD "SUPER POWERS."
EXPLODING JUNKIES--SOME *POWER.*
OFFICERS, WE'VE GOT REPORTS OF ANOTHER BLAZE ON THE WEST END...
OKAY, WE'RE GOOD HERE, MARSHAL.
NOT SO FAST, GUYS...I THINK THE FIRE STARTED *OUTSIDE.* THERE LOOKS TO BE TRACES OF AN ACCELERANT ON THE EXTERIOR WALLS. WE NEED TO GET THE FIRE MARSHAL TO CHECK THIS THOROUGHLY.
KID, SOMETIMES THE MOST OBVIOUS ANSWER IS THE *SIMPLE ONE.* LOOK AROUND YOU WE'RE SURROUNDED BY A THESE JUNKIES WHO MOR THAN LIKELY BLAZED UP AND STARTED THIS.
COTHAM FIRE DEPT
GCPD
IF WE COULD JUST GET THE PROPER EQUIPMENT, WE COULD--
LISTEN, BARRY--YOU DON'T KNOW WHAT THIS CITY IS LIKE IN THE DARK.
OUR RESOURCES ARE SPREAD THIN AS IT IS. WE CAN'T WASTE THEM ON HUNCHES, OKAY?
WHAT ABOUT THE PATIENTS WHO DIED IN HERE?! NO WAY THE FIRE STARTED INSIDE. ALL THE PATIENTS WERE STABILIZED AND IN RECOVERY. SOMEONE WANTED THEM DEAD!
WE HAVE TO AT LEAST LOOK INTO THE POSSIBILITY--
NO, WE DON'T.
WE HAVE TO GO WHERE WE ARE NEEDED THE MOST.
DRUG ADDICTS AREN'T AT THE TOP OF OUR LIST, KID. WE'LL GET BACK TO THIS IN DUE TIME. LET'S GO...
NO.
I'M STAYING HERE BEFORE THE STORM WASHES ALL THE EVIDENCE AWAY.
SUIT YOURSELF, KID. SAVE THE DEAD, WHILE WE GO ON PROTECTING THE LIVING.

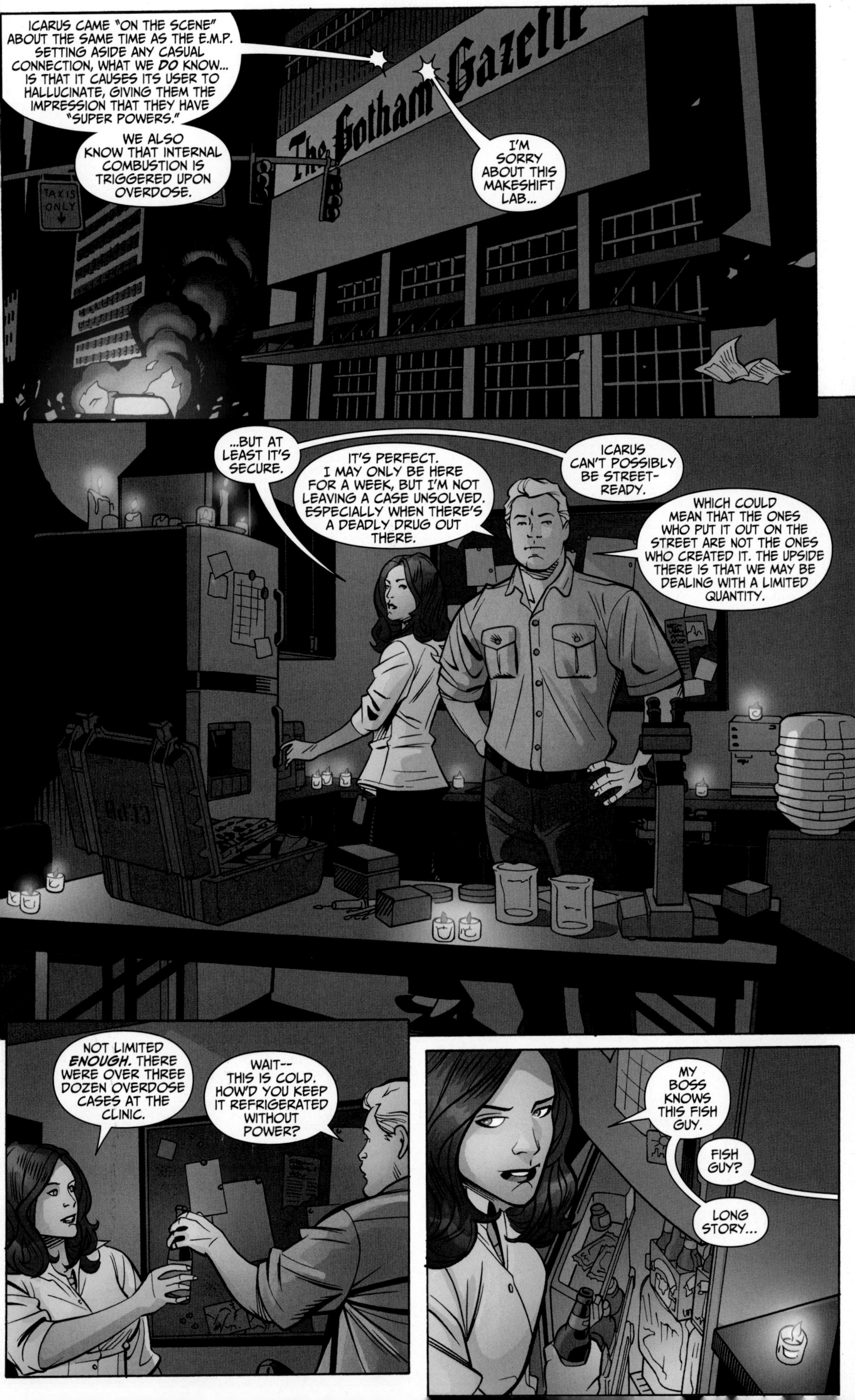

ICARUS CAME "ON THE SCENE" ABOUT THE SAME TIME AS THE E.M.P. SETTING ASIDE ANY CASUAL CONNECTION, WHAT WE *DO* KNOW... IS THAT IT CAUSES ITS USER TO HALLUCINATE, GIVING THEM THE IMPRESSION THAT THEY HAVE "SUPER POWERS."
WE ALSO KNOW THAT INTERNAL COMBUSTION IS TRIGGERED UPON OVERDOSE.
The Gotham Gazette
TAXIS ONLY
I'M SORRY ABOUT THIS MAKESHIFT LAB...
...BUT AT LEAST IT'S SECURE.
IT'S PERFECT. I MAY ONLY BE HERE FOR A WEEK, BUT I'M NOT LEAVING A CASE UNSOLVED. ESPECIALLY WHEN THERE'S A DEADLY DRUG OUT THERE.
ICARUS CAN'T POSSIBLY BE STREET-READY.
WHICH COULD MEAN THAT THE ONES WHO PUT IT OUT ON THE STREET ARE NOT THE ONES WHO CREATED IT. THE UPSIDE THERE IS THAT WE MAY BE DEALING WITH A LIMITED QUANTITY.
NOT LIMITED *ENOUGH.* THERE WERE OVER THREE DOZEN OVERDOSE CASES AT THE CLINIC.
WAIT-- THIS IS COLD. HOW'D YOU KEEP IT REFRIGERATED WITHOUT POWER?
MY BOSS KNOWS THIS FISH GUY.
FISH GUY?
LONG STORY...

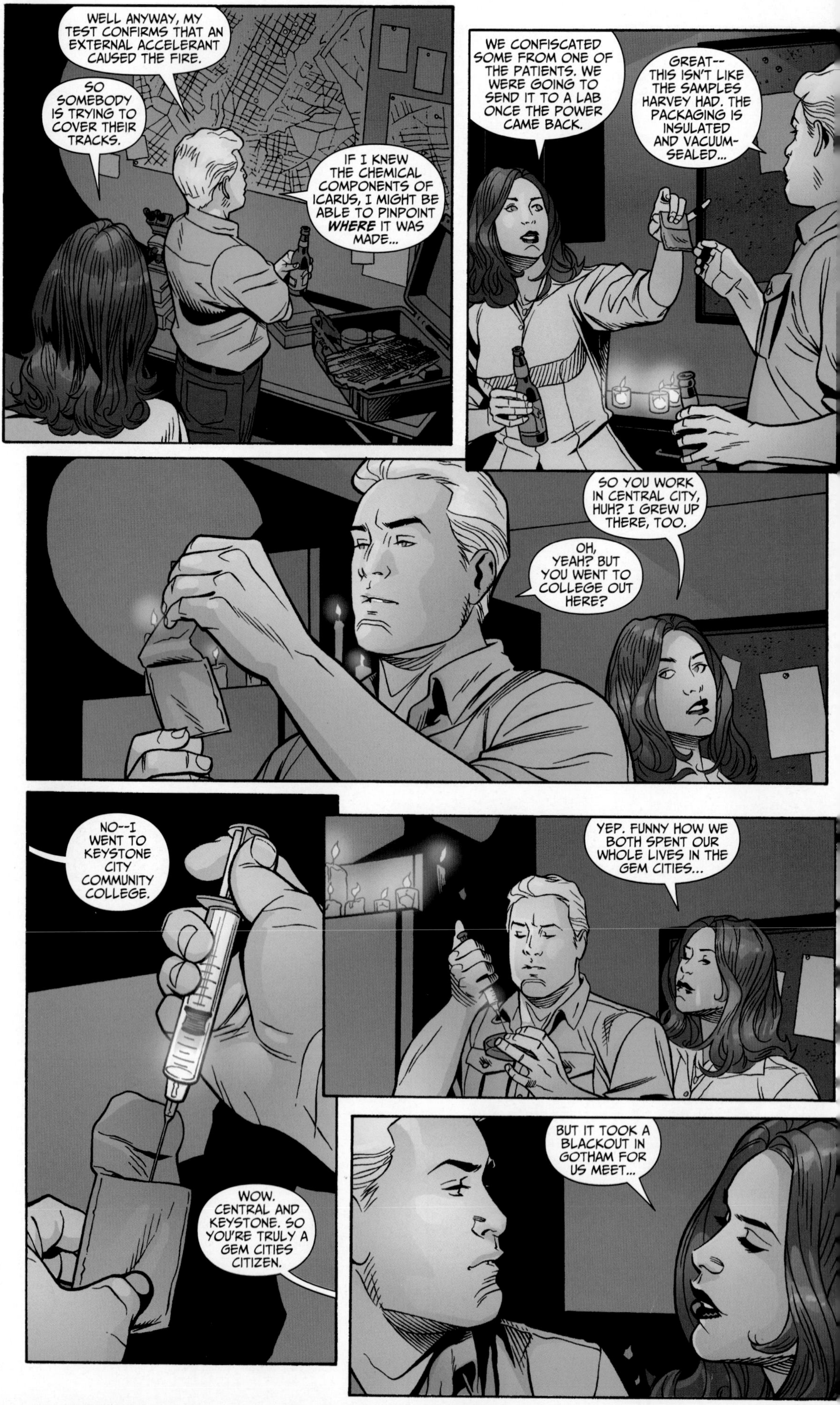

WELL ANYWAY, MY TEST CONFIRMS THAT AN EXTERNAL ACCELERANT CAUSED THE FIRE.
SO SOMEBODY IS TRYING TO COVER THEIR TRACKS.
IF I KNEW THE CHEMICAL COMPONENTS OF ICARUS, I MIGHT BE ABLE TO PINPOINT *WHERE* IT WAS MADE...
WE CONFISCATED SOME FROM ONE OF THE PATIENTS. WE WERE GOING TO SEND IT TO A LAB ONCE THE POWER CAME BACK.
GREAT-- THIS ISN'T LIKE THE SAMPLES HARVEY HAD. THE PACKAGING IS INSULATED AND VACUUM-SEALED...
SO YOU WORK IN CENTRAL CITY, HUH? I GREW UP THERE, TOO.
OH, YEAH? BUT YOU WENT TO COLLEGE OUT HERE?
NO--I WENT TO KEYSTONE CITY COMMUNITY COLLEGE.
WOW. CENTRAL AND KEYSTONE. SO YOU'RE TRULY A GEM CITIES CITIZEN.
YEP. FUNNY HOW WE BOTH SPENT OUR WHOLE LIVES IN THE GEM CITIES...
BUT IT TOOK A BLACKOUT IN GOTHAM FOR US MEET...

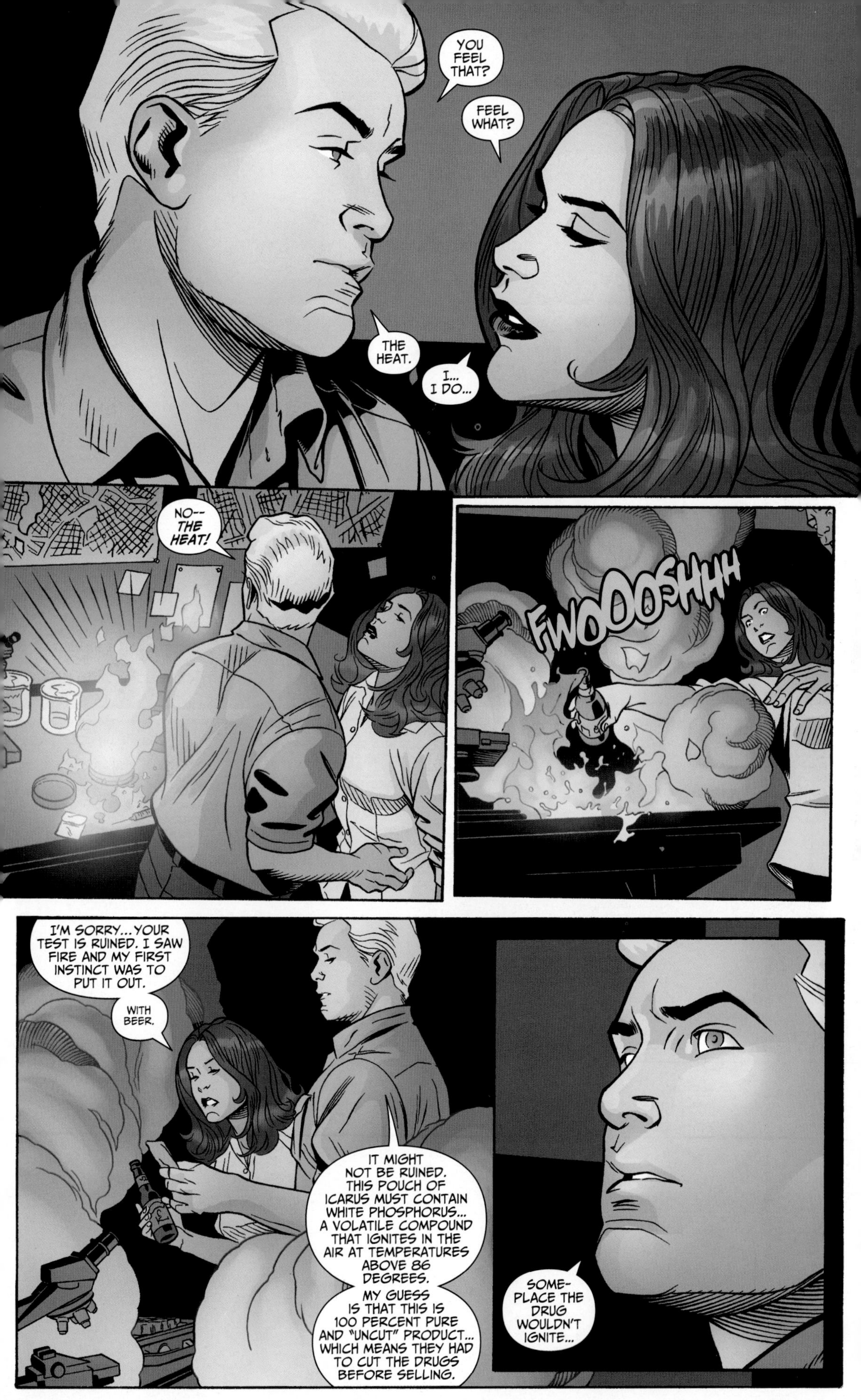

YOU FEEL THAT?
FEEL WHAT?
THE HEAT.
I... I DO...
NO-- THE HEAT!
FWOOOOSHHH
I'M SORRY...YOUR TEST IS RUINED. I SAW FIRE AND MY FIRST INSTINCT WAS TO PUT IT OUT.
WITH BEER.
IT MIGHT NOT BE RUINED. THIS POUCH OF ICARUS MUST CONTAIN WHITE PHOSPHORUS... A VOLATILE COMPOUND THAT IGNITES IN THE AIR AT TEMPERATURES ABOVE 86 DEGREES.
MY GUESS IS THAT THIS IS 100 PERCENT PURE AND "UNCUT" PRODUCT... WHICH MEANS THEY HAD TO CUT THE DRUGS BEFORE SELLING.
SOME-PLACE THE DRUG WOULDN'T IGNITE...

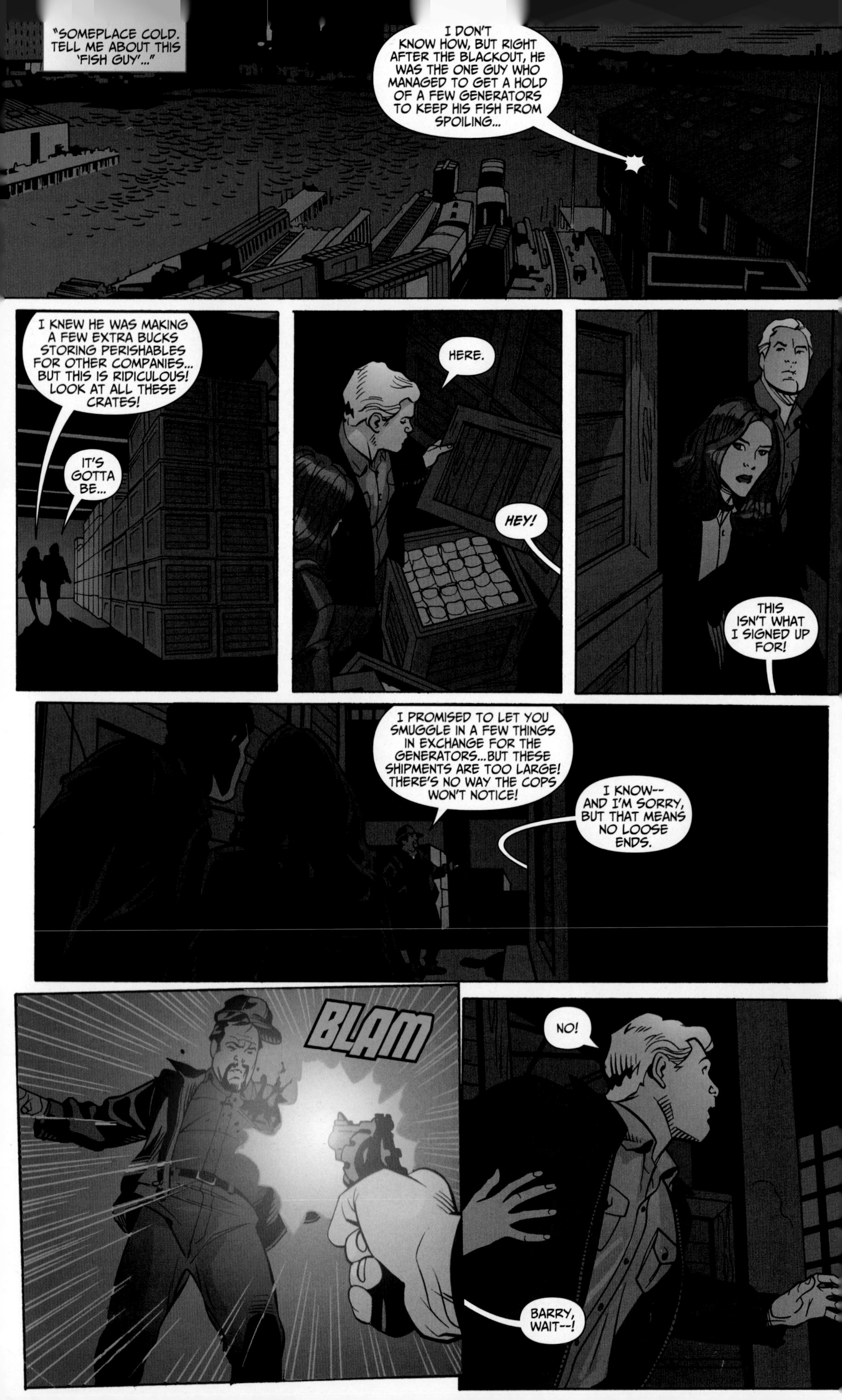
"SOMEPLACE COLD. TELL ME ABOUT THIS 'FISH GUY'..."
I DON'T KNOW HOW, BUT RIGHT AFTER THE BLACKOUT, HE WAS THE ONE GUY WHO MANAGED TO GET A HOLD OF A FEW GENERATORS TO KEEP HIS FISH FROM SPOILING...
I KNEW HE WAS MAKING A FEW EXTRA BUCKS STORING PERISHABLES FOR OTHER COMPANIES... BUT THIS IS RIDICULOUS! LOOK AT ALL THESE CRATES!
IT'S GOTTA BE...
HERE.
HEY!
THIS ISN'T WHAT I SIGNED UP FOR!
I PROMISED TO LET YOU SMUGGLE IN A FEW THINGS IN EXCHANGE FOR THE GENERATORS...BUT THESE SHIPMENTS ARE TOO LARGE! THERE'S NO WAY THE COPS WON'T NOTICE!
I KNOW-- AND I'M SORRY, BUT THAT MEANS NO LOOSE ENDS.
BLAM
NO!
BARRY, WAIT--!

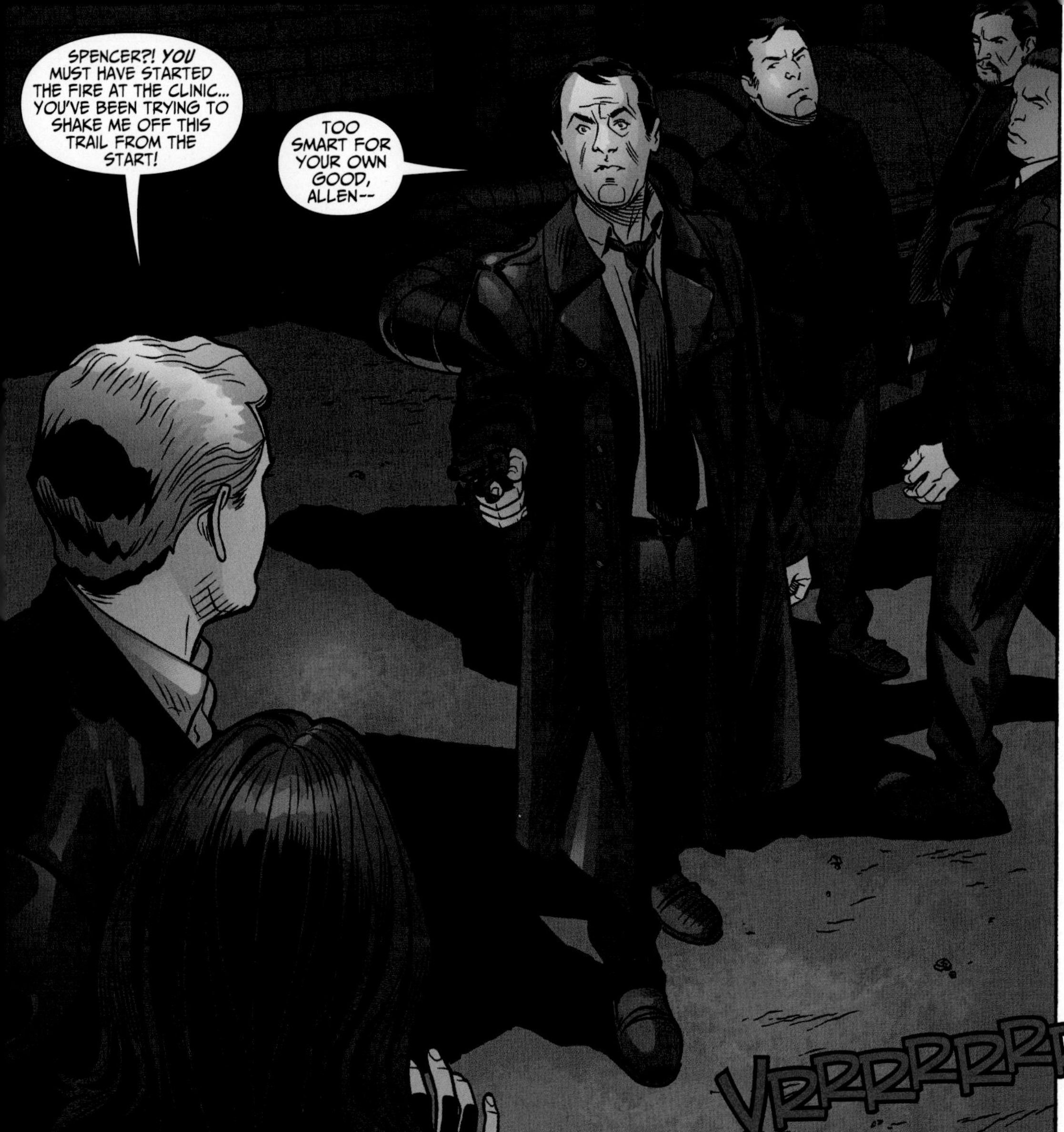
SPENCER?! YOU MUST HAVE STARTED THE FIRE AT THE CLINIC... YOU'VE BEEN TRYING TO SHAKE ME OFF THIS TRAIL FROM THE START!
TOO SMART FOR YOUR OWN GOOD, ALLEN--
VRRRRRRR

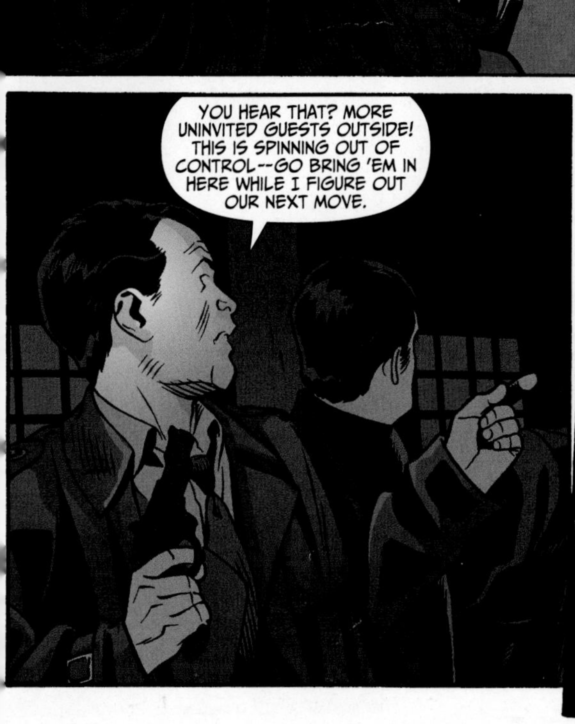
YOU HEAR THAT? MORE UNINVITED GUESTS OUTSIDE! THIS IS SPINNING OUT OF CONTROL--GO BRING 'EM IN HERE WHILE I FIGURE OUT OUR NEXT MOVE.

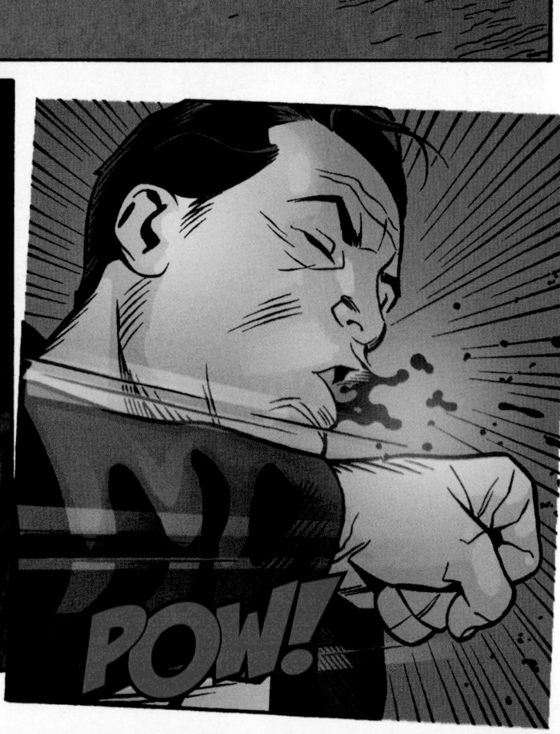
POW!

WHAT THE HELL KIND OF TROUBLE HAVE YOU DRAGGED ME INTO, ALLEN?

YA LOST, OFFICER? DONUT SHOP'S A HALF MILE BACK. HOW 'BOUT YOU GO GET A DOZEN, AND WE WON'T HAVE TO POUND YA INTO JELLY.

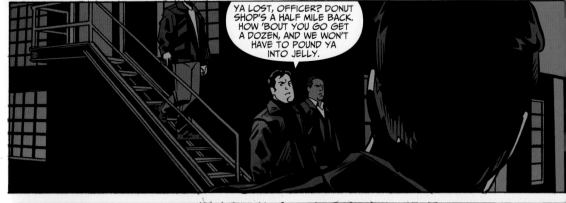

I'LL PASS. I'M MORE OF A SAVORY KINDA GUY...

GOOD. 'CAUSE I HATE COPS.

BAM

BAM

BAM

CRAP...

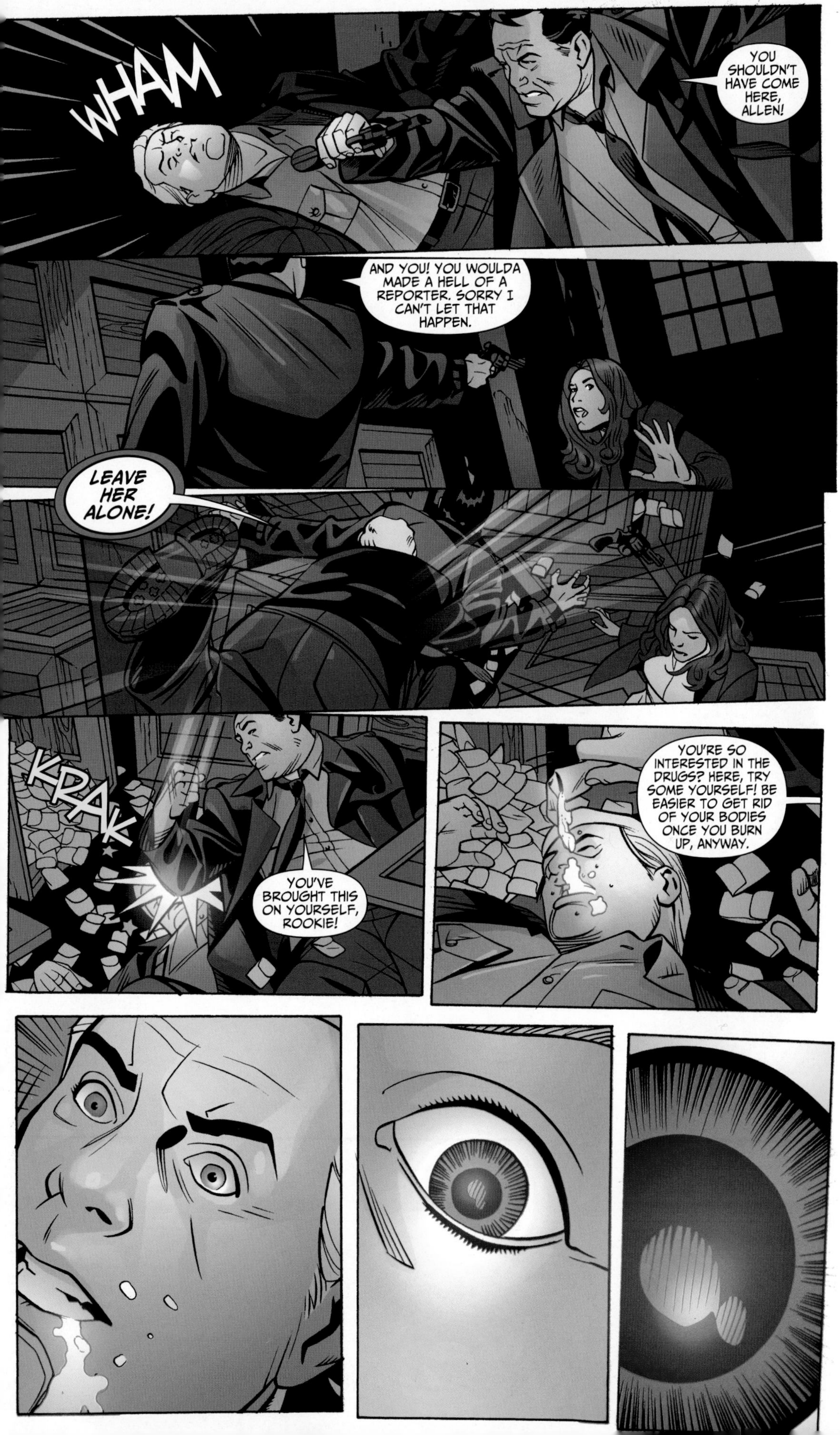
WHAM
YOU SHOULDN'T HAVE COME HERE, ALLEN!
AND YOU! YOU WOULDA MADE A HELL OF A REPORTER. SORRY I CAN'T LET THAT HAPPEN.
LEAVE HER ALONE!
KRAK
YOU'VE BROUGHT THIS ON YOURSELF, ROOKIE!
YOU'RE SO INTERESTED IN THE DRUGS? HERE, TRY SOME YOURSELF! BE EASIER TO GET RID OF YOUR BODIES ONCE YOU BURN UP, ANYWAY.

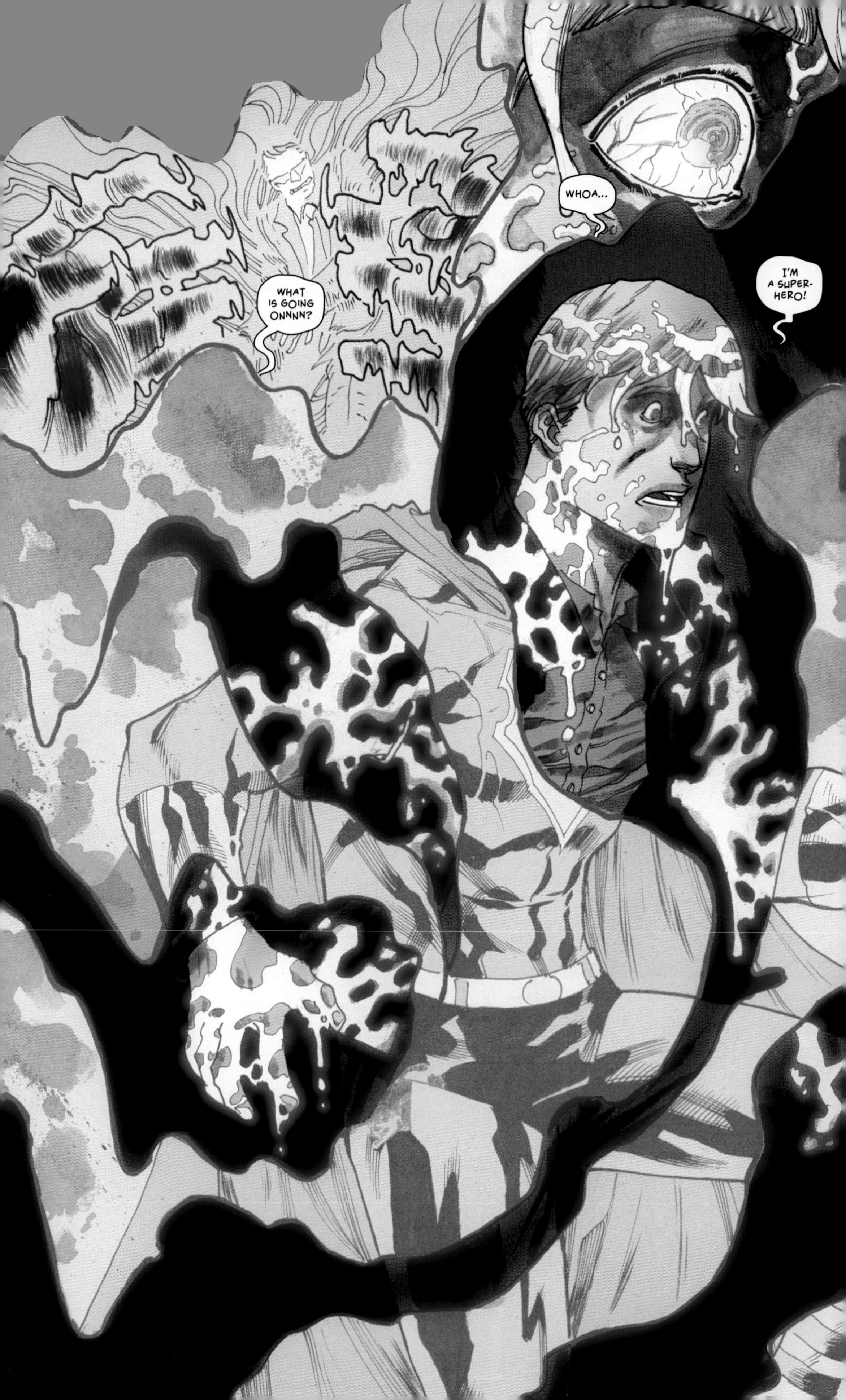
WHAT IS GOING ONNNN?
WHOA...
I'M A SUPER-HERO!

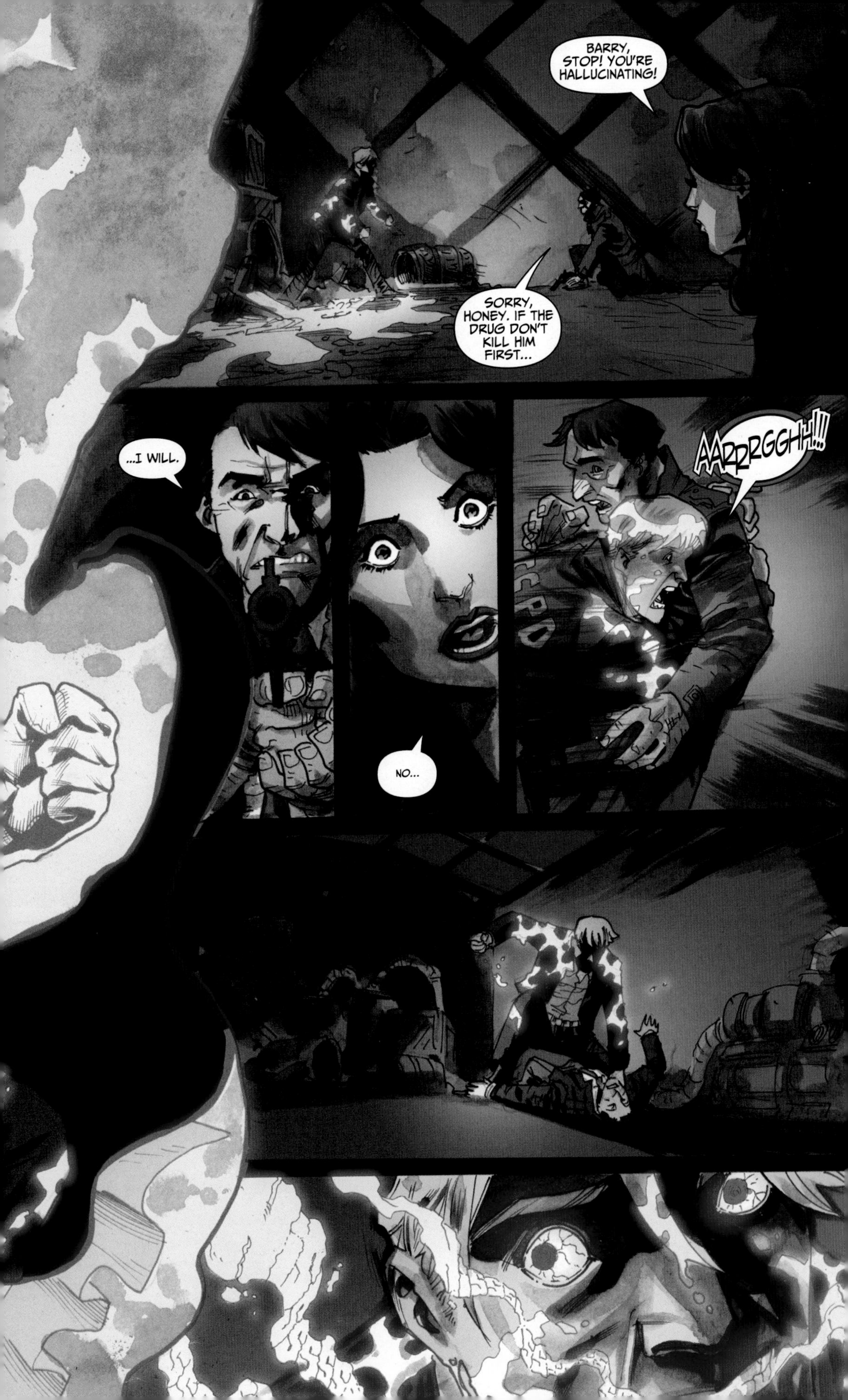
BARRY, STOP! YOU'RE HALLUCINATING!
SORRY, HONEY. IF THE DRUG DON'T KILL HIM FIRST...
...I WILL.
NO...
AARRRGGHH!!!

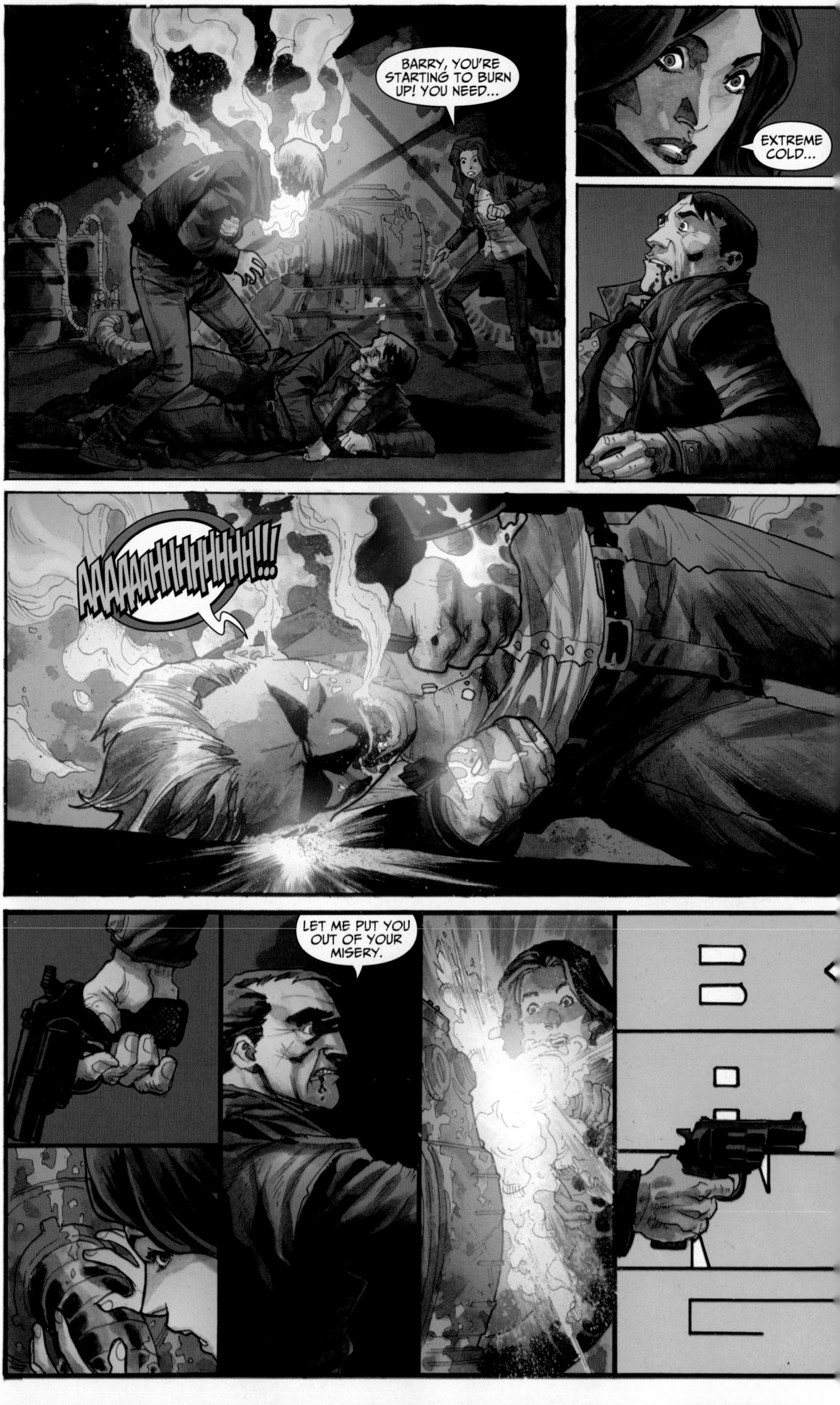

BARRY, YOU'RE STARTING TO BURN UP! YOU NEED...
EXTREME COLD...
AAAAAHHHHHHH!!!
LET ME PUT YOU OUT OF YOUR MISERY.

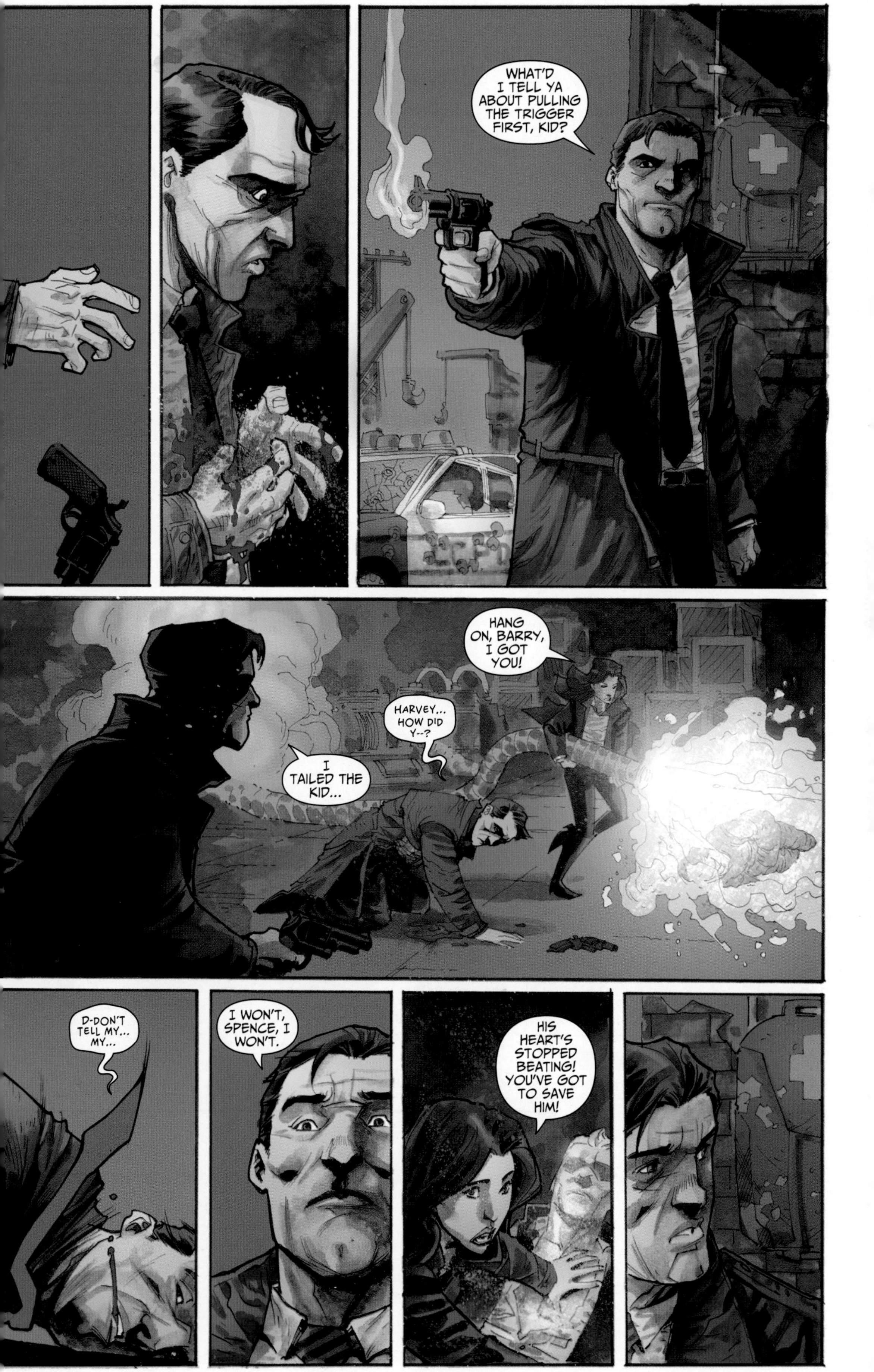

WHAT'D I TELL YA ABOUT PULLING THE TRIGGER FIRST, KID?
HANG ON, BARRY, I GOT YOU!
HARVEY... HOW DID Y--?
I TAILED THE KID...
D-DON'T TELL MY... MY...
I WON'T, SPENCE, I WON'T.
HIS HEART'S STOPPED BEATING! YOU'VE GOT TO SAVE HIM!

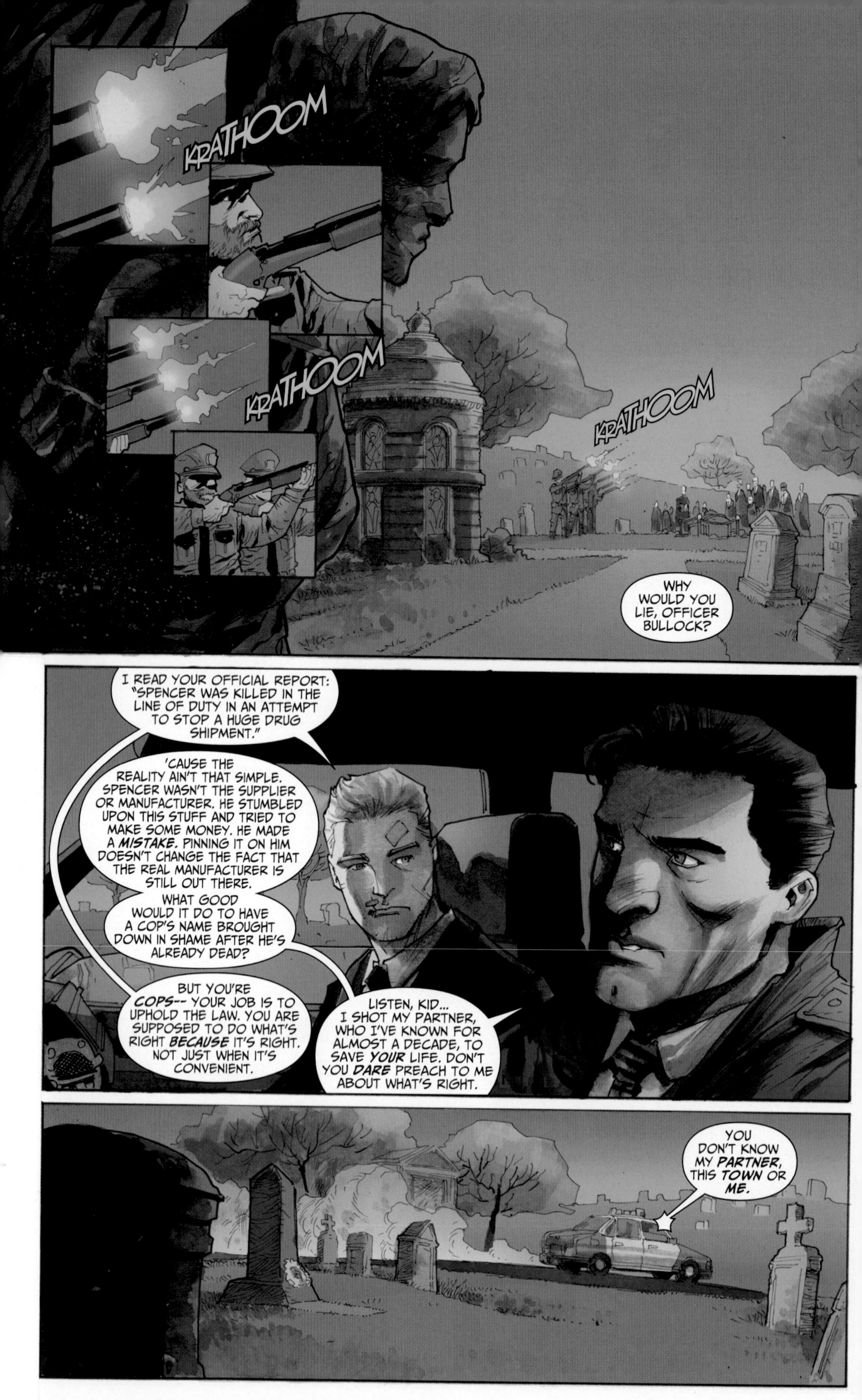
KRATHOOM
KRATHOOM
KRATHOOM
WHY WOULD YOU LIE, OFFICER BULLOCK?
I READ YOUR OFFICIAL REPORT: "SPENCER WAS KILLED IN THE LINE OF DUTY IN AN ATTEMPT TO STOP A HUGE DRUG SHIPMENT."
'CAUSE THE REALITY AIN'T THAT SIMPLE. SPENCER WASN'T THE SUPPLIER OR MANUFACTURER. HE STUMBLED UPON THIS STUFF AND TRIED TO MAKE SOME MONEY. HE MADE A MISTAKE. PINNING IT ON HIM DOESN'T CHANGE THE FACT THAT THE REAL MANUFACTURER IS STILL OUT THERE.
WHAT GOOD WOULD IT DO TO HAVE A COP'S NAME BROUGHT DOWN IN SHAME AFTER HE'S ALREADY DEAD?
BUT YOU'RE COPS-- YOUR JOB IS TO UPHOLD THE LAW. YOU ARE SUPPOSED TO DO WHAT'S RIGHT BECAUSE IT'S RIGHT. NOT JUST WHEN IT'S CONVENIENT.
LISTEN, KID... I SHOT MY PARTNER, WHO I'VE KNOWN FOR ALMOST A DECADE, TO SAVE YOUR LIFE. DON'T YOU DARE PREACH TO ME ABOUT WHAT'S RIGHT.
YOU DON'T KNOW MY PARTNER, THIS TOWN OR ME.

BEING AN OUTSIDER, IT'S EASY FOR YOU TO SIT IN JUDGMENT. TRY GETTING UP IN THE MORNING AND WORKING THE NARROWS, OR CRIME ALLEY.

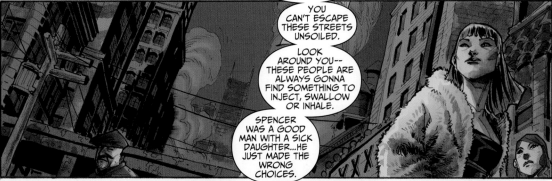

YOU CAN'T ESCAPE THESE STREETS UNSOILED.

LOOK AROUND YOU-- THESE PEOPLE ARE ALWAYS GONNA FIND SOMETHING TO INJECT, SWALLOW OR INHALE.

SPENCER WAS A GOOD MAN WITH A SICK DAUGHTER...HE JUST MADE THE WRONG CHOICES.

HE DID IT TO SAVE THE LIFE OF SOMEONE HE LOVED. NOBODY WINS HERE...BUT AT LEAST THIS WAY HIS FAMILY GETS A PENSION AND A LITTLE LIFE INSURANCE.

THINGS AIN'T ALWAYS SO BLACK AND WHITE. SOMETIMES YOU GOTTA LIVE IN THE GRAY.

BUT HOW ARE YOU ANY DIFFERENT FROM THE VIGILANTES OUT THERE?

TAP TAP

BETTER GO--DON'T WANT YOU TO MISS YOUR BUS.

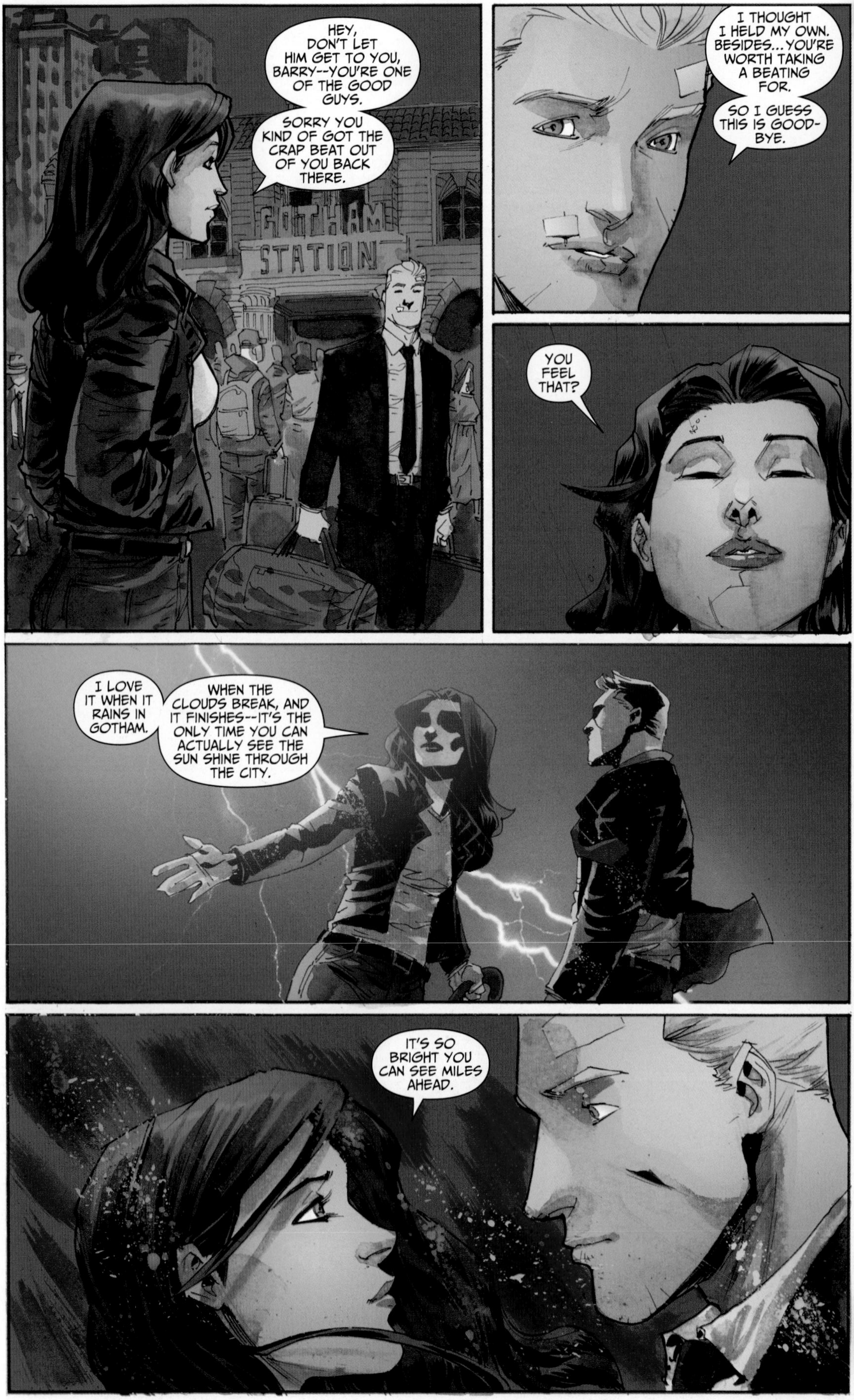
HEY, DON'T LET HIM GET TO YOU, BARRY--YOU'RE ONE OF THE GOOD GUYS.
SORRY YOU KIND OF GOT THE CRAP BEAT OUT OF YOU BACK THERE.
GOTHAM STATION
I THOUGHT I HELD MY OWN. BESIDES...YOU'RE WORTH TAKING A BEATING FOR.
SO I GUESS THIS IS GOOD-BYE.
YOU FEEL THAT?
I LOVE IT WHEN IT RAINS IN GOTHAM.
WHEN THE CLOUDS BREAK, AND IT FINISHES--IT'S THE ONLY TIME YOU CAN ACTUALLY SEE THE SUN SHINE THROUGH THE CITY.
IT'S SO BRIGHT YOU CAN SEE MILES AHEAD.

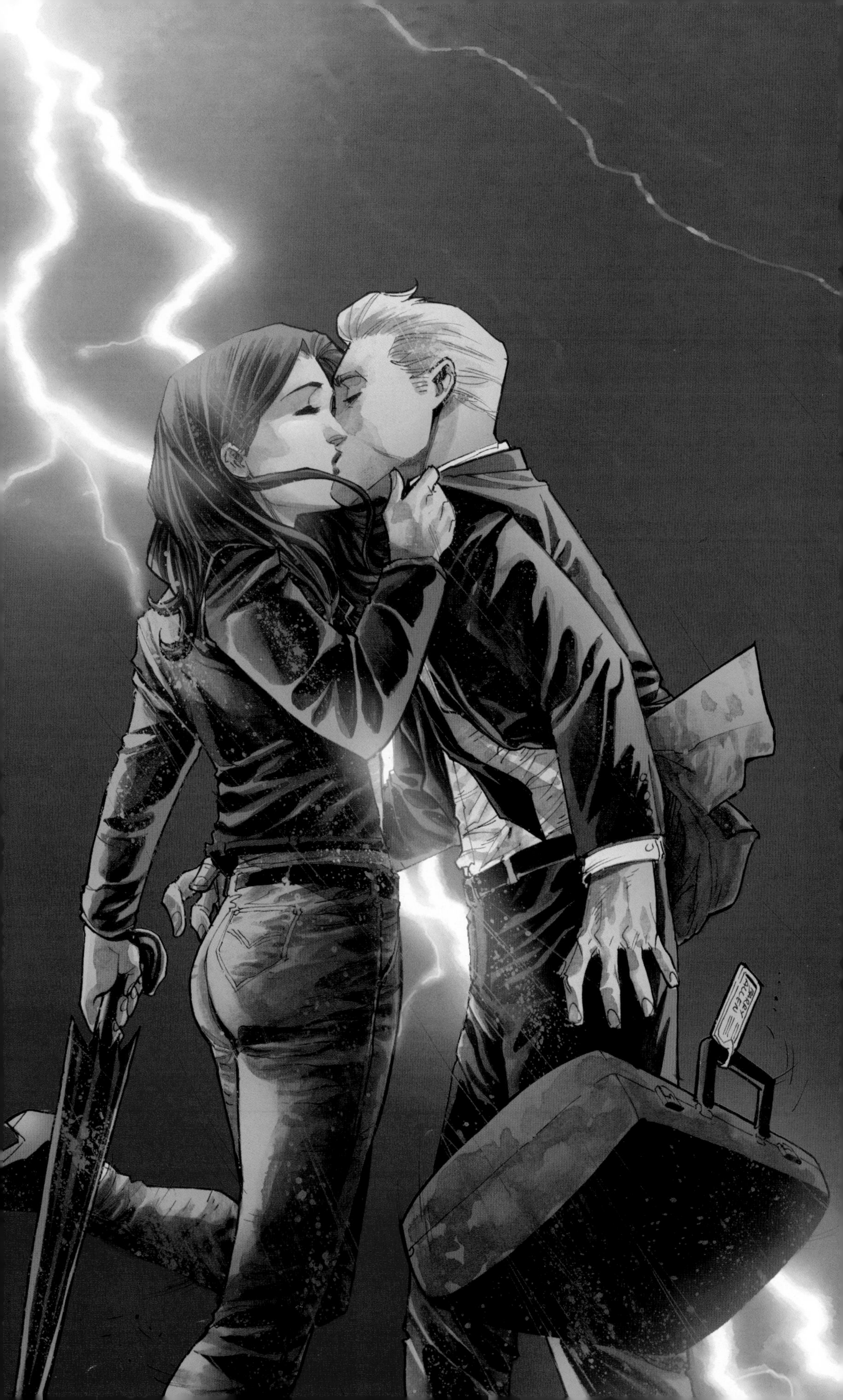
BARRY
ALLEN

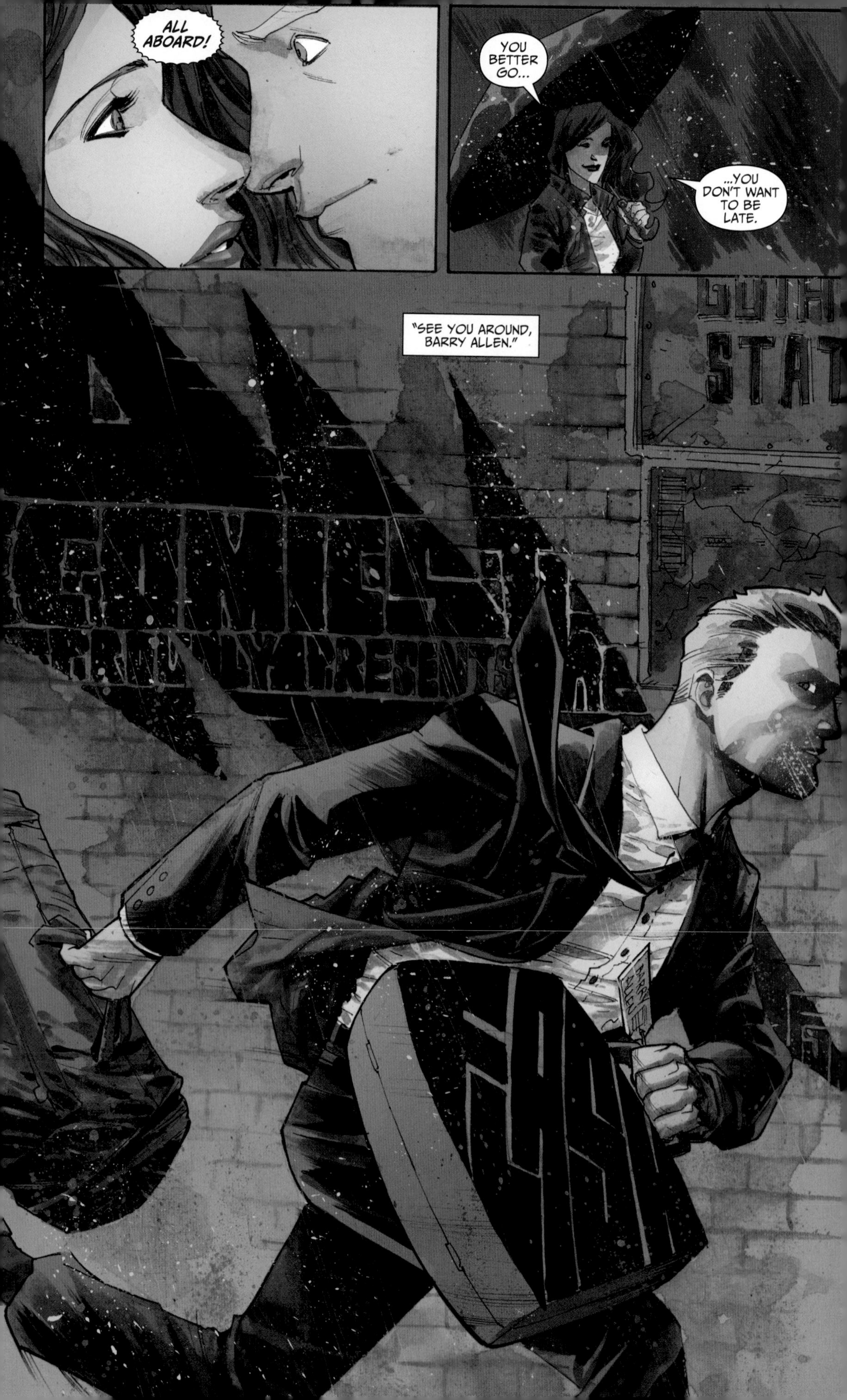
ALL ABOARD!
YOU BETTER GO...
...YOU DON'T WANT TO BE LATE.
"SEE YOU AROUND, BARRY ALLEN."

Pencils for THE FLASH #24 page 20

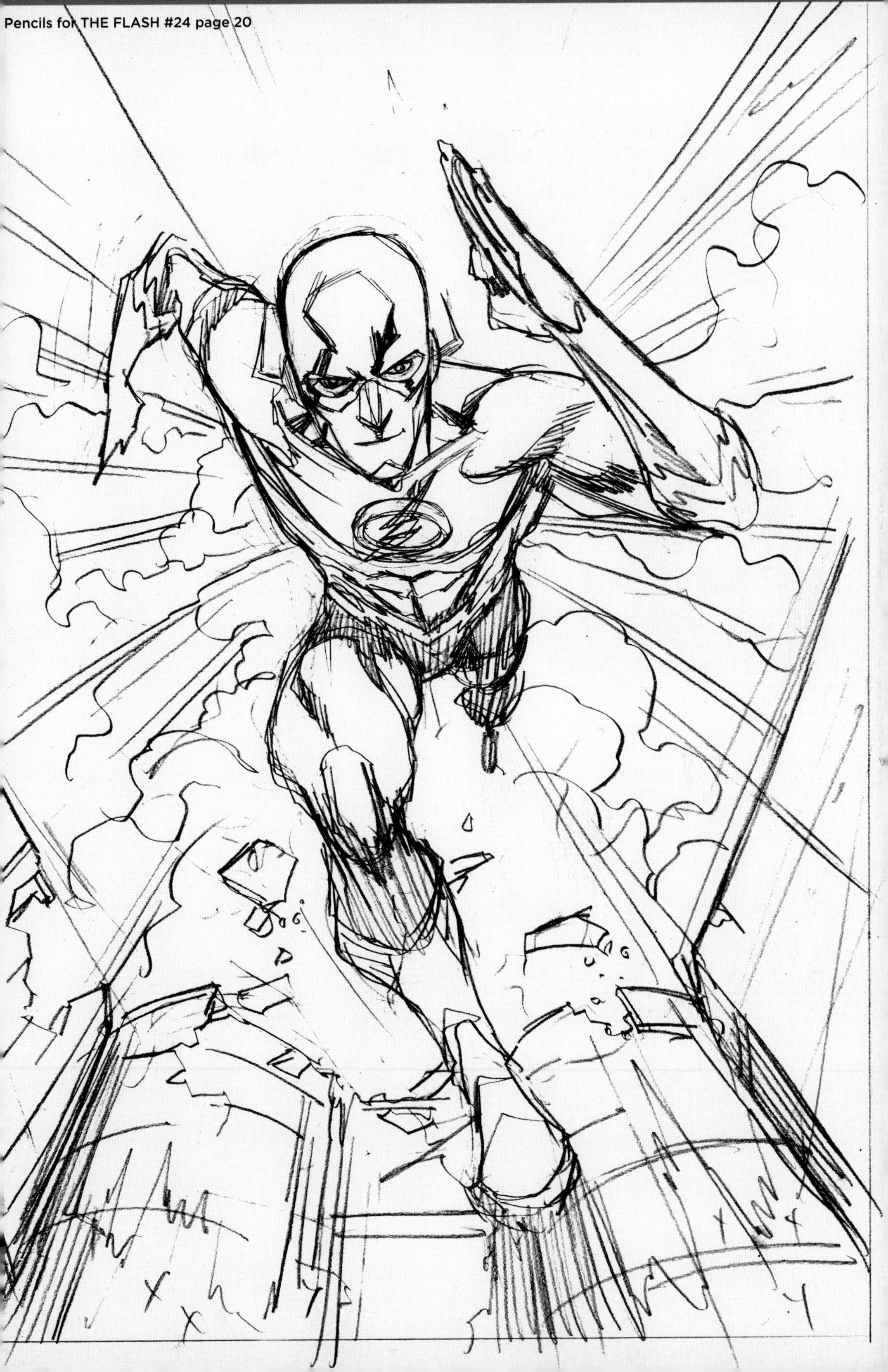

THE FLASH #25 page 27 pencils and finishes

THE FLASH #20 page 20 pencils and finishes

THE FLASH #20 pages 4 & 5 finishes

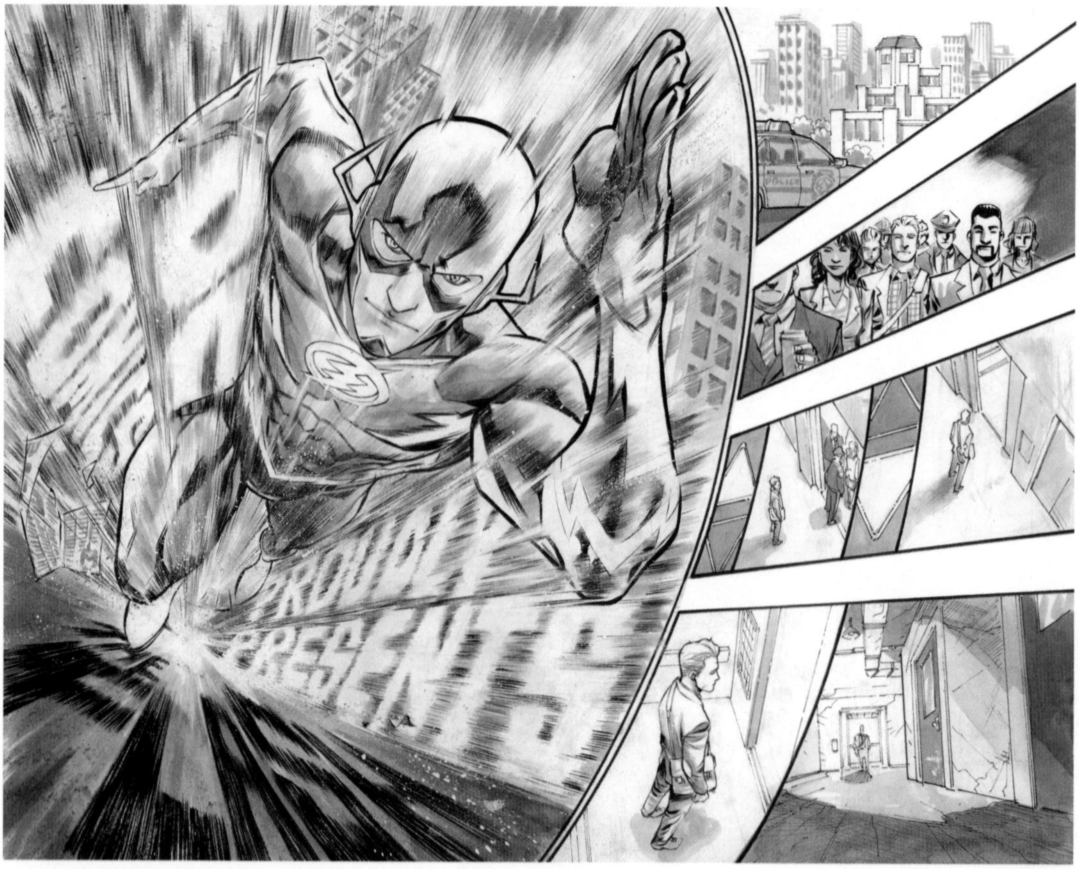

THE FLASH #20 pages 12 & 13 finishes

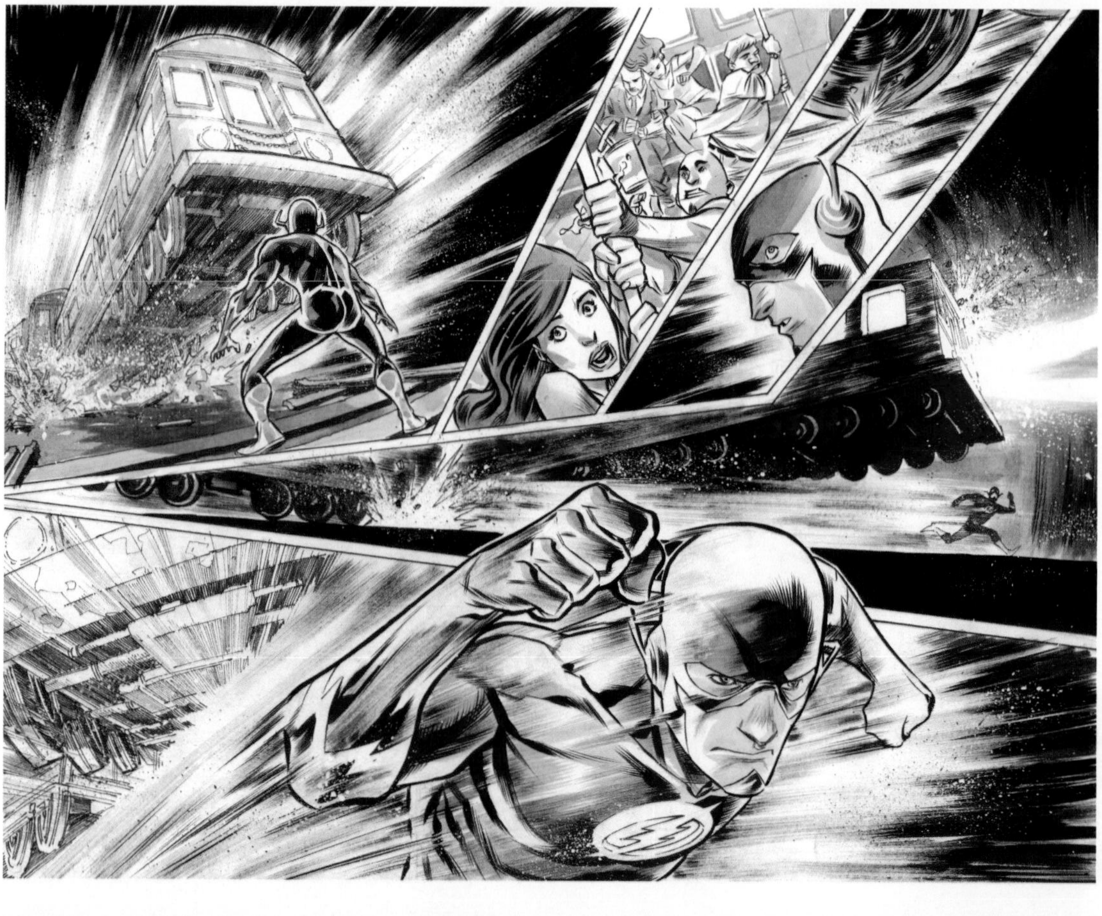

THE FLASH #20 pages 14 & 15 finishes

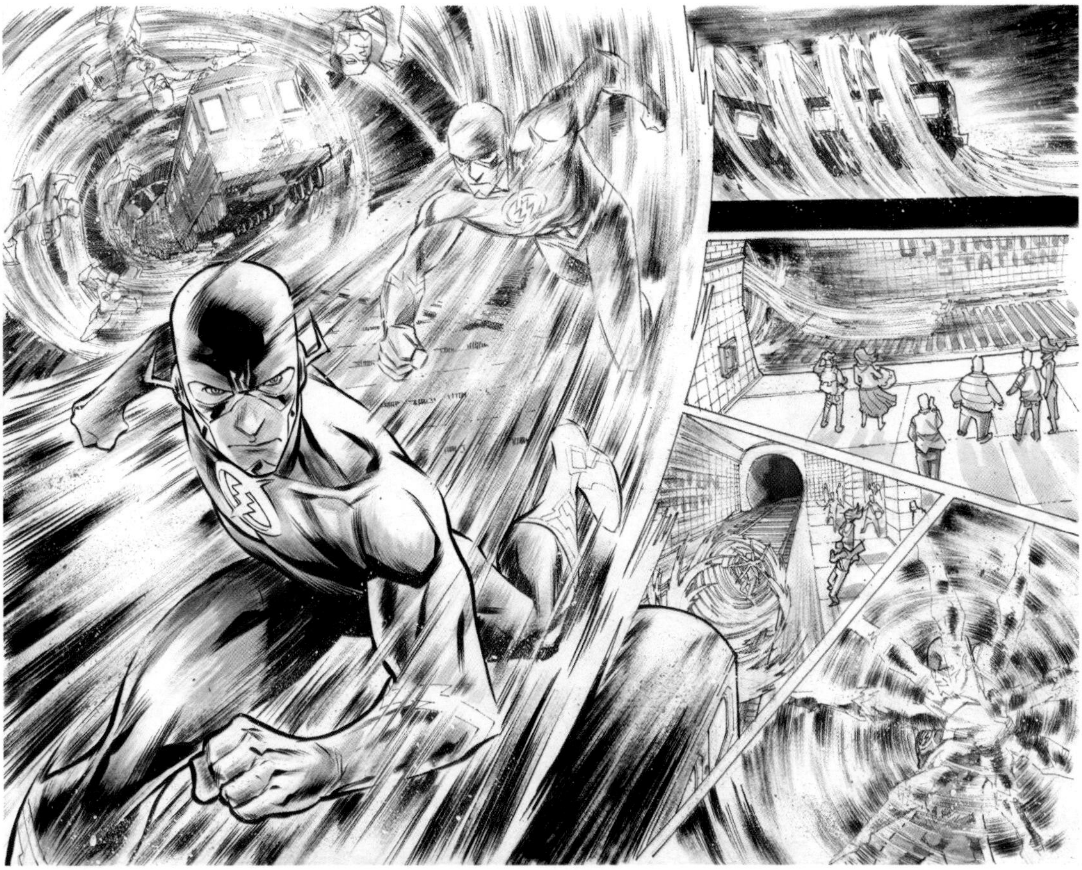
STATION

THE FLASH #21 pages 2 & 3 finishes

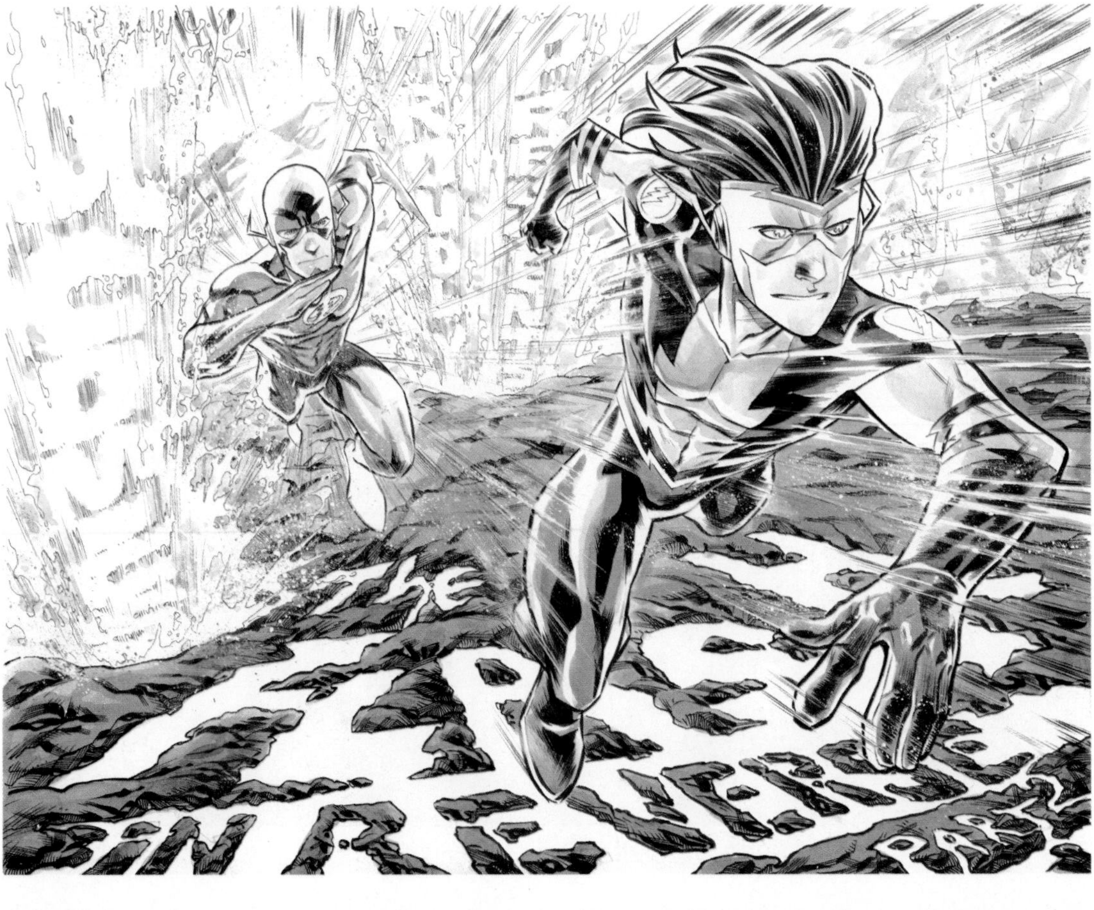

THE FLASH #25 page 28 finishes

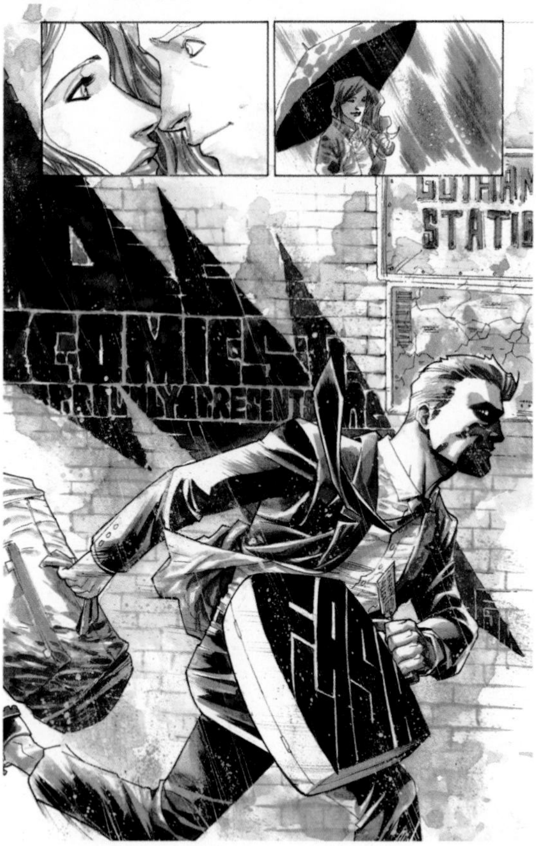
COMICS

THE FLASH #21 page 20 finishes

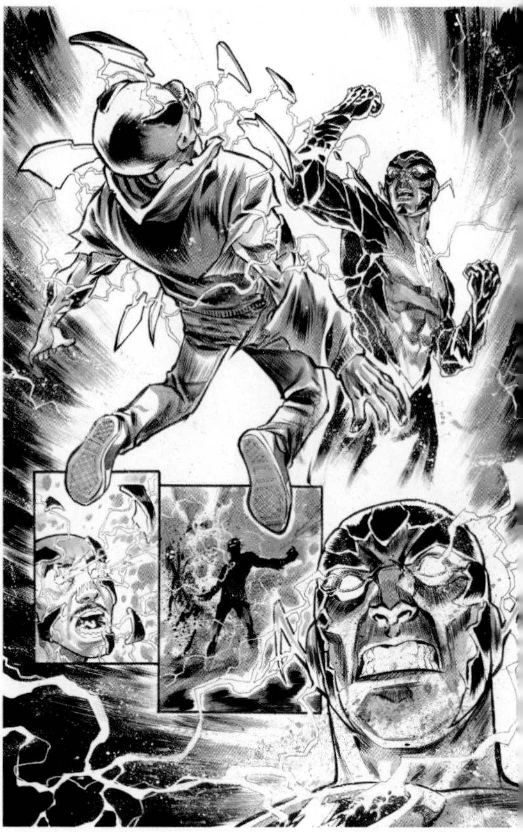

THE FLASH #22 pages 2 & 3 finishes

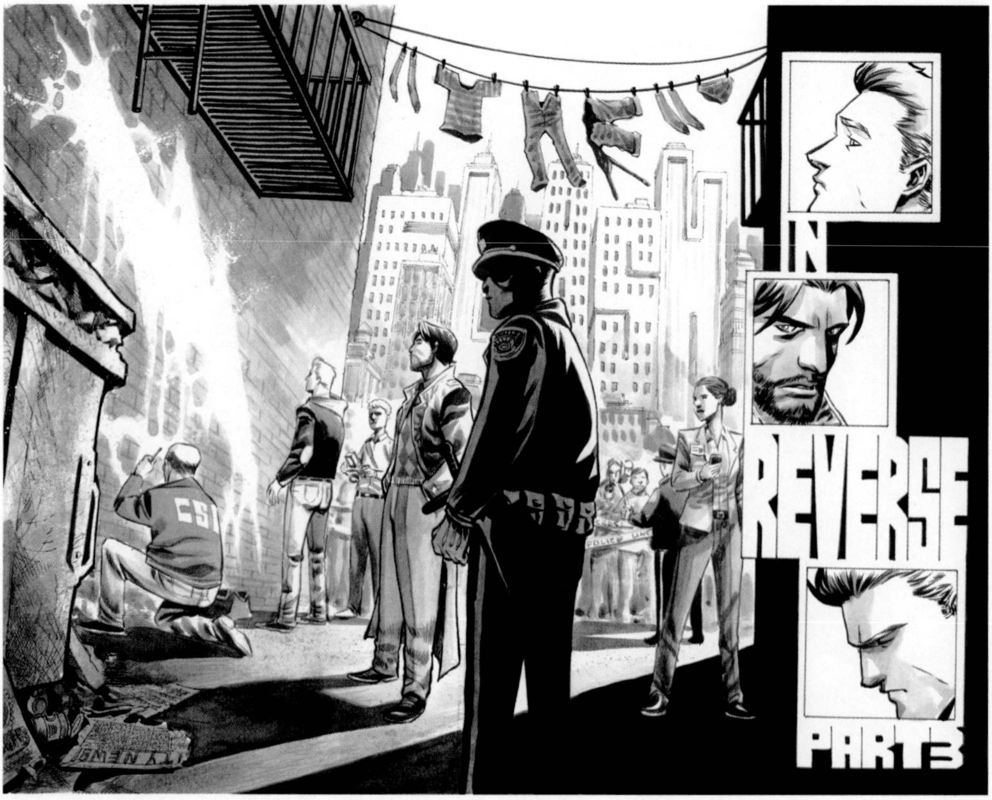
CSI
IN
REVERSE
PART 3

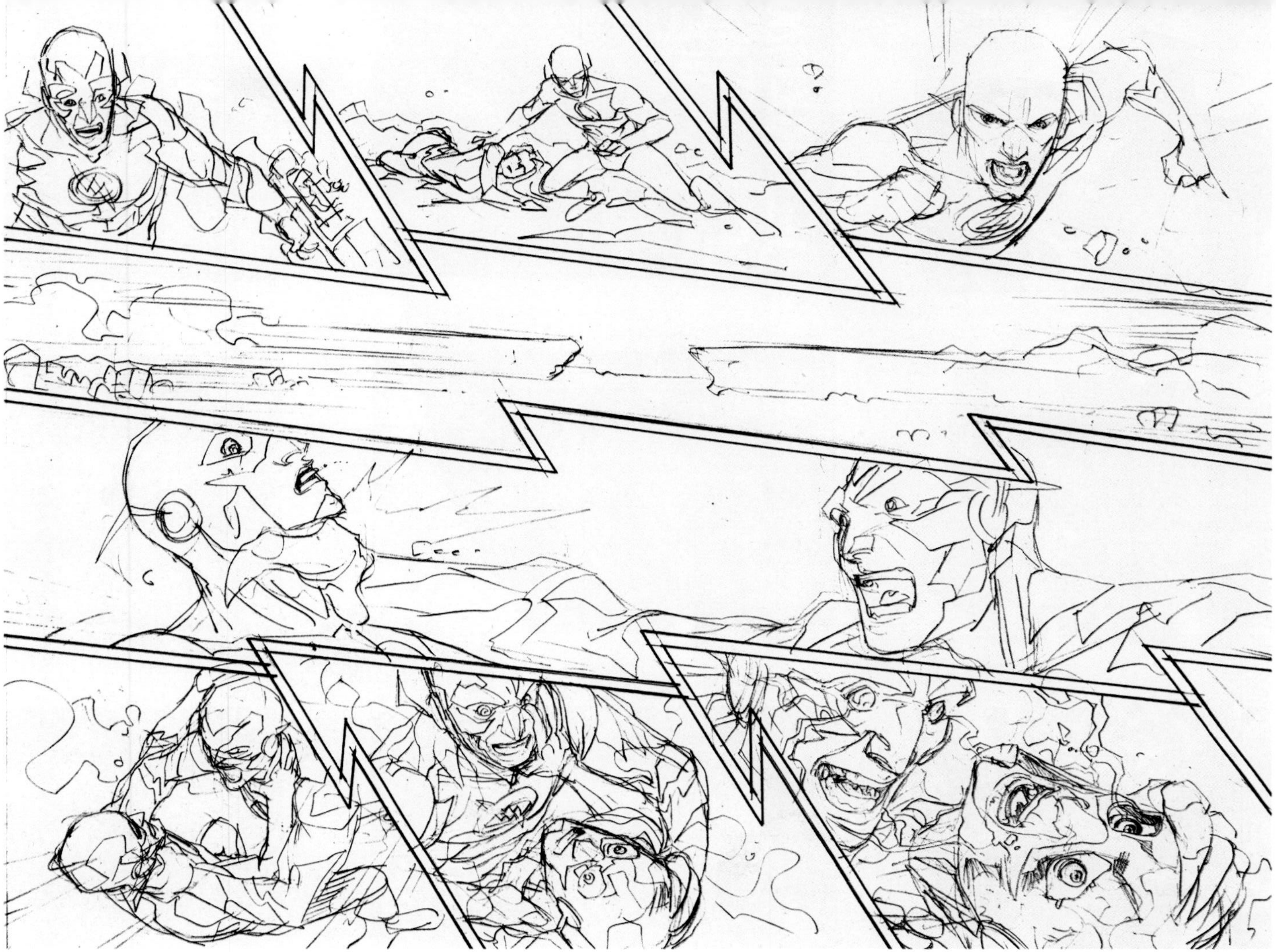

THE FLASH #23 pages 18 & 19 pencils

Cover layouts for THE FLASH #23-25

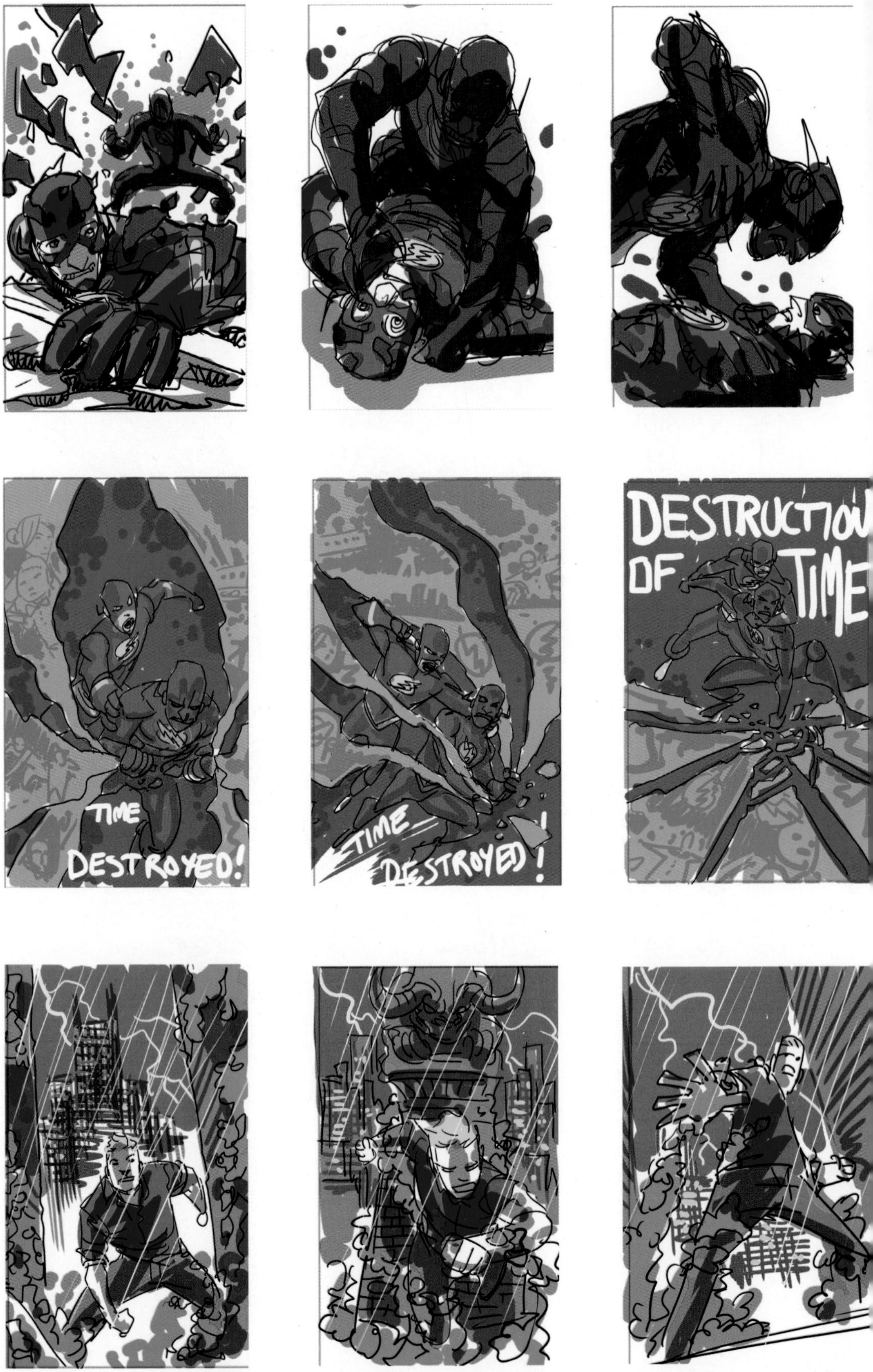
TIME
DESTROYED!
TIME
DESTROYED!
DESTRUCTION
OF TIME

THE FLASH #24 interior layout

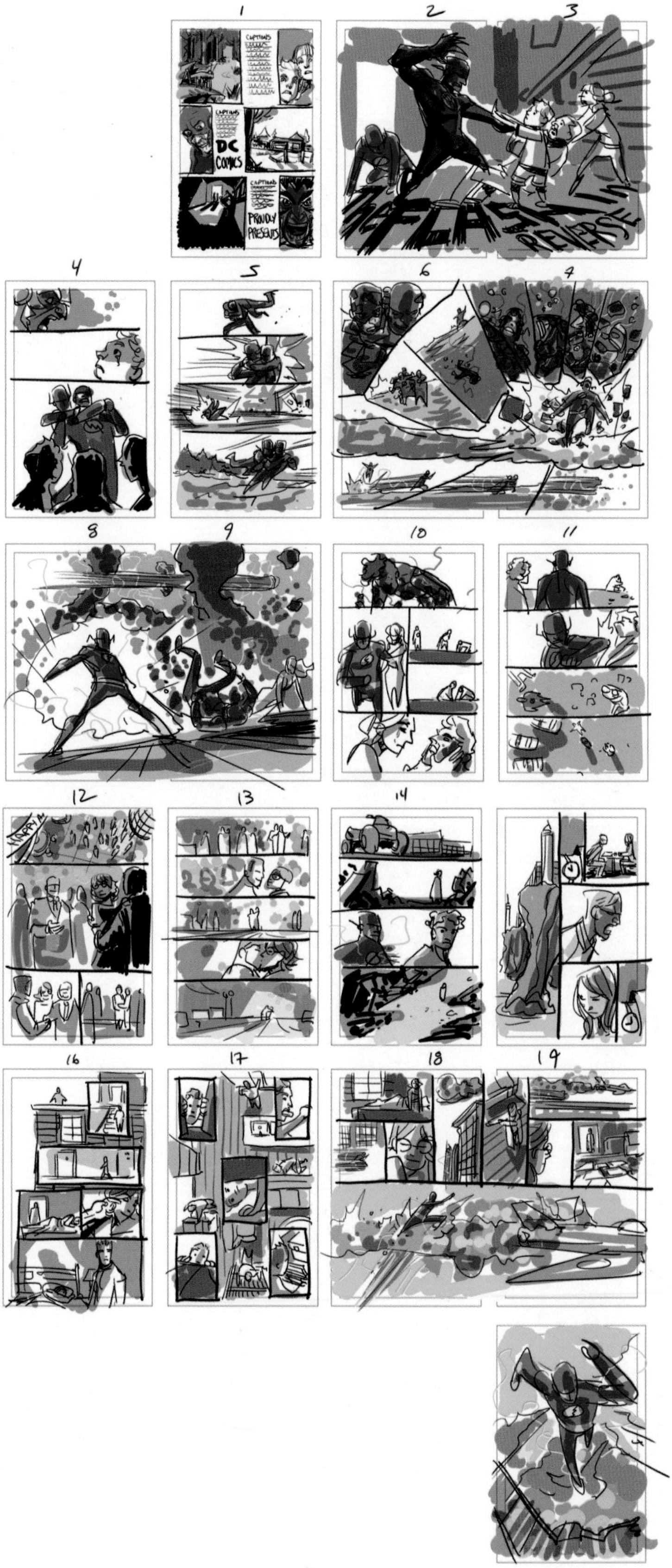

CAPTIONS
CAPTIONS
DC COMICS
CAPTIONS
PROUDLY PRESENTS

Alternate unused version of THE FLASH #24 interior layout

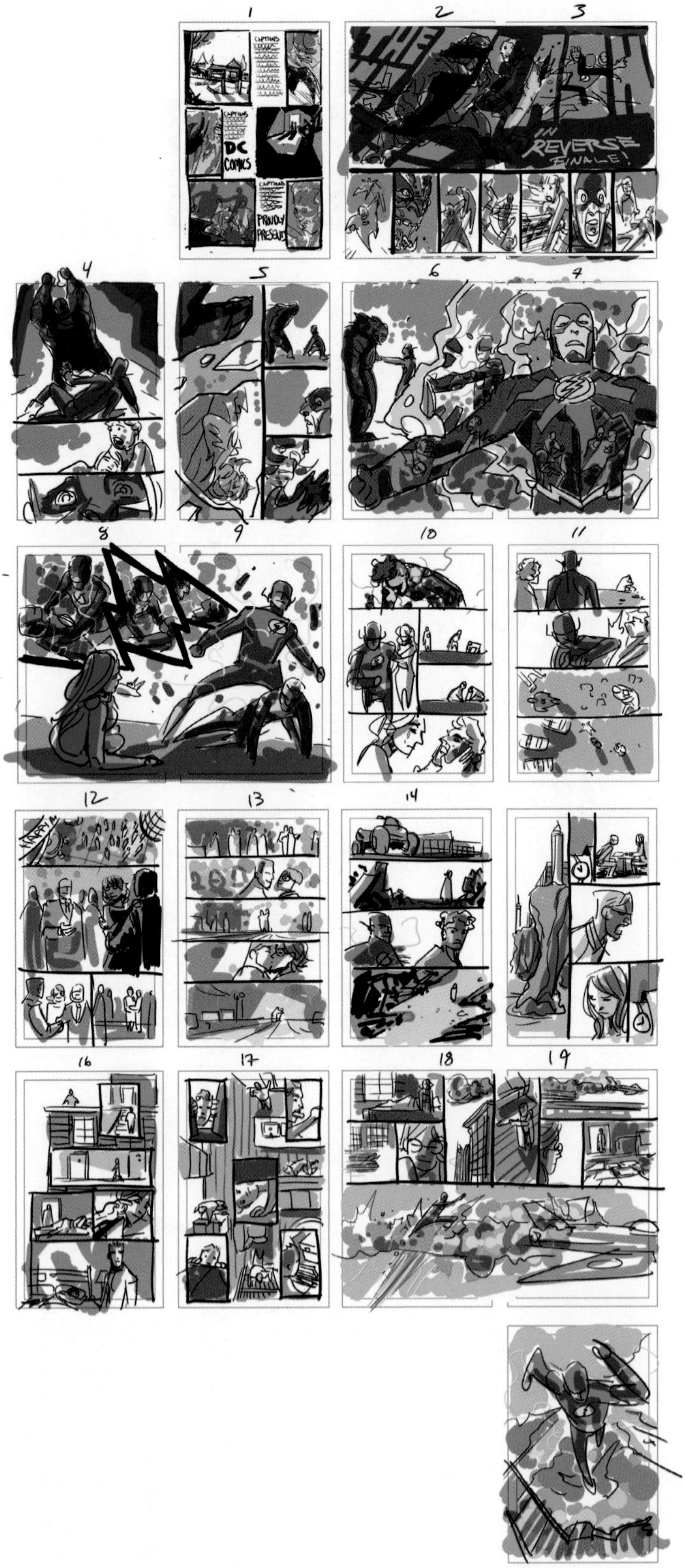
DC
COMICS
IN
REVERSE
FINALE!